Professional Windc

Professional
Windows® Embedded CE 6.0

Professional
Windows® Embedded CE 6.0

Samuel Phung

WILEY

Wiley Publishing, Inc.

Professional Windows® Embedded CE 6.0

Published by
Wiley Publishing, Inc.
10475 Crosspoint Boulevard
Indianapolis, IN 46256
www.wiley.com

Copyright © 2009 by Wiley Publishing, Inc., Indianapolis, Indiana

Published simultaneously in Canada

ISBN: 978-0-470-37733-8

Manufactured in the United States of America

10 9 8 7 6 5 4 3 2 1

Library of Congress Cataloging-in-Publication Data

Phung, Samuel, 1960-
    Professional Windows embedded CE 6.0 / Samuel Phung.
      p. cm.
    Includes index.
    ISBN 978-0-470-37733-8 (paper/website)
      1. Embedded computer systems—Programming.   2. Real-time data processing.   3. Microsoft
Windows (Computer file)   I. Title.
  TK7895.E42P49 2008
  005.26—dc22

                   2008037338

About the Author

Samuel Phung has worked for more than 20 years in both the hardware and software areas of the computer industry. In the late 1980s, he worked for computer hardware companies. In the early 1990s, he led a financial database software development team, developing software for the banking industry. Later he led a software team developing Windows-based telephony applications for a venture capital-funded startup. In the late 1990s, he became engaged with the Windows Embedded product team, starting with Windows NT 4.0 Embedded. He has been working with Windows Embedded CE since version 2.12 was introduced.

He currently works for ICOP Technology, Inc., in El Monte, California, where he is responsible for strategic business development for the North American region. Among his Windows Embedded activities is initiating ICOP local-language web sites supporting the Taiwan, China, and Japan regions. He also maintains a personal web site, www.embeddedpc.net, to provide Windows Embedded information resources for new developers.

Phung graduated from California State University Long Beach (CSULB) in 1984 with an EE degree.

About the Technical Editors

Todd Meister has been developing using Microsoft technologies for more than 10 years. He's been a technical editor on more than 50 titles ranging from SQL Server to the .NET Framework. He is an assistant director for computing services at Ball State University in Muncie, Indiana. He and his wife, Kimberly, live in central Indiana with their four children. Contact Todd at tmeister@sycamoresolutions.com.

Dan Francis has been working professionally in software development since he was 15 and is currently a software engineering manager for a Fortune 50 company. He lives with his wife and twin daughters in northern Maryland. Contact Dan at DanielEFrancis@gmail.com.

Credits

Acquisitions Editor
Katie Mohr

Development Editors
William Bridges
Tom Dinse

Technical Editors
Todd Meister
Daniel Francis

Production Editor
Kathleen Wisor

Copy Editor
Cate Caffrey

Editorial Manager
Mary Beth Wakefield

Production Manager
Tim Tate

**Vice President and
Executive Group Publisher**
Richard Swadley

Vice President and Executive Publisher
Joseph B. Wikert

Project Coordinator, Cover
Lynsey Stratford

Proofreader
Publication Services, Inc.

Indexer
Robert Swanson

Acknowledgments

Going through the experience of writing a book for the first time has helped me realize the amount of work, effort, and support needed to get a book to print. I could not have done it without the supporting team working behind the scenes to help me.

First, I thank Sondra Webber at Microsoft and Katie Mohr at Wiley for making this book possible. I thank William Bridges at Wiley for reviewing my writing, providing valuable input, and helping correct many of the mistakes I made. I thank Todd Meister and Dan Francis for reviewing the technical contents.

Without the hard work of the Windows Embedded team at Microsoft, the Windows Embedded CE product would not be where it is today. My thanks to Mike Hall, Susan Loh, Gabriel Spil, Travis Hobrla, Riki June, and the Windows Embedded CE development team for posting useful information and answering my questions over the years. I also recognize James Y. Wilson, Avi Kcholi, Steve Maillet, Chris Tacke, Alex Feinman, Maarten Struys, David Heil, Bill Ma, Richard Lee, Paul Yao, Paul Tobey, Douglas Boling, and other Windows Embedded MVPs who contributed their time and knowledge to the news group and posted a large pool of technical resources online to benefit others. The base provided by this group of MVPs helped me gain valuable knowledge and resolved countless problems.

I also thank the following individuals who went out of their way and provided help beyond what was expected:

> Ratheesh Rajan with the Windows Embedded CE BSP team
>
> Jason Summerour from Robotics Connection
>
> Chester Fitchett and Don Ha from Phidgets, Inc.

Most of all, I thank my wife, Ann, for her understanding, patience, and support while I took time away from the family to work on the book.

Contents

Contents

Contents

Contents

Contents

Introduction

Windows Embedded CE is a 32-bit, native, hard, real-time, small-footprint operating system developed by Microsoft to address the needs of handheld, mobile, and embedded devices. With support for multiple processor architectures, Windows Embedded CE can be adapted to a variety of devices like Smartphones, PocketPCs, set-top boxes, thin-client terminals, digital cameras, DVRs, VoIP, point-of-sale, point-of-information, network routers, wireless projectors, industrial automation, home and building automation, robotics, data acquisition, and human–machine interfaces.

In today's fast-paced, unforgiving technology market, rapid application development, fast time-to-market, manageable development risks, and cost are key factors contributing to the success of any product development project. With its low-cost licenses, along with the developer-friendly Visual Studio environment and large pool of professional Visual Studio developers, Windows Embedded CE is an attractive operating system for developing a new generation of intelligent, multimedia, connected, and service-oriented embedded devices.

Views differ on likely market size and opportunities for Windows Embedded CE technology. While some CE-enabled products have strong visibility, such as the Windows Mobile Smartphone, Pocket PC, GPS navigation device, Zune media player, and Windows CE Thin Client terminal, many other devices are not visible to end-users, even though they may be using the devices daily. These devices are built to provide a set of designated functions, such as test instrument, data acquisition device, industrial automation controller, digital video recorder, printer, human–machine interface terminal, self-serve kiosk, and multimedia appliance. The companies building these devices use the Windows Embedded CE kernel technology and develop their own applications and appropriate user interfaces for the particular device. When the device powers on, it displays a splash screen with information to identify the device and the company while booting. After the boot process is completed, the device displays the application's user interface, specifically designed for the device.

In the past, when referring to embedded development, many developers were thinking of low-cost 8-bit and 16-bit microcontrollers, with limited functionality, requiring the use of low-level, difficult-to-master programming languages and a user-unfriendly development environment. Rapidly evolving silicon technology, delivering faster and smaller processors, makes it possible to build smaller-footprint embedded controllers with faster processors while lowering the cost.

A new generation of 32-bit, high-performance, low-power, and small-footprint computing hardware is now readily available at low cost. These, coupled with Windows Embedded CE, provide the platform to develop a new breed of products. Companies can develop new products with additional features while lowering development time, maintenance, and product cost. This has changed the development landscape for the embedded-device market by enabling the Visual Studio developer, using Visual Basic, Visual C++, or C#, to develop new kinds of embedded devices. Embedded development is tightly coupled with writing software code and developing or finding appropriate hardware. The growing availability of embedded hardware, with support for Windows Embedded CE, helps expand the market and opportunities for CE.

Here are some of the new 32-bit embedded controllers built with the Vortex86 family of x86 processors, with costs ranging from under $100 to $200.

Introduction

The Vortex86SX-6117 (shown in Figure I-1) is an embedded controller, built with a 300-MHz x86 processor, 128 MB RAM, 10/100 Mbps Ethernet, USB 2.0, RS-232, 16-bit GPIO, 2 MB SPI flash to emulate bootable floppy drive, and IDE interface to support bootable IDE flash storage. This embedded controller requires +5 V DC and 240 mA to operate, measures 1.96 × 3.14 inches, and costs less than $100.

Figure I-1

The Vortex86SX-6115 (Figure I-2) is an embedded controller, built with a 300-MHz x86 processor, 128 MB RAM, 10/100 Mbps Ethernet, two USB 2.0 host interfaces, three RS-232 serial ports, one RS-232/485 serial port, parallel port, 16-bit GPIO, 2 MB SPI flash to emulate bootable floppy drive, and IDE interface to support bootable IDE flash storage. This embedded controller requires +5 V DC and 360 mA to operate, measures 2.6 × 3.94 inches, and costs less than $150.

Figure I-2

The Vortex86SX-6150E (Figure I-3) is an embedded controller in PC/104 format, built with a 300-MHz x86 processor, 128 MB RAM, 10/100 Mbps Ethernet, USB 2.0, RS-232, 16-bit GPIO, 2 MB SPI flash to emulate bootable floppy drive, and IDE interface to support bootable IDE flash storage. This embedded controller requires +5 V DC and 360 mA to operate, measures 3.54 × 3.77 inches, and costs less than $150.

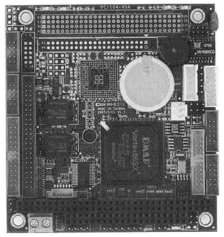

Figure I-3

The PDX-057T (Figure I-4) is a compact industrial panel PC with a 5.7-inch touch screen, providing 640 × 480 VGA display resolution. It's powered by a 600-MHz Vortex86DX processor with 256 MB RAM, integrated 10/100 Mbps Ethernet, USB 2.0, RS-232, Compact Flash, and Ultra-DMA IDE. This device measures 5.98 × 4.41 × 1.3 inches and requires +5 V DC at 1.04 A to operate.

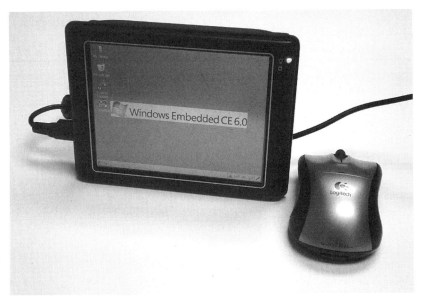

Figure I-4

The eBox-2300SX (Figure I-5) is a compact computing device, built with a 300-MHz x86 processor, 128 MB RAM, 10/100 Mbps Ethernet, three USB 2.0 host interfaces, two RS-232 serial ports, 24-bit GPIO, CompactFlash, and Ultra-DMA IDE interface to support bootable IDE flash storage. The eBox-2300SX is also available with an optional Wi-Fi 802.11 b/g wireless network interface. Measuring 4.5 × 4.5 × 1.375 inches, the basic version of eBox-2300SX, without wireless network and RS-232 ports, costs less than $100.

Figure I-5

The above five embedded devices represent a small sampling of the new breed of high-performance, small-footprint, and low-cost controllers available today. They are available from ICOP Technology and DMP Electronics. Additional product information is available from these web sites:

```
www.icoptech.com
www.compactpc.com.tw
```

In addition to supporting the x86 processor, Windows Embedded CE also supports the ARM, MIPS, and SH4 processors.

The combination of this embedded hardware and CE provides the development platform to support application development using Visual C++, C#, and Visual Basic. The Windows Embedded application development platform enables Visual Studio developers to adapt their existing skills with ease to developing a new breed of embedded device.

For the embedded developer new to this environment, the Windows Embedded CE and Visual Studio environment is efficient, developer-friendly, and easy to master. It's definitely a good investment, with strong ROI, to adopt Windows Embedded CE for your embedded development project.

Whom This Book Is For

This book is suitable for all developers new to the Windows Embedded CE development environment. It does not cover operating system architecture, programming concepts, or how to write efficient code or develop real-time applications.

This book's primary objective is to show you what resources are available as part of the Windows Embedded CE tool chains, where these resources are located, and how to use them. A series of exercises is provided, using simple and short examples.

If you are an embedded developer evaluating Windows Embedded CE, the information in this book will help shorten the time needed to go through the tool chains and set up the development environment.

If you are an existing Visual Studio developer programming in Visual C++, C#, or Visual Basic, this book will help broaden your opportunities and provide information to help you develop Windows Embedded CE applications quickly, using the skills you already have.

If you are a casual programmer or hobbyist, this book is definitely for you. We all like to tinker with toys (hardware). The CE development environment combines writing software code and developing or integrating embedded hardware, such as robotic and home automation projects. Whatever your programming skills may be, you can develop intriguing CE devices, using Visual C++, C#, or Visual Basic programming languages. With the help from this book, you'll be doing mostly fun stuff rather than pulling your hair out, trying to figure out how things should work.

What This Book Covers

This book talks about the Windows Embedded CE development environment and uses simple exercises to show how to perform different development tasks. These exercises are created with Windows Embedded CE 6.0 Platform Builder and Visual Studio 2005. Following is a list of the covered subjects:

- ❑ Windows Embedded CE Operating System overview
- ❑ Windows Embedded CE development environment overview
- ❑ Board Support Package
- ❑ Building customized runtime image
- ❑ Target device connectivity for image download
- ❑ Debugging and debugging tools
- ❑ Developing managed-code applications for Windows Embedded CE using Visual Studio
- ❑ Developing native-code applications for Windows Embedded CE using Visual Studio
- ❑ Autolaunch applications when Windows Embedded CE starts
- ❑ Deploying a Windows Embedded CE 6.0 device with BIOS Loader

How This Book Is Structured

Each chapter in this book is written with minimal dependency on the other chapters. Although it's recommended that you go through the chapters in order, the material in each chapter is self-contained. Following are brief descriptions of what's covered in each chapter:

Chapter 1: Windows Embedded CE

Overview information about CE 6.0 shows the timeline for different releases of earlier CE versions and information about differences between Windows Mobile and Windows Embedded CE.

Chapter 2: Development Environment and Tools

As part of learning new technology, it's important to understand the overall picture, related technologies, and development tools. This chapter provides information about the development environment and tools, focused for developers with different interests.

Chapter 3: Board Support Package

The board support package (BSP) is one of the critical components of CE, needed to develop the OS design, which, in turn, generates the runtime image. This chapter provides information about BSPs and shows how to create a customized one by cloning and modifying BSPs provided by Microsoft and third-party companies.

Chapter 4: Building a Customized CE 6.0 Runtime Image

This chapter provides information and samples showing how to use the Platform Builder tool to create a custom OS design project and compile a CE 6.0 OS runtime image from the OS design project.

Chapter 5: Connecting to Target Device

In this chapter, you'll learn how to configure target connectivity between the development workstation and the target device to download the runtime image to the target device.

Chapter 6: Debugging and Debugging Tools

Debugging and tracing potential problems are important for every development project. This chapter provides information showing how to debug a CE 6.0 runtime image running on a target device and provides information showing the tools that are available to help carry out the debugging function.

Chapter 7: Boot Loader Overview

After the CE runtime image is created, a boot loader is needed to launch the runtime image on the target device. This chapter provides an overview of the boot loader and shows how to use the BIOS Loader, the boot loader for devices built with the x86 processor.

Chapter 8: The Registry

The registry is another critical component for a CE device. This chapter provides information about the registry and using hive-based registry implementation for persisting registry settings.

Chapter 9: Testing with CETK

The CE Test Kit (CETK) is a useful tool provided as part of the Platform Builder installation. The CETK tool is used to test BSPs, device drivers, and applications. This chapter shows how to set up and use the CETK.

Chapter 10: Application Development

This chapter provides general application development information for CE.

Chapter 11: Visual C# 2005 Applications

This chapter steps through an exercise showing how to develop a C# managed-code application using the Visual Studio 2005 IDE and the emulator as the target device.

Chapter 12: VB 2005 Applications

This chapter steps through exercises to show how to develop VB 2005 managed-code applications using the Visual Studio 2005 IDE and the eBox-4300-MSJK, a compact computing device as the target device. It also covers using the CoreCon connection framework to establish a connection between the Visual Studio 2005 development workstation and the eBox-4300-MSJK target device to deploy the VB 2005 application to the target device. This chapter works through the process and creates a complete serial port communication program using VB 2005 and the .NET Compact Framework.

Chapter 13: Native-Code Applications

In Chapter 13, you'll step through exercises showing how to develop Visual C++ native-code applications using the Visual Studio 2005 IDE, and how to use the Platform Builder IDE to develop Win32 native-code applications.

Chapter 14: Autolaunch Applications

A CE device is designed to perform designated functions and launches a custom application designed for the device when powered on. This chapter provides information showing different methods available to launch an application when CE starts.

Chapter 15: Customizing the UI

This chapter provides examples showing how to launch the custom user interface (UI) when CE starts, to replace the standard Explorer shell.

Chapter 16: Thin-Client Applications

This chapter works through the process of creating thin-client applications using the provided design templates and takes you through simple exercises showing how to generate customized versions of thin-client applications that can be adopted and used for different kinds of information appliance applications.

Chapter 17: Home Automation Applications

Using the home automation application as an example, this chapter works through an exercise using the eBox-4300-MSJK and Phidget devices to develop a managed-code application, interacting with the hardware to read sensor data and turn external devices on and off.

Chapter 18: RFID Security Access Control Applications

Continuing from Chapter 17, using the eBox-4300-MSJK and Phidgets RFID reader, this chapter works through a simple exercise showing how to interact with the RFID reader to read data from RFID tags.

Chapter 19: Robotic Applications

This chapter works through two simple robotic applications using the eBox-4300-MSJK as the target device and the Serializer Robot Controller to provide robotic control.

Chapter 20: Deploying a CE 6.0 Device

During the development phase, the target device, boot loader, and runtime image were configured for development purposes. This chapter steps through the process to deploy a CE 6.0 device, using the eBox-4300-MSJK as the target device. The exercise in this chapter steps through the process to develop an OS design using the Windows Network Projector design template, generates the runtime image, and configures the eBox-4300-MSJK with the BIOS Loader. When completed, the exercise in this chapter transforms the eBox-4300-MSJK device into a Windows Network Projector system, capable of upgrading the existing computer projector to become a Windows Network Projector.

Appendix A: Windows Embedded CE References

There is a large pool of information resources available for Windows Embedded CE. This appendix provides references to some of these resources.

Appendix B: Installation and Software

The Windows Embedded CE 6.0 R2 development environment requires multiple pieces of software and updates for the software. Improper installation and missing software are the two major causes for many of the problems encountered by developers new to the CE development environment. This appendix provides information regarding installation and the software needed to work through the exercises in the book.

Appendix C: Sample Applications and OS Design Projects

A series of OS design and application development exercises is provided throughout this book. Some of these projects require certain versions of the programming library and BSP to function. When attempting to compile and build the sample project files provided as part of the software for this book, using mismatched versions of libraries and BSPs will generate errors. This appendix provides more detailed information about the sample projects provided with this book and shows how to modify the projects to support different versions of the libraries or BSPs, when possible. This appendix also provides information about additional sample projects.

What You Need to Use This Book

To work through the exercises in this book, you will need to have the following software installed:

- ❑ Visual Studio 2005
- ❑ Visual Studio 2005 Service Pack 1
- ❑ Visual Studio 2005 sp1 upgrade for Vista (only needed for Windows Vista machine)
- ❑ Windows Embedded CE 6.0
- ❑ Windows Embedded CE 6.0 Service Pack 1
- ❑ Windows Embedded CE 6.0 R2
- ❑ ICOP_eBox4300_60E_BSP.msi board support package
- ❑ VS2005_CoreCon_X86_WINCE600.msi CoreCon component for x86 processor
- ❑ VS2005_CoreCon_ARMV4I_WINCE600.msi CoreCon component for ARMV4I processor

To work through the exercises in some of the chapters involving hardware, you'll need the following hardware:

❑   eBox-4300-MSJK

www.embeddedpc.net/ebox4300/

❑   Phidget devices

www.phidgets.com

❑   Stinger CE Robot

www.roboticsconnection.com/p-78-stinger-windowsce-kit.aspx

Conventions

To help you get the most from the text and keep track of what's happening, I've used several conventions throughout the book.

> *Notes, tips, hints, tricks, and asides to the current discussion are offset and placed in italics like this.*

As for styles in the text:

❑   I show URLs and code within the text like so: `persistence.properties`.

❑   I present code in two different ways:

```
I use a monofont type with no highlighting for most code examples.
I use gray highlighting to emphasize code that's particularly important in the
present context.
```

Source Code

As you work through the examples in this book, you may choose either to type in all the code manually or to use the source code files that accompany the book. All of the source code used in this book is available for download at www.wrox.com. Once at the site, simply locate the book's title (either by using the Search box or by using one of the title lists) and click the Download Code link on the book's detail page to obtain all the source code for the book.

> *Because many books have similar titles, you may find it easiest to search by ISBN; this book's ISBN is 978-0-470-37733-8.*

Once you download the code, just decompress it with your favorite compression tool. Alternately, you can go to the main Wrox code download page at www.wrox.com/dynamic/books/download.aspx to see the code available for this book and all other Wrox books.

Errata

We make every effort to ensure that there are no errors in the text or in the code. However, no one is perfect, and mistakes do occur. If you find an error in one of our books, like a spelling mistake or faulty piece of code, we would be very grateful for your feedback. By sending in errata, you may save another reader hours of frustration, and at the same time, you will be helping us provide even higher-quality information.

To find the errata page for this book, go to www.wrox.com and locate the title using the Search box or one of the title lists. Then, on the Book Details page, click the Book Errata link. On this page, you can view all errata that have been submitted for this book and posted by Wrox editors. A complete book list including links to each book's errata is also available at www.wrox.com/misc-pages/booklist.shtml.

If you don't spot "your" error on the Book Errata page, go to www.wrox.com/contact/techsupport.shtml and complete the form there to send us the error you have found. We'll check the information and, if appropriate, post a message to the book's Errata page and fix the problem in subsequent editions of the book.

p2p.wrox.com

For author and peer discussion, join the P2P forums at p2p.wrox.com. The forums are a Web-based system for you to post messages relating to Wrox books and related technologies and interact with other readers and technology users. The forums offer a subscription feature to e-mail you topics of interest of your choosing when new posts are made to the forums. Wrox authors, editors, other industry experts, and your fellow readers are present on these forums.

At http://p2p.wrox.com, you will find a number of different forums that will help you not only as you read this book, but also as you develop your own applications. To join the forums, just follow these steps:

1. Go to p2p.wrox.com and click the Register link.

2. Read the terms of use and click Agree.

3. Complete the required information to join as well as any optional information you wish to provide, and click Submit.

4. You will receive an e-mail with information describing how to verify your account and complete the joining process.

   You can read messages in the forums without joining P2P, but in order to post your own messages, you must join.

Once you join, you can post new messages and respond to messages other users post. You can read messages at any time on the Web. If you would like to have new messages from a particular forum e-mailed to you, click the "Subscribe to this Forum" icon by the forum name in the forum listing.

For more information about how to use the Wrox P2P, be sure to read the P2P FAQs for answers to questions about how the forum software works as well as many common questions specific to P2P and Wrox books. To read the FAQs, click the FAQ link on any P2P page.

1

Windows Embedded CE

While the traditional Windows desktop operating system (OS) developed by Microsoft was designed to run on well-defined and standardized computing hardware built with the x86 processor, Windows Embedded CE was designed to support multiple families of processors.

This chapter provides an overview of CE and improvements for the latest Windows Embedded CE 6.0 R2 release. Multiple Windows Embedded products, including Windows Embedded CE, are being promoted and supported by the same business unit within Microsoft, the Windows Embedded Product group.

What Is Embedded?

Embedded is an industry buzz word that's been in use for many years. Although it's common for us to hear terms like embedded system, embedded software, embedded computer, embedded controller, and the like, most developers as well as business and teaching professionals have mixed views about the embedded market.

To fully understand the potential offered by the Windows Embedded product family, we need to have good understanding about what's considered an embedded device and embedded software.

Before getting into talking about Windows Embedded products, let's take a brief look at what embedded hardware and software are.

Embedded Devices

A computer is an electronic, digital device that can store and process information. In a similar fashion, an embedded device has a processor and memory and runs software.

While a computer is designed for general computing purposes, allowing the user to install different operating systems and applications to perform different tasks, an embedded device is generally developed with a single purpose and provides certain designated functions. Often the embedded device is designed as a closed system and does not allow applications from other developers to run on the system.

Throughout our daily lives, each of us interacts with multiple embedded devices. Here's a listing of some of the more common ones:

- Telephone, car phone, and mobile phone

- VCR, video CD player, DVD player/recorder, digital video recorder/player

- Remote control for TV, audio system, DVD player, garage door opener, security systems for automobiles and other devices

- Credit card reader, cash register, and self-service kiosk

- Digital camera, camcorder, digital photo frame, and gaming console

- Fax machine, copy machine, and printer

The above list contains only a few of the more common devices. It would take a much longer list to cover all embedded devices.

Embedded Software

Many software development projects use similar programming languages, such as the C language, with different operating systems and running on different types of hardware.

Fundamentally, the overall software development process should be the same regardless of the type of project. In an ideal situation, a competent project manager should evaluate the project thoroughly and establish the best possible development process to accomplish the tasks. Developers should use due diligence and apply their best efforts to reduce development time and to develop efficient code that can run on computing hardware in a way that minimizes resources used and cost of the product.

In the real world, it's the business manager's responsibility to deliver more profit while lowering costs. To the development team, this translates into having to solve more difficult problems with fewer resources.

The key difference between developing an embedded application and developing an application for the desktop computer has to do with the specifications for the application.

Application for Desktop Computer

When developing applications for the desktop computer, the developer expects the application will run on a computer with at least a monitor, keyboard, and mouse. The monitor is expected to be able to display VGA or higher display resolution. In the current market, even the cheapest monitor can support a 1024 × 768 display resolution.

In general, when developing application for the desktop computer, the developer doesn't need to give much consideration to the user interface or the display monitor, keyboard and mouse. In addition, the developer can safely assume that the typical computer will have a 1.0 Ghz or faster processor with

512 MB or more in system memory; this assumption is used in measuring the application performance needed to meet certain user requirements.

In a nutshell, when developing applications for the desktop computer, the developer can make a general assumption about the target hardware needed for running the application.

Application for Embedded Device

When developing applications for embedded devices, the developer must study and understand all the hardware features available, and how the end user will interact with and use the device.

Many embedded devices do not have a display monitor. For those built with display, the screen size is very small, with low resolution. This is true of such devices as the Windows Mobile smartphone, GPS navigation devices, and portable media players. Most embedded devices are not designed with keyboard and mouse to capture user input, and they use a limited number of special function keys to process user input.

To minimize cost, most embedded devices are built with slower processors and less system memory than desktop computers.

Thus when developing applications for embedded devices, the developer must consider the limited user interface and limited system memory as well as the slower processor. In addition to developing efficient code to maximize the user's experience, the developer also has to take great care to avoid memory leaks. Many of these embedded devices are on constantly once they go into service; examples are the Windows Mobile smartphone, security monitoring systems, and network appliances. Even a very small amount of memory leakage will accumulate over time and become a serious flaw in the device.

Embedded Devices and Software

A desktop application that consumes 30 to 50 MB of system memory is not considered to be using a lot of memory, when the whole system has 1 GB or more. But an embedded device may have only 64 MB of system memory to be shared between RAM and the file system. An application that consumes more than 1 MB of memory in this scenario is considered to be using a very big chunk of memory. But there also are embedded devices equipped with high performance processors and huge amounts of system memory in the industrial automation and aerospace industries.

In summary, we cannot classify embedded devices based on processor speed, memory resources, or product footprint. An embedded device is designed with embedded software to provide a set of designated primary functions, and will perform these primary function throughout its useful life.

The Windows Embedded Family

The Windows Embedded CE, Windows XP Embedded, and Windows Embedded Point of Service operating systems are products of Microsoft's Windows Embedded product group. Developers new to CE may be thinking it's a scaled-down version of the Windows desktop OS. But while CE shares some common development tools with the desktop Windows OS, the CE kernel is distinctively different from the desktop Windows OS.

I provide a brief overview of the other Windows Embedded products below to help you better understand the differences between them.

Windows XP Embedded

Windows XP Embedded (XPe) is a componentized version of the Professional edition of Windows XP, with some added features designed specifically to support the embedded device market. Microsoft announced a new name for this product, Windows Embedded Standard, on April 15, 2008.

Using a development tool called Target Designer and a properly configured design template, OS, device drivers, and application components, the developer can build a componentized XPe image with a significantly smaller footprint than the Professional edition of Windows XP.

The XPe image can be configured to boot from the network, removable USB storage, or CD-ROM. This OS includes the Write Filters component. When implemented in XPe, the Write Filters feature can configure the storage partition as Read Only to support devices subject to frequent unexpected loss of power. Without the Write Filters, Windows XP system shutoff due to unexpected loss of power might corrupt the file system and prevent it from functioning normally.

Since XPe is binary-compatible with the Professional edition of Windows XP, applications written for Windows XP can work with XPe with the proper components configured for the OS.

Windows Embedded Point of Service

The Windows Embedded Point of Service (WEPOS) is designed for point-of-service devices in the retail and hospitality markets that need to connect to a variety of peripherals, such as the following:

❑   ATMs for banking transactions

❑   Full-featured point-of-sale and point-of-service terminals

❑   Kiosks

WEPOS can be installed from a CD and does not require a development tool to generate the OS runtime image as XPe does. WEPOS is binary-compatible with the Professional edition of Windows XP.

Windows Embedded CE 6.0

CE is not binary-compatible with any version of the desktop Windows OS. Other than the common *Windows* term in the product name, Windows Embedded CE is not a scaled-down version of the desktop Windows OS and does not share the common desktop OS kernel.

CE is not a port from the desktop Windows. It is an embedded OS designed from the ground up to support a new generation of small-footprint, smart, connected, and service-oriented embedded devices. It was designed to support embedded devices with less system memory, less storage space, and a slower processor compared to the desktop PC. Since its inception in 1996, each new version of this OS has been improved with added features while maintaining the following design criteria:

- **Small Footprint** — Scalable footprint depends on selected components.

- **Modular Architecture** — Componentized operating system enables the OEM to make decisions about components to be included in the final runtime image.

- **Real-Time Support** — Provides bounded, deterministic response times.

- **Supports Broad Range of Hardware** — x86, ARM, MIPS, and SH-4

- **Efficient Power Management** — Provides uniform power management libraries.

- **Efficient Development Tools** — Applications can be developed with C/C++, C#, and Visual Basic using the Visual Studio Integrated Development Environment.

- **Efficient Debugging and Testing Tools** — These include the Windows Embedded CE Test Kit (CETK); CoreCon, which is a connectivity framework providing connectivity between the VS2005 development workstation and CE device; Kernel Independent Transport Layer (KITL); and Remote Tools.

Before the current CE 6.0 version, the earlier version of CE was limited to supporting 32 concurrent running processes and could address only 32 MB of virtual memory in each process. The latest version, CE 6.0, has been redesigned to remove these limits. The latest OS kernel can support up to 32,000 simultaneous processes and can access up to 2 GB of virtual memory in each process. The new kernel also includes an improved file system that supports larger storage media, larger individual file size, and encryption for removable media.

On April 15, 2008, Microsoft announced that it would change the Windows Embedded CE product name to *Windows Embedded Compact* for the next release of this OS.

Modular and Compact OS

Windows Embedded CE is a highly modular operating system. Each CE runtime image is made up of a collection of OS components, selectable from the platform builder development tool's component library. The collection of OS components consists of device drivers, hardware interfacing libraries, programming libraries, networking libraries, applications, and other software technology frameworks.

The device manufacturers, using the platform builder, can develop and configure a customized CE designed to include only the needed components to support the hardware and the application on the device. All unnecessary components are excluded from the final OS runtime image to yield the smallest possible image size.

The platform builder tool and the associated OS design wizard provide an intuitive integrated development environment to help create the initial OS design with help from the OS design wizard and a library of preconfigured design templates. The platform builder provides a component library listing all available components to further configure the OS design.

With a smaller OS runtime footprint, it takes less system memory, less storage, and fewer processor resources to run. Devices with smaller OS run time take less time to boot up, which helps provide an efficient device. By minimizing the OS footprint, the device can be built with less expensive hardware.

Real-Time Operating System

Windows Embedded CE is a hard real-time operating system, providing reliable core services to support embedded system designs that demand low-latency, deterministic, real-time system performance.

CE has the following features required by a real-time system:

❑ **Preemptive Multithreading** — Determines when a context switch should occur.

❑ **Prioritized Thread Scheduling** — Uses a priority-based time-slice algorithm to schedule threads.

❑ **Priority Inversion Prevention** — When a lower-priority thread is sharing the same resource with a higher-priority thread, priority inversion can occur when the lower-priority thread and the higher-priority thread are competing for the same resource.

❑ **Predictable Thread Synchronization** — When multiple threads compete for resources, it's necessary to manage and synchronize thread priority. Otherwise, priority inversion can occur.

There are hard real-time and soft real-time systems. A soft real-time system can miss its bounded time response, missing the timing deadline once in a while, and still maintain a reasonable level of acceptable performance. For example, a Voice over IP (VoIP) device may delay the delivery of voice packets once in a while and end up dropping some of the packets because of network traffic loading, but still provide acceptable performance. A hard real-time system cannot miss any of its bounded time responses. When a hard real-time system misses a bounded time response, it causes major system failure. Imagine what happens when an automobile's electronic brake system fails to engage in a timely manner while the automobile is traveling at high speed and needs to make an urgent stop to avoid a collision. In a real-time system, the bounded time response means that the system must respond to service an event, such as the interrupt, within a maximum allowable time defined by the system. Otherwise, a major failure will occur.

Supported Hardware

Windows Embedded CE is designed to run on hardware built with x86, ARM, MIPS, and SH4 processors.

Business statistics indicate that only about 2 percent of the total number of microprocessors are used to build desktop PCs. The other 98 percent are used to build non-PC devices for the embedded market.

The ability to support four processor families enables Windows Embedded CE to reach a much broader market than the PC market and creates broader employment opportunities for the "embedded" developer and development of new types of devices.

Most hardware vendors have reference platforms with the necessary device drivers, Board Support Package (BSP), and Software Development Kit (SDK) to support CE. The BSP is a collection of device drivers and OEM Adaptation Layer (OAL) code for the hardware.

Microsoft maintains a long list of embedded processor boards and systems with BSP available to support Windows Embedded CE.

> **The following URL provides a list of hardware with BSPs for the OS.**
>
> `http://msdn.microsoft.com/en-us/embedded/aa714506.aspx`
>
> **If this URL is broken, search** `www.microsoft.com` **using the "Windows CE" and "supported BSP" keywords.**

New Features in CE 6.0 R2

About a year after the initial CE 6.0 release, CE 6.0 R2 was released with additional features and improvements. CE 6.0 R2 is delivered as an overlay to the originally installed CE 6.0. For the development workstation that already has CE 6.0 installed, the CE 6.0 R2 installation will keep the existing BSPs and OS designs previously created. The CE 6.0 R2 installation incorporates all the Quick Fix Engineering (QFE) and updates that have been released for CE 6.0. Following are the key features added for CE 6.0 R2:

- ❑ The flash driver and Secure Digital controller drivers have been improved. The Secure Digital controller driver has been updated to support the Secure Digital 2.0 specification. The Secure Digital 2.0 provides better performance and enables faster speeds for SDIO modules. It also supports higher-capacity memory cards, up to 32 GB.

- ❑ A new USB smart-card reader driver has been added to support the USB Chip/Smart Card Interface Devices Specification.

- ❑ The ATAPI storage driver has been upgraded to include support for the Serial ATA disk controller.

- ❑ The BIOSLoader has been upgraded to overcome the 2-GB limit of the old FAT16 file partition.

- ❑ A Pluggable Font technology has been added to enable a third-party font engine to be used.

- ❑ Three Board Support Packages (BSPs) were added — an x86-based HP/Compaq t5530 thin-client BSP, an SH4-based ST7109 BSP, and an ARMV4I-based Marvel PXA270 BSP.

- ❑ The Terminal Services Client has been improved. RDP 5.2 has been upgraded to RDP 6.0, which brings the RDP stack for Windows Embedded CE in line with the stack used for Windows Vista. RDP 6.0 also provides support for spanning a remote desktop session across multiple local displays. The RDP 6.0 update also provides significant improvement in security through Secure Socket Layer (SSL), Transport Layer Security (TLS), Network Level Authentication (NLA), and Server Authentication.

- ❑ Internet Explorer (IE) 6.0 has improved significantly. It has been updated to provide better security and performance. The IE team back-ported some of the algorithms to increase performance for IE 7.0 to IE 6.0 for Windows Embedded CE.

- ❑ Added support for Web Services on Device (WSD). *WSD* is a Microsoft implementation of the Devices Profile for Web Services standard. WSD provides a method for a discovery protocol to take place between new devices being attached to the network and devices already on the network.

Customizable UI

Many devices built on top of the Windows Embedded CE technologies don't present themselves as CE devices. Often, the users of these devices don't know that they're using a CE device, even after years of usage.

An OEM device built with Windows Embedded CE typically powers up to a custom splash screen, launches a custom application at start-up, and provides the user interface unique to the device, without showing any of the standard Windows desktop or UI.

The Windows Embedded CE's User Interface (UI) is customizable by the OEM to create a unique look and feel for the CE device. Sample UI skins with source code are provided along with the platform builder installation.

> **The Zune from Microsoft is built on top of Windows Embedded CE. The Zune is being sold as a portable MP3 Video player. A majority of Zune users don't know that the Zune application is running on CE.**

Wired and Wireless Connectivity

Windows Embedded CE enables you to build scalable wired and wireless devices that connect mobile and embedded devices into existing infrastructures.

CE provides broad wireless support for Personal Area Networks (PANs), Local Area Networks (LANs), and Wide Area Networks (WANs), including Bluetooth, IrDA, and 802.11 WiFi.

CellCore, a set of wireless mobile communication service components, added to the CE 6.0 release, provides the following added features to Windows Embedded CE:

❑ **Radio Interface Layer (RIL)** — Handles the communication between CellCore and the radio hardware.

❑ **Telephony** — The Telephony programming elements that are applicable to CellCore, which include Extended TAPI (ExTAPI), Assisted TAPI, and Telephony Service Provider (TSP) API.

❑ **Wireless Application Protocol (WAP) API** — The WAP API is an open standard for wireless communication to access the Internet from the mobile device.

❑ **Short Message Service (SMS) Providers** — The SMS is a communication protocol for sending short text messages between mobile devices.

❑ **Subscriber Identity Module (SIM) Management** — The SIM is a small smart card, containing identification and other data, used in the mobile phone.

Using CE, you can remotely authenticate, authorize, administer, and update new applications and operating system services on the device.

Graphics and Multimedia

Windows Embedded CE includes graphics and multimedia technology similar to the desktop, provides multimedia streaming capabilities to the device, and supports the various protocol and streaming formats required for audio and video playback of either local files or streamed data over a network connection.

A large set of graphics and multimedia components are included with CE:

- ❑ AlphaBlend API
- ❑ Direct3D, DirectDraw, DirectShow
- ❑ DVD-Video, DVR Engine
- ❑ Still Image Encoders and Decoders
- ❑ Multiple Monitor Support
- ❑ G.711, GSM 6.10 and IMA ADPCM Audio Codec
- ❑ MP3, MPEG-1 Layer 1 and 2 Audio Codec, MP4, WMA, WMA, WMV Codec
- ❑ Windows Media Player OCX 7
- ❑ Digital Rights Management (DRM)
- ❑ Streaming Media Playback

> **Windows Embedded CE's graphic and multimedia components enable device manufacturers to build a networked media device, a television set-top box, media player, multimedia electronic picture frame, digital video recorder, and more.**

Multilanguage, International Localization

Windows Embedded CE provides Multilingual User Interface (MUI), locale-specific support, Input Method Manager (IMM), and Input Method Editor (IME) to support devices localized for different international markets.

Windows Embedded CE provides an efficient development environment for the device manufacturer to develop the initial device in one language and be able to port the same design with minimum code change for different international markets. This flexibility enables the device manufacture to minimize development cost and shorten development time.

The Windows Embedded CE includes international languages support and can be built and localized for more than 130 different regions. Here is a list of languages it can support:

Arabic	Farsi	Kazah	Slovak
Armenian	Finnish	Konkani	Slovenian
Baltic	French	Korean	Spanish
Basque	FYRO Macedonian	Latvian	Swahili
Belarusian	Galician	Latin	Swedish
Bulgarian	Georgian	Lithuanian	Syriac
Catalan	German	Malay	Tamil
Chinese	Greek	Marathi	Tatar
Croatian	Gujarati	Mongolian	Telugu
Cyrillic	Hebrew	Norwegian	Thai
Czech	Hindi	Polish	Turkish
Divehi	Hungarian	Portuguese	Ukrainian
Dutch	Icelandic	Punjabi	Urdu
English (US)	Indonesian	Romanian	Uzbek
English (Worldwide)	Italian	Russian	Vietnam
Estonian	Japanese	Sanskrit	
Faeroese	Kannada	Serbian	

Real-Time Communication and VoIP

Windows Embedded CE includes Real-Time Communication (RTC) and Voice over IP (VoIP) components, which can be employed for communication using audio and text messaging in real time.

Windows Embedded CE provides an RTC Client API built on the Session Initiation Protocol (SIP), enabling you to build CE devices to make and receive calls from any SIP client. The RTC Client API uses the following industry standard protocols:

- ❏ Session Initiation Protocol (SIP)

- ❏ Session Description Protocol (SDP)

- ❏ Real-Time Transport Protocol (RTP)

- ❏ Public Switched Telephone Network/Internet Interworking (PINT)

For the CE 6.0 release, a new set of VoIP components was added to help the OEM take advantage of the CE platform to design and build VoIP devices. In addition to the core VoIP communication component, the VoIP application suite, with source code provided, was added to CE 6.0 to improve functionality. The VoIP application suite includes the following components:

❑ **Homescreen Application** — Provides the shell functionality as the core of a phone application with features to launch other applications and provide network status, voice-mail and e-mail message status, and system monitoring.

❑ **Phone Application** — Provides the user interface to dial a phone number to initiate a phone call. The phone application also provides the user interface to the VoIP stack.

❑ **Settings Application** — Provides the user interface to configure system settings for the VoIP application suite.

❑ **Bootstrap Application** — This application connects to a server and downloads the provisioning information for the phone.

OS Design Templates

Windows Embedded CE provides a set of OS design templates. An OS design template contains a predefined selection of CE components to use as the starting point for a new OS design to develop a customized CE runtime image. The following OS design templates are included with CE Platform Builder and provide starting points for developing the various devices noted:

❑ **Digital Media Receiver** — Music and video playback and storage devices

❑ **Enterprise Terminal** — Thin client, point of sale, point of information, kiosk, and other types of information appliance devices

❑ **Enterprise Web Pad** — Portable Internet appliance devices with large display screens using a touch screen to capture user input

❑ **Gateway** — Wireless access points, network routers, and other type of devices requiring Internet connection sharing features

❑ **Industrial Controller** — Human Machine Interface (HMI) devices for industrial automation and control applications

❑ **Internet Appliance** — Browser-based Internet appliances using standard keyboards and monitors

❑ **IP Phone Advanced** — Video phones with QVGA touch screens, using VoIP to save cost, and with advanced provisioning and conference calling

❑ **IP Phone Basic** — Basic Internet-based telephone devices using VoIP

❑ **Set-Top Box** — Television set-top boxes able to display Internet and media contents

❑ **Small-Footprint Device** — Small-footprint devices with a minimal set of system components

❑ **Windows Network Projector** — Windows network projects. Using the Connect to Windows Network Projector feature, a Windows Vista computer can redirect its display contents to the Windows Network Projector.

❑ **Windows Thin Client** — Windows-based thin-client terminals

To develop a customized OS runtime image, select the OS design template with the closest features to the type of device you are working with, and add or remove components to meet the design goal.

Developing CE Applications

The Windows Embedded CE operating system is based on the Win32 application programming interface (API). CE is designed to be a compact small-footprint operating system. The CE version of the Win32 API is a subset of the Win32 API for Windows XP and does not include all the function calls available with the Windows XP Win32 API.

CE uses the UTF16 Unicode character encoding standard. This is a common practice for embedded systems design and helps make it easier to port applications to support other languages.

In addition to the Win32 API, CE provides support for the following programming frameworks:

❑ Active Template Library (ATL)

❑ ActiveX

❑ Microsoft Component Object Module (COM)

❑ Microsoft Foundation Classes (MFC)

❑ .NET Compact Framework

The Windows Embedded CE Platform Builder is a plug-in for the Visual Studio (IDE) to develop OS design, device driver, BSP, and OAL hardware interfacing codes.

While it's possible to develop native code applications using the development environment provided by the platform builder tool, application development using Visual C++, Visual C#, or Visual Basic within Visual Studio provides a better environment to develop both managed and native code application.

Testing and Debugging

Windows Embedded CE provides an effective and easy-to-use testing and debugging environment, enabling the developer to test and debug the OS runtime image and applications running on the actual hardware and to insert breakpoints in the source files to halt program execution while the code is actually running on the hardware. This level of combined hardware and software debugging enables the developer to trace the codes to pinpoint problem areas quickly.

CE provides the following debugging connection and testing tools:

❑ Kernel Independent Transport Layer (KITL)

❑ CoreCon

❑ CE Test Kit (CETK)

The platform builder tool provides the following remote tools that use the KITL connection to perform the debugging function. KITL is used to provide the connection to debug the OS runtime image on the hardware:

- Remote File Viewer
- Remote Heap Walker
- Remote Zoom In
- Remote Process Viewer
- Remote Registry Editor
- Remote System Information
- Remote Performance Monitor
- Remote Spy
- Remote Kernel Tracker
- Remote Call Profiler

When developing CE applications using the Visual Studio 2005 IDE, the CoreCon connection is the mechanism used to establish a link between the development workstation and the CE device. After the CoreCon connection is established, a Visual C++, Visual C#, or Visual Basic application development session can download the compiled application binary to the CE device for debugging. It's possible to insert a breakpoint at the proper line of source code to halt application execution while running on the CE device and enable stepping through the code line-by-line to trace the source code and analyze application behavior.

The CETK tool can run stand-alone or within the platform builder tool. The CETK tool provides the facilities to test the BSP, device driver, and application. Microsoft also uses the same CETK tool to certify the board support package and device driver for its certification program.

I'll work through sample exercises in subsequent chapters covering each of these debugging and testing resources.

What Can Windows Embedded CE Do?

With the correct combination of hardware, Windows Embedded CE is suitable for a broad range of applications.

The CE operating system's real-time capability enables it to be a good platform for time-critical systems where desktop Windows cannot accomplish the goal without acquiring additional expensive third-party software.

The CE operating system can run on low-cost, power-efficient embedded hardware with limited system memory and flash storage, housed in a small enclosure. This can be wall-mounted to function as the main controller for an always-on, low-power, environment-friendly home automation system. While a Windows XP machine may be able to perform these tasks, it is not able to meet the "low-cost," "power-efficient," and "environment-friendly" aspects of the equation.

As computer technology advances, new possibilities are created. Imagine what you could do with a $90, 32-bit embedded controller with the following features:

- ❑ 300-MHz Vortex86SX CPU with 128 MB system memory
- ❑ 64-MB bootable flash storage with Windows Embedded CE 6.0 installed
- ❑ 10/100-Mbps Ethernet interface
- ❑ 2 Serial ports
- ❑ Parallel port
- ❑ 2 USB 2.0 host interface
- ❑ 16 general purpose input output (GPIO) control pins
- ❑ Powered by a single 5-V DC @ less than 500 mA
- ❑ Supporting Visual Basic, C#, and Visual C++ within the Visual Studio 2005 IDE

Using the Vortex86SX controller with some glue logic components and linking them to a few relays, sensors, and motors, you can create a range of interesting, intelligent, and functional applications that can integrate and communicate with your desktop computer, portable computer, or even the mobile phone you carry at all times. Among these applications are:

- ❑ Home automation system controller
- ❑ Intelligent building or HVAC controller
- ❑ Robotic controller
- ❑ Security system
- ❑ Greenhouse system controller
- ❑ Industrial automation controller

Summary

This chapter provides an overview of CE and a brief look at the other products within the Windows Embedded product family. It also covers CE's key features, development environment, and debugging and testing tools.

2

Development Environment and Tools

As part of the process in learning any new skill, the keys to mastering the skill quickly and effectively are knowing the available tools and resources to help perform a given task and then lots of practice.

In this chapter, I review the CE development tools and the installation process and where the OS components, utilities, and sample code are installed.

Windows Embedded CE Platform Builder

The tool used to develop the CE design and generate the custom OS runtime image is called the *Platform Builder*. In each of the previous releases of CE, the Platform Builder tool was the stand-alone tool dedicated to supporting CE-related development.

For the 6.0 release, the Platform Builder is a Visual Studio plug-in that requires VS2005 to run. The plug-in allows building BSPs, creating device drivers, building runtime images, and exporting SDKs to support application development.

In a typical CE development project, the Platform Builder within the VS2005 IDE is used to perform one or more of the following tasks:

- ❏ Develop the OS design and generate the OS runtime image from the OS design.
- ❏ Develop the device driver code and compile the device driver binary.
- ❏ Develop the programming library code and generate the programming library binary.
- ❏ Develop the application code and compile the application executable.

Throughout every CE development project, compiling and generating the binary for the device drivers and programming libraries, compiling the application executable, and generating the OS runtime image are common tasks that need to be performed over and over again. Depending on the development workstation's processor speed and performance, many of these compilation processes may take anywhere from 10 minutes to well over 30 minutes. Under certain conditions, a full project compilation is not needed to generate the necessary result. With good understanding about the build system and the Platform Builder tool, unnecessary full compilation can be avoided to save precious development time.

It's definitely well worth the time spent to explore and become familiar with the Platform Builder tool. Figure 2-1 is a screen capture of the Platform Builder IDE.

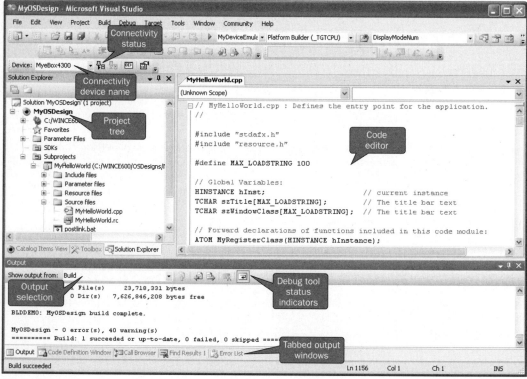

Figure 2-1

Windows Embedded CE 6.0 Installation

One of the most important keys to setting up a proper development environment is to have the development tools installed properly with all the needed components.

Improperly installed development tools, missing components, and not keeping up with the necessary updates and fixes are known to cause problems and can result in a build system that's not able to complete the project compilation process to generate the necessary binaries, not able to connect to the target device to transfer the OS runtime image, and not able to connect to the target device for debugging and application development.

As part of the CE 6.0 installation, depending on the supported processors selected during the installation process, the size of the installation can be well over 10 GB and take quite a bit of time to install even on a fast computer. In addition to the development tools, each new OS design project may take up more than 1 GB of storage space after compilation. To ensure that adequate storage space is available to work through an OS design project, the development workstation must have sufficient available storage space to accommodate the development tools and still have the necessary storage for the new OS design projects.

Microsoft specified that 18 GB of storage space is required on the installation drive and 1 GB of available space on the system drive. In addition, each OS design project will require an additional 1 to 2 GB of storage space.

It's always good practice to have a little more than what is needed to prevent problems down the road. It's best to reserve 30 to 40 GB of storage space for the installation and future OS design projects.

As part of the development process, there will be situations in which we need to create multiple instances of the sample project to debug and trace problems. In addition, there is a need to keep separate OS design projects developed for different purposes.

> The exercises in this book are developed using the default installation. It's strongly recommended that you install all software using the default recommended installation directory to drive C.

Supported Processors

CE is designed to support four families of processors (CPUs): ARM MIPS, SuperH, and x86. There are different derivatives of these four families available from vendors, with different features and costs.

Microsoft provides CPU support libraries for all four supported processor families as a starting point to help the hardware vendors lower the development effort to create the BSPs needed to support their hardware platforms. The CPU support libraries provided by Microsoft are in the following directory:

_WINCEROOT\PLATFORM\COMMON

The CE installation includes support by default for the ARMV4I processor. To develop the OS design for the other processor families, we need to explicitly include support for the targeted processors.

I use the eBox-4300, a compact computing device built with an x86 processor, to work through some of the exercises in this book. You need to include support for the x86 processor family with the installation. During the CE 6.0 installation process, select support for both the ARMV4I and x86 processors, as shown in Figure 2-2.

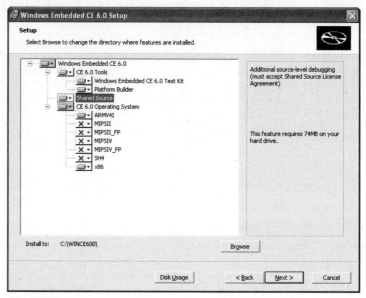

Figure 2-2

Installation Sequence

When done correctly, we need only install the development tools once. Otherwise, to fix a bad installation or deal with a workstation with questionable development tools installation, we may have to uninstall and reinstall everything from scratch.

We must invest a little bit of patience and time and follow the recommended sequence to properly install all the needed development tools and ensure a proper development environment.

As of the writing of this book, CE 6.0 R2 has been released. Following is the installation sequence to install CE 6.0 R2. Please consult product installation information if you are using a different release of CE.

> **After each installation step, launch the newly installed software to ensure that it has been properly installed before moving on to execute the next installation step.**

1. Install Visual Studio 2005.

2. Install Windows Embedded CE 6.0.

3. Install Visual Studio 2005 SP1 URL to download VS2005 SP1:

```
www.microsoft.com/downloads/
details.aspx?FamilyID=bb4a75ab-e2d4-4c96-b39d-37baf6b5b1dc&DisplayLang=en
```

> **In the event the link is broken, visit** `http://download.microsoft.com` **and search using the Visual Studio 2005 Service Pack 1 keyword.**

4. Install the Visual Studio 2005 SP1 update for Vista (skip this step for a Windows XP machine). URL to download the VS2005 SP1 update for Vista:

```
www.microsoft.com/downloads/
details.aspx?FamilyID=90e2942d-3ad1-4873-a2ee-4acc0aace5b6&DisplayLang=en
```

> **In the event the link is broken, visit** `http://download.microsoft.com` **and search using the VS2005 SP1 Update for Vista keyword.**

5. Install the Windows Embedded CE 6.0 SP1 URL to download the CE 6.0 SP1:

```
www.microsoft.com/downloads/
details.aspx?FamilyID=bf0dc0e3-8575-4860-a8e3-290adf242678&DisplayLang=en
```

> **In the event the link is broken, visit** `http://download.microsoft.com` **and search using the Windows Embedded CE 6.0 Service Pack 1 keyword.**

In the event the link is broken, visit `http://download.microsoft.com` *and search using the Windows Embedded CE 6.0 Service Pack 1 keyword.*

6. Install the Windows Embedded CE 6.0 R2 update URL to download the CE 6.0 R2 update:

```
www.microsoft.com/downloads/
details.aspx?FamilyID=f41fc7c1-f0f4-4fd6-9366-b61e0ab59565&DisplayLang=en
```

> **In the event the link is broken, visit** `http://download.microsoft.com` **and search using the Windows Embedded CE 6.0 R2 keyword.**
>
> **By default, the CE 6.0 installation program includes support for the ARMV4I processor; be sure to include support for the targeted processor during the installation process. For the exercises in this book, select ARMV4I and x86 as the supported processors.**
>
> **The emulator is used for some of the exercises in this book. The Microsoft Device Emulator 1.0 is installed with Windows Embedded CE 6.0 installation. Under Windows Vista, the Microsoft Device Emulator 1.0 does not function correctly. You need to install the Device Emulator update to 2.0 or later for it to function correctly under Windows Vista. As of the writing of this book, the Microsoft Device Emulator 3.0 is available for download from Microsoft download. To locate and download the updated Device Emulator, visit Microsoft download at** `http://download.microsoft.com` **and search for the Microsoft Device Emulator 3.0 download.**

Quick Fix Engineering and Update

It's good practice to keep your development environment up to date and install updates and quick fix engineering (QFE) updates as they become available. Microsoft releases QFE for Windows Embedded CE monthly to correct known issues and releases a year-end rollup to include all QFEs released during the year.

Some of these updates and QFEs install new components to the development workstation. It's important to install updates and QFEs in chronological order to prevent new files being overwritten by older files.

To work through the exercises in this book, CE 6.0 and the R2 update are needed.

As of the writing of this book, the following update QFE is available and should be installed — Windows Embedded CE 6.0 R2 Update Rollup 2007:

```
www.microsoft.com/downloads/details.aspx?FamilyID=2447c25f-782b-4378-a
228-f18af8c59aa3&DisplayLang=en
```

Windows Embedded CE Terminology

Every development environment has a set of commonly used terms, some of which may be common to other development and some that are unique to the specific development environment. It's important to know the key terms used in the CE environment. Many CE technical papers and application notes make use of these terms. Following is a listing of some of the common terms used in CE:

❏   Board Support Package (BSP)

❏   Catalog

❏   Component

❏   Design template

❏   Hardware Platform

❏   Module

❏   OEM Adaptation Layer (OAL)

❏   OS Design

❏   OS Runtime Image

❏   Target Device

Board Support Package (BSP)

The *Board Support Package (BSP)* is a set of software components combining the necessary OEM Adaptation Layer code, device drivers, and configuration files for a specific hardware platform. Several reference BSPs provided by Microsoft are installed by default along with the CE installation, such as the following:

❏   The Aruba Board BSP is installed when support for the ARMV4I processor is included in the installation.

❏   The CEPC BSP is installed when support for the x86 processor is included in the installation.

❏   The Device Emulator BSP is installed when support for the ARMV4I processor is included in the installation.

❏   The H4Sample OMAP2420 BSP is installed when support for the ARMV4I processor is included in the installation.

❏   The MainstoneIII PXA27X BSP is installed when support for the ARMV4I processor is included in the installation.

❑   The HP Compaq t5530 Thin Client BSP is installed by the CE 6.0 R2 update.

❑   The Voice over IP PXA270 BSP is installed by the CE 6.0 R2 update.

The BSPs installed along with the CE 6.0 installation and R2 update are listed in the \BSP node on the Platform Builder's component catalog, as shown in Figure 2-3.

Figure 2-3

The BSPs provided by third-party companies are listed in the \Third Party\BSP node on the Platform Builder's component catalog, as shown in Figure 2-4.

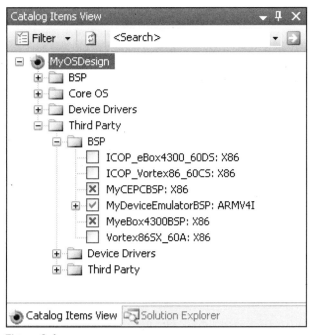

Figure 2-4

It's likely that you will use the BSP provided by the same company producing the hardware platform you use to develop the CE solution. If the hardware platform company does not have a CE BSP for its hardware, you will need to roll your own.

> A good starting point from which to roll your own BSP is to clone one of the Microsoft-provided reference BSPs, with the same CPU architecture as your hardware, and modify the cloned BSP to fit the hardware you are working with.

The files for all the installed BSPs, including Microsoft-provided and third-party BSPs, are located in the C:\WINCE600\PLATFORM\ directory. The C:\WINCE600 directory is the default installation path for the CE components.

> The C:\WINCE600\PLATFORM directory is represented by the _PLATFORMROOT variable, as seen throughout this book and the Windows Embedded CE document.

Catalog

The *Catalog* is a container for available OS features, modules, and components. Following are some examples of different groups of catalog items that CE has:

- ❏ Board support package (BSP)
- ❏ Device driver
- ❏ Application
- ❏ File system component
- ❏ Shell and user interface
- ❏ Third-party\BSP

Component

A *CE Component* can be a device driver, library, application, or utility that can be added to an OS design.

Figure 2-5 is a screen capture image showing some of the device driver components within the Platform Builder's components catalog.

Figure 2-5

Design Template

A *Design Template* contains a set of pre-selected OS components for a category of devices and is used to form the starting point for an OS design project.

Hardware Platform

The *Hardware Platform* is used to refer to the physical hardware for running CE and applications.

Module

A *Module* can be an EXE or DLL file, which can be included as part of a CE runtime image.

OEM Adaptation Layer (OAL)

The *OEM Adaption Layer (OAL)* is the low-level code acting as the interface between the hardware and CE.

OS Design

The *OS Design* is a collection of operating system components, application projects, BSPs, and configuration files. The OS Design Project contains the files, references to the files, system settings, and compilation directives needed to generate the CE runtime image.

OS Runtime Image

The *OS Runtime Image* is the binary generated from the OS Design Project and contains the OS and its associated software. The default name for the OS runtime image file is *nk.bin*. Upon a successful compilation of the OS Design Project, the nk.bin runtime image is generated in the OS Design Project's Release folder.

Target Device

The *Target Device* is generally referred to as the hardware platform used in the CE development project. When using the emulator to work through the exercises and samples in this book, the emulator is considered to be the target device. When using the eBox-4300 to work through the exercises and samples, the eBox-4300 is considered to be the target device.

Windows Embedded CE Environment Variables

CE uses different types of environment variables to configure the OS design and provides uniform vocabularies that represent the drive path and configuration string. These environment variables can be separated into two general types:

❏ The environment variable contains information such as drive path and system information.

❏ The environment variable is used to configure the OS design and control the functionality to be included or excluded in the OS design.

The environment variables can be set or cleared from the platform builder IDE, the command prompt build window, and the OS design configuration batch file.

The environment variables can be used to configure and customize the OS design to include or exclude components from the runtime image.

Below is a listing of different groups of environment variables:

- ❑ BSP environment variables
- ❑ BSP_NO environment variables
- ❑ IMG environment variables
- ❑ PRJ environment variables
- ❑ Miscellaneous environment variables

> **The environment variables are different between different versions of CE. Some of the variables in the earlier version have been removed. When searching for information relating to CE environment variables, you may find information from other versions, which may or may not be applicable to the version you are working on.**

BSP Environment Variables

BSP environment variables define optional support available with a board support package. This group of environment variables is used to include certain components with the OS design.

Table 2-1 lists some of the BSP environment variables and the affected components.

Table 2-1: BSP Environment Variables and Affected Components

BSP_DISPLAY_RAGEXL	Adds the ATI display driver to the configuration.
BSP_DISPLAY_FLAT	Adds the FLAT display driver to the configuration.
BSP_DISPLAY_RFLAT	Adds the rotated-FLAT display driver to the configuration.
BSP_DISPLAY_S3V	Adds the S3 Virge display driver to the configuration.
BSP_NIC_DP83815	Adds the DP83815 (MacPhyter) NDIS miniport driver to the configuration.
BSP_NIC_ISLP2NDS_PCMCIA	Adds the Intersil miniport driver to the configuration.
BSP_NIC_NE2000_ISA	Adds the ISA NE2000 NIC driver to the configuration.
BSP_NIC_NE2000_PCI	Adds the PCI NE2000 NIC driver to the configuration.
BSP_NIC_NE2000_PCMCIA	Adds the PCMCIA NE2000 NIC driver to the configuration.
BSP_NIC_PCX500_PCMCIA	Adds the Cisco miniport driver to the configuration. Supports the Cisco Aironet 340/350 series.
BSP_NIC_RTL8139	Adds the RTL8139 NIC driver to the configuration.
BSP_NIC_RTL8180	Adds Nativewifi RTL8180 wireless support and set to AP mode.

BSP_NIC_RTL8180_STA	Adds Nativewifi RTL8180 wireless support and set to the default STA mode.
BSP_NIC_XIRCCE2_PCMCIA	Adds the XIRCOM miniport driver to the configuration.
BSP_PCCARDATADISK	Uses Atapi.dll instead of Atadisk.dll for the ATA storage cards.
BSP_CREDSVC_IN_DEVICE	Enables the credential manager and sets it for operation in `devices.exe`, even if the OS design includes `services.exe`.
BSP_DISPLAY_MQ200	Adds the MQ200 display driver to the configuration.
BSP_DISPLAY_NOP	Adds the stub display driver to the configuration.
BSP_NIC_DC21X4	Adds the DEC21140 NDIS miniport driver to the configuration.
BSP_NIC_AR6K_PCMCIA	Adds the AR6000 WiFi CF adapter to the configuration.
BSP_NIC_AR6K_SDIO	Adds the AR6000 WiFi SDIO adapter to the configuration.
BSP_NIC_E100BEX	Adds the Intel EtherExpress PRO Ethernet Network driver for Intel i82559 PCI NIC.
BSP_NOTIFY_IN_DEVICE	Enables the notification subsystem engine for operation in `device.exe`.By default, if the variable is not set and `services.exe` is included in the OS design, the engine runs in `services.exe`.
BSP_SDHC_ELLEN	Assigns the standard SDIO host controller to the TE4370 Evaluation Board.

Table 2-1 (like Tables 2-2 through 2-6) is taken from the Microsoft Developers Network. The full list of the BSP environment variables is also available from the network's URL:

```
http://msdn2.microsoft.com/en-us/library/aa909549.aspx
```

> **Hardware manufacturers may establish their own BSP environment variables unique to their hardware and BSP to include device drivers for their hardware with the OS runtime image.**

BSP_NO Environment Variables

BSP_NO variables are used to define options not supported by the BSP or hardware platform.

For example, if your target device does not have audio function, the BSP_NOAUDIO can be set to exclude all audio components from getting into the final OS runtime image.

Table 2-2 lists some of the BSP_NO environment variables and the affected components.

Table 2-2: BSP_NO Environment Variables

BSP_NOAUDIO	Excludes support for audio.
BSP_NOCOMCARD	Excludes support for ComCard and Com 16550 serial drivers.
BSP_NODISPLAY	Excludes support for displays.
BSP_NOETHER	Excludes support for Ethernet.
BSP_NOGSM	Excludes support for the CSMI and RIL drivers. This is applicable only to the TI FSample BSP.
BSP_NOIDE	Excludes support for IDE device.
BSP_NOPCCARD	Excludes support for PC card.
BSP_NOPCIBUS	Excludes support for the PCI bus.
BSP_NOPCMCIA	Excludes support for PCMCIA
BSP_NORNDIS	Excludes support for RNDIS.
BSP_NOSHAREETH	Exclude support for shared Ethernet.
BSP_NOTOUCH	Excludes support for touch drivers.
BSP_NOUSB	Excludes support for USB.

The full list of the BSP_NO environment variables is available from the MSDN URL:

        http://msdn2.microsoft.com/en-us/library/aa908645.aspx

> **Hardware manufacturers may establish their own BSP_NO environment variables to exclude functions not supported by their hardware platform.**

IMG Environment Variables

The *IMG environment variables*, when set, remove modules from the OS design and leave the associated registry entries in the OS design intact. The IMG environment variable is also used to configure the memory footprint for the image.

The IMG environment variables are available for your convenience during development and are not to be used in a shipped product.

Table 2-3 lists the IMG environment variables and the affected components.

Table 2-3: IMG Environment Variables

IMGAUTH	Enables runtime images to be keyed to a specific device, ensuring that the images are flashed only on the selected device.
	When the device is booted, it validates the runtime image signature by ensuring that the signature matches the hardware device ID.
IMGAUTOFLUSH	Enables automatic flushing of events to the release directory.
	This must be used with IMGCELOGENABLE.
IMGCELOGENABLE	Adds celog.dll to the OS design and initializes event logging when the runtime image boots.
IMGEBOOT	Reserves space for the boot loader in ROM.
IMGFLASH	Enables flashing the runtime image into ROM.
IMGHDSTUB	Adds OS Awareness for hardware-assisted debugging.
IMGNODEBUGGER	Excludes debugger support from the OS design.
	When set to 0, the OS design must also contain these files for the debugger to run: Hd.dll, Kd.dll, OsAxsT0.dll, and OsAxsT1.dll.
IMGNOKITL	Selects a kernel that is not KITL-enabled.
IMGSHIMENABLE	Includes the kernel-side portion of the Application Verifier tool in the runtime image.
	If this is included in the runtime image, it loads at boot time.
IMGDUALPORTRIL	Configures the RIL driver to use an MUX driver instead of a raw serial driver.
IMGKCOVER	Enables code coverage.
IMGMULTIBIN	Enables multi-XIP regions in the runtime image.
IMGNOLOC	Excludes localization functionality from the runtime image.
IMGNORDPINGWE	Enables the RDP core, mstsax.dll, to be hosted in the same process as the container application, `cetsc.exe`, for debugging and testing.
IMGNOREDIR	Excludes redir from the OS design.
IMGNOSHAREETH	Excludes VMINI support from the OS design.
	Setting this environment variable might require you to perform a rebuild of the BSP.
	To perform a rebuild from a command prompt build window, navigate to the root directory for the BSP, and enter the following command:
	`Build -c`
IMGNOTAHOMA	Excludes Tahoma true-type font from the OS design.
IMGOSCAPTURE	Adds `OSCapture.exe` to the OS design. It starts buffering events in RAM when the runtime image boots.

Table 2-3

IMGPROFILER	Selects a profiling-enabled kernel.
IMGRAM16	Configures the runtime image for 16 MB of RAM.
IMGRAM32	Configures the runtime image for 32 MB of RAM.
IMGRAM64	Configures the runtime image for 64 MB of RAM.
IMGRAM128	Configures the runtime image for 128 MB of RAM.
IMGRAM256	Configures the runtime image for 256 MB of RAM.
IMGRAM512	Configures the runtime image for 512 MB of RAM.
IMGRILCOM1	Configures the RIL driver to open COM1 instead of COM2 for the AT command/response port.
IMGSIGN	Includes the signature extension block in the ROM header.
IMGTINYFSRAM	Set FSRAMPERCENT, which minimizes the amount of RAM allocated for the file system.
IMGTRUSTROMONLY	Sets ROMFLAGS, which configures the runtime image to trust only modulus in ROM.

The full list of the IMG environment variables is available from the MSDN URL:

> http://msdn2.microsoft.com/en-us/library/aa909715.aspx

PRJ Environment Variables

The *PRJ environment variables* enable project-specific functionality in the OS design.

Table 2-4 lists the PRJ environment variables.

Table 2-4: PRJ Environment Variables

PRJ_BOOTDEVICE_ATAPI	Enables ATAPI as the boot device.
	— If PRJ_ENABLE_FSREGHIVE is set, the hive registry is located on the device.
	— If PRJ_ENABLE_FSMOUNTASROOT is set, the device is mounted as the root file system.
PRJ_BOOTDEVICE_MSFLASH	Enables MSFLASH as the boot device.
	— If PRJ_ENABLE FSREGHIVE is set, the hive registry is located on the device.
	— If PRJ_ENABLE_FSMOUNTASROOT is set, the device is mounted as the root file system.

PRJ_BTH_PAN_BRIDGE	Configures a Bluetooth personal access network (PAN) to be a network access point using layer-2 bridging.
PRJ_BTH_PAN_GN	Configures a Bluetooth PAN to be a group of ad hoc networks.
PRJ_BTH_PAN_ROUTER	Configures a Bluetooth PAN to be a network access point using layer-3 routing.
PRJ_ENABLE_DBFLUSH_THREAD	Enables automatic flushing of the database volume periodically.
PRJ_ENABLE_FSREGHIVE	Controls whether the hive-based registry is enabled by default.
PRJ_ENABLE_FSMOUNTASROOT	Enables mounting of an external volume as the root file system. The device selected for mounting is defined by setting PRJ_BOOTDEVICE_ATAPI or PRJ_BOOTDEVICE_MSFLASH.
PRJ_ENABLE_REGFLUSH_THREAD	Enables automatic flushing of the registry periodically.
PRJ_NAS_CACHE	Enables the default FAT disk cache on the target device to improve network authentication server (NAS) performance.
PRJ_NAS_DOGFOOD	Enables backward compatibility with versions of Windows 98 and earlier and configures all adapters on the device to use the Server Message Block (SMB) file sharing protocol.

The full list of the PRJ environment variables is available from the MSDN URL:

```
http://msdn2.microsoft.com/en-us/library/aa908861.aspx
```

Miscellaneous Environment Variables

Table 2-5 contains miscellaneous environment variables.

Table 2-5: Miscellaneous Environment Variables

BUILD_MULTIPROCESSOR	Used by `build.exe` in the IDE.
	Specifies the number of processes launched simultaneously when running a build. This number can be more or less than the number of processors on the development workstation.
	The default setting is 1.
	It might take several trials to determine the optimal setting for your development workstation, which depends on factors including the number of processors, amount of RAM, and disk performance.
	The optimal setting decreases the amount of time the platform builder requires to complete a build. A setting larger than the optimal one can increase the amount of time required.
BUILDREL_USE_COPY	Used by buildrel.bat when copying files into the flat release. By default, buildrel.bat uses copylink to copy files. If you experience a sharing violation during the copy phase, you can set `BUILDREL_USE_COPY=1` to instruct buildrel.bat to use xcopy.
BUILDWARNISERROR	Specifies that `build.exe` treats warnings as errors. This includes instances such as passing an invalid parameter to `build.exe`, and parsing warning when reading sources and dirs files.
	When BUILDWARNISERROR is set to 1 in a sources or sources.cmn file, `build.exe` exits after a warning is generated.
	You can choose to set this environment variable globally in a sources.cmn file, and unset it locally in a sources file.
CPLMAIN_LP	Set to L to specify the Handheld PC (H/PC) style Control Panel.
	Set to P to specify the Windows Mobile powered PDA-style Control Panel.
LOCALE	Used by `Makeimg.exe`. Defines the target locale for localizing the build environment.
PBCONFIG	Defines the combination of BSP and debug or release settings for the current build.
RI_SUPPRESS_INFO	Specifies that output from Romimage is limited to a list of errors and the completion list.
	To limit the output from Romimage on the Build tab of the output windows; set `RI_SUPPRESS_INFO` to all.
_TGTCPUFAMILY	Defines the CPU family for a BSP.
_TGTPLAT	Defines the name of the BSP.

WINCEDEBUG=retail	Specifies whether debugging information is generated in object files.
	This environment variable is case-sensitive.
	Does not generate debugging information in the object files. The object files are placed in the Release directory.
	Because this setting allows compiler optimization, using the debugger is not recommended. The debugger could highlight the wrong source line if the compiler rearranges code.
WINCEDEBUG=debug	Generates debugging information in the object files. The object files are placed in the Debug directory.
	Compiler optimizations are disabled.
WINCEREL=1	Releases the built components into the _FLATRELEASEDIR directory and into the Public directory.
	When you have a build set up, you can make incremental changes, rebuild a component, and make a new runtime image without rerunning the Build Release tool, buildrel.bat.
WINCEREL=	Releases the built components only into the Public directory.
WINCESHIP	Specifies whether this build is for shipping or testing. This is only available in the release configuration and is hidden in the debug configuration.
	When set, the OS does not generate debug messages.
_WINCEOSVER	Defines the OS version.
	For CE 6.0, the default value is 600.

There is another group of miscellaneous environment variables that can be used to specify directory path, as shown in Table 2-6.

Table 2-6: Miscellaneous Environment Variables

_WINCEROOT	Defines the root directory.
_FLATRELEASEDIR	Defines the directory where the released source code and binary files will be placed.
PBWORKSPACEROOT	Defines the location of the current platform builder workspace.
_PLATFORMROOT	Defines the location of the Platform directory.
	The default is _WINCEROOT\Platform.

Table 2-6

_PRIVATEROOT	Defines the location of an alternate root directory, such as the directory to contain a different Set Environment variable tool, setenv.bat. You can set this variable to point to a directory of your choice. The default is _WINCEROOT\Private.
_PROJECTOAKROOT	Defines the location of the Oak directory for your project. During the build process, Build.exe places the files it builds in this directory. The default is _PROJECTROOT\Oak.
_PROJECTROOT	Defines the location of the project you are building.
_PUBLICROOT	Defines the location of the public projects. The default is _WINCEROOT\Public.
_SDKROOT	Defines the location of the tools you use to build projects, such as the command-line compiler, linker, debugger, and runtime libraries. The default is _WINCEROOT\SDK
_TGTPROJ	Defines the name of the current active workspace.
USING_PB_WORKSPACE	Specifies whether you are working in a build environment opened from the IDE. If this is set, the build environment was launched from the IDE. Otherwise, this is not present in setenv.bat.

Windows Embedded CE Files and Directories

One of the first few things we need to know while learning about CE is where things are. The Visual Studio 2005 and CE installation installs huge numbers of files to the development workstation.

In addition to the Platform Builder, associated utilities, and tools, the CE installation also installs a large collection of device drivers, software components, sample applications, and the source code for a large percentage of these components.

The default CE 6.0 installation installs the Platform Builder program and utilities to the C:\Program Files\Microsoft Platform Builder\6.00\ folder. The software components and libraries needed to compose the OS runtime image are installed to the C:\WINCE600\ folder. For CE development and this book's objective, the software components, libraries, and codes are located in the C:\WINCE600\ folder and subfolders. Table 2-7 provides a listing of the folders for the various software components installed by CE. Take some time to explore and browse through the C:\WINCE600\ directories and subdirectories.

Table 2-7: Windows Embedded CE Directories

_WINCEROOT\3rdParty	This directory is not created by default during the CE installation. Some third-party components create this directory during the installation.
_WINCEROOT\OSDesigns	The default location for user-created OS design projects.
_WINCEROOT\Others	A repository of various run times, samples, and components.
_PLATFORMROOT\	Stores the hardware-specific files and is the default location for all BSPs, including BSPs provided by Microsoft and third-party companies.
_PUBLICROOT\	Contains the platform-independent components and CE configuration. Some third-party components may be installed to this directory.
_SDKROOT\	Contains tools and binaries to support created platforms.
_PRIVATEROOT\	Contains Microsoft-shared source codes for the CE operating system.

The C:\WINCE600\ directory is represented by the _WINCEROOT variable. The C:\WINCE600\PLATFORM directory is represented by the _PLATFORMROOT variable.

The Platform Directory

The *Platform directory* (_PLATFORMROOT) contains BSPs and hardware-specific files. Table 2-8 lists the subdirectories under the Platform directory. Microsoft-provided BSP as well as third-party BSP are installed under the Platform directory.

Table 2-8: The Platform Directory

\ARUBABOARD	Contains BSP files for the ArubaBoard development kit.
\CEPC	Contains BSP files for the CE PC-based hardware platform.
\COMMON	Contains files common to all hardware platforms.
\DEVICEEMULATOR	Contains BSP files for the CE-based virtual hardware platform.
\H4SAMPLE	Contains BSP files for the TI OMAP2420 SDP (H4Sample) hardware platform.
\MAINSTONEIII	Contains BSP files for the Intel PXA27x MainstoneIII hardware platform.
\T5530	Contains BSP files for the HP Compaq t5530 Thin Client hardware platform.
\VOIP_PXA270	Contains BSP files for the sample VoIP platform using the Marvell PXA270 processor.

The Public Directory

The *Public directory* contains the platform-independent components and CE configurations. For a CE 6.0 installation with support for the ARMV4I and X86 processors, there are 2,500 folders and more than 46,000 files, occupying almost 6 GB of storage. There are production-quality device drivers, reference device drivers, sample shell applications, sample media applications, sample VoIP applications, sample speech applications, sample web applications, sample FTP applications, sample telnet applications, sample web service for devices, and more. And all of these come with their source code.

Needless to say, there's a lot of really good stuff under the Public directory. This is the treasure chest for those of you looking for functional sample codes. Table 2-9 lists the Public directory's subdirectories and provides general description about the contents.

Table 2-9: The Public Directory

\CEBASE	Contains components that support both the headless-based and display-based devices.
\CELLCORE	Contains the communication components to take advantage of the mobile communication network.
\COMMON	Contains OS components that are common to all CE designs.
\DATASYNC	Contains components that support data synchronization between a Windows-based desktop computer and CE-based device.
\DCOM	Contains components that support the Distributed Component Object Model (DCOM).
\DIRECTX	Contains components that support Microsoft DirectX, waveform audio, the DVD-Video API, and Windows Media.
\GDIEX	Contains components that support the Imaging API.
\IE	Contains components that support Microsoft Internet Explorer 6 for CE.
\NETCFV2	Contains components that support the Microsoft .NET Compact Framework version 2.
\NETCFV35	Contains components that support the Microsoft .NET Compact Framework version 3.5.
\RDP	Contains components that support the Remote Desktop Protocol (RDP).
\SCRIPT	Contains components that support the Microsoft JScript 5.5 development system, the Microsoft Visual Basic Scripting Edition (VBScript) 5.5 programming language.
\SERVERS	Contains components that support the HTTP Server Extension interface.

\SHELL	Contains components that support the standard shell, Explorer Browser, and CEShell module.
\SHELLSDK	Contains components that support API compatibility for the Pocket PC 2002 shell and use AYGShell API extensions.
\SPEECH	Contains components that support the Microsoft Speech Application Programming Interface (SAPI).
\SQLCE	Contains SQLCE components that support Microsoft SQL Server CE 2.0.
\VOIP	Contains components that support Voice over IP (VoIP) applications and services based on the SIP standard.
\WCEAPPSFE \WCESHELLFE	These two directories contain components that support CE application modules, WordPad, and Inbox.

Third-Party Components

There are three general types of third-party components found in the CE development environment:

❑   BSPs

❑   Device drivers

❑   Programming libraries

Third-party components may come in the form of the self-installation package with an MSI or EXE extension. Not all third-party components come in a self-installable package. It's common for third-party components to come in the form of binary files with associated registry entries, utilities, and manual installation instructions showing where to create the folder and place the files.

All third-party company BSPs are installed to the _PLATFORMROOT directory and show up on the \Third Party\BSP node within the Platform Builder's components catalog.

Third-party company device drivers and software components may be installed to the _PUBLICROOT or the _WINCEROOT\3rdParty directory and show up on the \Third Party node within the Platform Builder's components catalog.

Building CE Runtime Images

To get to the phase of developing the OS design and generating the OS runtime image, we need to have a target hardware platform for the project. Before diving into building the CE runtime image, let's take a brief look at the CE device development process.

A typical CE device development project may involve some or all of the following steps. Some of the steps may take place concurrently and in parallel:

1. Identify the hardware platform and hardware vendor for the project.

2. Identify additional hardware peripherals needed for the project.

3. Acquire or develop the CE BSP for the hardware platform.

4. Acquire or develop the CE device driver for the additional peripherals.

5. Develop the OS design and generate the CE runtime image to run on the hardware.

6. Develop the application.

7. Build the prototype.

8. Debug and test.

> **Selecting a hardware platform that comes with a quality Windows Embedded BSP and device drivers will help save development time and minimize development risk. Working with hardware vendors who understand the Windows Embedded development environment and have a strong software support team will help eliminate a lot of aggravation during the development process.**

To continue and cover the build process to generate the CE runtime image, I make the following assumptions:

❑   The hardware platform has been selected.

❑   There is a quality BSP for the hardware platform.

❑   There is a quality boot loader for the hardware platform.

❑   CE device drivers are available for all the hardware peripherals.

Based on the above assumptions, let's go through the following steps to create an OS design and build and generate an OS runtime image for the targeted hardware platform:

1. Create a new OS design with help from the OS Design Wizard.

2. Add additional components from the CE Platform Builder's components catalog to customize the OS design.

3. Develop the application and include the application in the OS design.

4. Set environment variables, add additional components to the project, and edit the project registry entries to further customize the OS design.

5. Build and generate the OS runtime image.

Summary

This chapter provides a high-level overview and covers the following subjects about the CE development environment, what is available within CE Platform Builder, and the VS2005 IDE:

- Visual Studio 2005 and CE 6.0 installation sequence
- Supported processors
- CE terminology
- CE environment variables
- Development processes

3

Board Support Package

The Board Support Package is one of the critical components needed to develop the OS design to generate the CE runtime image.

A complete technical reference covering the Board Support Package (BSP) topic for Windows Embedded CE could expand into a whole book. In this chapter, I simply provide a high-level overview of BSPs and how to clone and customize existing BSPs.

BSP Overview

The *Board Support Package* is a common name referring to a software library required to load and run the operating system on a supported hardware device. Developing the BSP is one of the important steps to provide Windows Embedded CE support for the targeted hardware. If one is not already available, creating a BSP to support the target hardware is usually one of the first steps in the early stage of development. BSP development typically includes the following:

- ❑ Develop the boot loader.
- ❑ Develop the OEM Adaptation Layer (OAL).
- ❑ Develop the device drivers.
- ❑ Develop the OS runtime image configuration files.

In general, the BSP is provided by the hardware manufacturer or the hardware development team. Although the application developer does not need to be concerned about BSP development, knowing how the BSP is developed and the BSP's structure can be helpful in writing code for applications involving hardware control, in helping save precious development time, and in minimizing hardware-related coding problems.

Windows Embedded CE is designed to support multiple CPU architectures, such as ARM, MIPS, SuperH, and x86. Microsoft provides CPU support libraries for all four of the supported CPU architectures. All BSPs reference and make use of these CPU support libraries. These libraries are in the following directory:

    _WINCEROOT\PLATFORM\COMMON

Microsoft provides several reference BSPs with the Windows Embedded CE. Depending on which supported CPUs were selected during the Windows Embedded CE Platform Builder installation, different BSPs are installed to the _WINCEROOT\PLATFORM directory. For the installation process covered in Chapter 2, in addition to the default support for the ARMV4I processor, support for the x86 processor was selected. Based on the CE Platform Builder installation in Chapter 2 with support for ARMV4I and x86 processors selected, the following BSP folders are present under the _WINCEROOT\ PLATFORM directory on your workstation:

- ❑ \ARUBABOARD — This folder is for the ARUBABOARD BSP. This BSP supports the Aruba reference development board, built with an ARM processor.

- ❑ \CEPC — This folder is for the CEPC BSP. This BSP supports target devices built with an x86 processor.

- ❑ \COMMON — This folder contains common codes and components that may be used by all BSPs.

- ❑ \DEVICEEMULATOR — This folder is for the DEVICEEMULATOR BSP. This BSP is used to develop OS designs and generate runtime images for the emulator.

- ❑ \H4SAMPLE — This folder is for the H4SAMPLE BSP. This BSP supports target devices built with the OMAPP2420 processor, an ARM derivative.

- ❑ \MAINSTONEIII — This folder is for the MAINSTONEIII BSP. This BSP supports the Mainstone reference development board, built with the PXA27X processor, an ARM derivative.

- ❑ \T5530 — This folder is for the HP Compaq T5530 Thin Client BSP. This BSP supports the HP Compaq T5530 Thin Client device, built with an x86 processor.

- ❑ \VOIP_PXA270 — This folder is for the Voice over IP PXA270 BSP. This BSP supports a Voice over IP reference hardware, built with the PXA270 processor, an ARM derivative.

By default, all the BSPs are installed to the _WINCEROOT\PLATFORM folder. Each BSP is installed into a separate subfolder, and each BSP's folder name is the same as the BSP name shown on the CE Platform Builder's component catalog.

The component catalog lists the BSPs provided by Microsoft separate from the BSPs provided by the other third-party companies. The BSPs provided by Microsoft are listed under the BSP node on the component catalog; the ones provided by third-party companies are listed under the Third Party\BSP node on the component catalog.

Starting with CE 5.0, Microsoft introduced the Production Quality OAL Initiative (PQOAL), a directory organization for BSP. It's not required that a developer follow the PQOAL BSP directory organization. However, by doing so, it will take a lot less effort to port an existing BSP to support future releases of Windows Embedded CE. If you already have a CE 5.0 BSP for a hardware platform and need to port the BSP to support CE 6.0, it's recommended that you first port the CE 5.0 BSP to meet the PQOAL format before attempting to port the BSP to CE 6.0.

> **Application notes are available on MSDN showing how to port a CE 5.0 BSP to CE 6.0. Search with the "Porting a CE 5.0 BSP to CE 6.0" keywords.**

Even if you do not have an existing CE 5.0 BSP to port to 6.0, it's a good time investment to find and read this article. It provides good reference information about the CE 6.0 BSP architecture, and lots of useful references.

Table 3-1 is a listing of the recommended directory structure for a Windows Embedded CE 6.0 PQOAL BSP.

Table 3-1: Directory Structure for Windows Embedded CE 6.0 PQOAL BSP

Folder Name	Description
_PLATFORMROOT\Catalog	Contains the component catalog file with .pbcxml extension.
_PLATFORMROOT\Cesysgen	Contains makefile for filtering the configuration files.
_PLATFORMROOT\Files	Contains registry files and files for image layout.
_PLATFORMROOT\Src	Contains source code for the BSP.
_PLATFORMROOT\Src\Bootloader	Boot loader-specific code
_PLATFORMROOT\Src\Common	Code common to the boot loader and OAL
_PLATFORMROOT\Src\Drivers	BSP-specific drivers
_PLATFORMROOT\Src\Inc	BSP-specific include files
_PLATFORMROOT\Src\OAL\OALlib	Hardware-specific OAL codes for the BSP
_PLATFORMROOT\Src\OAL\OALexe	Links OAL code with common codes.
_PLATFORMROOT\Src\Kitl	KITL source code

The _PLATFORMROOT variable is used to represent the BSP directory. The full BSP directory is _WINCEROOT\PLATFORM\<BSP Name>.

In the previous release of Windows Embedded CE, the kernel, OAL, and KITL are linked together to make the kernel executable, nk.exe.

For CE 6.0, these three parts are broken into kernel.dll, oal.exe, and kitl.dll. By separating these three components, it helps make it easier for the OEM to maintain the BSP codes when Microsoft releases updates to the kernel. In the previous release, when Microsoft released a kernel update, the OEM had to take the updated kernel and link it again with the OAL to produce a new nk.exe. For CE 6.0, the OEM only has to distribute the new kernel.dll.

BSP Development

Developing BSP code from the ground up is quite challenging, involving device driver development and the use of low-level assembly code. One of the approaches in developing a BSP for a new hardware platform is to clone one of the existing BSPs, with the same CPU architecture as the new hardware, and modify the BSP codes to support the new hardware.

To develop the BSP for a new hardware, the detailed technical information for the hardware is needed, including the schematic for the circuitry. The BSP development process typically involves the following steps:

1. **Develop the boot loader** — The boot loader initializes the hardware, places the OS runtime image into memory, and triggers the OS start-up routine.

2. **Develop the OEM Adaptation Layer (OAL) code** — The OAL is the interface between the kernel and the hardware. The kernel uses the OAL routines to communicate with the hardware.

3. **Develop the device drivers** — CE device drivers that support the specific hardware and I/O peripheral on the hardware device.

4. **Develop the OS runtime image configuration files** — Configuration files, including registry, binary image builder, filesystem, database, and locale-specific string files, are used to configure how the OS runtime image is built.

> **The BSP Wiki provides lots of useful technical information related to BSP development:** http://channel9.msdn.com/wiki/default.aspx/CeDeveloper .WindowsCEBSP.

One common method many developers use to develop the BSP for new hardware is to clone one of the sample BSPs provided by Microsoft, designed to support the same CPU architecture as the new hardware, and then customize the cloned BSP to support the new hardware.

For this chapter, we will clone the following three BSPs and customize them to support the exercises in the later chapters:

❑ **The Device Emulator BSP** — To support exercises running on the emulator, this BSP is installed to the development workstation during the CE Platform Builder installation process.

❑ **The CEPC BSP** — To support the common desktop PC or laptop computer built with the x86 processor, this BSP is installed to the development workstation when support for the x86 processor is selected.

❑ **The ICOP_eBox4300_60E BSP** — This BSP is provided by a third-party company to support the eBox-4300 target device. It is installed to the system after the CE Platform Builder installation. The installation file for this BSP, ICOP_eBOX4300_60E_BSP.msi, is provided as part of the software that comes with this book. This BSP is available for download from the following URL:

www.embeddedpc.net/ce6book

> **You need to install the ICOP_eBox4300_60E_BSP.msi file to work through the cloning exercise for this BSP.**

In the above three BSPs, the Device Emulator BSP supports the emulator, a virtual target device. The CEPC BSP supports a class of target devices built with the x86 processor, not targeting a specific device. The ICOP_eBox4300_60E BSP is designed to support the eBox-4300 target hardware, a real target device.

The Device Emulator and the CEPC BSPs are provided by Microsoft, from the VS2005 IDE. Both these BSPs are presented in the BSP folder.

The ICOP_eBox4300_60E BSP is provided by a third-party company. From the VS2005 IDE, this BSP is presented in the Third-Party folder.

The three BSPs — CEPC, Device Emulator and ICOP_eBox4300_60E — are different. Each has unique components. One of the purposes for the cloning exercises is to show that the BSP cloning utility works the same way for different type of BSPs.

From the VS2005 IDE's Catalog Items View window, all BSPs not provided by Microsoft are presented in the Third-Party folder, including the BSP cloned from a Microsoft-provided BSP.

Let's launch the VS2005 IDE to work through the exercises. When starting the VS2005 IDE after installing the CE Platform Builder, you may see the Platform Builder Environment Settings screen shown in Figure 3-1.

Figure 3-1

Depending on your preference, the Visual Studio development environment can be customized to expose different sets of convenience features for Visual C++, Visual C#, Visual Basic, or Platform Builder. Click No to keep the existing settings, and continue.

Cloning the Device Emulator BSP

The Device Emulator BSP is provided to support the emulator. By cloning this BSP, we are creating a duplicate of the BSP. We can make changes to the cloned BSP without affecting the original codes. From the VS2005 IDE, select Tools ⇨ Platform Builder for CE 6.0 ⇨ Clone BSP to start the Clone Board Support Package wizard, as shown in Figure 3-2.

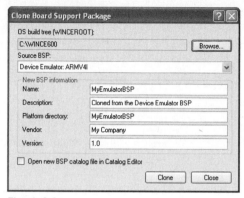

Figure 3-2

From the Source BSP selection, select the Device Emulator: ARMV4I BSP. In the "New BSP information" section, enter **MyEmulatorBSP** as the Name for the new BSP and **MyEmulatorBSP** for the "Platform directory." We will use the MyEmulatorBSP in the later chapters, and it's good to use the same *MyEmulatorBSP* name. The Vendor and Version information are used for information and version control purposes and do not have any impact on how the BSP functions. Click Clone to clone the BSP.

After the MyEmulatorBSP is successfully cloned, a MyEmulatorBSP folder containing the clone BSP codes is created in the _WINCEROOT\PLATFORM directory. We will use this BSP in the later chapters to develop OS design and generate runtime images for the emulator.

Cloning the CEPC BSP

The CEPC BSP is one of the reference BSPs included as part of the Windows Embedded CE Platform Builder installation when the x86 CPU support is selected. This is a general BSP with the core components to support all hardware built with the x86 CPU, including the eBox-4300 device referenced in this book.

If you have an old computer or laptop sitting around that has a 486 or better CPU with 32 MB or more system memory and a hard drive, you can clone the CEPC BSP and modify the cloned BSP to support the old hardware you have. While you may not be able to make use of all the peripherals available (because of the lack of a device driver for Windows Embedded CE), you can generate a simple Windows Embedded CE runtime image that can run on the hardware.

From the VS2005 IDE, select Tools ⇨ Platform Builder for CE 6.0 ⇨ Clone BSP to start the Clone Board Support Package wizard. Select CEPC from the Source BSP selection. Enter **MyCEPCBSP** as the Name and "Platform directory" for the new BSP. Enter the BSP Description, Vendor, and Version information as shown in Figure 3-3.

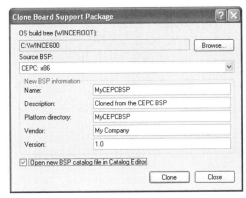

Figure 3-3

Click to enable the "Open new BSP catalog file in Catalog Editor" checkbox, and click Clone to clone the BSP. After the BSP is cloned, the Catalog editor within VS2005 will open the cloned MyCEPCBSP for editing, as shown in Figure 3-4.

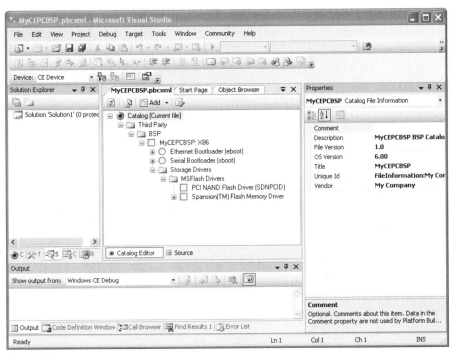

Figure 3-4

> Here is another method to open the MyCEPCBSP Catalog file for editing. Navigate to the BSP's Catalog directory, _PLATFORMROOT\MyCEPCBSP\CATALOG; right-click on the MyCEPCBSP.pbcxml file; and select Open With ⇨ Microsoft Visual Studio 2005.

Remove Components from BSP

From the VS2005 IDE, expand the Storage Drivers and MSFlash Drivers nodes on the MyCEPCBSP.pbcxml tab. For the typical x86 hardware, it's not likely that we need the PCI NAND Flash Driver and the Spansion Flash Memory Driver. Position the mouse pointer over each of these two components, right-click, and select Remove to remove these two components from the cloned MyCEPCBSP.

In Chapter 4, we will generate OS runtime images using this cloned BSP to run on eBox-4300. The eBox-4300 has the Realtek-8100 Ethernet interface and uses the Realtek-8139 device driver, available as a component within the Windows Embedded CE component catalog. So let's add the Realtek-8139 device driver to this cloned MyCEPCBSP.

Add Component to BSP

From the VS2005 IDE, with the MyCEPC.pbcxml Catalog file open, position the mouse pointer over the MyCEPCBSP: x86 node, right-click, and select Add Catalog Item. A new catalog item will be added to the BSP. Click to highlight the newly added catalog item. From the Properties window on the right side of the VS2005 IDE, enter **Realtek-8139 Ethernet Driver** as the title and **BSP_NIC_RTL8139** as the Sysgen variable.

Since all x86 hardware uses the ATAPI storage device, let's add the ATAPI driver to the cloned BSP. Follow the same steps to add the Realtek-8139 Ethernet driver above and create a component for the ATAPI Storage Driver. Enter **ATAPI Storage Driver** as the title and **SYSGEN_ATAPI** as the Sysgen Variable.

The VGA Linear (Flat) Framebuffer driver supports the majority of displays used for the PC. Follow the same steps to create a new component for the VGA Linear (Flat) Framebuffer driver. Enter **VGA Linear (Flat)** as the title and **BSP_DISPLAY_FLAT** as the Sysgen Variable.

With the additional device driver components, the MyCEPCBSP.pbcxml tab on the VS2005 IDE should look like Figure 3-5.

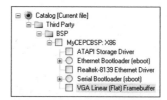

Figure 3-5

By adding these device driver components as subcomponents within the BSP, it helps group these components within the BSP node and provides a graphical view for reviewing which components are included in the OS design.

There are multiple methods to add device drivers to an OS design. The Realtek-8139, ATAPI, and VGA Linear (Flat) drivers can be added to an OS design by selecting each driver from the component catalog in the Catalog Items View window.

Another method to add the Realtek-8139 and VGA Linear (Flat) drivers to the OS design is by setting the following BSP environment variables. The BSP environment variables can be set from the Environment Variables page, which can be accessed from the OS design's property pages.

- ❏ BSP_NIC_RTL8139
- ❏ BSP_DISPLAY_FLAT

In this section, in addition to cloning the CEPC BSP, we added the following three components to the cloned MyCEPCBSP:

- ❏ ATAPI storage driver
- ❏ Realtek-8139 Ethernet driver
- ❏ VGA Linear (Flat) Framebuffer display driver

Clone Public Code to BSP

Although the above three components are added to the MyCEPCBSP, we are using the respective environment variables — SYSGEN_ATAPI, BSP_NIC_RTL8139, and BSP_DISPLAY_FLAT — to include each of these three device driver components into the BSP. The source code and binary files for these three components are located under the _PUBLICROOT directory.

In the event that we need to modify the component's source code, we need to clone the source code for the component to be part of the BSP folder. Let's work through the following exercise to clone the VGA Linear (Flat) Framebuffer display driver source code to the MyCEPCBSP BSP, and name the cloned version *MyVGA* display driver:

1. Create a folder for the MyVGA display driver under the following directory: _PLATFORMROOT\MyCEPCBSP\SRC\Drivers\.

2. Copy all files from _PUBLICROOT\Common\Oak\Drivers\Display\VGAFlat to the above folder.

3. Rename *ddi_flat.def* to **MyVGA.def**.

The Platform Builder's build system uses the directive within the Sources file to build the binary for this driver. The Sources file is copied to the _PLATFORMROOT\MyCEPCBSP\SRC\Drivers\MyVGA in the earlier step.

To configure the build system to build as part of the MyCEPCBSP BSP, we need to use a text editor to make the following changes to the Sources file:

1. Find and remove the following line of code:

```
DOSYSGEN=1
```

Since the MyVGA is not part of the Public code, the system-wide Sysgen command does not take effect here.

2. Find the following line of code:

```
TARGETNAME=DDI_FLAT_LIB
```

Change the above line of code to the following:

```
TARGETNAME=MyVGA
```

3. Change the library name from DDI_FLAT to MyVGA.

4. Find the following line of code:

```
TARGETTYPE=LIBRARY
```

Change the above line to the following:

```
TARGETTYPE=DYNLINK
```

5. Change the build target type from generating a library file to generating a DLL file.

6. Find the following line of code:

```
TARGETDEFNAME=ddi_flat
```

Change the above line of code to

```
TARGETDEFNAME=MyVGA
```

7. Change the binary filename from *ddi_flat* to **MyVGA**.

8. Add the following line of code near the beginning of the file:

```
RELEASETYPE=PLATFORM
```

9. Find the following line of code:

```
DEFFILE=ddi_flat.def
```

Change the above line of code to

```
DEFFILE=MyVGA.def
```

10. Find the following line of code:

```
WINCETARGETFILE0=$(_COMMONOAKROOT)\lib\$(_CPUINDPATH)\$(TARGETDEFNAME).def
```

Change the above line of code to

```
WINCETARGETFILE0=$(_TARGETPLATROOT)\lib\$(_CPUINDPATH)\$(TARGETDEFNAME).def
```

11. Add the following TARGETLIBS entries after the SOURCELIBS line:

```
TARGETLIBS=\
    $(_COMMONSDKROOT)\lib\$(_CPUINDPATH)\Coredll.lib \
    $(_COMMONSDKROOT)\lib\$(_CPUINDPATH)\Ceddk.lib \
    $(_SYSGENOAKROOT)\lib\$(_CPUINDPATH)\gpe.lib \
    $(_SYSGENSDKROOT)\lib\$(_CPUINDPATH)\ddguid.lib \
```

With the above modifications to the Sources file, the cloned MyVGA display driver source code can be compiled to generate the myvga.dll binary in the build release directory.

To verify that you have performed all the steps without error, go through the following steps to build the MyVGA display driver source code to generate the myvga.dll binary file:

1. From the Solution Explorer window within the VS2005 IDE, expand the PLATFORM\ MyCEPCBSP\src\drivers folder.

2. Right-click on the MyVGA node and select Build, as shown in Figure 3-6, to build the MyVGA display driver code.

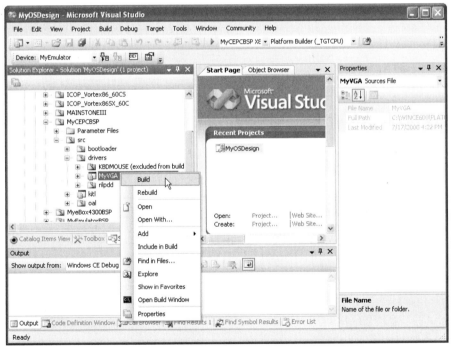

Figure 3-6

The build should be able to complete without error, as indicated by the VS2005's output window, as shown in Figure 3-7.

Figure 3-7

3. Check to verify that the myvga.dll is generated in the following build release directory:

_MyOSDesign\MyOSDesign\RelDir\MyCEPCBSP_x86_Release

At this point, we have successfully generated the MyVGA.dll binary to the build release directory.

When the build system compiles the VGA Linear (Flat) display driver in the Public directory, it goes through a different process. The source code gets compiled into ddi_flat.lib first. Then, during the Sysgen phase, the ddi_flat.lib library file is compiled into ddi_flat.dll. The libraries needed to link to during this step are specified in the _PUBLICROOT\Common\cesysgen\makefile directory.

When the build system compiles the cloned MyVGA display driver code in the BSP directory, there is no Sysgen involved. The code is compiled to myvga.dll directly. The TARGETLIBS added to the Sources file specifies to the build system which libraries to link to during compilation to generate the myvga.dll binary.

Next, we need to add the following entry, using a test editor, to the end of the Dirs file in the _PLATFORMROOT\MyCEPCBSP\SRC\Drivers directory, to configure the build system to compile the source code for the MyVGA display driver:

```
MyVGA  \
```

Next, we need to add the registry entries for the MyVGA display driver. Using the same environment variable naming convention as the VGA Linear (Flat) display driver, we will use the BSP_DISPLAY_MYVGA variable for this driver, and add the following registry entries to the end of the _PLATFORMROOT\MyCEPCBSP\Files\Platform.reg registry file:

```
IF BSP_DISPLAY_MYVGA
[HKEY_LOCAL_MACHINE\System\GDI\Drivers]
    "Display"="MyVGA.dll"
ENDIF ; BSP_DISPLAY_MYVGA
```

The cloned MyVGA display driver gets its settings from the boot loader via the BOOT_ARGS structure that is passed to the OS. You can change the code to read the settings from the registry instead. Take a look at the GPEFlat class constructor in the _PLATFORMROOT\MyCEPCBSP\SRC\Drivers\MyVGA\ Gpeflat.cpp file.

Next, we need to add the following entry to the platform.bib file's Modules section, in the _PLATFORMROOT\MyCEPCBSP\Files\ directory:

```
IF BSP_DISPLAY_MYVGA
    MyVGA.dll    $(_FLATRELEASEDIR)\MyVGA.dll    NK    SHK
ENDIF BSP_DISPLAY_MYVGA
```

Then we need to work through the following steps to modify the MyCEPCBSP BSP file to replace the VGA Linear (Flat) display driver with MyVGA display driver:

1. Close the current VS2005 session.

2. From Windows Explorer, navigate to the following directory:

   C:\WINCE600\Platform\CATALOG\.

3. Right-click over the MyCEPCBSP.pbcxml and select Open With ➪ Microsoft Visual Studio 2005, as shown in Figure 3-8, to launch the MyCEPCBSP.pcbxml file with VS2005 IDE.

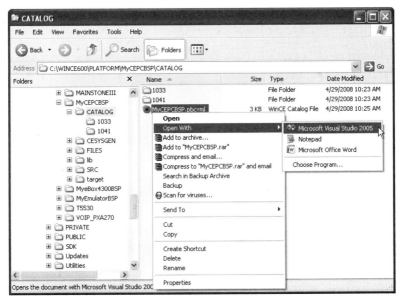

Figure 3-8

4. From the VS2005 IDE, expand the Third Party\BSP\MyCEPCBSP:X86 folder.

5. Right-click over the VGA Linear (Flat) and select Properties.

6. From the VGA Linear (Flat) Properties window, change the Title entry from *VGA Linear (Flat)* to **MyVGA**.

7. Change the Sysgen Variable entry from *BSP_DISPLAY_FLAT* to **BSP_DISPLAY_MYVGA**.

8. From VS2005 IDE, select File ➪ Save All, and close the VS2005 IDE.

We have successfully completed all the steps to clone the CEPC BSP to MyCEPCBSP and have cloned the VGA Linear (Flat) display driver's source code from the Public directory to the BSP directory.

Cloning the ICOP_eBox4300_60E BSP

The ICOP_eBox4300_60E BSP is a third-party company BSP needed to support the eBox-4300 compact computer. Before the cloning process, the eBox4300_60E BSP must be installed on the development station.

If you have not already installed the ICOP_eBox4300_60E BSP, it's available as part of the software with this book. You can also download this BSP from the following URL: www.embeddedpc.net/ce6book.

With the ICOP_eBox4300_60E BSP installed, from the VS2005 IDE select Tools ⇨ Platform Builder for CE 6.0 ⇨ Clone BSP to start the Clone Board Support Package wizard. Select ICOP_eBox4300_60E from the Source BSP selection. Enter **MyeBox4300BSP** as the name and "Platform directory" for the new BSP. Enter BSP Description, Vendor, and Version information, as shown in Figure 3-9.

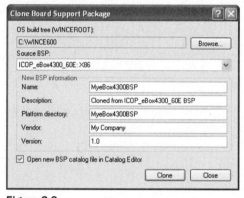

Figure 3-9

Click to enable the "Open new BSP catalog file in Catalog Editor" checkbox, and click Clone to clone the BSP. After the BSP is cloned, the Catalog editor within VS2005 will open the cloned MyeBox4300BSP for editing, as shown in Figure 3-10.

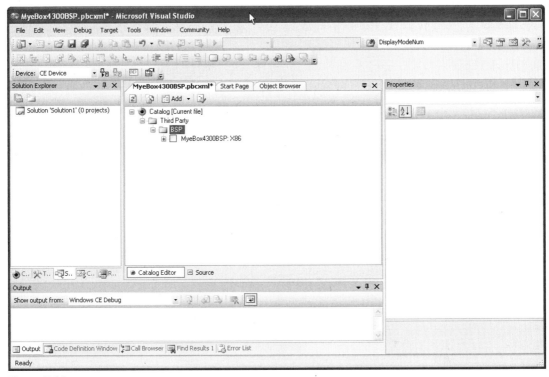

Figure 3-10

All BSPs, from Microsoft or third-party companies, are physically stored in the _WINCEROOT\ PLATFORM directory. When viewing from the VS2005 IDE, in the Catalog Items View window, BSPs provided by Microsoft are listed under the BSP node, and BSPs from third-party companies are listed under the Third-Party\BSP node. The cloned BSP is treated the same as a third-party BSP, and listed under the Third-Party\BSP node.

We will use this BSP in later chapters to develop OS designs, generate runtime images, and develop sample applications for the eBox-4300 target device.

BSP Components, Files, and Folders

The BSP cloning exercise in the previous section cloned two Microsoft-provided BSPs, the Device Emulator and CEPC BSPs, and one third-party company BSP, the ICOP_eBox4300_60E BSP. Each of these three BSPs is a little different from the others. The Device Emulator BSP does not support real hardware and is developed around the ARM processor architecture. The CEPC BSP is a good reference BSP, which can be used as the starting point to develop a customized BSP for any hardware built with an x86 CPU. The ICOP_eBox4300_60E is a customized BSP to support the eBox-4300, a hardware device built with an x86 CPU.

Reviewing the components and file folder structure for all three of the cloned BSPs shows many similarities between them. For this section, we will use the cloned MyeBox4300BSP to review the BSP components, files, and folders.

The eBox-4300 is a compact device built with an x86 processor. With the exception that it does not have a built-in floppy or CD-ROM drive, it has all the common I/O peripherals found on the desktop PC:

- VGA video output
- PS/2 keyboard and mouse input
- IDE interface to support IDE storage devices
- CompactFlash slot
- Three USB host interfaces
- Two serial ports
- Ethernet
- Audio output and microphone input

The MyeBox4300BSP.bat configuration file, a batch command file with the same name as the BSP, is located at the root of the BSP folder and executes a series of commands for setting the environment variables to include or exclude components for the BSP. For the MyeBox4300BSP, the configuration file is located in the _WINCEROOT\PLATFORM\MyeBox4300BSP directory. To view or edit the file content, navigate to the _WINCEROOT\PLATFORM\MyeBox4300BSP directory from within Windows Explorer, right-click over the MyeBox4300BSP.bat file, and select Edit. You can also use a text editor, such as notepad.exe, to view the MyeBox4300BSP.bat file contents.

```
@REM
@REM
@REM      Windows Embedded CE 6.0 BSP version: E
@REM      Last updated to support eBox-4300:   June 25, 2008
@REM      Last updated by:                      Samuel Phung
@REM
@REM
@REM

REM BSP_DEBUGSERIAL=1
set BSP_SERIAL2=1

set BSP_USB_OHCI=
set BSP_USB_UHCI=1
set BSP_USB_EHCI=1

REM set BSP_DISPLAY_VIA=1

set BSP_WAVEDEV_UAM3059=1
set BSP_WAVEDEV_UAMHDA=1
Set BSP_NIC_RTL8139=1

Set SYSGEN_SERDEV=1
Set SYSGEN_FATFS=1
```

```
Set SYSGEN_ATAPI=1

Set SYSGEN_FSRAMROM=1
Set SYSGEN_FSREGHIVE=1

Set PRJ_BOOTDEVICE_ATAPI=1
Set PRJ_ENABLE_FSREGHIVE=1
Set PRJ_ENABLE_FSMOUNTASROOT=1
```

Each line within the MyeBox4300BSP.bat file, without the REM preceding the line, is a command to set the designated environment variable for the build.

❑   With the REM preceding, the BSP_DEBUGSERIAL variable is not set. When this variable is set, the first available serial port is allocated to send serial debugging messages.

❑   The BSP_SERIAL2 variable is set to include the components needed to support the two serial ports.

❑   The BSP_USB_OHCI variable is set to blank to keep the Open Host Controller Interface USB components out of the OS design.

❑   The BSP_USB_UHCI variable is set to include the Universal Host Controller Interface USB components to support the USB host interface.

❑   The BSP_USB_EHCI variable is set to include the Enhanced Host Controller Interface USB components to support the USB host interface.

❑   The BSP_DISPLAY_VIA variable is set to include the VIA CN/CX display driver components to support the integrated video hardware. With the REM preceding the line, this variable is not set. To include the VIA CN/CX display driver to the OS design, select this component from the component catalog during the OS design development process. This variable is not set for the following two reasons:

   ❑   The display driver needs to be excluded from the OS design to generate a headless (without user interface) runtime image.

   ❑   To create the OS design using the ICOP_eBox4300_60E BSP with the VGA Linear (Flat) display driver.

❑   The BSP_WAVEDEV_UAM3059 and BSP_WAVEDEV_UAMHDA variables are set to include the components to support the sound hardware.

❑   The BSP_NIC_RTL8139 variable is set to include the driver and components to support the Realtek-8100 Ethernet interface.

❑   The SYSGEN_SERDEV variable is set to include the necessary components to support the serial device.

❑   The SYSGEN_FATFS variable is set to include the necessary components to support the FAT filesystem.

❑   The SYSGEN_ATAPI variable is set to include the ATAPI storage driver components.

❑   The SYSGEN_FSRAMROM variable is set to include the components to support the RAM and ROM filesystem.

❑   The SYSGEN_FSREGHIVE variable is set to include the Hive-based registry components with the OS design.

❑   The PRJ_BOOTDEVICE_ATAPI variable is set to enable the IDE storage as the boot device. ATAPI is the device driver for IDE storage devices.

❑   When the PRJ_ENABLE_FSREGHIVE variable is set, the Hive registry is located on the ATPI (IDE storage) device.

❑   When the PRJ_ENABLE_FSMOUNTASROOT variable is set, the ATAPI (IDE storage) device mounts as the root filesystem.

The REM (remark) at the beginning of the line is used to make remarks. All the entries with REM at the beginning of the line will be ignored and excluded from execution.

Under the _PLATFORMROOT\MyeBox4300BSP\CATALOG folder, there is a MyeBox4300BSP.pbcxml file. The Windows Embedded CE Platform Builder tool scans this file for information about the MyeBox4300BSP and lists the BSP on the component catalog based on the description provided in this file.

The Makefile in the _PLATFORMROOT\MyeBox4300BSP\CESYSGEN folder is used for filtering the OS runtime configuration files.

The _PLATFORMROOT\MyeBox4300BSP\FILES folder contains the following OS runtime image configuration files:

❑   **config.bib** — The config.bib file contains the entry used to configure the OS runtime image's memory structure.

❑   **platform.bib** — The platform.bib file contains the entry used to configure the files and modules to be included in the OS runtime image.

❑   **platform.dat** — The platform.dat file defines the RAM filesystem's directories, files, and links for an OS runtime image created during a cold boot.

❑   **platform.db** — The platform.db file defines the databases to be included in the object store of an OS runtime image created during a cold boot.

❑   **platform.reg** — The platform.reg file defines the registry keys and values for an OS runtime image created during a cold boot.

> During the OS design's build process, all the runtime image configuration files are merged into one set of configuration files after being copied to the build release directory.
>
> ❑   All the binary image builder files, files with the .bib extension, merge into the ce.bib file in the release directory.
>
> ❑   All the registry files, files with the .reg extension, merge into the reginit.ini file in the release directory.
>
> ❑   All the filesystem files, files with the .dat extension, merge into the omotpbj.dat file in the release directory.
>
> ❑   All the database files, files with the .db extension, merge into the initdb.ini file in the release directory.

The subfolders in the _PLATFORMROOT\MyeBox4300BSP\src folder contain the boot loader, device drivers, and OAL code for the BSP to support the targeted hardware.

- ❑ The BOOTLOADER folder contains boot loader codes for the BSP to support the targeted hardware.

- ❑ The COMMON folder contains codes that are common to the boot loader and OAL.

- ❑ The DRIVERS folder contains device driver codes for the BSP to support the targeted hardware's peripherals.

- ❑ The INC folder contains the include files for the BSP.

- ❑ The KITL folder contains the KITL codes for the BSP specific to the supported hardware.

- ❑ The OAL folder contains OAL hardware interfacing codes for the BSP to support the targeted hardware.

- ❑ The x86 folder contains the x86 CPU support library and codes cloned from the _ PLATFORMROOT\COMMON folder and customized for the BSP to support the targeted hardware.

With a properly configured BSP, the process of developing an OS design is simple and straightforward.

When an OS design fails to complete the build process, other than because of errors within the OS design project itself, it's generally caused by the BSP.

During the OS design build process, the code within the BSP directory is compiled into libraries and modules, which may be needed by the other components within the OS design to generate the runtime image. When the build process has problems building the libraries or modules for the BSP, the OS design build engine will not be able to locate the compiled libraries or modules and will raise an error, which, in turn, prevents the OS design project from completing the build process and generating an OS runtime image for the project.

> **The build error problems typically are caused by missing files, incorrect build configuration files, or missing or wrong references to dependency files.**
>
> **Reviewing the files in each of the source-code folders within the BSP directory will show there are Dirs or Sources files in each of the source-code folders. The Dirs file lists the folders for the build system to go through and build the source files. The Sources file contains entries to set the path for the include and header files, source-code configuration, target name, release type, and so on.**
>
> **To learn more about the build system, search MSDN with the "Windows Embedded CE DIRS SOURCES and Build System" keywords.**

Adding Files and Modules to the BSP

Files and modules, such as the background graphic for the Windows Embedded CE desktop, device drivers, or application support libraries, can be added to the BSP. All OS designs developed with the BSP will include these files and modules in the OS runtime image it generates.

Replacing the Desktop Background Graphic

By default, all OS runtime images generated from an OS design with a Windows shell will use the graphic shown in Figure 3-11 as the desktop background.

Figure 3-11

The default graphic, windowsce_vgal.jpg or windowsce_vgal.bmp, is located in the _PUBLICROOT\ SHELL\OAK\FILES directory. When the JPEG decoder component is included in the OS design, the windowsce_vgal.jpg file is used as the background graphic. When the jpeg decoder component is not included in the OS design, the windowsce_vgal.bmp file is used as the background graphic. In most cases, the windowsce_vgal.jpg file is more likely to be used as the background graphic.

To change the desktop background graphic for the OS runtime images generated from the BSP to show a custom graphic, we need to replace the default graphics.

Following are the steps to add a graphic file to use as the background image for the desktop:

1. Create a JPEG graphic file, approximately 512 × 60 pixels, and name the file *windowsce_vgal.jpg*.

2. Make a duplicate of the windowsce_vgal.jpg file, convert it to bitmap format, and name the file *windowsce_vgal.bmp*.

3. Copy the windowsce_vgal.jpg and windowsce_vgal.bmp files to the BSP's Files directory, _PLATFORMROOT\<BSP name>\Files.

During the build process, all the files in the BSP's Files directory are copied to the OS design's build release directory. Since the files in the BSP directory are copied to the build release directory after the files under the Public directory, the windowsce_vgal.jpg and windowsce_vgal.bmp files under the _PLATFORMROOT\<BSP name>\Files directory are copied to the build release directory later, overwriting the two files from the _PUBLICROOT\SHELL\OAK\FILES directory.

During the make image phase, the windowsce_vgal.jpg file is renamed *windowsce.jpg* and included in the final runtime image.

Adding Files to the BSP

As part of the task of customizing a BSP, there may be a need to add data files, programs, or utilities to the BSP, to be included in the OS runtime image created with the BSP.

To add the mydata.txt file to the BSP, go through the following steps to include the file in the BSP:

1. Place a copy of the mydata.txt file in the BSP's Files directory.

2. Use a text editor to add the following code to the Files section of the platform.bib file. The platform.bib file is located in the BSP's Files directory.

```
MYDATA.txt          $(_FLATRELEASEDIR)\MYDATA.txt          NK
```

The above is a binary image builder (BIB) file entry. The *mydata.txt* is the filename to be included in the runtime image. The $(_FLATRELEASEDIR)\MYDATA.TXT is the source, where the file is located. The NK variable represents the destination. The empty space between the three variables can be tabs or multiple spaces to keep them apart.

3. After the NK variable, additional flags can be added to set file attributes, such as S, H, K, and Q. Following is an example:

```
MyDriver.DLL     $(_FLATRELEASEDIR)\AudioDriver.DLL          NK     SHK
```

In the above example, the AudioDriver.dll in the build release directory is to be included in the runtime image as MyDriver.dll. The SHK file attributes set MyDriver.dll to be a system file, hidden and loaded in kernel mode.

During the build process, all the files from the BSP's Files directory are copied to the Release directory. After the file-copying phase, all the files with the BIB (Binary Image Builder) file extension in the Release directory are merged into the ce.bib file. The ce.bib file is the final configuration file used to configure which files are to be included in the OS runtime image.

The BIB configuration files, with the .bib extension, are used to configure which files or modules are to be included in the runtime image. The BIB files are just plain text files with keywords defining different sections. The *Modules* keyword identifies the modules section. The *Files* keyword identifies the files section. The BIB files also contain configuration settings to determine how to load the modules and files into the memory when the runtime image is launched.

The BIB files have the following four different sections:

- ❑ **Memory** — This section defines the available physical memory and specifies the starting address, size, and type of memory. The Memory section is usually found in the config.bib file located in the BSP's Files directory.

- ❑ **Config** — This section defines the configuration options for romimage.exe. The Config section is usually found in the config.bib file.

- ❑ **Modules** — This section specifies the modules to be included in the runtime image and how the modules are loaded into memory.

- ❑ **Files** — This section specifies the files to be included in the runtime image.

Summary

In this chapter you got a high-level overview of the BSP, files and directories for the BSP, and the general development process for the BSP. The cloning exercises and the exercise to add files to the BSP provided the basic information showing how you can clone a reference BSP and customize it to support your target hardware.

The following chapters use the cloned BSPs from this chapter to create the OS design, generate an OS runtime image, and develop sample applications.

Building a Customized CE 6.0 Runtime Image

In this chapter, we will go through the steps to create an OS design, include additional components from the component catalog, set environment variables to further customize the OS design, and generate a CE 6.0 runtime image.

To work through the exercise in this chapter, you need to have the following software components already installed on the development workstation. The installation steps for these software components were covered in Chapter 2.

- ❏ Visual Studio 2005

- ❏ Visual Studio 2005 SP1

- ❏ Visual Studio 2005 SP1 update for Vista

    This item is needed for workstations using Windows Vista. If you are using Windows XP, skip this item.

- ❏ Windows Embedded CE 6.0

- ❏ Windows Embedded CE 6.0 SP1

- ❏ Windows Embedded CE 6.0 R2

If you don't have all the software components installed, follow the steps provided in Chapter 2.

To build a CE 6.0 runtime image, we will go through the following steps:

1. Create the OS design project.

2. Select the Board Support Package.

3. Select additional needed components from the CE 6.0 component catalog.

4. Generate the OS runtime image from the OS design project.

> **Depending on the development workstation's processor speed and available system memory, a typical OS design project takes anywhere from 15 minutes to well over 30 minutes to build.**

Creating the Initial OS Design

When creating a new OS design project, VS2005 launches the OS design wizard and steps through the OS design project creation process, providing templates we can select and use as the starting point for a custom OS design.

Launch VS2005 and select File ⇨ New ⇨ Project from the VS2005 IDE to bring up the New Project screen as shown in Figure 4-1.

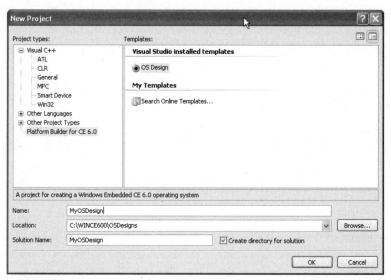

Figure 4-1

VS2005 provides a common integrated development environment (IDE) for Visual Basic, Visual C#, Visual C++, Visual J#, and CE 6.0 projects. To create an OS design project for CE 6.0, from the "Project type" selection on the left pane, select "Platform Builder for CE 6.0"; from the Templates selection on the right pane, select "OS Design," and enter a project name for the OS design. We will use this OS design project and components from this OS design for other chapters. To avoid confusion in following the exercises in this book, enter **MyOSDesign** as the project name and click OK to continue. At this point, the OS Design Wizard starts running, as shown in Figure 4-2.

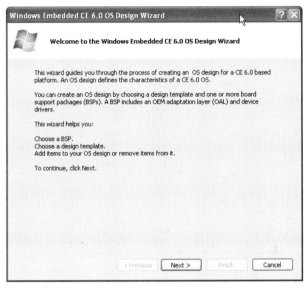

Figure 4-2

The OS Design Wizard

The OS Design Wizard will go through a series of steps, presenting different options for each step to select the BSP, the OS design template, application media components, multimedia components, and application components for the OS design, and create the initial development environment for the project.

In the following section, we'll step through each of the OS Design Wizard steps, selecting the components for the project, and reviewing the components presented by the OS Design Wizard in each step.

To advance to the next step, click on Next to bring up the Board Support Packages (BSP) selection screen, as shown in Figure 4-3.

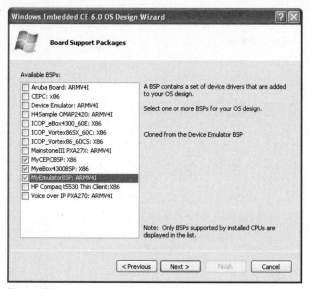

Figure 4-3

The BSP selection screen lists all the BSPs currently installed on your development station, including the three cloned BSPs, MyCEPCBSP, MyeBox4300BSP, and MyEmulatorBSP, from the exercise in Chapter 3. The ICOP_Vortex86_60CS and ICOP_Vortex86SX_60C BSPs are from third-party companies. Unless these BSPs are installed separately, they are not present on your workstation.

Multiple BSPs can be selected for each OS design project. Each BSP is developed to support unique hardware. By selecting multiple BSPs, the OS design can be configured to generate multiple OS runtime images, one for each of the selected BSPs to support the hardware associated with the BSP.

For the exercise in this chapter, select the following BSPs from the available BSPs as shown in Figure 4-3:

❑ **MyCEPCBSP** — This is selected to support the target device built with an x86 processor. When using an old computer or laptop as the target device, the My CEPCBSP can be used to develop the OS runtime image to support the target device.

❑ **MyEmulatorBSP** — This is selected to support the *emulator*, a virtual target device provided to simulate a development environment without the need for the actual hardware.

❑ **MyeBox4300BSP** — This is selected to support the *eBox-4300*, a third-party device built with an x86 processor.

Although all three BSPs are selected to support the same OS design project, each BSP is designed to support different target devices with different hardware. Separate OS runtime images will need to be generated from the OS design for each of the three selected BSPs. By selecting multiple supported BSPs in the same OS design, we can generate multiple unique OS runtime images, each to support a designated target device.

Other than the components specific to support the unique hardware features for the target device, all the images will have the same common OS components and include a programming library. This is useful for developers working on hardware-independent applications and who need to test and debug the applications running on different hardware platforms.

Click Next to bring up the Design Templates selection screen, as shown in Figure 4-4.

Figure 4-4

The Design Templates step presents different template categories. Some of the template categories provide multiple templates:

❑ **Consumer Media Device** — This category provides the starting templates to create SetTopBox and Digital Media devices.

❑ **Custom Device** — This category provides a blank template and lets you choose the components to be included in the initial OS design.

❑ **Industrial Device** — This category provides the starting templates to create Industrial Controller, Internet Appliance, and Gateway devices.

❑ **PDA Device** — This category provides the starting templates to create Mobile Handheld and Enterprise Web Pad devices.

❑ **Phone Device** — This category provides the starting templates to create IP Phone devices.

❑ **Small Footprint Device** — This category provides the minimum set of components as the starting point for your OS design.

❑ **Thin Client** — This category provides the starting templates to create Windows Thin Client, Enterprise Terminal, and Windows Network Projector devices.

For the exercise in this chapter, select the Industrial Device category and click on Next to bring up the Design Template Variants screen, as shown in Figure 4-5.

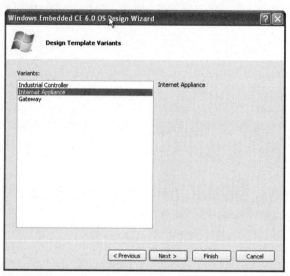

Figure 4-5

For each of the OS Design Template categories, the OS Design Wizard provides one or more template variants to choose from. For this book's exercises, select Internet Appliance and click on Next to bring up the Application Media component selection screen, as shown in Figure 4-6.

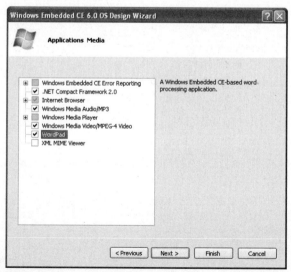

Figure 4-6

The OS Design Wizard's application and media selection step provides the option for you to include the application, media components, and programming library with the OS design. This step provides a short list of common application and media components. After the initial OS design project is created, additional application and media components from the component catalog can be added to the OS design to provide additional functionality.

In the step shown in Figure 4-6, the ".NET Compact Framework 2.0" library component is included to support managed-code applications. Internet Explorer 6.0 is added to be the web browser function. The Windows Media components are added to provide basic multimedia functionality.

At this point, the Finish option is provided to complete the initial OS design project.

Select Networking Communications Components

Let's advance to the next step to review additional options provided by the OS Design Wizard. Click on Next to bring up the Networking Communications components selection. From the Network Communications screen, expand the Local Area Network (LAN), Personal Area Network (PAN), and Wide Area Network (WAN) nodes, as shown in Figure 4-7, to see the available selections under these three options.

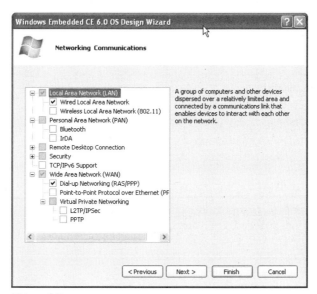

Figure 4-7

Networking communication is an important commodity for modern embedded devices. The components in this step provide the following functions:

❑ The Local Area Network (LAN) components provide the necessary libraries and utilities for local area networking support, such as Ethernet and Remote Access Service (RAS). The LAN components provided here include the LAN library and configuration utility for the OS design.

❑ The Personal Area Network (PAN) components provide the necessary support library and utility to provide Personal Area Network support, such as IrDA and Bluetooth. The PAN components provided here include the PAN library and configuration utility for the OS design.

❑ The Remote Desktop Connection components provide the necessary support library and utility to establish a remote desktop session.

❑ The Security components provide the necessary support library and utility to provide security- and encryption-related functions.

❑ The TCP/IPv6 component provides the necessary support library and utility to support the newer TCP/IPv6 network stack.

❑ The Wide Area Network (WAN) provides the necessary support library and utility to support Dial-up, Point-to-Point, and Virtual Private networking.

> **For the networking feature to function properly, in addition to the Networking Communications components selected in this step, device driver components for the network hardware need to be included in the OS design, in the later steps.**

The available selections represent a fraction of all the available networking and communication components. After the initial OS design is created, additional networking and communication components can be added to the OS design from the component catalog. Click on Next to advance to the wizard's last step, shown in Figure 4-8.

Figure 4-8

Security Warning

After the OS Design Wizard's final step, a security warning screen, as shown in Figure 4-9, will pop up, showing that some of the selected components have potential security issues. Click Acknowledge to close the warning screen.

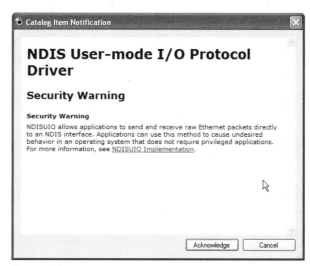

Figure 4-9

OS Design Project Folders and Files

After the OS Design Wizard has completed all the steps to set the initial configuration for the OS design, it generates a project folder with subfolders and files, which make up the initial project for the OS design.

In the first step, *MyOSDesign* was entered as the name of the project. VS2005 creates a solution folder with the same name in the _WINCEROOT\OSDesigns\MyOSDesign folder and creates several subfolders and files under the _WINCEROOT\OSDesigns\MyOSDesign (\MyOSDesign). Following are descriptions for the subfolders and files created by VS2005:

❑   The \MyOSDesign\MyOSDesign subfolder contains the file for the OS design project.

❑   The \MyOSDesign\MyOSDesign.sln is the VS2005 solution file.

❑   The \MyOSDesign\MyOSDesign\MyOSDesign.pbxml is the Platform Builder project file for the OS design.

❑   Three BSPs were selected to support the OS design. Think of this as combining three OS designs into one, where the only difference between the three is the supported hardware. There is a separate set of build release directories for debug and release modes, for each of the selected BSPs, under the \MyOSDesign\MyOSDesign\RelDir directory. Since each BSP will have one debug and one release mode build release directory, a total of six directories is created under the \MyOSDesign\MyOSDesign\RelDir directory.

❑ MyCEPCBSP_x86_Debug is the debug mode build release directory for the MyCEPCBSP board support package.

❑ MyCEPCBSP_x86_Release is the release mode build release directory for the MyCEPCBSP board support package.

❑ MyEmulatorBSP_ARMV4I_Debug is the debug mode build release directory for the MyEmulatorBSP board support package.

❑ MyEmulatorBSP_ARMV4I_Release is the release mode build release directory for the MyEmulatorBSP board support package.

❑ MyeBox4300BSP_x86_Debug is the debug mode build release directory for the MyeBox4300BSP board support package.

❑ MyeBox4300BSP_x86_Release is the release mode build release directory for the MyeBox4300BSP board support package.

❑ The three folders in the \MyOSDesign\MyOSDesign\Wince600 directory contain SYSGEN files for the three selected BSPs.

OS Design Project View from VS2005 IDE

At this point, the OS Design Wizard has completed the task of creating the initial OS design. The VS2005 IDE should look similar to Figure 4-10.

Figure 4-10

Although the colors don't show here, there is a green checkmark on MyCEPCBSP: X86 and a red X mark on MyEmulatorBSP: ARMV4I and MyeBox4300BSP: X86. The checkmark indicates that MyCEPCBSP is the active BSP. Any build or SYSGEN command will result in generating files for the active BSP only.

The Device Drivers and Third Party folders, under the MyOSDesign\Third Party folder, are not installed by default and may not be present on your workstation. These two folders are created when installing third-party company device drivers and programming libraries.

To generate the OS runtime image for each of the included BSPs, we need to set each of the BSPs as the active BSP, one at a time, to generate an OS runtime image for the active BSP.

To change the current active BSP, from VS2005 IDE, select Build ⇨ Configuration Manager to bring up the Configuration Manager screen, as shown in Figure 4-11, and select the BSP from the list of "Active solution configurations."

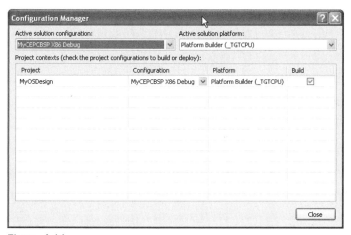

Figure 4-11

Six configurations are listed in the "Active solution configuration" dropdown list:

❑ **MyCEPCBSP x86 Debug** — This is the configuration for generating a debug OS runtime image to support the target device built with an x86 processor associated with MyCEPCBSP, which is based on the x86 processor.

❑ **MyCEPCBSP x86 Release** — This is the configuration for generating a release OS runtime image to support the target device built with an x86 processor associated with MyCEPCBSP, which is based on the x86 processor.

❑ **MyEmulatorBSP ARMV4I Debug** — This is the configuration for generating a debug OS runtime image to support the target device associated with MyEmulatorBSP, which is based on the ARM processor.

❑ **MyEmulatorBSP ARMV4I Release** — This is the configuration for generating a release OS runtime image to support the target device associated with MyEmulatorBSP, which is based on the ARM processor.

❏ **MyeBox4300BSP x86 Debug** — This is the configuration for generating a debug OS runtime image to support the target device associated with MyeBox4300BSP, which is based on the x86 processor.

❏ **MyeBox4300BSP x86 Release** — This is the configuration for generating a release OS runtime image to support the target device associated with MyeBox4300BSP, which is based on the x86 processor.

For the exercise in this chapter, select MyEmulatorBSP ARMV4I Release as the active BSP, and click Close to continue.

Review OS Design Catalog Items

If it's not already present, from the VS2005 IDE click on the "Catalog Items View" tab. Under the Third-Party\BSP folder, expand the MyEmulatorBSP: ARMV4I folder and subfolders to review the components associated with this BSP, as shown in Figure 4-12.

Figure 4-12

Some of the catalog items listed in Figure 4-12 are from third-party companies, installed separately from the CE installation, and are not present on your workstation.

The Catalog items with a checkmark (actually in green on your screen) are manually selected. The catalog items with a solid green square are needed by other selected components and are included in the OS design as part of the dependency check done automatically by the Platform Builder tool.

When clicking on the Filter option at the "Catalog Items View" tab's top left corner, three options are shown:

❏ **User-selected Catalog Items Only** — When this option is selected, only manually selected Catalog items are shown.

❏ **User-selected Catalog Items and Dependencies** — When this option is selected, only manually selected Catalog items and dependencies are shown.

❏ **All Catalog Items in Catalog** — When this option is selected, all Catalog items are shown.

To become familiar with the "Catalog Items View" options, select each option and review the Catalog items shown on the "Catalog Items View" tab. After completing this exercise, set the Filter to "All Catalog Items in Catalog."

Searching for Catalog Items

The "Catalog Items View" tab provides the search function to search for a Catalog item using the partial name or the associated SYSGEN variable. Set the "Catalog Items View" to "All Catalog Items in Catalog."

Let's search for a few items to get familiar with this feature. On the "Catalog Items View" Search entry, enter **SYSGEN_ATAPI** and click on the little square (green on your screen) with an arrow pointing to the right, just next to the Search entry, to execute the search function. The "Catalog Items View" displays and highlights the ATAPI PCI Support catalog item, as shown in Figure 4-13.

Figure 4-13

Remote Display Application

Let's do another search. This time, enter **Remote Display** in the search entry, and click on the little green square to execute the search. The "Catalog Items View" displays and highlights the "Remote Display Application" item, as shown in Figure 4-14.

Figure 4-14

Let's select and include the Remote Display Application in the OS design. This application provides a function similar to the Remote Desktop available with Windows XP, enabling remote access to the Windows XP desktop. The Remote Display Application, when active, enables remote access to the Windows Embedded CE desktop by executing the client application, `cerhost.exe`.

The `cerhost.exe` **application is located at C:\WINCE600\PUBLIC\COMMON\ OAK\BIN\i386\cerhost.exe.**

With the Remote Display Application, the target device's CE 6.0 desktop can be accessed using the development station's display, keyboard, and mouse, and this will help save valuable desk space.

Adding Catalog Items to the OS Design

Windows Embedded CE is a componentized OS. The Platform Builder tool includes user-selected catalog items and dependencies, and will not include unnecessary catalog items. If a needed catalog item is not included in the OS design manually and is not triggered by dependencies factored to be included, it will not be in the final OS runtime image.

Use the Search feature to locate and add the following Catalog items to the OS design:

❑ **CAB File Installer/Uninstaller** — This Catalog item is needed to support application installation and uninstall.

❑ **USB Storage Class Driver** — This is a class driver needed to support USB mass storage devices.

At this point, all of the needed Catalog items are included in the OS design.

OS Design Build Options

The Build options help control how the OS runtime image is built. To bring up the Build option setting screen, select Project ➪ MyOSDesign Properties, which will bring up the MyOSDesign Property Pages, and then expand the Configuration Properties node and select "Build options," as shown in Figure 4-15.

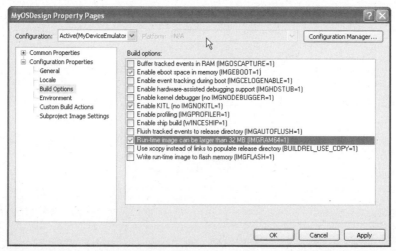

Figure 4-15

For this exercise, enable the following Build options:

❏ **Enable eboot space in memory** — Select this option to reserve memory space for the boot loader to save parameter data, such as display resolution and debug serial port settings, and enable the OS to read the data at boot time.

❏ **Enable KITL** — Select this option to enable the Kernel Independent Transport Layer (KITL), the communication link between the development workstation and target device for debugging.

❏ **Run-time image can be larger than 32 MB** — When this option is selected, the IMGRAM64 environment variable is set to configure the runtime image to use 64 MB of system memory.

A corresponding environment variable is linked to each of the Build options. Manually setting the environment variable associated with the Build option has an effect equivalent to selecting the Build option here.

Following are general descriptions for each of the Build options. Some of the Build options may have dependencies not available with all the hardware.

❏ **Buffer Tracked Events in RAM (IMGOSCAPTURE=1)** — Select this option to include the `oscapture.exe` application with the image. This application records data from the event tracking subsystem.

❏ **Enable eboot space in memory (IMGEBOOT=1)** — Select this option to reserve space in the config.bib file and enable the boot loader to save data that the OS can read at boot time.

❏ **Enable event tracking during boot (IMGCELOGENABLE=1)** — Select this option to enable the event-tracking subsystem.

❏ **Enable hardware-assisted debugging support (IMGHDSTUB=1)** — Select this option to support hardware-assisted debugging. This option is automatically enabled if Watson SYSGEN variables to support Windows error reporting are enabled.

❏ **Enable kernel debugger (no IMGNODEBUGGER=1)** — Select this option to enable the debugger to connect and pass debugging information from the target device to the development station.

❏ **Enable KITL (no IMGNOKITL=1)** — Select this option to enable KITL (Kernel Independent Transport Layer) for the OS image, which enables communication between the development station and the target device for debugging.

❏ **Enable profiling (IMGPROFILER=1)** — Enable this option to build a runtime image that supports the kernel profiler.

❏ **Enable ship build (WINCESHIP=1)** — When this option is selected, the resulting OS image does not output debug messages. When this option is not selected, the OS provides verbose debug messages to aid debugging. This option is available for the Release build only and is hidden when the Debug build configuration is used.

❏ **Flush tracked events to release directory (IMGAUTOFLUSH=1)** — Select this option to flush events to the release directory. When this option is selected, it also turns on event tracking.

❏ **Runtime image can be larger than 32 MB (IMGRAM64=1)** — Selecting this option is equivalent to setting the IMGRAM64 environment variable to build an OS image for hardware with 64 MB of memory.

❑ **Use xcopy instead of links to populate release directory (BUILDREL_USE_COPY=1)** —
During the build process, the Build system uses copylink to copy files. If you experience sharing
violation during the copy phase, select this option to copy files to the release directory.

❑ **Write runtime image to flash memory (IMGFLASH=1)** — Select this option to allow the
runtime image to be written to flash memory after download. This feature is not supported by
all hardware.

OS Design: Environment Variables

In addition to the Build option in the previous section, additional environment variables can be set for
the OS design from the OS Design Property Pages.

For example, to set the BSP_NOAUDIO environment variable and exclude all audio components from
the runtime image, we need to do the following:

1. From VS2005 IDE, select Project ➪ MyOSDesign Properties to bring up the MyOSDesign
Property Pages. This is the same MyOSDesign Property Pages from the previous section about
Build options.

2. On the left pane, expand the Configuration Properties node and click on Environment to bring
up the Environment Variables setting utility. To set an environment variable for the OS design,
click on New and enter the variable name and associated value, as shown in Figure 4-16.

Figure 4-16

> **The above step is an example showing how to set an environment variable for an OS
> design project. Do not include this with your project.**

Environment variables play a big part in how the OS design builds, enables, and disables certain key
features and configures how the OS runtime image is generated.

To learn more about different environment variables and their associated functions, look up "BSP
environment variables" in the Windows Embedded CE documentation.

Generating the OS Runtime Image

The Platform Builder goes through a fairly complex system to build, compile, and generate the OS runtime
image. One of the following chapters will cover the Windows Embedded CE build system in depth.

The build process to generate a runtime image from the OS design is lengthy. Depending on the
development station's performance, it may take anywhere from 15 to 30 minutes or more to generate
the runtime image.

From VS2005 IDE, select Build ⇨ Build Solution to generate the OS runtime image.

> **Only the OS runtime image supporting the active BSP, the MyEmulatorBSP, is generated. To generate an additional OS runtime image to support another BSP, we need to change the active solution configuration to the other BSP and execute the Build Solution or SYSGEN command.**

During the build process, VS2005 IDE's output window displays the module and library currently being built, as shown in Figure 4-17.

Figure 4-17

When the build is finished, VS2005 IDE's output windows display the build results, as shown in Figure 4-18.

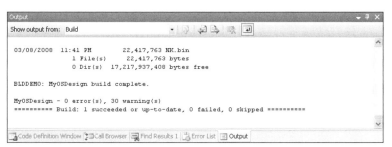

Figure 4-18

When the build process is completed with one or more errors, the build will have failed to generate an OS runtime image. In order to generate an OS runtime image, the build must not have any errors. Figure 4-18 indicates that the build resulted in 30 warnings, but without any errors. A CE 6.0 OS runtime image has been successfully generated.

Let's take a look at some of the files generated from the build process to help better understand the build system.

Since there are multiple layers of directories involving very long entries for the folder names, let's use the _MyOSDesign variable to represent the C:\WINCE600\OSDesigns\MyOSDesign\MyOSDesign folder.

The active solution configuration is set to the MyEmulatorBSP ARMV4I Release. The OS runtime image is generated in the following folder:

_MyOSDesign\RelDir\MyEmulatorBSP_ARMV4I_Release

The OS runtime image, nk.bin, along with more than 1,000 objects, is generated in the above folder.

In addition to showing build information during the build process and presenting warnings and errors to the VS2005 IDE's output windows, the information from the output windows is logged to the following files:

- ❑ **_WINCEROOT\Build.log** — This is a very long file, logging all of the build activities.

- ❑ **_WINCEROOT\Build.wrn** — This file logs all the warning messages. These warning messages are included in the Build.log file as well.

- ❑ **_WINCEROOT\Build.err** — This file logs all the error messages. When the build is successful, the Build.err file is not created.

> **When the Platform Builder builds or rebuilds any OS design project, a new set of the build.log, build.wrn, and build.err files is created in the _WINCEROOT\ directory, overwriting the old files from the previous build. Unless the build has an error, the build.err file is not created.**

OS Runtime Image for MyCEPCBSP

In the beginning of this chapter, an OS design project was created supporting three BSPs — MyCEPCBSP, MyEmulatorBSP, and MyeBox4300BSP. In the previous step, a release mode OS runtime image was generated for the MyEmulatorBSP to support the emulator.

To generate another release mode OS runtime image for the MyCEPCBSP to support the target device built with the x86 processor, we need to change the active BSP to MyCEPCBSP x86 Release. From VS2005 IDE, select Build ⇨ Configuration Manager to bring up the Configuration Manager screen, as shown in Figure 4-19.

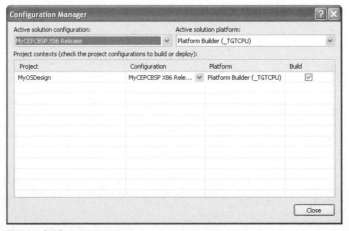

Figure 4-19

From the "active solution" configuration, select MyCEPCBSP x86 Release as the "active solution" configuration and click on Close.

The old computer or laptop you may have sitting in the garage with a 486 or better CPU and 64 MB or more of system memory, along with any size IDE hard drive that can boot to DOS, can be used as the target device to work through the exercises in this book.

The most efficient way to transfer the OS runtime image generated from the OS design to the target device is through an Ethernet connection. The MyCEPCBSP's boot loader has built-in support for an Ethernet card built with the Realtek-8100, Realtek-8139, and most NE2000-compatible Ethernet cards.

There is a good chance the old PC or laptop computer you have already has one of the supported Ethernet cards. If not, it's worth the effort to find an NE2000-compatible card, or an Ethernet card built with the Realtek-8139 or Realtek-8100 controller.

> **I found several Ethernet cards in March 2008, built with the Realtek-8139 controller, for less than $10 at the local computer store. You can probably obtain such cards from a computer recycler or surplus store.**

To support these Ethernet cards, we need to include one or more of the following device drivers in the OS design:

- ❑ NE2000-compatible ISA card
- ❑ NE2000-compatible PCI card
- ❑ NE2000-compatible PCMCIA card
- ❑ Realtek RTL8139

Since the above Ethernet drivers are specific to the MyCEPCBSP and may not be needed by the other BSP, we should configure the build process to include these drivers for the OS runtime image generated from this BSP. To accomplish this, we can set the appropriate BSP environment variables from MyOSDesign's properties.

From the VS2005 IDE, select Project ⇨ MyOSDesign Properties to bring up the MyOSDesign Property Pages screen. On the left pane, click on the Environment node to access the Environment variables settings and perform the following steps:

1. Click New to bring up the Environment Variable entry screen.
2. For the Variable name, enter **BSP_NIC_RTL8139**.
3. For the Variable value, enter **1**.

4. Click OK to complete the Environment Variable setting process.

5. Repeat the above steps for the BSP_NIC_NE2000_PCI and BSP_NIC_NE2000_ISA environment variables, as shown in Figure 4-20.

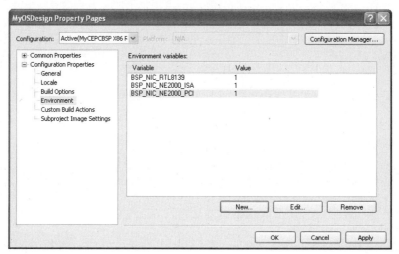

Figure 4-20

6. Click Apply, followed by OK, to continue.

> The environment variable setting in Figure 4-20 is unique to the current active BSP. The components associated with these environment variables are included with the OS runtime image for the current active BSP and do not have any impact on the other BSPs.

After the "Environment variables" settings process, from the VS2005 IDE, select Build ⇨ Build Solution to generate the release mode OS runtime image for the MyCEPCBSP. When the build process is completed, the OS runtime image, nk.bin, is generated in the following directory along with more than 1,000 other components:

```
_MyOSDesign\RelDir\MyCEPCBSP_x86_Release
```

OS Runtime Image for MyeBox4300BSP

To generate a release mode OS runtime image for the MyeBox4300BSP to support the eBox-4300 target device, we need to change the active BSP to MyeBox4300BSP x86 Release. From the VS2005 IDE, select Build ⇨ Configuration Manager to bring up the Configuration Manager screen, as shown in Figure 4-21.

From the "Active solution configuration," select MyeBox4300BSP x86 Release as the active solution configuration and click Close.

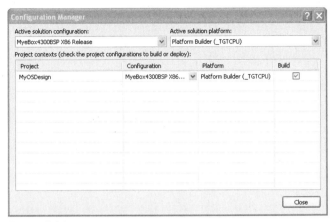

Figure 4-21

The eBox-4300 is a compact computing device, with the following common peripherals found on the typical personal computer:

❏ 500-Mhz CPU, 512 MB DDR2 RAM

❏ VGA , Serial ports, PS/2 keyboard, and mouse

❏ USB 2.0 host interface, supporting USB boot and able to load an OS from a USB storage device

❏ Sound function with audio-out and microphone interface

❏ IDE interface, supporting IDE hard drive and IDE flash storage

The ICOP_eBox4300_60E BSP includes all needed CE 6.0 device drivers for the eBox-4300 to launch a CE 6.0 runtime image. The MyeBox4300BSP is cloned from the ICOP_eBox4300_60E BSP and inherently has all its features.

Although the display driver is included in the MyeBox4300BSP, it's not included in the OS design by default. From the Catalog Items View window, expand the Third-Party\BSP folder, followed by expanding the MyeBox4300BSP: x86 folder and selecting the VIA CN/CX display driver, as shown in Figure 4-22.

Figure 4-22

To enable the eBox-4300, running CE 6.0, to persist registry settings and install the program after a power reset, we need to include the Hive-based registry component, mount the file system at the root, and designate the IDE storage as the boot device for the OS runtime image. To accomplish this, we need to set the following three environment variables before building the OS runtime image:

- ❏   `PRJ_ENABLE_FSREGHIVE = 1`
- ❏   `PRJ_ENABLE_FSMOUNTASROOT = 1`
- ❏   `PRJ_BOOTDEVICE_ATAPI = 1`

The above three environment variables have already been set by the BSP's configuration file, MyeBox4300BSP.bat. This is a batch command file located in the root of the BSP folder and executes a series of commands to set the environment variables to include components to the OS design. Using a text editor to view this file, we can see the following three lines of code in this batch file:

```
Set PRJ_ENABLE_FSREGHIVE=1

Set PRJ_ENABLE_FSMOUNTASROOT=1

Set PRJ_BOOTDEVICE_ATAPI=1
```

The MyeBox4300BSP.bat is located in the following directory:

       _WINCEROOT\Platform\MyeBox4300BSP

The eBox-4300 target device is built with 512 MB of system memory. To generate an OS runtime image to take advantage of all available memory, we need to set the IMGRAM512 environment variable. To set this variable, select Project ⇨ Properties from the VS2005 IDE to bring up the MyOSDesign Property Pages. On the left pane, expand the Configuration Properties node and click on the Environment node to bring up the Environment variables settings tab to set the variable, as shown in Figure 4-23.

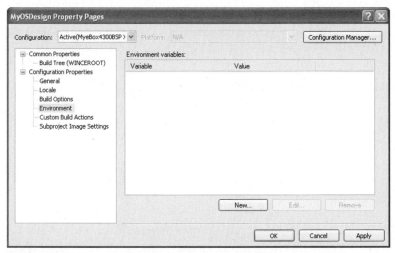

Figure 4-23

From the MyOSDesign Property Pages screen, click on the New button to bring up the Environment Variable screen, as shown in Figure 4-24.

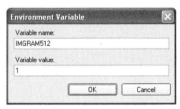

Figure 4-24

From the Environment Variable screen, enter IMGRAM512 for the Variable name and **1** for the Variable value, and click OK to continue.

From the MyOSDesign Property Pages screen, click Apply and then OK to close the MyOSDesign Property Pages screen.

To generate the runtime image from this OS design, select Build ⇨ Build Solution from the VS2005 IDE to start the build process and generate the release mode OS runtime image for the active BSP, MyeBox4300BSP, to support the eBox-4300 target device.

Summary

In this chapter, we created an OS design project and included support for three BSPs — MyEmulatorBSP, MyCEPCBSP, and MyeBox4300BSP, with help from the OS Design Wizard. After the initial OS design was created, we further customized the OS design and generated release mode OS runtime images for each BSP.

The exercise in this chapter covered the common steps and scenarios for the development of an OS design project.

5

Connecting to Target Device

Windows Embedded CE runtime images were generated from the exercise in Chapter 4. To launch these runtime images to the designated target devices, we need to establish connections between the target devices and the development workstation.

The OS design in Chapter 4 was created to support three BSPs. Each BSP is designed to support one particular family of target devices. The OS design was created to generate three different sets of OS runtime images for the three supported BSPs. Each set of OS runtime images consists of one release mode and one debugging mode runtime image.

This chapter goes over the process to establish connections between the development station and the three target devices — the emulator, eBox-4300, and CEPC — and to transfer the OS runtime image from the development station to the target device after each connection is established.

Target Device Connectivity

After the runtime image is generated from the OS design, the development station needs to establish connectivity with the target device to download the image to the device.

The three common connectivity options are

- ❏ Ethernet
- ❏ USB
- ❏ Serial

To work with the emulator, the configuration for target device connectivity provides the device emulator (DMA) option to establish a connection to the emulator.

Connecting to Emulator

As part of the Windows Embedded CE 6.0 installation, the emulator is installed along with the Platform Builder tool when ARM processor support is selected. To use the emulator as the target device for debugging, the OS runtime image must be generated to support the DeviceEmulator BSP. In Chapter 3, the MyEmulatorBSP was cloned from the DeviceEmulator BSP. The OS runtime image in Chapter 4 was generated to support the MyEmulatorBSP, the same as in supporting the DeviceEmulator BSP. Therefore, the resulting OS runtime image will be able to load and launch on the emulator.

Since the MyOSDesign project was created with support from three different BSPs, to establish connectivity to the emulator, we need to select the MyEmulatorBSP as the active BSP. Work through the following steps to select the MyEmulatorBSP as the active BSP:

1. Launch VS2005 IDE, and open the MyOSDesign project.

2. From the VS2005 IDE, select Build ⇨ Configuration Manager to bring up the Configuration Manager screen.

3. From the Configuration Manager screen, select MyEmulatorBSP ARMV4I Release, from the Active solution configuration selection, as the active BSP, and click Close to continue.

With the MyOSDesign project open and the MyEmulatorBSP set as the active BSP, select Target ⇨ Connectivity Options to bring up the Target Device Connectivity Options screen, as shown in Figure 5-1.

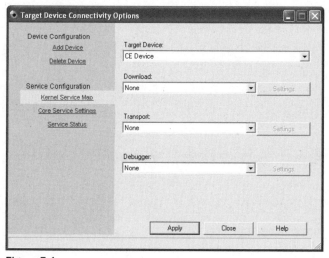

Figure 5-1

Creating the MyEmulator Target Device Profile

Multiple target device profiles can be established to help save time when working with multiple OS design projects. Each device profile is configured to support one target device. When using the Ethernet connection as the option for downloading a runtime image to the target device, the target connectivity service uses the Ethernet controller's Media Access Control (MAC) address to identify the target device and will only download the image to the device configured to work with the active device profile.

Work through the following steps to create a device profile for the emulator, and name this profile *MyEmulator*:

1. From the Target Device Connectivity Options screen, on the top left of the screen, click on the Add Device option, to bring up the Add New Target Device screen; then enter **MyEmulator** as the new target device name, as shown in Figure 5-2.

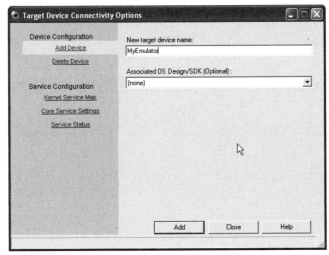

Figure 5-2

2. Use the default entry, "(none)," for the Associated OS Design/SDK (Optional) entry, and click Add to continue.

3. After clicking Add, the Target Device Connectivity Options screen brings up the screen to configure settings for the MyEmulator device profile, as shown in Figure 5-3.

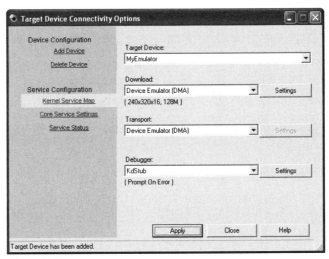

Figure 5-3

Configuring the MyEmulator Target Device Settings

Work through the following steps to configure the MyEmulator target device settings:

1. From the Target Device Connectivity Options screen, select Device Emulator (DMA) for both the Download and Transport options.

2. For the Debugger option, select KdStub.

3. From the Target Device Connectivity Options screen, click on the topmost Settings button to bring up the Emulator Properties screen, as shown in Figure 5-4.

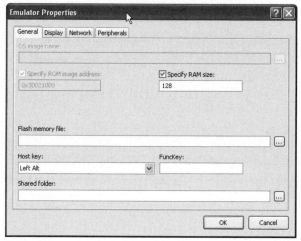

Figure 5-4

The OS runtime image generated in Chapter 4 for the emulator was generated with the IMGRAM64 environment variable. This variable was set by one of the build options. The runtime image can be larger than 32 MB. The emulator must be configured to have at least 64 MB of RAM to support the image.

Work through the following steps to configure the emulator with 128 MB of RAM:

1. On the General tab, select the checkbox to enable "Specify RAM size," and enter 128 to allocate 128 MB as the available RAM for the emulator.

The emulator's display resolution can be configured to display in different resolutions, not necessarily matching any of the common display resolutions. To prove the point, let's work through the following steps to configure the emulator to display in 640 × 300 resolution:

2. Click on the Display tab to bring up the display settings configuration screen.

3. Enter **640** for "Screen width" and **300** for "Screen height," and select **16** "bits per pixel" for "Color depth," as shown in Figure 5-5.

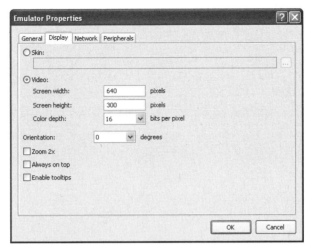

Figure 5-5

We need to configure a network interface for the emulator to enable network access. Take the following steps to configure network settings:

1. Click on the Network tab to bring up the network settings configuration screen, as shown in Figure 5-6.

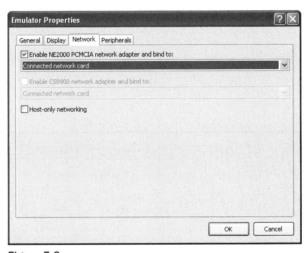

Figure 5-6

2. From the Network tab, select the "Enable NE2000 PCMCIA" checkbox.

3. From the dropdown list box, select "Connected network card."

With the above network configuration, the emulator will connect to the network through the development workstation's active network connection.

4. For the exercises in this book, the default settings on the Peripherals tab are just fine. Click OK to continue.

> While the Emulator Properties screen is active, click on the Peripherals tab to review the settings available on this tab. Some of these settings can be useful in creating the environment to simulate certain operating environments and help the application developer write appropriate codes for the environment. For example, setting the remaining-battery level to 10 percent in the battery-operated device simulation section can help an application developer write code responding to a low-battery condition.

At this point, on the Target Device Connectivity Options screen, the Download option should be showing "Device Emulator (DMA)," the Transport option should be showing "Device Emulator (DMA)," and the Debugger option should be showing "KdStub," as shown in Figure 5-7.

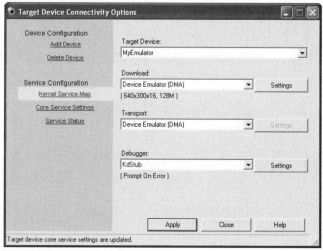

Figure 5-7

5. Click Apply followed by Close to complete the Target Device settings for the MyEmulator profile.

Downloading Runtime Image to the Emulator

The OS design is now configured to download the runtime image generated from the exercise in Chapter 4 to the emulator, using the MyEmulator target device profile.

To download the image to the emulator, select Target ⇨ Attach Device from the VS2005 IDE. The Figure 5-8 screen, Download Runtime Image to MyEmulator, shows the progress as the image is being transferred to the emulator. Depending on the development workstation's performance and available memory, this process can go very quickly.

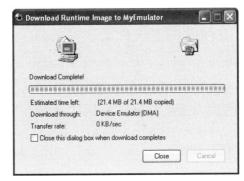

Figure 5-8

After the runtime image download process is completed, the emulator will launch with the downloaded CE 6.0 runtime image, as shown in Figure 5-9.

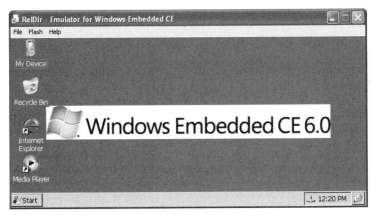

Figure 5-9

To shut down the emulator, select File ⇨ Exit from the Emulator screen.

Connecting to eBox-4300-MSJK

In Chapter 4, the MyeBox4300BSP was added to the OS design. The OS runtime image generated with MyeBox4300BSP is designated to support the eBox-4300-MSJK, an x86 compact computer, as shown in Figure 5-10.

Figure 5-10

The exercises in the remainder of this chapter require the use of an eBox-4300-MSJK. If you do not have an eBox-4300-MSJK, you can skip to the next chapter.

A monitor, keyboard, and mouse connected to the eBox-4300-MSJK are needed to view the output and enter commands for the exercises in this section.

> **For more information about the eBox-4300-MSJK and where to purchase the device, visit** www.embeddedpc.net/ebox4300**.**

The connection between the eBox-4300-MSJK and the development workstation is established through an Ethernet link. Both the development workstation and the eBox-4300-MSJK must be connected to the same Ethernet network segment and assigned IP addresses in the same subnet.

For the exercises in this book, the eBox-4300-MSJK is configured with the following:

- ❑ 256 MB internal IDE bootable flash storage
- ❑ IDE bootable flash storage to boot to DOS 6.22
- ❑ loadcepc.exe (DOS boot loader)
- ❑ Eboot.bin (Ethernet boot loader)
- ❑ Nk.bin (Windows Embedded CE runtime image)

Connecting to eBox-4300-MSJK with DHCP

To continue with this exercise, an eBox-4300-MSJK is needed. In a typical setup, both the development workstation and the eBox-4300-MSJK are connected to an Ethernet network with DHCP service to assign IP addresses dynamically, similar to the network setup as shown in Figure 5-11.

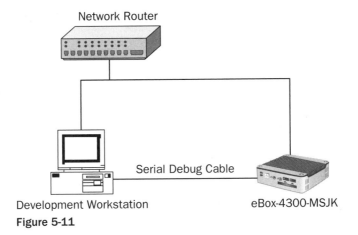

Figure 5-11

The serial debugging cable (null serial modem cable) connects the eBox-4300-MSJK's COM1 with the development workstation's serial port. From the development workstation, set the Hyper Terminal to 38400 baud, 8 data bits, no parity, and 1 stop bit to capture debugging messages from the eBox-4300-MSJK.

> The Hyper Terminal program is not available for Windows Vista, but the Hyper Terminal program from Windows XP will work in Vista.
>
> To use the Hyper Terminal program from Windows XP, create a directory on the Windows Vista machine and name the directory \HyperTerm, copy the hypertrm.dll from the Windows XP machine's \Windows\System32 directory, and the hypertrm.exe from the \Program Files\Windows NT directory, to the \HyperTerm directory on the Windows Vista machine.
>
> After the above two files are copied to Windows Vista, you can launch the Hyper Terminal program by executing the hypertrm.exe executable.

Once the runtime image is downloaded and launched on the target device, it's more efficient to use the Ethernet connection for debugging messages. However, before the runtime image is fully launched, the Ethernet connection may not be available for debugging purposes. The serial debugging cable, connecting the target device and the development workstation, provides another means to capture debugging messages. As the loadcepc.exe boot loader launches, the loadcepc.exe sends serial debugging messages to a designated COM port. When launching a CE runtime image built in debugging mode, the OS runtime sends serial debugging messages to the serial port as the runtime image is launching.

If you are continuing from the previous exercise, the active configuration for the MyOSDesign project is set to MyEmulatorBSP ARMV4I Release. We need to configure the OS design and set the MyeBox4300BSP as the active BSP. Go through the following steps to configure the OS design:

1. From the VS2005 IDE, select Build ⇨ Configuration Manager to bring up the Configuration Manager screen, as shown in Figure 5-12.

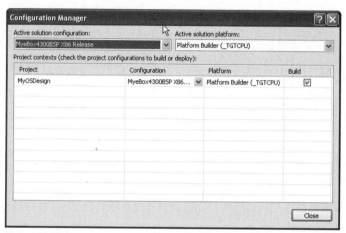

Figure 5-12

2. From the Configuration Manager screen, change the "Active solution configuration" to MyeBox4300BSP X86 Release, and click Close to continue.

> An OS runtime image generated from the OS design with MyeBox4300BSP set as the active configuration is needed to complete this exercise. If the OS runtime image has not been generated, select Build ⇨ Build Solution to generate it.

Creating the MyeBox4300 Target Device Profile

Let's create a target device profile, MyeBox4300, and use this device profile to connect to the eBox-4300-MSJK.

Work through the following steps to create the MyeBox4300 device profile:

1. Select Target ⇨ Connectivity Options to bring up the Target Device Connectivity Options screen.

2. From this options screen, click on the Add Device option from the top left of the screen to bring up the Add New Target Device screen.

3. Enter **MyeBox4300** as the new target device name, and click Add to continue.

Configuring the MyeBox4300 Target Device Settings

After the MyeBox4300 profile is created, go through the following steps to configure the MyeBox4300 device settings:

1. Select Ethernet for both the Download and Transport options, and select KdStub for the Debugger option, as shown in Figure 5-13.

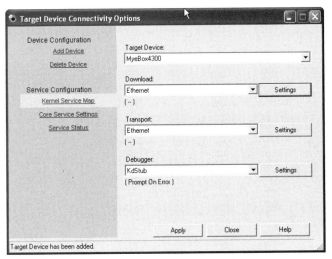

Figure 5-13

2. Click on the topmost Settings button on the right to bring up the Ethernet Download Settings screen, as shown in Figure 5-14.

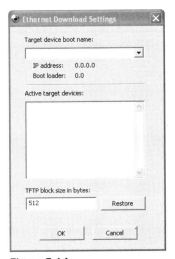

Figure 5-14

At this point, the MyeBox4300 target device profile is not associated with any device yet. The Ethernet Download Settings screen is waiting for bootme messages from a target device over the Ethernet connection, which can be used to associate with the MyeBox4300 device profile.

In the following steps, you will power on the eBox-4300-MSJK and launch the `loadcepc.exe` boot loader to send bootme messages to the Ethernet Download Settings screen, and associate the eBox-4300-MSJK with the MyeBox4300 device profile:

1. Turn on the eBox-4300-MSJK's power. After power is on, the eBox-4300-MSJK boots to DOS and displays four command options, as shown in Figure 5-15.

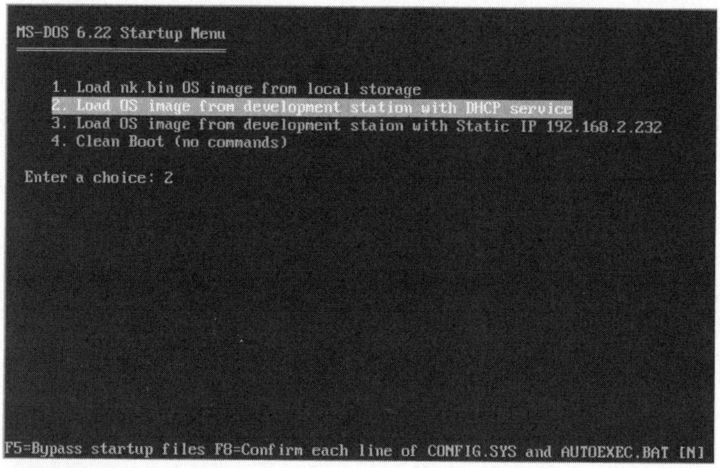

Figure 5-15

2. From the keyboard connected to the eBox-4300-MSJK, use the arrow-up or arrow-down key to select option 2: "Load OS image from development station with DHCP service," and press Enter to launch the DOS boot loader, running on the eBox-4300-MSJK.

The eBox-4300-MSJK is preconfigured to boot to DOS and launch the autoexec.bat batch file, and provides a selection menu with four options. The following list shows the actual DOS command lines associated with each of the four options:

1. When the first option is selected, load the nk.bin OS image from local storage, which launches the runtime image, nk.bin, from local storage, using the following command line:

```
Loadcepc /C:0 nk.bin
```

The `/C:0` switch in the above command line disables the serial debugging message port. When this switch is set to `/C:1`, COM1 is allocated for sending serial debugging messages.

2. When the second option is selected, load the OS image from the development station with DHCP service; this launches the Ethernet boot loader, eboot.bin, and sends bootme messages over the Ethernet connection to request and download the runtime image from the development workstation, using the following command line:

```
Loadcepc /L:1024x768x32 /C:0 /e:0:0:0 eboot.bin
```

3. When the third option is selected, load the OS image from the development station with Static IP 192.168.2.232. This launches the Ethernet boot loader, eboot.bin, with a static IP address, 192.168.2.232, and sends bootme messages over the Ethernet connection to request and download the runtime image from the development workstation, using the following command line:

```
Loadcepc /L:1024x768x32 /C:0 /e:0::192.168.2.232 eboot.bin
```

4. When the fourth option is selected, "Clean Boot (no commands)," the autoexec.bat batch file terminates without launching any command.

    As the DOS boot loader (`loadcepc.exe`) is executing on the eBox-4300-MSJK, it broadcasts a series of bootme messages over the Ethernet connection.

    As the bootme messages reach the development workstation, with the Ethernet Download Settings screen active, the eBox-4300-MSJK is listed in the "Active target devices" window as CEPC1039, as shown in Figure 5-16.

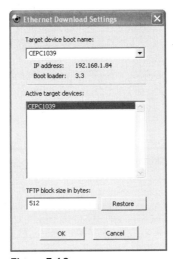

Figure 5-16

CEPC1039 is the device identification for the eBox-4300-MSJK used for this exercise; the 1039 numeric portion of the device identification is the decimal equivalent for 040F in hex, derived from the eBox-4300-MSJK's Ethernet MAC address. In this case, the full MAC address for the eBox-4300-MSJK is 44 4D 50 09 04 0F in hex.

In a classroom or lab environment, where there may be multiple eBox-4300-MSJKs booting and sending bootme messages at about the same time, multiple target devices will show up in the "Active target devices" window. To ensure you are associating the correct target device, make sure the eBox-4300-MSJK you are using is the only device booting and sending bootme messages. Or, find a utility to read the eBox-4300-MSJK's MAC address, translate the last four digits of the MAC address from hex to decimal, and use this information to identify the unit you're working with in a multidevice environment.

3. From this Ethernet Download Settings screen, Figure 5-16, click to highlight the detected device in the "Active target devices" list. The same device ID will show up on the "Target device boot name" selection at the top.

4. Click OK to continue.

5. On the Target Device Connectivity Options screen, click Apply followed by Close to save the settings and continue.

Downloading the Runtime Image to eBox-4300-MSJK

To download the OS runtime image to the eBox-4300-MSJK, select the Target ⇨ Attach Device from the VS2005 IDE to bring up the Download Runtime Image to the MyeBox4300 screen, as shown in Figure 5-17; if this step is performed before the `loadcepc.exe` boot loader has timed out and stopped sending the bootme messages, the image download process will be delayed briefly.

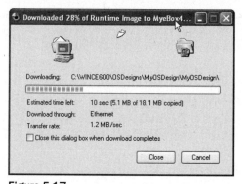

Figure 5-17

If the process does not begin, however, you'll need to reset the eBox-4300-MSJK's power to launch the `loadcepc.exe` boot loader again. After the eBox-4300-MSJK has powered on, select option 2: "Load OS image from development station with DHCP service" to launch the `loadcepc.exe` boot loader again.

After the OS runtime image is downloaded to the eBox-4300-MSJK, it will launch and show a Windows Embedded CE 6.0 desktop similar to Figure 5-18, from the eBox-4300-MSJK's display.

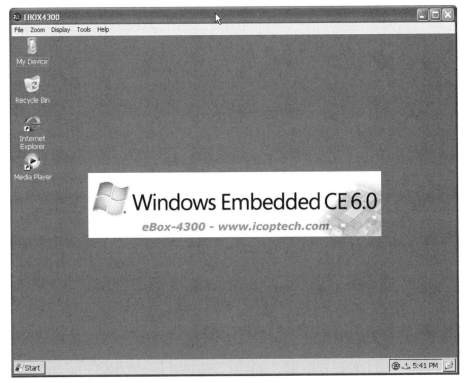

Figure 5-18

Connecting to eBox-4300-MSJK with Static IP

In the event that the DHCP is not available, both the development workstation and the eBox-4300-MSJK must be connected either to the same LAN, to the same Ethernet network hub, or directly to each other using a crossover Ethernet cable, with the proper static IP address configured to establish the communication.

Since a crossover Ethernet cable is provided as part of the eBox-4300-MSJK purchase, let's use this crossover cable to connect the eBox-4300-MSJK directly to the development workstation, as shown in Figure 5-19. A crossover Ethernet cable is made with the transmitting signal from one end of the cable, connected to the receiving signal on the other end of the cable.

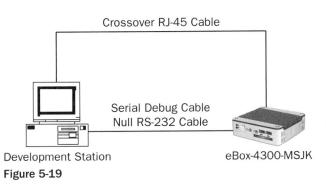

Crossover RJ-45 Cable

Serial Debug Cable
Null RS-232 Cable

Development Station   eBox-4300-MSJK

Figure 5-19

When connected with a crossover Ethernet cable, the eBox-4300-MSJK's Ethernet transmitting signal will go to the development workstation's Ethernet receiver, and the development workstation's Ethernet transmitting signal will go to the eBox-4300-MSJK's Ethernet receiver.

Connecting both the development station and eBox-4300-MSJK to a network hub, with normal Ethernet cable, yields the same result.

Both the development workstation and the eBox-4300-MSJK's static IP addresses must be set to the same subnet.

Other than the network connection and static IP address setting, the steps to download the runtime image from the development workstation to the eBox-4300-MSJK for this section are similar to the earlier section on connecting to eBox-4300-MSJK with DHCP.

Let's assume that we did not work through any of the steps in the earlier section on connecting to eBox-4300-MSJK with DHCP. We'll now work through the following steps to create the MyeBox4300 target device profile, configure MyeBox4300 target device settings, and download the runtime image to the eBox-4300-MSJK.

Configuring Static IP Address for eBox-4300-MSJK

The eBox-4300-MSJK is preconfigured to boot to DOS and launches a selection menu with four options, when powered up. The third option, loading the OS image from the development station with Static IP 192.168.2.232, will launch the loadcepc.exe boot loader using a preconfigured IP address, 192.168.2.232.

The situation is different when, for some reason, you need to change and use a different IP address from 192.168.2.232 for the eBox-4300-MSJK. As an example, let's use 192.168.100.201 as the IP address for the eBox-4300-MSJK. Work through the following steps to change the static IP address:

1. Use a text editor to edit the autoexec.bat, located in the eBox-4300-MSJK's flash storage.

2. Locate the following line of code:

```
Set NET_IP=192.168.2.232
```

3. Change the IP address in the above line of code, in the autoexec.bat file, to the following:

```
Set NET_IP=192.168.100.201
```

With the above modification, when the third option is selected from the selection menu, the static IP address 192.168.100.201 will be used.

The above steps show how to change the static IP address, used by the loadcepc.exe boot loader.

Continuing with the exercise, let's use the preconfigured IP address for the eBox-4300-MSJK, 192.168.2.232.

Configuring a Static IP Address for the Development Workstation

In order for the development workstation to communicate with eBox-4300-MSJK, the IP address for the development workstation must be configured to 192.168.2.xxx, where the xxx value can be any value from 1 to 255, except 232, which is used by the eBox-4300-MSJK. For our purpose, let's use 192.168.2.101 and work through the following steps to configure the development workstation's IP address:

1. Launch the Control Panel from the development workstation's start menu.

2. From the Control Panel, double-click on the Network Connections icon to bring up the Network Connections screen.

3. Right-click on the Local Area Connection icon and select Properties, to bring up the Local Area Connection Properties screen, as shown in Figure 5-20.

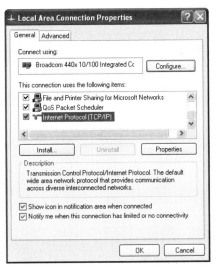

Figure 5-20

4. From the Local Area Connection Properties screen's General tab, select Internet Protocol (TCP/IP) and click on Properties, to bring up the Internet Protocol (TCP/IP) Properties screen.

5. From the Internet Protocol (TCP/IP) Properties screen, click the "Use the following IP address" button, and enter **192.168.2.101** for the "IP address" and **255.255.255.0** for the "Subnet mask," as shown in Figure 5-21.

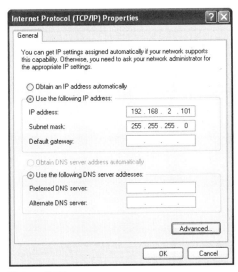

Figure 5-21

6. From the Internet Protocol (TCP/IP) Properties screen, click OK to save the settings and close this screen.

7. From the Local Area Connection Properties screen, click Close to continue.

Creating the MyeBox4300 Target Device Profile

Work through the following steps to create the MyeBox4300 target device profile:

1. Select Target ⇨ Connectivity Options to bring up the Target Device Connectivity Options screen.

2. From the Target Device Connectivity Options screen, click on the Add Device option from the top left of the screen to bring up the Add New Target Device screen.

3. Enter **MyeBox4300** as the new target device name, and click Add to continue.

> If you've already worked through the steps to create the MyeBox4300 target device profile in the previous section, skip the above steps.

Configuring the MyeBox4300 Target Device Settings

After the MyeBox4300 profile is created, go through the following steps to configure the MyeBox4300 device settings:

1. Select Ethernet for both the Download and Transport options, and select KdStub for the Debugger option.

2. Click on the topmost Settings button on the right to bring up the Ethernet Download Settings screen, as shown in Figure 5-22.

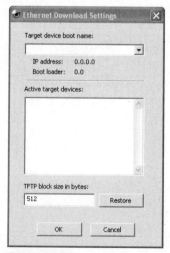

Figure 5-22

At this point, the Ethernet Download Settings screen is waiting for bootme messages from the eBox-4300-MSJK, over the Ethernet connection, which can be used to associate with the MyeBox4300 device profile.

In the following steps, we will power up the eBox-4300-MSJK and launch the loadcepc.exe boot loader, using a static IP address, to send bootme messages to the Ethernet Download Settings screen, and associate the eBox-4300-MSJK with the MyeBox4300 device profile.

1. Turn on the eBox-4300-MSJK's power.

2. After power is on, the eBox-4300-MSJK boots to DOS and displays four command options, as shown in Figure 5-23.

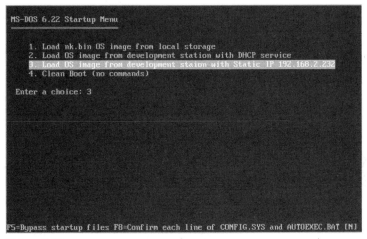

Figure 5-23

3. From the keyboard connected to the eBox-4300-MSJK, use the arrow-up or arrow-down key to select option 3: "Load OS image from development station with Static IP 192.168.2.232." Press Enter to launch the loadcepc.exe boot loader with the associated command-line options.

As the loadcepc.exe boot loader is executing on the eBox-4300-MSJK, using 192.168.2.232 as the static IP address, it broadcasts a series of bootme messages over the crossover Ethernet cable connection to the development workstation.

As the bootme messages reach the development workstation, with the Ethernet Download Settings screen active, the eBox-4300-MSJK is listed in the Active target devices window as CEPC1039, as shown in Figure 5-24.

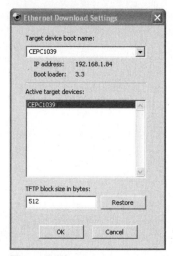

Figure 5-24

CEPC1039 is the device identification for the eBox-4300-MSJK used for this exercise. The 1039 numeric portion of the device identification is the decimal equivalent for 040F in hex, derived from the eBox-4300-MSJK's Ethernet MAC address. In this case, the full MAC address for the eBox-4300-MSJK is 44 4D 50 09 04 0F, in hex.

4. From the Ethernet Download Settings screen, Figure 5-24, click to highlight the detected device in the "Active target devices" list. The same device ID will show up on the "Target device boot name" selection at the top.

5. Click OK to continue.

6. On the Target Device Connectivity Options screen, click Apply followed by Close to save the settings and continue.

Downloading the Runtime Image to eBox-4300-MSJK

To download the OS runtime image to the eBox-4300-MSJK, select Target ⇨ Attach Device from the VS2005 IDE to bring up the Download Runtime Image to the MyeBox4300 screen, as shown in Figure 5-25. If this step is performed before the `loadcepc.exe` boot loader has timed out and stopped sending bootme messages, the image download process will be delayed briefly.

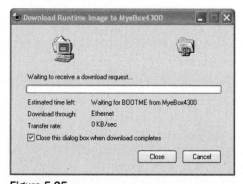

Figure 5-25

If the image download process fails to start after 20 seconds, you'll need to reset the eBox-4300-MSJK's power to launch the `loadcepc.exe` boot loader again. As in the original step, after the eBox-4300-MSJK has powered up, select option 3 to load the OS image from the development workstation with static IP 192.168.2.232, thus launching the `loadcepc.exe` boot loader again.

After the OS runtime image is downloaded to the eBox-4300-MSJK, it will launch and show a Windows Embedded CE 6.0 desktop from the eBox-4300-MSJK's display.

Connecting to the CEPC

The *CEPC* is an abbreviated term referring to a PC running Windows Embedded CE, or Windows Embedded CE PC. The CEPC BSP is designed to provide basic processor support for all computing devices built with a 32-bit x86 processor.

If the x86 computing device is built with a 32-bit x86 processor and able to run DOS, with 32 MB or more memory, it can support a CE runtime image built with the VGA Linear (Flat) display driver.

> **Other hardware components such as the Ethernet and audio hardware require CE device drivers to function.**

With the following minimum requirements, you can use an older PC as the CEPC target device:

- ❑ 486 or better processor
- ❑ 64 MB or more RAM
- ❑ Floppy drive that is bootable (available with most older PCs)
- ❑ At least one serial port (also available with most older PCs)
- ❑ VGA output with support for 640 × 480 or better display resolution

Ideally, if there is an NE2000 compatible or Realtek-8139 network interface, the runtime image downloading process will be much quicker.

Otherwise, we can use the serial port to download the runtime image to the CEPC target device. However, this is slow — it takes about 30 minutes to download a 20-MB image.

Creating the CEPC Boot Floppy Disk

First, we need to prepare a bootable floppy disk with the `loadcepc.exe` boot loader and other associated files. A floppy disk image file, CepcBoot.144, and the utility program, `makeimagedisk.exe`, to extract the floppy image file onto a floppy disk, are provided as part of the CE 6.0 platform builder installation, in the following directory: \Program Files\Microsoft Platform Builder\6.00\cepb\utilities.

Go through the following steps to make the CEPC bootable floppy disk:

1. Place a blank floppy disk in your development workstation's floppy drive.
2. Launch the `makeimagedisk.exe` utility program.

3. From the MakeImageDisk program screen, click Open to bring up the file selection screen. Navigate to the \Program Files\Microsoft Platform Builder\6.00\cepb\utilities directory and select the CepcBoot.144 file, as shown in Figure 5-26.

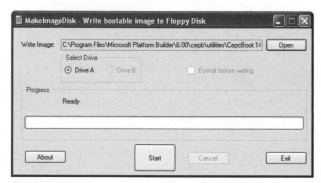

Figure 5-26

4. Click on the Start button to create the CEPC bootable floppy disk.

In addition to the DOS system files, the following files are provided on the CEPC floppy disk:

❑ **Eboot.bin** — Ethernet boot loader for CE

❑ **Loadcepc.exe** — DOS boot loader for CE

❑ **Sboot.bin** — Serial boot loader for CE

❑ **Vesatest.exe** — This is a test utility, used to test whether the PC's display can support the VESA display mode. When executed on the target device, it lists all of the valid Flat driver modes, as shown in Figure 5-27. Valid Flat driver modes are the different display resolutions supported by the VGA Linear (Flat) display driver.

```
SYS      COM         9,432 05-31-94   5:22a
HIMEM    SYS        29,136 09-30-93   4:20a
README   TXT        13,591 01-28-04   5:50p
CONFIG   SYS           688 01-28-04   5:50p
VESATEST EXE         7,121 01-28-04   5:50p
SBOOT    BIN        27,107 07-17-06   3:18p
AUTOEXEC BAT         4,101 07-07-06   4:08p
LOADCEPC EXE       100,464 07-18-05  10:35a
EBOOT    BIN       105,175 07-17-06   3:18p
         10 file(s)        351,460 bytes
                           957,952 bytes free

A:\>vesatest
Vesa BIOS Version: 2.0

    640x 400x 8    640x 480x 8    800x 600x 8   1024x 768x 8   1280x1024x 8
    640x 480x32    800x 600x16    800x 600x32   1024x 768x16   1024x 768x32
   1280x1024x16   1024x 768x 4   1024x 768x 8   1600x1200x 8   1600x1200x16
   1600x1200x16   1600x1024x 8    800x 512x 8    800x 512x16    800x 512x32
    896x 600x 8    896x 600x16    896x 600x32   1152x 768x 8   1152x 768x16
   1152x 768x32

Number of valid FLAT driver modes: 26

A:\>_
```

Figure 5-27

❏ **Config.sys** — DOS configuration file, responsible for launching the device driver and other system libraries when DOS starts.

❏ **Autoexec.bat** — This batch file launches when DOS starts.

When the CEPC target device boots up with this floppy, the selection menu shown in Figure 5-28 is presented when the system starts.

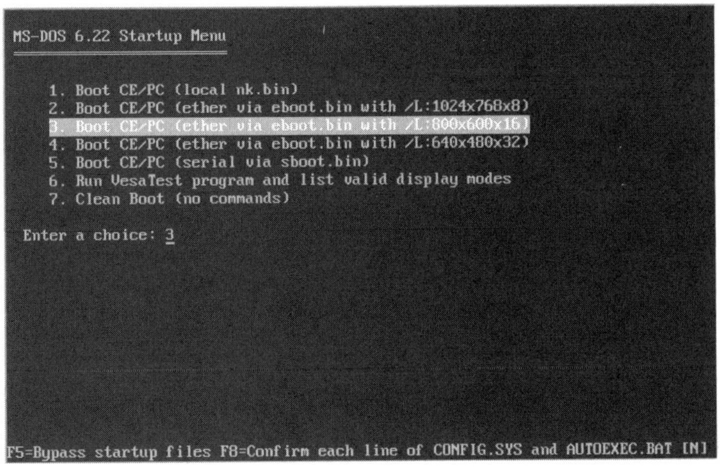

Figure 5-28

Following is a listing of the code in the autoexec.bat file associated with each of the menu selections in Figure 5-28.

❏ When option 1 is selected, Boot CE/PC (local nk.bin), the following block of code in the autoexec.bat file will execute, to launch the OS runtime image, nk.bin, from the local storage:

```
:CEPC_LOCAL
REM ##############################################################
REM     Launch LOADCEPC using a local NK.BIN image.
loadcepc /v nk.bin
goto END
```

107

❑   When option 2 is selected, Boot CE/PC (ether via eboot.bin with /L:1024 × 768 × 8), the following block of code in the autoexec.bat file will execute, to launch the Ethernet boot loader, eboot.bin, with 1024 × 768 display resolution in 8-bit color:

```
:CEPC_1024
REM ##############################################################
REM     Set RES=/L:1024x768x8 for use with FLAT display driver.
REM
REM     Format
REM              /L:DXxDYxBPP[:PXxPY] in DECIMAL!!!!
REM


set RES=/L:1024x768x8
goto WITHRES
.


.
:WITHRES
REM ##############################################################
REM     Here we actually Launch LOADCEPC using the RES, NET_IOBASE,
REM     and NET_IRQ env vars we just set above based on menu
REM     selections.

loadcepc /v /e:%NET_IOBASE%:%NET_IRQ%:%NET_IP% %RES% eboot.bin
goto END
```

❑   When option 3 is selected, Boot CE/PC (ether via eboot.bin with /L:800 × 600 × 16), the following block of code in the autoexec.bat file will execute, to launch the Ethernet boot loader, eboot.bin, with 800 × 600 display resolution in 16-bit color:

```
:CEPC_800
REM ##############################################################
REM     Set RES=/L:800x600x16 for use with FLAT display driver.
REM
REM     Format
REM              /L:DXxDYxBPP[:PXxPY] in DECIMAL!!!!
REM
set RES=/L:800x600x16
goto WITHRES
.


.
:WITHRES
REM ##############################################################
REM     Here we actually Launch LOADCEPC using the RES, NET_IOBASE,
REM     and NET_IRQ env vars we just set above based on menu
REM     selections.

loadcepc /v /e:%NET_IOBASE%:%NET_IRQ%:%NET_IP% %RES% eboot.bin
goto END
```

❑   When option 4 is selected, Boot CE/PC (ether via eboot.bin with /L:640 × 480 × 32), the following block of code in the autoexec.bat file will execute, to launch the Ethernet boot loader, eboot.bin, with 640 × 480 display resolution in 32-bit color:

```
:CEPC_640
REM ################################################################
REM     Set RES=/L:640x480x32 for use with FLAT display driver.
REM
REM     Format
REM             /L:DXxDYxBPP[:PXxPY] in DECIMAL!!!!
REM

set RES=/L:640x480x32
goto WITHRES
.
.
.
:WITHRES
REM ################################################################
REM     Here we actually Launch LOADCEPC using the RES, NET_IOBASE,
REM     and NET_IRQ env vars we just set above based on menu
REM     selections.

loadcepc /v /e:%NET_IOBASE%:%NET_IRQ%:%NET_IP% %RES% eboot.bin
goto END
```

❑   When option 5 is selected, Boot CE/PC (serial via sboot.bin), the following block of code in the autoexec.bat file will execute, to launch the serial boot loader, sboot.bin, with 800 × 600 display resolution in 16-bit color:

```
:CEPC_SERIAL
REM ################################################################
REM     Launch LOADCEPC on SBoot for a serial port download.

loadcepc /v /L:800x600x16 sboot.bin
goto END
```

❑   When option 6 is selected, Run VesaTest program and list valid display modes, the following block of code in the autoexec.bat file will execute to list all valid VESA display modes:

```
:VESATEST
REM ################################################################
REM     Launch VESATEST program.  VESATEST will display the
REM     VESA BIOS Version number and list all of the available
REM     video modes that are supported by the FLAT driver.
REM
REM      Note: VESATEST.EXE is an internal tool that is provided AS-IS
REM      with no testing or support, hence use at your own risk. We do
REM      not provide any redistribution rights either.

vesatest
goto END
```

❑   When option 7 is selected, Clean Boot (no commands), the autoexec.bat batch file terminates without launching any command.

Connecting to CEPC with the Serial Port

In this section, we will work through the process of connecting to the CEPC target device using the serial port to download the runtime image.

For the exercise in this section, we will use an old Pentium PC with 128 MB of RAM, two serial ports, and a 3.5-inch floppy drive. The two serial ports are configured as follows:

❑ The first serial port is configured as COM1 with IRQ 4 and 3F8 I/O base address.

❑ The second serial port is configured as COM2 with IRQ 3 and 2F8 I/O base address.

To work through the exercise in this section, we need a null RS-232 serial modem cable to connect the CEPC target device with the development workstation. We also need to configure the MyOSDesign to set the MyCEPCBSP as the active BSP.

Go through the following steps to configure the MyOSDesign and set MyCEPCBSP as the active BSP:

1. Launch the VS2005 IDE and open the MyOSDesign project.

2. From the VS2005 IDE, select Build ⇨ Configuration Manager to bring up the Configuration Manager screen.

3. From the Configuration Manager screen, select MyCEPCBSP x86 Release as the active BSP from the Active solution configuration selection, and click Close to continue.

Creating MyCEPCSerial Target Device Profile

Work through the following steps to create the MyCEPCSerial target device profile:

1. From the VS2005 IDE, select Target ⇨ Connectivity Options to bring up the Target Device Connectivity Options screen.

2. From this options screen, click on the Add Device option at the top left of the screen to bring up the Add New Target Device screen.

3. Enter **MyCEPCSerial** as the new target device name, and click Add to continue.

Configuring MyCEPCSerial Target Device Settings

1. Select Serial for both the Download and Transport options, and select KdStub for the Debugger option, as shown in Figure 5-29.

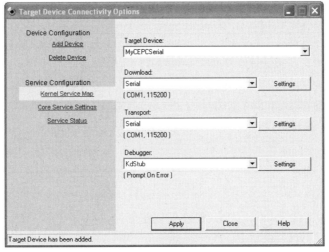

Figure 5-29

By default, the serial port setting is configured to operate at 115200 baud with 8 data bits, no parity, and one stop bit.

2. From the Target Device Connectivity Options screen, click Apply followed by Close to continue.

Downloading Runtime Image to CEPC

Work through the following steps to download the runtime image to the CEPC target device:

1. From the VS2005 IDE, select Target ⇨ Attach Device to bring up the Download Runtime Image to the MyCEPCSerial screen, as shown in Figure 5-30.

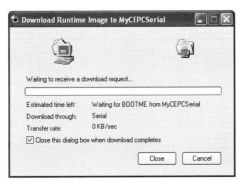

Figure 5-30

2. Power on and boot the CEPC target device using the CEPC boot floppy.

3. As the CEPC target device boots and shows the DOS selection menu, select option 5, Boot CE/PC (serial via sboot.bin), to launch the `loadcepc.exe` with the sboot.bin serial boot loader.

4. As the runtime image download process begins, the Download Runtime Image to MyCEPCSerial screen displays the download progress.

> It takes about 30 minutes to download a 20-MB image file, using the serial connection.

After the runtime image is downloaded to the CEPC target device, it will launch and show a Windows Embedded CE 6.0 desktop from the CEPC target device's display.

Connecting to CEPC with Ethernet

If the CEPC target device has an NE2000-compatible or Realtek-8139 Ethernet interface, the steps to establish connectivity and download a runtime image to the CEPC target device are very similar to the exercise we covered in an earlier section of this chapter, for the eBox-4300-MSJK target device.

Using the CEPC bootable floppy to boot the CEPC target device, follow the same steps as in the exercise for the earlier section, for the eBox-4300-MSJK, to establish a connection to the CEPC target device and download the runtime image.

Summary

In this chapter, we worked through multiple exercises showing the steps to establish a connection between the CE platform builder development workstation and the emulator, eBox-4300-MSJK, and CEPC target devices.

For the eBox-4300-MSJK, we worked through two separate exercises to connect to the eBox-4300-MSJK using the Ethernet connection and the Ethernet boot loader. One of the exercises is done in the environment with DHCP services to provide the IP address. The other exercise is done using a crossover Ethernet cable that connects the eBox-4300-MSJK to the development workstation directly, using a static IP address.

For the CEPC target device, we worked through the exercise to connect to the CEPC target device using a null RS-232 serial modem cable and downloaded the runtime image to the CEPC target device using `loadcepc.exe` with sboot.bin, a serial boot loader.

6

Debugging and Debugging Tools

In most embedded development projects, there are multiple options and methods to reach the same design goals. Throughout the development process, even with the best engineering team, you are expected to spend a great deal of time and resources to look for alternative ways to improve system performance, debug, and identify problem areas. A productive debugging environment can help minimize the time and effort you need to spend for debugging, which can have a direct impact on the project's cost, schedule, and success.

The Windows Embedded CE Platform Builder and Visual Studio 2005 development environment provides an efficient debugging environment, with easy-to-use debugging tools, to help minimize the needed efforts for debugging and to resolve design deficiencies.

Many different options and resources are available to help with the debugging process. Some options are from Microsoft, some are from third-party vendors and may require additional debugging hardware, and some are undocumented processes from other developers sharing their knowledge. In this chapter, we will attempt only to cover the common debugging tools available within the Platform Builder tool.

Chapters 4 and 5 covered the steps to create the OS design, generate the OS runtime image from the OS design, and establish connection between the development workstation and target device to download the CE runtime image to the target device. In this chapter, we will use the same OS design project, from Chapters 4 and 5, to work through the exercise and show the debugging environment and tools available within Windows Embedded CE.

Debugging Environment

The Windows Embedded CE Platform Builder tool provides an effective and efficient debugging environment with easy-to-use debugging tools. The CE debugging tools provide the mechanism for us to launch an application on the target device, view the target device's filesystem, evaluate the target device's system performance, and edit its registry entries. The debugging tools also make it possible to step through the source code for the OS and applications. Being able to step through the source code while it's being executed lets the developer observe system behavior.

CETK

Windows Embedded CE provides a separate testing environment, the CE Test Kit (CETK), to test BSPs and device drivers. It is also the tool Microsoft uses internally to test Windows Embedded CE BSPs and device drivers for its certification program.

The CETK can run as a stand-alone tool or within the VS2005 IDE.

- ❑ To launch the CETK from the VS2005 ID, select Tools ⇨ Windows CE Test Kit.
- ❑ To launch the CETK as a stand-alone tool from the Windows desktop, select Start ⇨ All Programs ⇨ Windows Embedded CE 6.0 ⇨ Windows Embedded CE 6.0 Test Kit.

In Chapter 9, the CETK tool is covered in more detail.

CoreCon

A connection framework called *CoreCon* is available to support the VS2005 IDE. It enables a VS2005 application development session to connect to a Windows Embedded CE target device. When developing a VS2005 application, with an established CoreCon connection to the target device, we can download the VS2005 application to the CE target device, launch the application, inject breakpoints, and step through the code as it runs on the target device.

Different versions of CoreCon support the VS2008 IDE and VS2008 with Service Pack 1 (SP1). The CoreCon binaries are shipped with each version of Visual Studio. The binary for each version is different from the others and only works for the intended version — CoreCon for VS2008 will not work with VS2008 with SP1 installed, and CoreCon for VS2005 will not work under VS2008.

Debugging and Release Configuration

The OS design can be configured to generate a debugging-mode and release-mode OS runtime image. When properly configured, it's possible to use a release-mode OS runtime image to perform many of the debugging functions. An OS runtime image generated from the debugging-mode configuration is usually about twice the size of an image generated from the same project in release-mode configuration. An OS runtime image generated in debugging mode can output far more debugging messages than the release-mode image can.

The additional debugging messages provide more details about the components and modules being launched. Unless you are developing low-level hardware code, the runtime image generated in debugging mode sends out too much detailed information not needed by the application developer. Also, additional components are added to the OS design to generate the debugging-mode runtime image, which affects the system's performance and can have an impact on certain types of applications during development. For application developers, generating a runtime image in release mode with KITL enabled will provide sufficient debugging messages for application development. A release-mode runtime image built with KITL has little impact on system performance and enables the developer to see near-real-life user experience while debugging the application. We will work through the exercise in this chapter using the release-mode image.

The MyOSDesign project in Chapter 2 was created with support for three different BSPs. There are two separate configurations — release mode and debugging mode — for each of the supported BSPs. The MyOSDesign has a total of six selectable configurations. Each configuration will require a separate build process to generate a unique OS runtime image. The debugging environment points only to active configurations. Settings and files from the other, non-active configurations do not have any impact on the active configuration.

For the exercise in this chapter, we will use the release-mode configuration for the MyEmulatorBSP. To set the MyOSDesign project to this configuration, select Build ⇨ Configuration Manager from the VS2005 IDE to bring up the Configuration Manager screen, and select MyEmulatorBSP ARMV4I Release from the "Active solution configuration" selection.

If you followed the exercises in the previous chapters, an OS runtime image has been generated with the Kernel Independent Transport Layer (KITL) build option enabled and can be used for the exercise in this chapter.

If you are not continuing from the previous chapter, open the MyOSDesign project and set the target device connectivity options to MyEmulator (refer to Chapter 5 for information about connecting to the target device). From the VS2005 IDE, select Target ⇨ Attach Device to download the OS runtime image to the emulator.

Debugging the OS Design Build

Not being able to complete the build process to generate an OS runtime image is one of the common problems encountered on a new OS design project. The problem may be caused by any one or a combination of the following:

- ❏ Incorrect entry in the OS design configuration file
- ❏ Incorrect entry in the subproject configuration file
- ❏ Incorrect entry in the Platform configuration file
- ❏ Missing file
- ❏ Incorrect directory reference to a needed file

To fix the problem, we need to know how and where to find its cause. To do this, we need to know the different build processes the Windows Embedded CE build system goes through to generate the OS runtime image.

The CE Build Process

The Windows Embedded CE build process involves the following five phases:

1. **Pre-SYSGEN Build** — During this phase, the build system compiles the source code provided by Microsoft under the Public directory. Since Microsoft also provides the binaries for these components, there is no need to compile the source code unless it has been changed. You should avoid directly modifying the source code under the Public directory. If you do need to modify this code, you should copy the code to a folder under your active project and modify it in this folder.

2. **System Generation (SYSGEN)** — The system generation phase filters the selected Windows Embedded CE components for your platform from the list of available components and links the OS component libraries into DLL or EXE modules.

3. **Post-SYSGEN Build** — This build phase compiles the BSP code, including the device drivers, OAL, and boot loader code. This phase also compiles the code for the OS design's subprojects.

4. **Build Release** — During this phase, the files from the System Generation and Post-SYSGEN Build phases are being copied to a single directory, the build release directory.

5. **Make Run-Time Image** — The Windows Embedded CE runtime image is generated in this phase upon a successful build.

During the build processes, the build system uses the OS design, platform, and source code configuration files to gather information for the build, such as the DIRS, Sources, Makefile, BIB, and REG files.

- **DIRS** — DIRS identifies the subdirectories that contain source code.

- **Sources** — Sources contains the macro variables needed to build the source code.

- **Makefile** — Makefile contains the variables needed to compile and link the source code.

- **BIB** — The Binary Image Builder file (with the .bib file extension) contains system memory configuration information and entries to control which files and modules are included in the OS runtime image.

- **REG** — The Registry file (with .reg file extension) contains registry entries for the system, applications, and device drivers.

Build Error — Missing File

To show one of the common errors, missing file or incorrect filename or path, we'll create an error condition and work through the exercise to show how to resolve the error.

To create an error for the build process, we will add an entry to the project.bib file, instructing the build system to include myfile.txt (the myfile.txt file does not exist) from the build release directory with the runtime image. Since the myfile.txt file is not available, the build system will raise an error and will not generate the runtime image.

To add the entry to the project's BIB file, from the VS2005 IDE, with the MyOSDesign project active, click on the Solution Explorer tab, expand the Parameter Files node, expand the MyEmulatorBSP: ARMV4I node, and double-click on project.bib to open this file in the center pane to view and edit the source code.

From the center pane, scroll to the end of the project.bib source file and enter the following entry, as shown in Figure 6-1:

```
MyFile.txt      $(_FLATRELEASEDIR)\MyFile.txt      NK
```

This BIB file entry will create an error in the make-image phase of the build process.

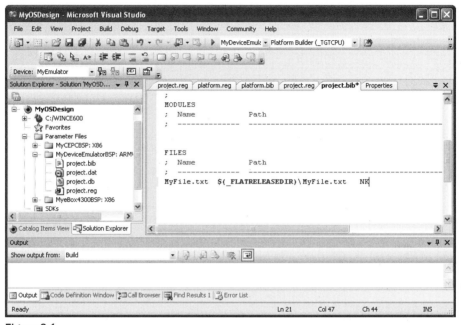

Figure 6-1

The above BIB file entry instructs the build system to include a file that does not exist, the myfile.txt file, in the runtime image. With this BIB file entry added, the build process will fail to generate a runtime image because of the error condition we created.

Let's go through the following process and build the OS design to see the error:

From the VS2005 IDE, select Build ⇨ Build Solution to build the project.

The build process will end with errors. The output window on the VS2005 IDE indicates that the build failed with errors, as shown in Figure 6-2.

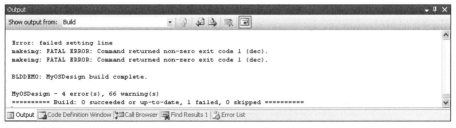

Figure 6-2

> **Depending on your development workstation's performance, the build process may take anywhere from 15 to well over 30 minutes.**

Since the error was created purposely, by adding a build instruction to include a file that does not exist and thus generating the build error, we know exactly what it is. In a real project, to trace the error and find the cause, we need to review the following files:

- ❏ **Build.err** — This file contains error information. The build.err file is not generated for a successful build.

- ❏ **Build.log** — This file logs all activities during the build process. The build.log file is generated for every build.

- ❏ **Build.wrn** — This file contains warning information. The build.wrn file is not generated for a build that does not have a warning.

All these files are located in the _WINCEROOT\ directory and contain build information for the last project that was built. A new build process will erase the existing build.err, build.log, and build.wrn files and generate new ones.

During the build process, in addition to logging the build process to the build.err, build.log, and build.wrn files, these build activities are displayed in the output windows on the VS2005 IDE, where you can view the build activities as they are being processed. The VS2005 IDE output window provides useful information about the build process and helps point out problems and errors. Using the build activities from the output window, we can resolve simple errors. When dealing with complicated errors, the build.err, build.log, and build.wrn files provide build activities information that you can review and forward to other developers to help find a solution to the problem.

> **When tracing complicated build- and compilation-related problems, it's good to keep copies of the build.err, build.log, and build.wrn files for each build session. Comparing the build.err, build.log, and build.wrn files between different build sessions, with different build configurations, can help identify problem areas.**

Using the default build settings, the warnings generated during the build process do not prevent the OS from building and generating a runtime image. The build settings can be changed to prevent the build system from generating a runtime image when a warning occurs. Many of the warnings are not critical and can be ignored. However, it's good practice to review the warning log file, build.wrn, to check for serious warnings.

In this case, since the error is happening in the make-image phase because of a missing file, the build.log file does not indicate any error condition.

> For a simple error such as a missing file, you can view the build result from the
> build output window in the VS2005 IDE to find and resolve the error quickly.
> The build.err, build.log, and build.wrn files are useful for tracing complicated errors,
> and this lets you reference the build errors with other developers by sending these
> log files to them and seeking resolution of the problem.

To review errors from the build process, view the build.err file content with a text editor, such as
notepad.exe. The build.err file contains the following entry:

```
BLDDEMO: Error(s) in makeimg phase. See C:\WINCE600\OSDesigns\MyOSDesign\
MyOSDesign\RelDir\MyEmulatorBSP_ARMV4I_Release\makeimg.out for details.
```

The entry in the build.err directs us to look at the makeimg.out file in the build release directory.

The makeimg.out file is a text file and can be viewed using notepad.exe or any text editor. At the end
of the makeimg.out file are entries indicating the build system encountered errors due to the missing file.
The build system could not find the myfile.txt file and treated this as a fatal error.

```
Error: Could not find file
'C:\WINCE600\OSDesigns\MyOSDesign\MyOSDesign\RelDir\
MyEmulatorBSP_ARMV4I_Release\Myfile.txt' on disk
Myfile.txt C:\WINCE600\OSDesigns\MyOSDesign\MyOSDesign\RelDir\MyEmulatorBSP_ARMV4I_
Release\Myfile.txt NK

Error: failed setting line
makeimg: FATAL ERROR: Command returned non-zero exit code 1 (dec).
makeimg: FATAL ERROR: Command returned non-zero exit code 1 (dec).
```

The error can be corrected by creating the myfile.txt file and placing the file in the build release directory.

We won't use the myfile.txt file for any other purpose — it was just needed to complete the build
process. Let's create the myfile.txt with a line of text, "Hello world," and place the file in the following
directory:

_MyOSDesign\MyOSDesign\RelDir\MyEmulatorBSP_ARMV4I_Release\

> To keep the above directory reference within one line for ease of reading, and
> subsequent reference to the same directory, the _MyOSDesign directory variable is
> used: _MyOSDesign = _WINCEROOT\OSDesigns\MyOSDesign.

Since we know that the build process failed during the make-image phase, we don't need to go through
the complete build process again. We can execute the make-image phase to generate the runtime image.
Select Build ⇨ Make Run-Time Image from the VS2005 IDE to generate the runtime image. The Make
Run-Time Image process should be able to complete without error and generate a runtime image.

The Make Run-Time Image process does not trigger the build system to go through the System Generation, Build Release phases and takes much less time to generate the runtime image. The previous step, adding the myfile.txt file to the build release directory, is a temporary fix and does not apply to the overall project. Without changing any of the MyOSDesign project settings, select Build ⇨ Build Solution from the VS2005 to build the project again. The build process will result in the same missing file error as before, since the myfile.txt file cannot be found.

> **During the build release phase, the build process deletes all the files in the build release directory and copies the files from the system generation and post-sysgen build phases to the build release directory.**

To make the myfile.txt a permanent part of the project, we need to make the following adjustments:

1. Create the MyFile folder in the _MyOSDesign\ directory, _MyOSDesign\MyFile\.

2. Create the myfile.txt file and save the file to the _MyOSDesign\MyFile\ directory.

3. Modify the BIB file entry, in the project.bib file, made in the earlier part of the exercise, to the following. You can modify this file from the VS2005 IDE as done previously.

```
Myfile.txt    $(_WINCEROOT)\OSDesigns\MyOSDesign\MyFile\Myfile.txt    NK
```

To make the above modification using a text editor, the project.bib file is located in the following directory:

_MyOSDesign\MyOSDesign\Wince600\MyEmulatorBSP_ARMV4I\OAK\Files

With the above changes, the project should be able to complete the build process and generate a runtime image without error. This is one method to include a single file or multiple files in the runtime image. To include multiple files, you need to add one BIB file entry for each additional file to the project.bib file and copy the file to the _MyOSDesign\MyFile\ directory.

Remote Tools

Windows Embedded CE Platform Builder provides the following remote tools to help with the debugging process. These remote tools can access the OS runtime image running on the target device remotely from the development workstation.

❑ File Viewer

❑ Heap Walker

❑ Zoom

❑ Process Viewer

❑ Registry Editor

❏ System Information

❏ Performance Monitor

❏ Spy

❏ Kernel Tracker

❏ Call Profiler

These remote tools can be accessed by selecting Target ➪ Remote Tools from the VS2005 IDE.

The Platform Builder remote tools communicate with the target device over a Kernel Independent Transport Layer (KITL). To use these remote tools, the OS runtime image must be built with the KITL build option enabled. All remote tools go through a similar process to establish a connection to the target device, using KITL. We will go through the detailed steps with one tool, the Remote File Viewer remote tool. For all other tools, the connection processes are the same.

Remote File Viewer

You can use the *Remote File Viewer tool* to view the files on the target device in much the same way as using Windows Explorer locally on the device. It's also possible to copy files to the target device using the Remote File Viewer.

To use the Remote File Viewer, perform the following steps:

1. With the MyOSDesign project active, download the OS runtime image to the emulator.

2. From the VS2005 IDE, select Target ➪ Remote Tools ➪ File Viewer to bring up the following Select a Windows CE Device screen, as shown in Figure 6-3.

Figure 6-3

3. From the "Select a Windows CE Device" screen, click to select the default device and click OK to continue. The following Connecting to Device screen, as shown in Figure 6-4, will show briefly.

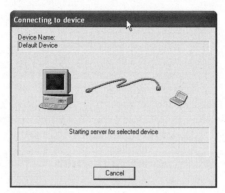

Figure 6-4

After the connection to the emulator is established, the Remote File Viewer tool will launch, as shown in Figure 6-5.

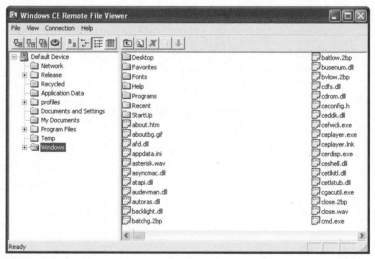

Figure 6-5

The Remote File Viewer functions similarly to the Windows File Explorer, providing a graphical user interface to navigate through the files and folders on the emulator, a CE target device.

The Windows Embedded CE filesystem does not have a drive letter to represent the storage device as the desktop Windows system does. As shown in the Remote File Viewer application user interface, Figure 6-5, the default device is the root of the filesystem. For the desktop Windows filesystem,

C:\WINDOWS\ is used to represent the WINDOWS folder under drive C. For the Windows Embedded CE filesystem, \WINDOWS\ is used to represent the WINDOWS folder in the root of the filesystem.

The \RELEASE\ folder is mapped to the workstation's active release folder, $(_MyOSDesign)\ MyOSDesign\RelDir\MyEmulatorBSP ARMV4I Release\.

_MyOSDesign = _WINCEROOT\OSDesigns\MyOSDesign.

The release folder can be used to copy files from the workstation to the target device. With the Remote File Viewer active, use the following steps to copy the 123MYDATA.txt file to the emulator:

1. Create a text file and name the file 123MYDATA.txt.

2. Copy the 123MYDATA.txt file to the workstation's active release folder, $(_MyOSDesign)\ MyOSDesign\RelDir\MyEmulatorBSP ARMV4I Release\.

3. From the Remote File Viewer user interface, select Connection ⇨ Refresh Selection to update the display contents.

4. From the Remote File Viewer user interface, click on the release folder. The 123MYDATA.txt file is listed, as shown in Figure 6-6.

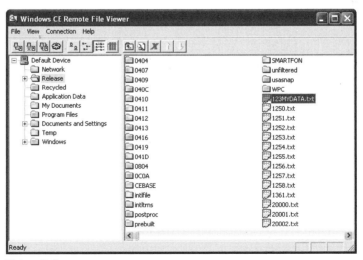

Figure 6-6

From the Windows CE Remote File Viewer screen, select File ⇨ Exit to terminate the Remote File Viewer application.

Remote Heap Walker

The *Remote Heap Walker tool* is used to examine heap layout and memory contents for each process running on the target device.

To use the Remote Heap Walker tool, an OS runtime image with KITL running on the CE target device is needed.

To use the Remote Heap Walker tool with the image running on the emulator, select Target ⇨ Remote Tools ⇨ Heap Walker from the VS2005 IDE, and use the same steps as in the Remote File Viewer to establish a connection with the emulator.

After the connection to the emulator is established, the Remote Heap Walker application will launch, as shown in Figure 6-7.

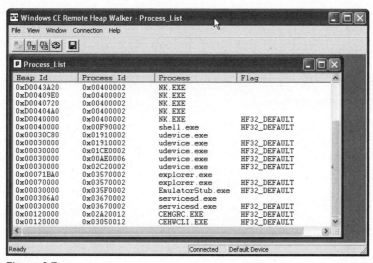

Figure 6-7

From the Remote Heap Walker Process_List, double-click on any one of the processes on the list to open a Heap_List window for the process. Double-click on the `explorer.exe` process to open the Heap_List window, as shown in Figure 6-8.

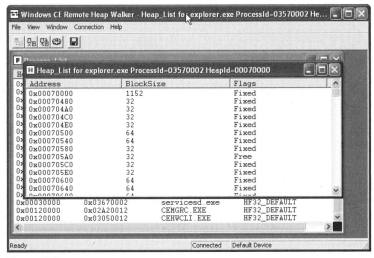

Figure 6-8

Double-click on any one of the Heap addresses on the Heap_List screen to open a Heap_Dump screen for the associated address, as shown in Figure 6-9.

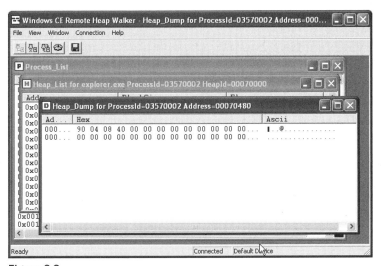

Figure 6-9

From the Windows CE Remote Heap Walker screen, select File ⇨ Exit to terminate the Remote Heap Walker application.

Remote Zoom-In

The *Remote Zoom-In tool* is used to capture the current screen image, in bitmap (.bmp) format, from the connected CE target device. The captured screen image can be saved to a bitmap file in the workstation's storage, which is useful for documentation and other purposes.

To use the Remote Zoom-In tool, an OS runtime image with KITL running on the CE target device is needed.

To use the Remote Zoom-In tool with the image running on the emulator, select Target ⇨ Remote Tools ⇨ Zoom from the VS2005 IDE, and use the same steps as with the Remote File Viewer to establish a connection with the emulator.

After the connection to the emulator is established, the Remote Zoom-In application will launch, as shown in Figure 6-10.

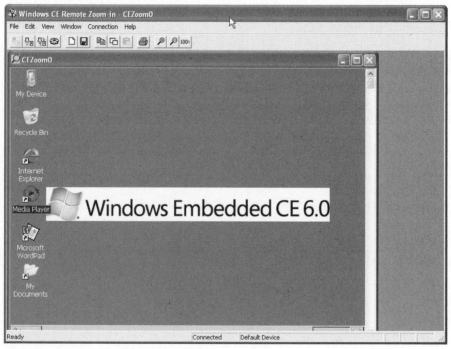

Figure 6-10

Within the same instance of the Remote Zoom-In tool, it's possible to capture and display multiple screen images from the same target device. Figure 6-10 shows the initial screen image captured from the emulator when the Remote Zoom-In tool was launched. From the emulator desktop, double-click on the Media Player icon to launch the program. After the Media Player is launched, from the Windows CE

Remote Zoom-In program screen, select Window ⇨ New Window to capture a new screen image from the emulator, as shown in Figure 6-11.

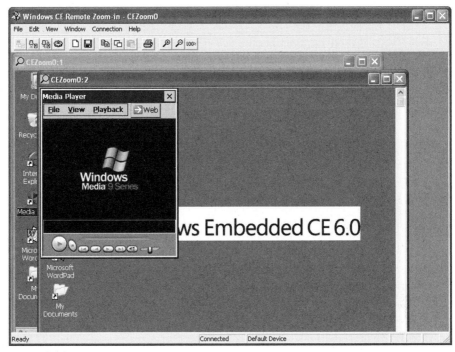

Figure 6-11

From the Windows CE Remote Zoom-In screen, select File ⇨ Exit to terminate the Remote Zoom-In application.

Remote Process Viewer

The *Remote Process Viewer* displays all running processes on the target device. The tool also displays the threads and modules associated with each running process.

To use the Remote Process Viewer tool, an OS runtime image with KITL running on the CE target device is needed.

To use the Remote Process Viewer with the image running on the emulator, select Target ⇨ Remote Tools ⇨ Process Viewer from the VS2005 IDE, and use the same steps as in the Remote File Viewer to establish a connection with the emulator.

After the connection to the emulator is established, the Remote Process Viewer application will launch, as shown in Figure 6-12.

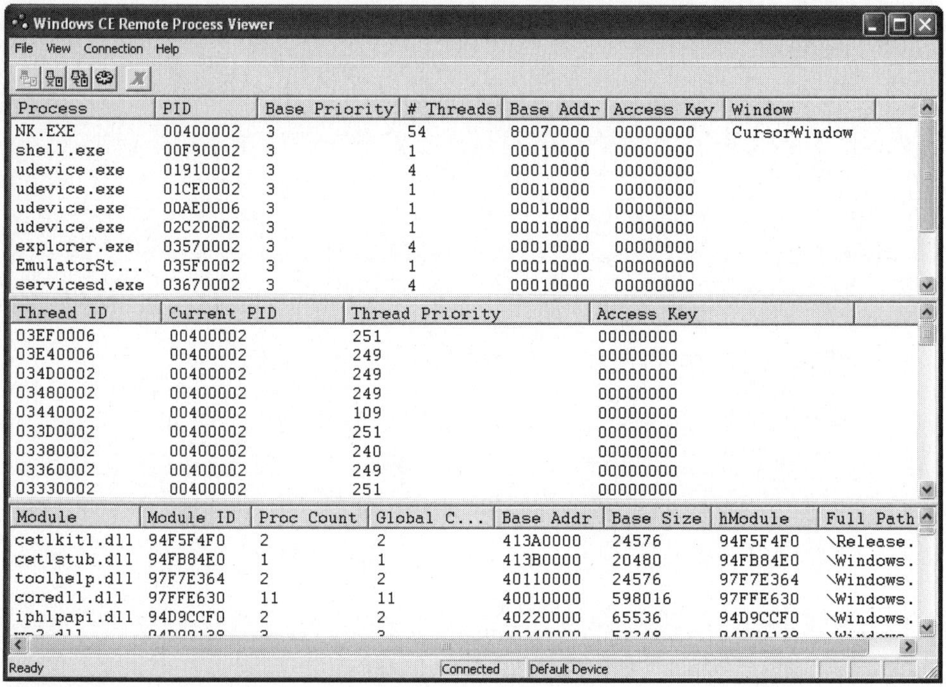

Figure 6-12

From the Windows CE Remote Process Viewer screen, when you click on different processes in the top Process pane, the Thread and Module panes will change to reflect the associated threads and modules.

Let's launch the Media Player application on the emulator to see how many threads and modules are associated with the Media Player. From the emulator desktop, double-click on the Media Player icon to launch the application. After the Media Player application is launched on the emulator desktop, then from the Windows CE Remote Process Viewer, select Connection ⇨ Refresh to update the display; from the screen's top pane, click to highlight the ceplayer.exe process, the Media Player process. The Remote Process Viewer user interface shows that there are two threads and 13 modules associated with the ceplayer.exe process, as shown in Figure 6-13.

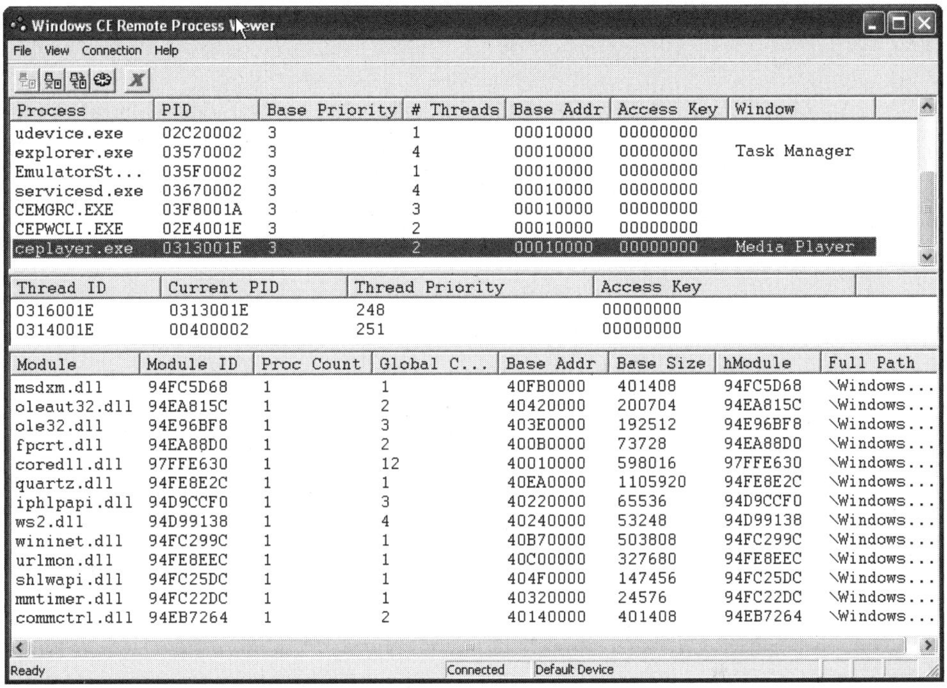

Windows CE Remote Process Viewer

File   View   Connection   Help

Process	PID	Base Priority	# Threads	Base Addr	Access Key	Window
udevice.exe	02C20002	3	1	00010000	00000000	
explorer.exe	03570002	3	4	00010000	00000000	Task Manager
EmulatorSt...	035F0002	3	1	00010000	00000000	
servicesd.exe	03670002	3	4	00010000	00000000	
CEMGRC.EXE	03F8001A	3	3	00010000	00000000	
CEPWCLI.EXE	02E4001E	3	2	00010000	00000000	
ceplayer.exe	0313001E	3	2	00010000	00000000	Media Player

Thread ID	Current PID	Thread Priority	Access Key	
0316001E	0313001E	248	00000000	
0314001E	00400002	251	00000000	

Module	Module ID	Proc Count	Global C...	Base Addr	Base Size	hModule	Full Path
msdxm.dll	94FC5D68	1	1	40FB0000	401408	94FC5D68	\Windows...
oleaut32.dll	94EA815C	1	2	40420000	200704	94EA815C	\Windows...
ole32.dll	94E96BF8	1	3	403E0000	192512	94E96BF8	\Windows...
fpcrt.dll	94EA88D0	1	2	400B0000	73728	94EA88D0	\Windows...
coredll.dll	97FFE630	1	12	40010000	598016	97FFE630	\Windows...
quartz.dll	94FE8E2C	1	1	40EA0000	1105920	94FE8E2C	\Windows...
iphlpapi.dll	94D9CCF0	1	3	40220000	65536	94D9CCF0	\Windows...
ws2.dll	94D99138	1	4	40240000	53248	94D99138	\Windows...
wininet.dll	94FC299C	1	1	40B70000	503808	94FC299C	\Windows...
urlmon.dll	94FE8EEC	1	1	40C00000	327680	94FE8EEC	\Windows...
shlwapi.dll	94FC25DC	1	1	404F0000	147456	94FC25DC	\Windows...
mmtimer.dll	94FC22DC	1	1	40320000	24576	94FC22DC	\Windows...
commctrl.dll	94EB7264	1	2	40140000	401408	94EB7264	\Windows...

Ready   Connected   Default Device

Figure 6-13

We can use the Remote Process Viewer application to terminate running processes. The Media Player application running on the emulator can be terminated by terminating the `ceplayer.exe` process from the Remoter Process Viewer. From the Remote Process Viewer application screen, click to highlight the `ceplayer.exe` process, and select File ⇨ Terminate Process to terminate it.

To terminate the Remote Process Viewer application, select File ⇨ Exit from the Windows CE Remote Process Viewer screen.

Remote Registry Editor

The *Remote Registry Editor* displays the target device's registry and makes it possible to add, delete, and modify registry keys and entries. The Remote Registry Editor is quite similar to the Registry Editor for the desktop Windows system.

When accessing the target device's registry, be very careful about the changes, additions, and deletions you are making to the registry. Improper registry entry changes can prevent the device from functioning as intended. With bad registry entries, a CE device may not be able to complete the boot process.

To use the Remote Registry Editor tool, an OS runtime image with KITL running on the CE target device is needed.

To use the Remote Registry Editor with the image running on the emulator, select Target ⇨ Remote Tools ⇨ Registry Editor from the VS2005 IDE, and use the same steps as in the Remote File Viewer to establish a connection with the emulator.

After the connection to the emulator is established, the Remote Registry Editor application will launch, as shown in Figure 6-14.

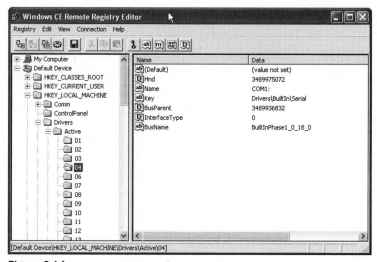

Figure 6-14

The Remote Registry Editor is a useful tool that enables you to view the actual registry entries on the target device. You can view and validate the device driver, application, and other system registry entries.

The registry entry under the [HKEY_LOCAL_MACHINE\Drivers\Active] key lists the active device drivers on the target device. You can view the registry entries in this section to see which device drivers are loaded.

You can make changes to the registry and reflect these changes to the running target device in real time. For example, you can change the device name registry entries for the emulator and view the changes on the emulator to see the immediate result.

Let's work through the following steps to change the emulator's device name, using the remote registry editor:

1. On the Windows CE Remote Registry Editor screen's left pane, click on the HKEY_LOCAL_ MACHINE\Ident key. On the right pane, double-click on the Name value to bring up the New String Value entry screen, and enter **MyEmulator** for the Value entry, as shown in Figure 6-15. Then click OK to continue.

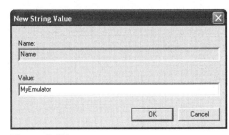

Figure 6-15

The above step changed the emulator's device name to *MyEmulator*. Go through the following steps to view the result from the system properties within the Control Panel:

2. From the emulator's desktop, click on Start ⇨ Settings ⇨ Control Panel to bring up the Control Panel screen.

3. From the Control Panel screen, double-click on the System icon to bring up the System Properties screen.

4. From the System Properties screen, click on the Device Name tab to show the device name. The entry should match what you entered from the Remote Registry Editor, *MyEmulator*, as shown in Figure 6-16.

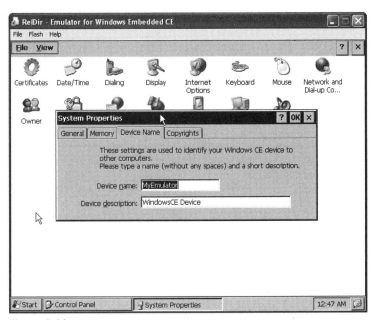

Figure 6-16

When making changes to the registry entries for certain device drivers or applications, the drivers or applications may need to be unloaded and reloaded in order for the new registry entries to take effect.

The Remote Registry Editor is able to export the target device's registry entries to a file and save to the workstation's storage as backup or reference.

Remote System Information

The *Remote System Information tool* displays system information, settings, and properties for the target device.

To use the Remote System Information tool, an OS runtime image with KITL running on the CE target device is needed.

To use the Remote System Information tool with the image running on the emulator, select Target ➪ Remote Tools ➪ System Information from the VS2005 IDE, and use the same steps as in the Remote File Viewer to establish a connection with the emulator.

After the connection to the emulator is established, the Remote System Information application will launch, as shown in Figure 6-17.

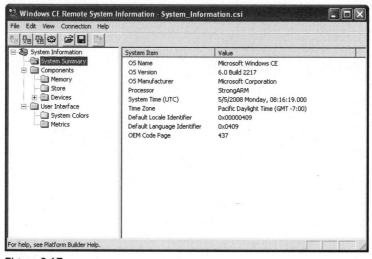

Figure 6-17

Remote Performance Monitor

The *Remote Performance Monitor tool* is a graphical tool for measuring performance. The Remote Performance Monitor application can track current activity on the target device and can view data from a log file. The Performance Monitor tool can be used to monitor system resources consumption and other performance-related issues for a CE target device.

To use the Remote Performance Monitor, an OS runtime image with KITL running on the CE target device is needed.

To use the Remote Performance Monitor tool with the image running on the emulator, select the Target ⇨ Remote Tools ⇨ Performance Monitor from the VS2005 IDE, and use the same steps as in the Remote File Viewer to establish a connection with the emulator.

After the connection to the emulator is established, the Remote Performance Monitor application will launch, as shown in Figure 6-18.

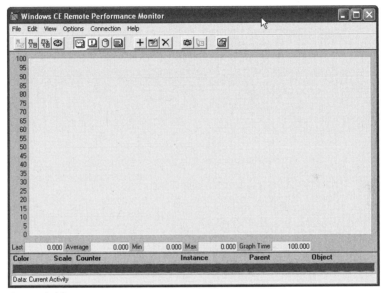

Figure 6-18

From the Windows CE Remote Performance Monitor screen, perform the following:

1. Select Edit ⇨ Add to Chart to bring up the Add to Chart screen, as shown in Figure 6-19.

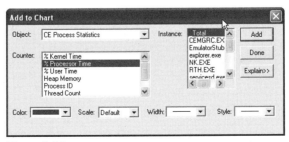

Figure 6-19

2. From the Add to Chart screen, in the Object list, select CE Process Statistics. In the Counter list, select % Processor Time. In the Instance list, select _Total, and click Add to continue.

3. From the Add to Chart screen, in the Object list, select CE Memory Statistics. In the Counter list, select Memory Load, and click Add to continue.

4. From the Add to Chart screen, in the Object list, select CE UDP Statistics. In the Counter list, select Datagrams Received/Sec, and click Add to continue.

5. From the emulator desktop, move the mouse rapidly, click the left mouse button on the empty portion of the screen to avoid activating other programs, and view the changing graph on the Remote Performance Monitor screen.

6. From the emulator desktop, launch Internet Explorer, and see the changing graph on the Remote Performance Monitor screen, as shown in Figure 6-20.

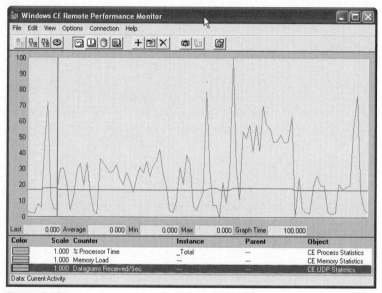

Figure 6-20

7. On the lower portion of the Remote Performance Monitor screen, click to highlight the last line, with "1.000 Datagrams Received/Sec" shown as the Scale Counter value.

8. From the Remote Performance Monitor screen, select Edit ⇨ Edit Chart Line to bring up the Edit Chart Line screen, as shown in Figure 6-21.

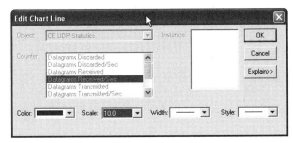

Figure 6-21

9. From the Edit Chart Line screen, on the Scale list, select 10.0, and click OK to continue.

10. From the emulator, navigate with Internet Explorer and see the changes on the Remote Performance Monitor, as shown in Figure 6-22.

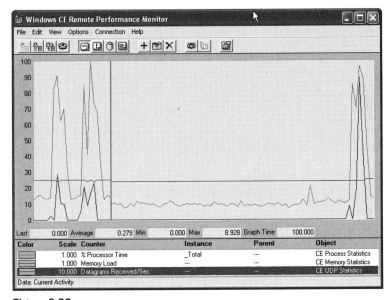

Figure 6-22

After changing the display scale for the Datagrams Received/Sec, the activities resulting from navigating the Internet with Internet Explorer become much more visible.

Remote Spy

Before CE 6.0, the *Remote Spy tool* was able to show Windows messages being delivered to processes running on the target device.

For CE 6.0, all processes run within their own 2-GB virtual memory space. A pointer within a process is only valid within that process address space. Owing to the change in memory architecture, the Remote Spy tool views Windows properties and cannot view Windows messages.

To use the Remote Spy tool, an OS runtime image with KITL running on the CE target device is needed.

To use the Remote Spy tool with the image running on the emulator, select Target ⇨ Remote Tools ⇨ Spy from the VS2005 IDE, and use the same steps as in the Remote File Viewer to establish a connection with the emulator.

After the connection to the emulator is established, the Remote Spy application will launch, as shown in Figure 6-23.

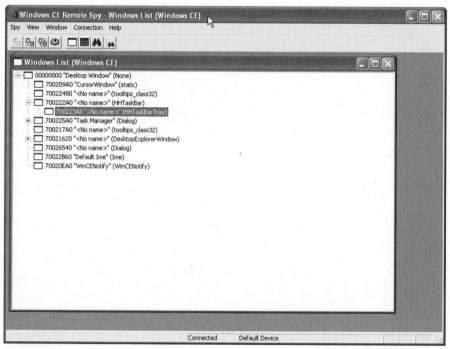

Figure 6-23

Let's work through the following steps to view the window properties for the Media Player application:

1. From the emulator's desktop, double-click on the Media Player icon to launch the Media Player.

2. From the Windows CE Remote Spy screen, select Spy ⇨ Windows List to bring up a new Windows List. After resizing the first Windows List on the left side and the second Windows List on the right, as shown in Figure 6-24, we can see there are additional icons listed.

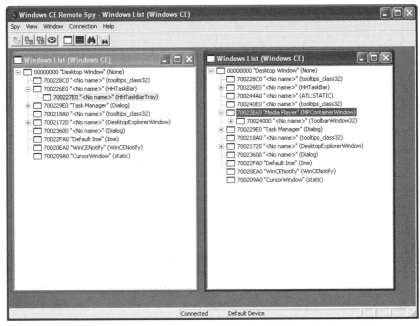

Figure 6-24

3. On the second Windows List, on the right side, within the Windows CE Remote Spy screen, click to highlight the "Media Player" (MPContainerWindow), as shown in Figure 6-24, and select Spy ⇨ Property to bring up the Window Property screen, as shown in Figure 6-25, to show the properties for the "Media Player" (MPContainerWindow) window.

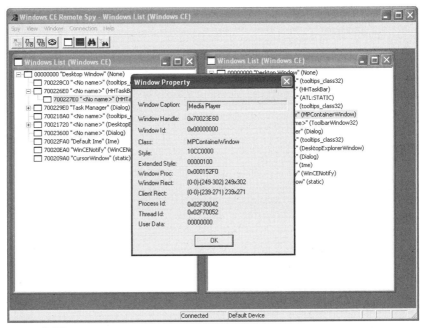

Figure 6-25

As pointed out above, the Remote Spy tool cannot display Windows messages. When we select Spy ➪ Messages to bring up the Messages screen, nothing is listed, as shown in Figure 6-26.

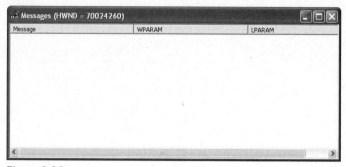

Figure 6-26

It's hoped that a work-around will be available soon to enable the Remote Spy tool to display Windows messages.

Remote Kernel Tracker

The *Remote Kernel Tracker tool* provides a graphical representation of the CE runtime and application events occurring on the target device.

The Remote Kernel Tracker can be launched in three different modes and will launch in the data collection mode by default:

1. **Data Collection Mode** — In this mode, the data are collected live from the target device and update the user interface in real time. This is the default mode that allows you to monitor system events as the events happen.

2. **Limited Buffer Mode** — This mode is the same as the data collection mode with a limited buffer set to collect the desired amount of data. The size of the buffer can be set from 1 MB to 100 MB.

3. **File Mode** — This mode allows you to view the collected data from a log file. You can save the collected data from the data collection mode or limited buffer mode and view the data using the file mode.

To use the Remote Kernel Tracker, an OS runtime image with KITL running on the CE target device is needed. In addition to KITL, in order to capture interrupts data, the runtime image needs to be generated with the Kernel debugger and Profiling options enabled.

To use the Remote Kernel Tracker with the image running on the emulator, select Target ➪ Remote Tools ➪ Spy from the VS2005 IDE, and use the same steps as in the Remote File Viewer to establish a connection with the emulator.

After the connection to the emulator is established, the Remote Kernel Tracker will launch, as shown in Figure 6-27.

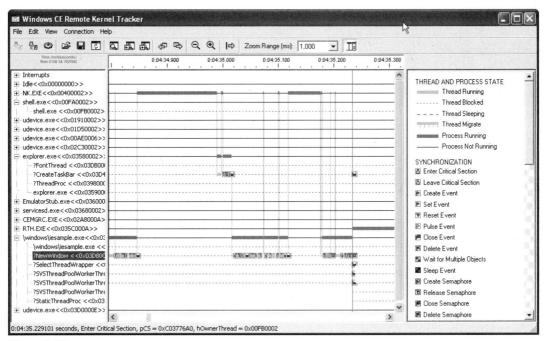

Figure 6-27

The left pane on the Remote Kernel Tracker user interface lists all the system's interrupts, processes, and threads. The center pane displays the events and state of the interrupts, processes, and threads in the system. The measuring scale on top of the center pane indicates the time since the system started. The right pane lists the description for the symbols used in the center pane to represent the threads, processes, and events.

More detailed information about an event is available by clicking on the Event node, as shown in Figure 6-28.

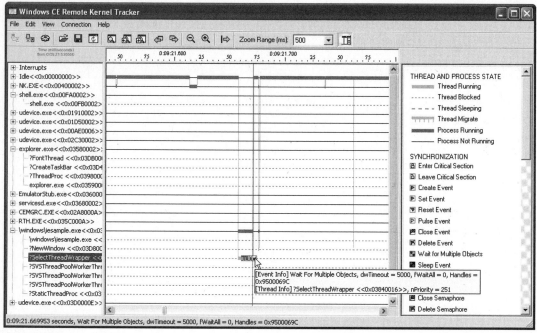

Figure 6-28

The Remote Kernel Tracer is useful for tracing low-level system behavior, enabling you to perform tasks such as locating transitions between threads, locating events on a thread, displaying properties for an event, determining the length of time between events, and more. It's well worth the time to learn how to use this tool.

> **Since there are a lot more application developers than low-level system developers, information about system-level debugging is not as widely available. The Windows Embedded CE development team's blog provides a good source of system-level and debugging information:**
>
> `http://blogs.gotdotnet.com/ce_base/`

Remote Call Profiler

The *Remote Call Profiler* is an application profiling tool. To use this tool, the application must be built with special flags to insert instrumentation hooks into the profiler's data collector. The hooks record every function entry and exit in the instrumented code. The hooks record the time each function starts and stops. The hooks can also detect nested function calls, so they can record data about a whole call graph instead of just the individual functions. However, the overhead caused by the instrumented code can distort the results.

Microsoft does not ship an instrumented version of the code.

Remote Target Control

The *Remote Target Control tool* enables you to send commands to control the target device remotely, to launch programs, and view running processes. It's also possible to terminate some of the target device's running processes from the workstation.

To use the Remote Target Control tool, an OS runtime image with KITL running on the CE target device is needed.

To use the Remote Target Control tool with the image running on the emulator, select Target ⇨ Target Control from the VS2005 IDE to launch the Remote Target Control tool to bring up the Remote Target Control command window, as shown in Figure 6-29.

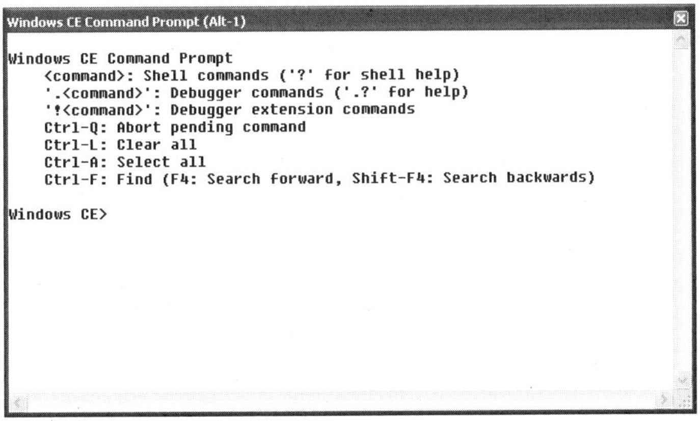

```
Windows CE Command Prompt (Alt-1)                                    ☒

Windows CE Command Prompt
     <command>: Shell commands ('?' for shell help)
     '.<command>': Debugger commands ('.?' for help)
     '!<command>': Debugger extension commands
     Ctrl-Q: Abort pending command
     Ctrl-L: Clear all
     Ctrl-A: Select all
     Ctrl-F: Find (F4: Search forward, Shift-F4: Search backwards)

Windows CE>
```

Figure 6-29

From the Remote Target Control command window, you can enter the following command to view the running processes on the emulator (the command is case-sensitive):

```
gi proc
```

All the processes running on the emulator are listed on the Remote Target Control window, as shown in Figure 6-30.

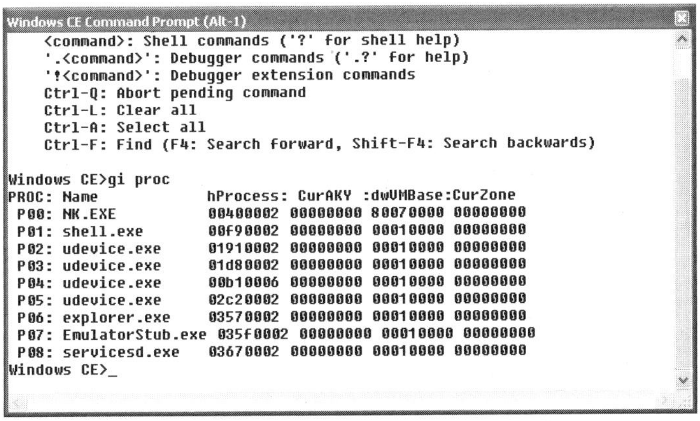

```
Windows CE Command Prompt (Alt-1)                                    ☒
     <command>: Shell commands ('?' for shell help)
     '.<command>': Debugger commands ('.?' for help)
     '!<command>': Debugger extension commands
     Ctrl-Q: Abort pending command
     Ctrl-L: Clear all
     Ctrl-A: Select all
     Ctrl-F: Find (F4: Search forward, Shift-F4: Search backwards)

Windows CE>gi proc
PROC: Name               hProcess: CurAKY :dwVMBase:CurZone
  P00: NK.EXE            00400002 00000000 80070000 00000000
  P01: shell.exe         00F90002 00000000 00010000 00000000
  P02: udevice.exe       01910002 00000000 00010000 00000000
  P03: udevice.exe       01d80002 00000000 00010000 00000000
  P04: udevice.exe       00b10006 00000000 00010000 00000000
  P05: udevice.exe       02c20002 00000000 00010000 00000000
  P06: explorer.exe      03570002 00000000 00010000 00000000
  P07: EmulatorStub.exe  035f0002 00000000 00010000 00000000
  P08: servicesd.exe     03670002 00000000 00010000 00000000
Windows CE>_
```

Figure 6-30

From the Remote Target Control command window, we can enter the following command to launch the Windows Media Player application on the emulator:

```
s ceplayer.exe
```

After the command is executed from the Remote Target Control command window, notice that the Windows Media Player application is launched on the emulator.

Now, execute the following command to view the running processes on the emulator again:

```
gi proc
```

All the processes running on the emulator, including the Windows Media Player application process, ceplayer.exe, are listed on the Remote Target Control window, as shown in Figure 6-31.

```
Windows CE Command Prompt (Alt-1)                                        ⊠
  P03: udevice.exe      01d80002 00000000 00010000 00000000
  P04: udevice.exe      00b10006 00000000 00010000 00000000
  P05: udevice.exe      02c20002 00000000 00010000 00000000
  P06: explorer.exe     03570002 00000000 00010000 00000000
  P07: EmulatorStub.exe 035F0002 00000000 00010000 00000000
  P08: servicesd.exe    03670002 00000000 00010000 00000000
Windows CE>s ceplayer.exe
Windows CE>gi proc
PROC: Name            hProcess: CurAKY :dwVMBase:CurZone
  P00: NK.EXE           00400002 00000000 80070000 00000000
  P01: shell.exe        00f90002 00000000 00010000 00000000
  P02: udevice.exe      01910002 00000000 00010000 00000000
  P03: udevice.exe      01d80002 00000000 00010000 00000000
  P04: udevice.exe      00b10006 00000000 00010000 00000000
  P05: udevice.exe      02c20002 00000000 00010000 00000000
  P06: explorer.exe     03570002 00000000 00010000 00000000
  P07: EmulatorStub.exe 035F0002 00000000 00010000 00000000
  P08: servicesd.exe    03670002 00000000 00010000 00000000
  P09: ceplayer.exe     02b0000a 00000000 00010000 00000000
Windows CE>_
```

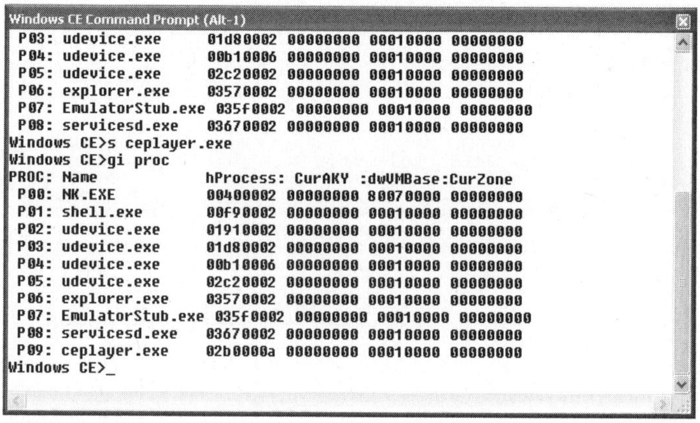

Figure 6-31

From the Remote Target Control command window, we can issue commands to terminate the process that is running on the target device.

From the list of running processes displayed in the Remote Target Control command window, as shown in Figure 6-31, we can see the Windows Media Player application process, ceplayer.exe, listed as P09, process 09. We can terminate the Windows Media Application process, currently running on the emulator, by entering the following kill process command from the Remote Target Control command window:

```
kp 09
```

> **If there are other programs or utilities running, the process number on your system may be different.**

After the command is executed from the Remote Target Control command window, notice that the Windows Media Player application is terminated on the emulator.

In this section, we work through a few exercises showing some of the useful commands supported by the Target Control command window. Following is the full list of commands supported by this command window:

- ❑ **?** — Displays the list of supported commands.

- ❑ **break** — Breaks into the Microsoft kernel debugger program.

- ❑ **dd** — Dumps DWORD values for a range of addresses to the display.

- ❑ **df** — Dumps DWORD values for a range of addresses to file.

- ❑ **dis** — Discards all memory that can be discarded.

- ❑ **gi** — Gets information on processes and processes with threads, modules, critical sections with threads waiting, and events.

- ❑ **log** — Displays the zones used by the event-tracking subsystem. You can also use this command to modify the zone for the event-tracking subsystem. This command only works when the event-tracking subsystem is active.

- ❑ **memtrack** — Controls the collection of memory-tracking data by the event-tracking subsystem. This command only works when the event-tracking subsystem is running.

- ❑ **mi** — Displays memory information.

- ❑ **prof** — Controls the kernel profiler. This command has an effect only on a CE OS built with profiling support.

- ❑ **s** — Starts a process.

- ❑ **run** — Runs a series of processes listed in a text file specified by the BatchFilename parameter.

- ❑ **win** — Dumps the list of windows currently displayed on the target device.

- ❑ **zo** — Performs debugging zone operations.

The above list of commands and descriptions for the Remote Target Control is taken from Microsoft Developers Network. The full list of commands is also available from the network's URL:

```
http://msdn.microsoft.com/en-us/library/ms937117.aspx
```

> **If the above URL is broken, go to** `http://msdn.microsoft.com` **and search for Target Control Debugging Commands.**

Serial Debug

The serial port is another connection available for debugging. By connecting a null RS-232 serial modem cable between the target device's serial port and the development workstation's serial port, with Hyper Terminal running on the development workstation, we can capture serial debugging messages from the target device.

Such messages can be a helpful debugging tool when

❑   Debugging boot loader-related issues.

❑   The runtime image is not able to launch far enough to use the KITL over the Ethernet to capture debugging messages.

❑   The target device has a serial connection but not an Ethernet one.

Let's use the MyOSDesign to work through the serial debugging exercise in this section. Take the following steps to configure the MyeBox4300BSP as the active BSP, and use the existing runtime image generated from the previous exercise:

1.   Launch VS2005 and open the MyOSDesign project.

2.   From the VS2005 IDE, select Build ⇨ Configuration Manager to bring up the Configuration Manager screen.

3.   From the Configuration Manager screen, select MyeBox4300BSP x86 Release as the active BSP from the "Active solution configuration," and click Close to continue.

Go through the following steps to launch Hyper Terminal, and configure it to capture serial debugging messages from the eBox-4300-MSJK target device:

1.   Connect a null RS-232 modem cable between eBox-4300-MSJK's COM1 and one of the available serial ports on the development workstation.

2.   Launch Hyper Terminal and enter **MyeBox4300** as the New Connection name. The click OK to bring up the Connect to Screen instruction.

3.   On Connect to Screen, select the serial port that is connected to the eBox-4300-MSJK from the "Connect using selection drop-down" list, and click OK to bring up the Properties screen.

4.   From the Properties screen, select 38400 for the bits per second selection, and use the default for the other settings. Click Apply followed by OK to continue.

The Hyper Terminal is launched and configured to communicate with the eBox-4300-MSJK and is ready to capture serial debugging messages.

Next, work through the following steps to download the runtime image to the eBox-4300-MSJK target device:

1. From the VS2005 IDE, select Target ⇨ Connectivity Options to bring up the Target Device Connectivity Options screen.

2. From this Options screen, select the MyeBox4300 target device profile, created in Chapter 5, and click Apply followed by Close to continue.

3. From the VS2005 IDE, select Target ⇨ Attach Device to initialize the runtime image download process.

4. Power up the eBox-4300-MSJK.

5. After the eBox-4300-MSJK is powered up and has launched the DOS selection menu, select option 2, to load the OS image from the development station with DHCP service.

As the eBox-4300-MSJK executes the `loadcepc.exe` and launches the Ethernet boot loader, serial debugging messages should begin to show in the Hyper Terminal's screen.

Following is a partial listing of the serial debugging messages captured:

```
Microsoft Windows CE Ethernet Bootloader Common Library Version 1.0 Built Apr  8
2003 05:35:15
Copyright (c) 2000-2001  Microsoft Corporation
Microsoft Windows CE Ethernet Bootloader 3.3 for CE/PC (May 21 2003)
Boot Args @ 0x1E246
PCI Device Configurations (3 PCI bus(es) present)...
=======================================================
 Bus, Device, Function = 0, 8, 0
 Vendor ID, Device ID  = 0x10EC, 0x8139
 Base Class, Subclass  = 2, 0 => NETWORK_CTLR
 Interrupt             = 10
 BaseAddress[0]        = 0xE800 (I/O)
 BaseAddress[1]        = 0xFCFFFC00 (Memory)
=======================================================
 Bus, Device, Function = 0, 15, 0
 Vendor ID, Device ID  = 0x1106, 0x5324
 Base Class, Subclass  = 1, 1 => MASS_STORAGE_CTLR
 Interrupt             = 255
 BaseAddress[4]        = 0xFC00 (I/O)
=======================================================
 Bus, Device, Function = 0, 16, 0
 Vendor ID, Device ID  = 0x1106, 0x3038
 Base Class, Subclass  = 12, 3 => SERIAL_BUS_CTLR
 Interrupt             = 10
 BaseAddress[4]        = 0xEC00 (I/O)
=======================================================
 Bus, Device, Function = 0, 16, 1
 Vendor ID, Device ID  = 0x1106, 0x3038
 Base Class, Subclass  = 12, 3 => SERIAL_BUS_CTLR
 Interrupt             = 11
 BaseAddress[4]        = 0xE480 (I/O)
```

```
===========================================================
Bus, Device, Function = 1, 0, 0
Vendor ID, Device ID  = 0x1106, 0x3157
Base Class, Subclass  = 3, 0 => DISPLAY_CTLR
Interrupt             = 0
BaseAddress[0]        = 0xC000000 (Memory)
BaseAddress[1]        = 0xFD00000 (Memory)
===========================================================
Bus, Device, Function = 2, 1, 0
Vendor ID, Device ID  = 0x1106, 0x3288
Base Class, Subclass  = 4, 3 => MULTIMEDIA_DEV
Interrupt             = 11
BaseAddress[0]        = 0xFEBFC000 (Memory)
===========================================================
FindAllPCINetCard: Searching for PCI Ethernet NIC ...
FindALLPCINetCard(0): Found Ethernet NIC (IRQ=10, IOBase=0xE801, Type=4).
FindPCINetCard:Argument IOBASE=0, IRQ=0,TYPE=4
FindPCINetCard:Found 1 PCI Ethernet NIC ...
FindPCINetCard: Found Ethernet NIC (IRQ=10, IOBase=0xE800).
RTL8139InitDMABuffer():: Start[0x20000]-[0x20000] - Size[0x20000]
Tx[0x20000] - Rx[0x201800] - RxLength[0x10000] - RxLengthBit[0x1800]
RTL8139Init()::  BaseIO[0xE800] : MemOffset[0x1]
RTL8139Init()::  TxBuff[0x20000] - RxBuff[0x201800] - LastRx[0x2117FF]
RTL8139Init:: MAC = 44-4D-50-09-04-0F
RTL8139 ethdbg library: AutoNegotiate..
RTL8139:: RTL8139HWSetMCRegs():: Set all to 0x00
Returned MAC Address:44:4D:50:09:04:0F
System ready!
Preparing for download...
Using device name: CEPC1039
Hit ENTER within 3 seconds to enter static IP address!InitDHCP():: Calling
ProcessDHCP()
ProcessDHCP()::DHCP_INIT
Got Response from DHCP server, IP address: 192.168.1.84

ProcessDHCP()::DHCP IP Address Resolved as 192.168.1.84, netmask: 255.255.255.0
Lease time: 86400 seconds
Got Response from DHCP server, IP address: 192.168.1.84
No ARP response in 2 seconds, assuming ownership of 192.168.1.84
+EbootSendBootmeAndWaitForTftp
Sent BOOTME to 255.255.255.255
Locked Down Link 1
Src IP 192.168.1.84 Port 0800   Dest IP 192.168.1.193 Port 0A46
EthDown::TFTPD_OPEN::boot.bin
-EbootSendBootmeAndWaitForTftp
```

When the runtime image is built in debugging mode, the serial debugging messages will be far more detailed.

Summary

This chapter provided an overview of the debugging environment and the build process to help you determine what to look for and where to look to resolve problems. I covered the tools available from the Platform Builder, and we worked through a short exercise showing how to use the tools along with an exercise showing how to trace a missing file error for the build process.

The information in this chapter provides the starting point for you to learn and become more familiar with the debugging environment and tools. Debugging and problem resolution are integral parts of software and hardware development. You should invest time and effort to understand and learn how to use the debugging environment and tools effectively. When you master the debugging environment and tools, it will save you countless hours and lots of aggravation.

7

Boot Loader Overview

In the previous chapter, I talked about the Board Support Package, the OS design, connecting to the target device, the debugging environment, and debugging tools. All of these development processes come into play after the boot loader.

In the Windows Embedded CE development environment, the boot loader is the first piece of code to develop for a new hardware platform and is needed to download the debug and release mode OS runtime images to the hardware platform. Unless you're developing brand-new hardware from the ground up, it's not likely that you need to develop new boot loader code from scratch.

In general, the hardware platform manufacturer is likely to have a platform that supports the Windows Embedded CE environment and provides the reference development hardware with a boot loader and a BSP to support that environment. Microsoft also provides a sample boot loader, with source code, as part of the Platform Builder installation, for developers to use as the starting point to create their own boot loaders.

What Is a Boot Loader?

For a hardware platform that requires an operating system (OS), the *boot loader* is the code responsible for launching that system. The boot loader is unique to each hardware platform. For many devices, immediately after power is applied to an embedded device, the boot loader is the first piece of code to be executed.

There are devices that ship without a boot loader. For these devices, the system reset process bootstraps the OS runtime image in the device's local storage. Although these devices may ship without the boot loader, one is needed during the development phase.

Since the boot loader is the first piece of code to run on the device, there isn't any code running in the background to help with debugging. To develop a boot loader, the developer must have a good understanding of the hardware platform, the processor, and the operating system.

The boot loader initializes the hardware platform to a known state and sets the stage for the OS to launch.

For x86 devices, the system BIOS is the first piece of code to be executed. The BIOS initializes the system hardware, after which it searches for a bootable storage device to boot from. The x86 system BIOS is considered to be a boot loader.

For a Windows Embedded CE device, the boot loader initializes the device's hardware and provides the necessary function to load the CE runtime image to the device's system memory from the device's local ROM or flash storage.

BIOS Loader–x86 BIOS Loader

The *BIOS Loader*, also referred to as the *x86 BIOS Loader*, is a boot loader designed to support x86 devices. It does not provide the functionality to initialize system hardware but is dependent on the system BIOS to initialize the hardware. The BIOS Loader is launched by the system BIOS.

The BIOS Loader launches the CE runtime image from the target device's local storage. When launched, the BIOS Loader reads the content from the boot.ini file, containing boot parameters, and parses the display resolution, network, debugging serial port, and other settings, placing the parsed parameters in a memory location where the CE runtime can read and launch the image based on these parameters. In order to read these parameters, the CE runtime image must be generated with the "Enable eboot space in memory build" option enabled.

In addition to launching the nk.bin CE runtime image, the BIOS Loader can launch the Eboot and Sboot loaders to download a runtime image from the development workstation.

A boot loader can launch another boot loader.

Eboot Loader

The *Eboot loader* (Ethernet boot loader) is a network boot loader designed to download the CE runtime image from the development station to the target device over a network connection. The Eboot loader is launched by another boot loader and cannot function by itself.

In a typical development environment, the Eboot loader broadcasts a "bootme" packet over the network connection when it runs. After establishing a connection with the CE development workstation, the Eboot loader initiates a Trivial File Transfer Protocol (TFTP) to download the runtime image from the development workstation.

Loadcepc

The *Loadcepc* is a DOS boot loader, designed to support x86 devices, and is provided as part of the CEPC BSP for use in the development process. The Loadcepc loader requires DOS to function.

The Loadcepc boot loader can launch the CE runtime image, nk.bin, from the target device's local storage.

The Loadcepc is also used to launch the Eboot loader, an eboot.bin file in the target device's local storage, which, in turn, sends "bootme" messages to the development workstation and downloads the CE runtime image.

It can also launch the Sboot loader, an sboot.bin file on the target device's local storage, to download the CE runtime image from the development station through a serial connection.

For the x86 device development environment, the Loadcepc and Eboot loaders combination is the most common boot loader usage. Using this combination of loaders, you can boot an x86 device with DOS, launch the Loadcepc loader, which, in turn, launches the Eboot loader to establish a link to the development station, and download the CE runtime image.

The Loadcepc is an executable that runs under the DOS operating system. Here are some Loadcepc usage samples:

```
; Launch the NK.BIN file, CE OS run-time image, with 2 parameters.
; The /C switch specify the COM port for sending serial debug messages.
; The /L switch specify the display resolution

Loadcepc /C:1 /L:1024x768x16 NK.BIN
```

```
; Launch the EBOOT.BIN file, Eboot loader with the following parameters.
; The /C switch specify the COM port for sending serial debug messages.
; The /L switch specify the display resolution
; This is used in the environment with DHCP service, and both the target
; device & development station are on the same subnet.

Loadcepc /C:1 /L:1024x768x16 EBOOT.BIN
```

```
; Launch the EBOOT.BIN file, Eboot loader with the following parameters
; The /e switch specify 0x320 I/O port, IRQ-5, 192.168.1.232 static IP
; for target device with a NE2000 interface.
; The /L switch specify the display resolution
;
Loadcepc /e:320:5:192.168.1.232 /L:800x600x16 EBOOT.BIN
```

A floppy disk image is provided in the platform builder, cepcboot.144, using the Loadcepc with various boot options. The floppy disk image is in the following directory:

\PROGRAM FILES\MICROSOFT PLATFORM BUILDER\6.00\CEPB\UTILITIES

The makeimagedisk.exe utility is also provided to load the image onto a floppy disk, in the same directory as above.

You can review the autoexec.bat and readme.txt files provided in the cepcboot.144 floppy image to see additional Loadcepc usage.

Romboot Loader

The *Romboot loader* is designed to replace the x86 system BIOS and resides in the flash storage generally occupied by the x86 system BIOS.

After power is supplied to the system, the Romboot loader initializes the system hardware, a task normally handled by the system BIOS, and launches the CE runtime image stored on the flash drive locally or launches an Eboot loader, which, in turn, downloads the CE runtime image from the development station over a network connection.

Sboot Loader

The *Sboot loader* is a serial boot loader designed to download the CE runtime image from the workstation to the target device over a serial connection. The Sboot loader is launched by another boot loader and cannot function by itself.

> Since the data transfer speed over a serial link is extremely slow compared to an Ethernet network link, the serial boot loader, sboot.bin, is not commonly used.

BIOS Loader for x86 Devices

To work through a boot loader exercise, we need to have hardware and the bootloader code written to support the hardware.

The BIOS Loader can support most x86 devices, including the typical desktop PC and notebook computer. An old desktop or notebook computer can be used as the x86 target device for the exercise, since these are easier to access than some of the other embedded devices. We will work through the boot loader exercise using the BIOS Loader.

To begin, let's look at how a typical x86 device goes through the boot process and uses the BIOS Loader to launch the CE runtime image.

x86 Device Boot Process

Similar to the typical personal computer, an x86 device goes through the following boot process to launch the Windows Embedded CE runtime image with the BIOS Loader:

1. After power is supplied to the system, the x86 processor jumps to the reset vector address and executes the BIOS code.

2. The BIOS code initializes the hardware and searches for a bootable storage device.

3. After detecting a bootable storage device, generally an IDE, the BIOS locates and loads the master boot sector (MBR) to the system memory.

4. As the MBR code runs, it searches for the boot sector image on a valid partition, loads the boot sector image into the system memory, and kick-starts the boot sector code.

5. As the boot sector code runs, it finds and loads the BIOS Loader.

6. As the BIOS Loader runs, it finds and loads the Windows Embedded CE runtime image into system memory and jumps to the starting address of the image to launch the image.

BIOS Loader Code

The BIOS Loader is included as part of the CEPC BSP, installed during the Windows Embedded CE Platform Builder installation when support for the x86 processor is selected. Since the MyCEPCBSP is cloned from the CEPC BSP, it has all the components and code that are part of the CEPC BSP, including the BIOS Loader.

The BIOS Loader is provided in compiled binary along with the source code. A set of bootable floppy disk images is also provided, with the necessary utility to prepare an IDE bootable storage device and launch the BIOS Loader, which, in turn, launches the CE runtime image.

The BIOS Loader floppy images, binary, and source codes can be found in the following directory:

_MYCEPCBSP\SRC\BOOTLOADER\BIOSLOADER\

> **_MYCEPCBSP = _WINCEROOT\PLATFORM\MYCEPCBSP**

There are five subdirectories under the above BIOS Loader directory:

1. BOOTSECTOR — This directory contains the boot sector code. This code is separated into four folders, each containing the code for the ExFAT, FAT12, FAT16, and FAT32 filesystems. The boot sector code is responsible for loading the BIOS Loader into system memory for the jump to the startup routine. When compiled, the boot sector image size is 512 bytes, fitting into one disk sector. A boot sector image, bset.img, is provided as part of the floppy disk image in the _WINCEROOT\PLATFORM\CEPC\SRC\BOOTLOADER\BIOSLOADER\DISKIMAGES directory. When preparing the IDE storage to boot to BIOS Loader, after formatting the storage device, the boot sector image is written to the device in the appropriate location by the cesys .exe utility.

2. DISKIMAGES — This directory contains two floppy disk images and two folders containing the files for each of the floppy images.

   ❑ BOOTDISK.144 — This is a bootable floppy image that will boot to the BIOS Loader and launch the included Eboot loader, sending "bootme" requests to download the CE runtime image from the workstation.

   ❑ SETUPDISK.144 — This is a bootable floppy image that will boot to MS DOS 6.22. This floppy contains the BIOS Loader binary and the necessary utility to prep an IDE storage device to boot using the BIOS Loader.

3. INIPARSER — This directory contains the code to parse the information from the boot.ini file.

4. LOADER — There are two subdirectories under this directory, \Fixed and \Floppy. The BIOS Loader code that supports booting from the floppy disk is in the \Floppy subdirectory. The code that supports IDE storage is in the \Fixed directory. Under the \Fixed directory are five directories containing the BIOS Loader code to support different filesystems, as follows:

    ❑   MAIN — Main code for the BIOS Loader to support the IDE storage device

    ❑   INC — Included header libraries

    ❑   EXFAT — Code to support the ExFAT filesystem

    ❑   FAT16 — Code to support the FAT16 filesystem

    ❑   FAT32 — Code to support the FAT32 filesystem

5. UTILITIES — This directory contains the code for three utilities, `bincompress.exe`, `cesys.exe`, and `disport.exe`.

    ❑   BINCOMPRESS directory — Code for `bincompress.exe`, the utility used to compress or decompress .bin runtime images for use with the BIOS Loader

    ❑   CESYS directory — Code for the `cesys.exe` utility used to copy the boot sector to the appropriate location on the storage device

    ❑   DISKPART directory — Code for the `diskpart.exe` utility. This utility can be used to prepare bootable storage partitions for ExFAT FAT16, and FAT32 filesystems.

Building the BIOS Loader Code

With the available BIOS Loader source code, you can change and customize the BIOS Loader to meet your specific needs.

For example, instead of launching the splash screen using the standard splash graphic filename, splash.bmp or splash.bmx, you can change the BIOS Loader code to launch the splash screen using a unique graphic filename, such as *mysplash.bmp* or *mysplash.bmx* graphic file, by changing the SPLASH_IMAGE_FILE_NAME and COMPRESSED_SPLASH_IMAGE_FILE_NAME variable in the splash.h header file, located in the following directory:

    _MYCEPCBSP\SRC\BOOTLOADER\BIOSLOADER\LOADER\FIXED\INC

Before CE 6.0 R2, the BIOS Loader supported only the FAT16 filesystem and had one set of code for the loader. The FAT16 filesystem limits the BIOS Loader to supporting file partitions of less than 2 GB.

For the Windows Embedded CE 6.0 R2 release, additional code was added to the BIOS Loader code base to support the ExFAT and FAT32 filesystems, which enabled the BIOS Loader to support file partitions much larger than 2 GB.

The BIOS Loader source code must be built and compiled within an active OS design project. Let's go through the following steps to set up the VS2005 IDE to compile the BIOS Loader code:

1. Start the VS2005 IDE and open the MyOSDesign project.

2. From the VS2005 IDE, Select Build ⇨ Configuration Manager to bring up the Configuration Manager screen.

3. From the "Active solution configuration" selection on the Configuration Manager screen, select MyCEPCBSP x86 Release, and click Close to continue.

4. From the VS2005 IDE, click the Solution Explorer tab.

5. From the Solution Explorer tab, click the C:\WINCE600 node and continue to expand the node until you can see the following node:

   \PLATFORM\MYCEPCBSP\SRC\BOOTLOADER\BIOSLOADER.

6. Right-click on the BIOS Loader node and select Build to compile the code, as shown in Figure 7-1.

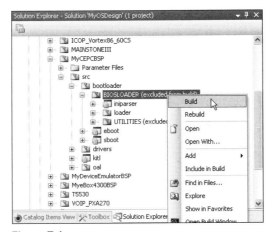

Figure 7-1

If you are working with CE 6.0, the build process is able to complete without error, and generates the BLDR binary file in the build release directory.

If the build process ends with an error, it's caused by the updated BIOS Loader source code from the CE 6.0 R2 update. Before CE 6.0 R2, the BIOS Loader provided support for the FAT16 filesystem only. The R2 update added support for ExFAT and FAT32 filesystems. The updated source code has been broken up into additional directories and places the code to support ExFAT, FAT16, FAT32, and Floppy filesystems into four separate directories. We need to remove some of the leftover code and correct the errors in the source code configuration files.

BIOS Loader Code Cleanup

To fix the build errors caused by the CE 6.0 R2 update, we need to go through the following steps to clean up the BIOS Loader source code and make changes to the source code configuration files in order for the code to complete the build process and generate the necessary binary files:

1. Navigate to the _MYCEPCBSP\SRC\BOOTLOADER\BIOSLOADER\LOADER directory using the Windows File Explorer, keeping the Dirs file and subfolders and deleting all other files in this directory. These are leftover files that should have been removed during the CE 6.0 R2 update installation process. The Dirs file is used by the Windows Embedded CE build system to identify the directories containing source code files that need to be built.

   _MYCEPCBSP=_WINCEROOT\PLATFORM\MYCEPCBSP

2. Open the sources.cmn file in the following directory with a text editor:

   _MYCEPCBSP

3. Add this entry to the sources.cmn file:

   _PLATLIB=$(_TARGETPLATROOT)\LIB

4. Open the boot.bib file in the following directory with a text editor:

   _MYCEPCBSP\SRC\BOOTLOADER\BIOSLOADER\LOADER\FIXED\EXFAT

   Locate the following entry:

```
nk.exe   $(_PROJECTROOT)\cesysgen\Platform\$(_TGTPLAT)\target\$(_TGTCPU)\
$(WINCEDEBUG)\bldr_exfat.exe    BLDR
```

   The above codes are all within the same line.

   Change the above line of code to the following:

```
Nk.exe     $(_PLATFORMROOT)\$(_TGTPLAT)\target\$(_TGTCPU)\$(WINCEDEBUG)
\bldr_exfat.exe    BLDR
```

5. Open the makebldr.bat file in the following directory with a text editor:

   _MYCEPCBSP\SRC\BOOTLOADER\BIOSLOADER\LOADER\FIXED\EXFAT

   Locate the following line of code (the third line), containing the bldr.nb0 filename:

```
Copy
%_PROJECTROOT%\cesysgen\platform\%_TGTPLAT%\target\%_TGTCPU%\%WINCEDEBUG%\bldr.nb0 bldr
```

   The above is a single line of code.

   Change the above line of code to the following:

```
Copy %_TARGETPLATROOT%\target\%_TGTCPU%\%WINCEDEBUG%\bldr.nb0 bldr
```

6. Open the boot.bib file in the following directory with a text editor:

_MYCEPCBSP\SRC\BOOTLOADER\BIOSLOADER\LOADER\FIXED\FAT16

Locate the following entry:

```
Nk.exe
$(_PROJECTROOT)\cesysgen\platform\$(_TGTPLAT)\target\$(_TGTCPU)\
$(WINCEDEBUG)\bldr_fat16.exe   BLDR
```

The above code is all within the same line.

Change the above line of code to the following:

```
Nk.exe
$(_PLATFORMROOT)\$(_TGTPLAT)\target\$(_TGTCPU)\$(WINCEDEBUG)\
bldr_fat16.exe    BLDR
```

7. Open the makebldr.bat file in the following directory with a text editor:

_MYCEPCBSP\SRC\BOOTLOADER\BIOSLOADER\LOADER\FIXED\FAT16

Locate the following line of code (the third line), containing the bldr.nb0 filename:

```
Copy %_PROJECTROOT%\cesysgen\platform\%_TGTPLAT%\target\%_TGTCPU%\%WINCEDEBUG%\
bldr.nb0 bldr
```

The above is a single line of code.

Change the above line of code to the following:

```
Copy %_TARGETPLATROOT%\target\%_TGTCPU%\%WINCEDEBUG%\bldr.nb0 bldr
```

8. Open the boot.bib file in the following directory with a text editor:

_MYCEPCBSP\SRC\BOOTLOADER\BIOSLOADER\LOADER\FIXED\FAT32

Locate the following entry:

```
Nk.exe
$(_PROJECTROOT)\cesysgen\platform\$(_TGTPLAT)\target\$(_TGTCPU)\$(WINCEDEBUG)\
bldr_fat32.exe   BLDR
```

The above code is all within the same line.

Change the above line of code to the following:

```
Nk.exe
$(_PLATFORMROOT)\$(_TGTPLAT)\target\$(_TGTCPU)\$(WINCEDEBUG)\bldr_fat32.exe     BLDR
```

9. Open the makebldr.bat file in the following directory with a text editor:

_MYCEPCBSP\SRC\BOOTLOADER\BIOSLOADER\LOADER\FIXED\FAT32.

Locate the following line of code (the third line), containing the bldr.nb0 filename:

```
Copy
%_PROJECTROOT%\cesysgen\platform\%_TGTPLAT%\target\%_TGTCPU%\%WINCEDEBUG%\
bldr.nb0 bldr
```

The above is a single line of code.

Change the above line of code to the following:

```
Copy %_TARGETPLATROOT%\target\%_TGTCPU%\%WINCEDEBUG%\bldr.nb0 bldr
```

10. Open the boot.bib file in the following directory with a text editor:

_MYCEPCBSP\SRC\BOOTLOADER\BIOSLOADER\LOADER\FLOPPY

Locate the following entry:

```
Nk.exe
$(_PROJECTROOT)\cesysgen\platform\$(_TGTPLAT)\target\$(_TGTCPU)\$(WINCEDEBUG)\
bldr_floppy.exe   BLDR
```

The above code is all within the same line.

Change the above line of code to the following:

```
Nk.exe
$(_PLATFORMROOT)\$(_TGTPLAT)\target\$(_TGTCPU)\$(WINCEDEBUG)\bldr_floppy.exe      BLDR
```

11. Open the makebldr.bat file in the following directory with a text editor:

_MYCEPCBSP\SRC\BOOTLOADER\BIOSLOADER\LOADER\FLOPPY

Locate the following line of code (the third line), containing the bldr.nb0 filename:

```
Copy
%_PROJECTROOT%\cesysgen\platform\%_TGTPLAT%\target\%_TGTCPU%\%WINCEDEBUG%\
bldr.nb0 bldr
```

The above is a single line of code.

Change the above line of code to the following:

```
Copy
%_TARGETPLATROOT%\target\%_TGTCPU%\%WINCEDEBUG%\bldr.nb0 bldr
```

Generating the BIOS Loader Binary

After cleaning up the code and changing the path in the source code configuration files, the BIOS Loader code is able to complete the build process and generate the binary file.

From the VS2005 IDE's Solution Explorer tab, right-click on the BIOS Loader node and select Build to compile the code, as shown in Figure 7-1.

If the build process still ends with an error, check to verify that the changes were made correctly. Sometimes the residual files from the previous failed build can cause problems. To fix this, you need to perform a clean build to eliminate the problem caused by these residual files. To perform a clean build, go through the following steps:

1. Select Build ⇨ Clean Solution from the VS2005 IDE.

2. After the Clean Solution process is done, select Build ⇨ Build Solution to build the OS design.

3. After the OS design finishes the build process, build the BIOS Loader code again.

The build.err and build.log files in the BIOS Loader directory provide information about the build process and error condition that can help identify the error. These files are located in the following directory:

_MYCEPCBSP\SRC\BOOTLOADER\BIOSLOADER

After building the BIOS Loader code from the VS2005 IDE, there is one more step to generate the BIOS Loader binary file. To generate this file to support a FAT16 filesystem, perform the following steps:

1. From the VS2005 IDE, click the Solution Explorer tab.

2. From the Solution Explorer tab, click on the C:\WINCE600 node and continue to expand the node until you can see the following node:

\PLATFORM\MYCEPCBSP\SRC\BOOTLOADER\BIOSLOADER\LOADER\FIXED\FAT16

3. Right-click on the FAT16 node and select Open Build Window, as shown in Figure 7-2, to bring up a DOS command window pointing to the FAT16 directory, under the Loader directory.

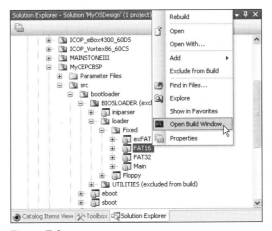

Figure 7-2

> To generate the BIOS Loader binary file for the FAT32 filesystem, use the same process and select Open Build Window for the FAT32 filesystem to bring up a DOS command window pointing to the FAT32 directory. Then go through the remaining steps to generate the BIOS Loader binary.

4. From the DOS command window, execute the following command: `makebldr`.

5. After the `makebldr` command is executed, a series of events takes place in the DOS command window, as shown in Figure 7-3.

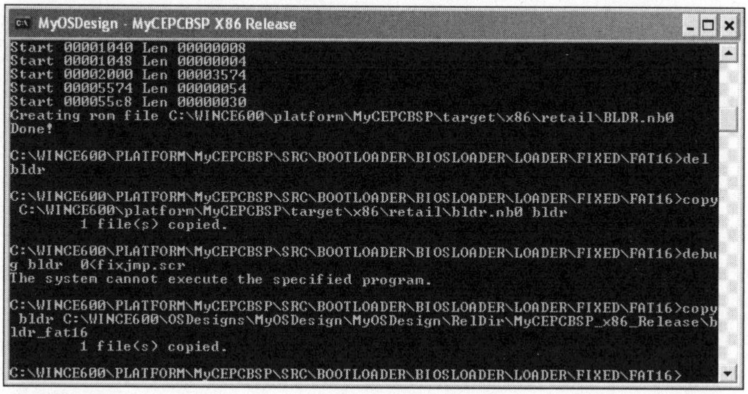

Figure 7-3

6. The FAT16 BIOS Loader binary file is generated in the OS design project's build release directory. Search for the bldr_fat16 (without file extension) file in the following directory:

    _MYOSDESIGN\MyOSDesign\RelDir\MYCEPCBSP_x86_Release\

> **_MYOSDESIGN=_WINCEROOT\OSDesigns\MyOSDesign**

The bldr_fat16 is the file needed to prepare a FAT16 file partition to boot using the BIOS Loader. When in use, the bldr_fat16 file must be renamed *bldr*.

By repeating the same steps to generate the BIOS Loader binary for the FAT16 filesystem for EXFAT and FAT32, the following BIOS Loader binary files will be generated in the same OS design build release directory:

❑ BLDR_EXFAT

❑ BLDR_FAT32

How to Use the BIOS Loader Binary

The steps in this section are applicable to all x86 target devices.

To prepare an IDE storage device to load the Windows Embedded CE runtime image using the BIOS Loader, we need the following additional file and utility:

❑ BOOTSECTOR image — This image launches the BIOS Loader.

❑ `cesys.exe` — This utility copies the boot sector image to the boot partition's first sector.

Two BIOS Loader floppy disk images are provided as part of the CEPC BSP. Since the MyCEPCBSP is cloned from the CEPC BSP, the following two floppy disk images are also cloned into the MyCEPCBSP directory:

❑   BOOTDISK.144 — This is a sample boot disk for downloading the OS runtime image from the development workstation using the BIOS Loader and Eboot to the target device.

❑   SETUPDISK.144 — This is a setup disk containing the setup utility, boot sector image, and BIOS Loader. This disk is bootable and can be used to prepare and set up an IDE hard drive or IDE flash storage with BIOS Loader.

The floppy disk images are located in the following directory:

_MYCEPCBSP\SRC\BOOTLOADER\BIOSLOADER\DISKIMAGES

The makeimagedisk.exe utility is also provided to copy the floppy disk images onto a floppy disk, in the following directory:

\PROGRAM FILES\MICROSOFT PLATFORM BUILDER\6.00\CEPB\UTILITIES

Here are the steps to create the bootable BIOS Loader setup floppy disk from the setupdisk.144 floppy image:

1.   Put a blank floppy disk in the development workstation's floppy drive.

2.   Execute the makeimagedisk.exe utility.

3.   From the MakeImageDisk program screen, click on Open and navigate to the following directory to select the setupdisk.144 floppy image file, as shown in Figure 7-4.

Figure 7-4

4.   Click on Start to write the image to the floppy disk.

The floppy disk created in the above steps is bootable. To prepare an IDE storage device with BIOS Loader, use this floppy disk as the startup disk to boot the x86 target device, and perform the following steps:

1.   Run the fdisk.exe utility to create an active partition.

2.   Run format.com to format the partition without any command-line parameter (do not make the partition bootable).

3. Execute the following command to prep the IDE storage device with the BIOS Loader:

```
;
; Assuming the IDE storage device is setup as drive C
; The MKDISK.BAT batch file perform the following tasks
; - Use CESYS.EXE utility to copy the Boot sector image to drive C
; - Copy the BLDR Biosloader to drive C
; - Copy the BOOT.INI file to drive C
; - Copy the SPLASH.BMX to drive C
; - Copy the EBOOT.BIX Eboot loader to driver C
;
MKDISK C:
```

4. After the IDE storage device is prepped with the BIOS Loader, copy the nk.bin Windows Embedded CE runtime image to the IDE storage device.

5. After the above step, reset the target device power. When the target device boots, the BIOS Loader will launch the nk.bin runtime image stored on the IDE storage device.

> Since a typical nk.bin Windows Embedded CE runtime image is larger than the capacity of a floppy disk, you need to use another method to copy the nk.bin image to the IDE storage. Many of the newer generation of x86 devices, such as the eBox-4300 compact computer, are capable of booting from USB bootable flash storage. The USB bootable flash storage is a convenient way to copy the nk.bin runtime image from the workstation to the target device.

For the target device built with a network interface, we can boot the device using a floppy drive or bootable USB flash with network service and copy the runtime image file, nk.bin, through the network connection.

Summary

The boot loader is the first piece of code to run on many devices. In this chapter, we provided a high-level overview about the boot loader, introduced the Loadcepc, BIOS Loader, Romboot loader, eboot.bin (Ethernet boot loader), and sboot.bin (serial boot loader).

We worked through an exercise to build the BIOS Loader code, creating the BIOS Loader boot floppy, and prepped the IDE storage with BIOS Loader.

Unless you are involved in developing CE support from the ground up for a target device, it's not likely that you need to perform serious boot-loader-related coding. CE has been around for more than 10 years, so most (if not all) of the key hardware vendors have a CE support package for their product, which typically includes the BSP and boot loader.

8

The Registry

The *registry* is a collection of data containing configurations, settings, and usage parameters for the operating system, device drivers, and applications. The registry is a critical part of the system.

The registry affects the operating system's boot process, device driver, and application loading process. Some device drivers and applications have dependencies and must be configured to load after certain components are loaded before launching. When the registry is not configured correctly, the system may not function properly and may even fail to complete the boot process.

This chapter takes a brief look at the CE registry and provides an overview of persisting registry settings and how the boot process can be affected by the registry.

Windows Embedded CE Registry

The registry data structure for Windows Embedded CE is similar to the registry data structure for desktop Windows. In addition to storing the configuration data and settings for the OS run time and installed device drivers, the Windows Embedded CE registry also stores configuration and usage parameters for applications. For some devices designed to support multiusers, the CE registry also stores user profile information.

The registry stores data in a tree structure. Each branch of the tree is called a *registry key*. Each registry key may contain other registry subkeys and entries. Each registry entry has a value, which can be a string or binary value. The registry data are stored in the registry entry. Think of the registry key and subkey as the file folders for registry data, which also provide the marker and grouping to store and identify the registry entry.

The Windows Embedded CE registry contains four root keys, as shown in Table 8-1.

Table 8-1: Registry Root Key

HKEY_CLASSES_ROOT	Stores information about file types.
HKEY_CURRENT_USER	Stores user data for the current active user.
HKEY_LOCAL_MACHINE	Stores data specific to the hardware platform, such as OS configuration, device drivers, and settings.
HKEY_USERS	Stores data for all users including a default user.

Within each registry key, there may be multiple entries and multiple subkeys. This is quite similar to the file folder structure, where there may be multiple files and subfolders under each folder.

For example, the main registry key for the Windows Embedded CE 6.0 Internet Explorer is as follows: HKEY_LOCAL_MACHINE\SOFTWARE\Microsoft\Internet Explorer.

Under the main registry key for the Internet Explorer application, there are four subkeys and one entry, as shown in Table 8-2.

Table 8-2: Internet Explorer Registry Subkeys and Entries

AboutURLS	Registry subkey with multiple entries under this subkey
ActiveX Compatibility	Registry subkey with multiple subkeys and entries under this subkey
Main	Subkey with one subkey underneath
Security	Subkey with multiple subkeys underneath
ProductID	A registry entry, with a string value, under the main Internet Explorer registry key

As mentioned above, the registry key and subkey structure is similar to the file folder and subfolder structure. A file folder may contain files and subfolders. A subfolder may contain files and other subfolders. A subfolder can be referred to as a folder.

Similar to the file folder structure, a registry key may contain registry entries and subkeys. A subkey may contain registry entries and other subkeys. A registry entry has an assigned value.

When referring to a registry key or subkey individually, we can refer to it as a registry key.

When referring to a registry key and its subkey as a group, the registry key and subkey references help identify and separate the child key from the parent key.

Windows Embedded CE supports two different types of registry implementation, RAM-based and hive-based registry.

RAM-Based Registry

The RAM-based registry implementation stores registry data within the object store. This is an efficient implementation for devices that rarely power off.

The object store functions much like the hard drive for the desktop PC, and provides storage support for the device's filesystem, databases, and system registry.

Devices such as the Windows Mobile Smartphone and PDA are typically built with battery-backed RAM. As part of the device's normal operation, during the power-off stage, the battery-backed RAM maintains the object store in the RAM, which also includes the registry data, to provide an "instant on" feature. With some of the earlier generations of these devices, implemented without the ability to persist registry data when the device lost power, the user data and settings stored in the object store were lost when power to the device failed.

Some of the newer generation of Windows Mobile Smartphones and PDAs do not require battery-backed RAM to persist registry data when the device powers off. When these devices power off, the registry and user application data are backed up to a non-volatile memory storage device, and the registry and user application data are restored when power resumes.

Hive-Based Registry

The hive-based registry implementation stores registry data in files, or hives, which can be stored on any filesystem. With hive-based registry, the device eliminates the need for backup. This implementation is designed for devices that typically go through the cold boot process when powered up by the end-user, and seldom go through the warm boot process.

For devices built with hive-based registry implementation, the registry data are broken into three different hives — the boot hive, system hive, and user hive. The *boot hive* contains system settings that are used when the system is booting up. The *system hive* contains all system data. The *user hive* contains user-related data. See Table 8-3.

Table 8-3: Hive-Based Registry Files

BOOT.HV	The boot hive is compiled as part of the OS runtime image. The boot hive contains system settings affecting the first boot phase.
SYSTEM.HV	When in use, the system hive is stored on the target device's local storage.
USER.HV	When in use, the user hive is stored on the target device's local storage.

A *registry hive* is a group of registry data, consisting of keys, subkeys, and entries within each key. Each registry entry is assigned a value, which can be a numerical value, a text string, a binary number, or other type of value.

Hive-Based Registry Triggers Two Boot Phases

The default registry settings are built as part of the runtime image. When the CE runtime image boots for the first time, the target device's local storage does not contain any registry data. The image launches with the default registry settings built in as part of the image.

During the initial boot, the system.hv and user.hv registry hives are created on the local storage. From the OS design's registry configuration, we can specify the directory where the system.hv and user.hv files are located.

A CE device with hive-based registry implementation goes through two boot phases when powered on. During the first boot phase, based on system configuration information provided by the boot hive, the system loads the kernel with minimum drivers to access the filesystem and the rest of the registry in the system and user hives. After the registry data are read, the system continues with the second boot phase to load the remaining components based on the configuration saved in the system and user hives.

> **When the hive-based registry implementation is not done correctly, it's common for the device to hang in the second boot phase.**

Persistent Registry with Hive-Based Registry

To use hive-based registry implementation to persist registry settings between power resets, the registry needs to be configured with the proper entries for hive-based registry to function.

The MSDN documentation provides the general guideline to implement hive-based registry, using the following steps:

1. Add the hive-based registry catalog item to the OS design.

2. Add the following registry entries to the OS design:

```
[HKEY_LOCAL_MACHINE\init\BootVars]
    "SystemHive"="<your system hive location>"
    "Flags"=dword:<your value>
    "DefaultUser"="<username>"
```

3. Wrap all the registry entries for starting the device driver during the first boot phase with the HIVE BOOT SECTION as follows:

```
; HIVE BOOT SECTION
    <your registry entries>
: END HIVE BOOT SECTION
```

4. Set the following flag bit for each driver that is loaded during the first boot phase to prevent it from loading again in the second boot phase:

```
[HKEY_LOCAL_MACHINE\Drivers\<driver name>]
    "Flags"=dword:1000
```

5. Configure the following Storage Manager profile registry for the filesystem:

```
[HKEY_LOCAL_MACHINE\System\StorageManager\Profiles\<ProfileName>\<FileSystemName>]
    "MountFlags"=dword:1
```

When the hive-based registry implementation is not done correctly, the system ordinarily hangs and is not able to complete the boot process.

It's simpler to show a working example than try to explain in words how things work.

Following are registry entries extracted from the ICOP_eBox4300_60E BSP, used to implement the hive-based registry.

The eBox-4300-MSJK uses the GenericIDE registry with the ATAPI storage driver. The following section of the registry entries is extracted from the genericide.reg registry file:

```
; This is a section of the registry to support the GenericIDE profile
; for the x86 target device.
;
; Each IDE interface supports two IDE device, Device0 and Device1
;
; Device0 is typically the boot device
;
; HIVE BOOT SECTION
[$(PCI_BUS_ROOT)\Template\GenericIDE]
  "Flags"=dword:1000
[$(PCI_BUS_ROOT)\Template\GenericIDE\Device0]
  "Flags"=dword:1000
; END HIVE BOOT SECTION
```

The above registry entry is extracted from the genericide.reg registry file in the following directory:

❑   _PUBLICROOT\Common\Oak\Drivers\Block\ATAPI.

There are multiple IDE hardware profiles. Your hardware may be using a different profile. Following are six different registry files to support different types of IDE controllers:

❑   Ali1543.reg

❑   genericide.reg

❑   geodeide.reg

❑   i82371.reg

❑   pdc20262.reg

❑   pcd40518.reg

Each of the six registry files above corresponds to an IDE storage device profile. Depending on the target device and BSP you are working with, the ATAPI driver may use any one of these six IDE registry files. The registry entries needed to implement hive-based registry are not the same for different types of IDE devices.

In addition to configuring the storage device registry, additional configuration registries are needed to configure the other peripherals, such as the data bus, needed by the storage device to function.

The following registry entries, for hive-based registry implementation, are extracted from the platform.reg file, part of the ICOP_eBox4300_60E BSP, in the _WINCEROOT\PLATFORM\ICOP_ eBox4300_60E\Files directory:

```
; HIVE BOOT SECTION
[HKEY_LOCAL_MACHINE\init\BootVars]
    ; Specify the storage location for the system.hv file
    "SYSTEMHIVE"="\\Registry\\system.hv"

    ; Specify the storage location for the user.hv file
    "PROFILEDIR"=\\Registry

    ; This entry carry over from the previous version
    ; Not needed for CE 6.0
    "Start DevMgr"=dword:1

    ; Default user setting
    "DefaultUser"="User"

    ; Start Storage manager and Device manager in the first boot phase
    "Flags"=dword:3

[HKEY_LOCAL_MACHINE\Drivers\Resources\IRQ]
 "Flags"=dword:1000

[HKEY_LOCAL_MACHINE\Drivers\Resources\IO]
 "Flags"=dword:1000

[$(PCI_BUS_ROOT)\Template\GenericIDE]
 "Flags"=dword:1000

[$(PCI_BUS_ROOT)\Template\GenericIDE\Device0]
 "Flags"=dword:1000

[HKEY_LOCAL_MACHINE\System\StorageManager\FATFS]
 "Flags"=dword:1000

[HKEY_LOCAL_MACHINE\System\StorageManager\Profiles\HDProfile\FATFS]
 "MountAsBootable"=dword:1

; END HIVE BOOT SECTION
```

The ICOP_eBox4300_60E BSP uses the IDE device profile in the genericide.reg registry file. The eBox-4300 is an x86 device. The above registry is a good reference to other x86 devices to implement hive-based registry.

Registry Flushing

Windows Embedded CE needs to flush the changes made to the registry to save the changes between power resets.

For devices with hive-based registry implementation that persists registry data to the target device's storage filesystem (external to the object store when changes are made to the device's registry), the changed registry data are not saved to the filesystem automatically. The registry needs to be flushed in order to save to the filesystem.

Aggressive registry flushing can be set with the following registry entry:

```
[HKEY_LOCAL_MACHINE\init\BootVars]
  "RegistryFlags"=dword:1 ; enables aggressive flushing
```

When the above registry entry is set, the changed registry data are automatically flushed.

Another method for setting the system to flush the registry automatically is to set the PRJ_ENABLE_ REGFLUSH_THREAD environment variable before generating the runtime image from the OS design. By setting this environment variable, the system flushes the registry periodically.

This aggressive and automated periodic registry flushing can cause performance issues for some systems. If the performance issues outweigh the automated registry flushing option, set the following registry to prevent background registry flushing, and implement a manual flushing process by calling the RegFlushKey function:

```
[HKEY_LOCAL_MACHINE\init\BootVars]
    "RegistryFlags"=dword:2 ; disable background flushing
```

With the above registry setting, the background registry flushing function is disabled. To flush and save updated registry entries to the filesystem, you need to implement code to flush the registry, similar to the following:

```
; Sample codes to flush the registry

#include "stdafx.h"

int WINAPI WinMain(HINSTANCE hInstance,
             HPINSTANCE hPrevInstance,
             LPTSTR lpCmdLine,
             int nCmdShow)
{
 RegFlushKey(HKEY_LOCAL_MACHINE);
 RegFlushKey(HKEY_CLASSES_ROOT);
 RegFlushKey(HKEY_CURRENT_USER);
 RegFlushKey(HKEY_USERS);
}
```

Windows Embedded CE Registry Files

When working on an OS design project, the final registry entries that get compiled into the OS runtime image may be coming from the following four sources of registry files:

- ❑ COMMON.REG — This registry file is common to all platforms and contains registry entries that are hardware-independent. This is a system-wide common file; don't edit or change the registry entry in this file. The file is located in the following directory:

  - ❑ _PUBLICROOT\COMMON\OAK\FILES

- ❑ PLATFORM.REG — This registry file contains registry entries for the hardware platform supported by the BSP. This file is part of the BSP in the following directory:

  - ❑ _PLATFORMROOT\<BSP name>\FILES.

- ❑ PROJECT.REG — This is the OS design project's registry file. All registry entries specific to the OS design should be entered in this registry file. This file is part of the OS design in the following directory:

  - ❑ _WINCEROOT\OSDesigns\<OS name>\<OS name>\WINCE600\<BSP name>\OAK\FILES.

- ❑ <Component>.REG — For each component (a device driver, an OS component, or an application programming library) included in the OS design, associated registry entries may be included in the project.

During the Windows Embedded CE build process, the build system combines all registry entries for the OS design project into one file, reginit.ini, in the OS design's build release directory.

Registry entries are the key components that provide the data to configure how the OS runtime image behaves, as well as device driver loading sequences and other system functions. Many problems associated with the function of peripherals or included OS components are caused by improper or missing registry entries.

Reviewing the registry to verify proper entries should be one of the troubleshooting steps.

Registry for Windows Embedded CE Components

When adding a component from the component catalog to the OS design, the default registry entries may not be configured for the component to load in active mode to perform the expected function.

When the expected feature is not working after adding a component from the component catalog to the OS design, check to make sure the proper registry entries are configured for the component to function.

Registry Entries for the FTP Server

Using the FTP Server component as an example, when the FTP Server component is added to the OS design, the registry for the FTP Server is not configured to accept incoming connections.

Here is a listing of the default registry entries added to the OS design, for the FTP Server:

```
[HKEY_LOCAL_MACHINE\COMM\FTPD]
    ; Set to 1 to accept incoming connections
    "IsEnabled"=dword:0
```

```
; When set to 1, user need to be authenticated to log-on
"UseAuthentication"=dword:1

; When set to 1, allow users to connect without
; providing verifiable credential
"AllowAnonymous"=dword:1

; When set to 1, unauthenticated users can
; copy files to and delete files from the server.
"AllowAnonymousUpload"=dword:0

; When set to 1, unauthenticated users can access the VROOTs
"AllowAnonymousVroots"=dword:0

; Set the default root directory
"DefaultDir"="\\Temp\\"

; Idle time out, in seconds
"IdleTimeout"=dword:12c

; To control logging
"DebugOutputChannels"=dword:2
"DebugOutputMask"=dword:17
"BaseDir"="\\Windows"
"LogSize"=dword:1000
```

The IsEnable registry entry is set to 0 by default. With this setting, the FTP server does not accept an incoming connection.

To enable the FTP server to accept an incoming connection, set the IsEnable registry entry to 1.

Serial Port Registry Entries

The serial port is one of the commonly used communication links in industrial automation, home automation, and robotics. The hardware provided by different vendors may have different serial port settings. The Windows Embedded CE development environment captures and uses one of the serial ports to send debugging messages and prevents the captured serial port from being used by other programs.

The default serial port registry entries for the CEPC BSP are configured to support serial port hardware with the settings shown in Table 8-4.

Table 8-4: Default CEPC BSP Serial Ports Registry Settings

Serial port	IRQ	I/O base address
COM1	3	0x2F8
COM2	4	0x3F8
COM3	5	0x2E8

The default CEPC BSP registry entries for the serial ports are as follows:

```
;   Partial Serial port registry entries for COM1
[HKEY_LOCAL_MACHINE\Drivers\BuiltIn\Serial]
  "SysIntr"=dword:13            ; IRQ-3
  "IoBase"=dword:02F8
  "DeviceArrayIndex"=dword:0    ; indicate this is the 1st device

;   Partial Serial port registry entries for COM2
[HKEY_LOCAL_MACHINE\Drivers\BuiltIn\Serial2]
  "SysIntr"=dword:14            ; IRQ-4
  "IoBase"=dword:03F8
  "DeviceArrayIndex"=dword:1    ; indicate this is the 2nd device

; Partial Serial port registry entries for COM3
[HKEY_LOCAL_MACHINE\Drivers\BuiltIn\Serial3]
  "SysIntr"=dword:15            ; IRQ-5
  "IoBase"=dword:02E8
  "DeviceArrayIndex"=dword:2    ; indicate this is the 3rd device
```

You may need to change the default CEPC BSP serial port registry entries to match the serial port configuration used by the hardware you are working with.

To support a hardware platform with four or more serial ports, additional registry entries need to be added. You can use the existing serial port registry entries as a template and change the appropriate entries to support COM4, as shown in the following sample entries:

```
[HKEY_LOCAL_MACHINE\Drivers\BuiltIn\Serial4]
  "SysIntr"=dword:1a            ; IRQ-10
  "IoBase"=dword:03E8
  "IoLen"=dword:8
  "DeviceArrayIndex"=dword:3    ; indicate this is the 4th device
  "Prefix"="COM"
  "IClass"="{CC5195AC-BA49-48a0-BE17-DF6D1B0173DD}"
  "Dll"="Com16550.Dll"
  "Order"=dword:0
  "Flags"=dword:10 ; User MOde: DEVFLAGS_LOAD_AS_USERPROC
[HKEY_LOCAL_MACHINE\Drivers\BuiltIn\Serial4\Unimodem]
  "Tsp"="Unimodem.dll"
  "DeviceType"=dword:0
  "DevConfig"=hex: 10,00, 00,00, 05,00,00,00, 10,01,00,00, 00, _
            0,4B,00,00, 00,00, 08, 00, 00, 00,00,00,00

#if ! (defined IMGPPC || defined IMGTPC)
 "FriendlyName"=LOC_FRIENDLYNAME_SERIAL4
#else (defined IMGPPC || defined IMGTPC)

{BEGIN MULTILANG}
; @BEGINASSOC LOCALE %LANGID%
[     HKEY_LOCAL_MACHINE\Drivers\BuiltIn\Serial4\Unimodem]
   "FriendlyName"=LOC_%LANGID%_FRIENDLYNAME_SERIAL3

; @ENDASSOC
{END MULTILANG}

#endif ! (defined IMGPPC || defined IMGTPC)
```

> IRQ conflict or the lack of IRQ can cause problems. Each serial port needs to have an assigned IRQ to work. Although it's possible to configure multiple serial ports to share the same IRQ, this implementation requires support from the device driver. The standard serial port driver from the CE catalog does not support IRQ sharing.

The eBox-4300-MSJK and many of the x86 computers use the following serial port settings:

❑   COM1-IRQ-4/0x3F8

❑   COM2-IRQ-3/0x2F8

The above settings are different from the default settings used by CE.

Following is the serial port registry extracted from the ICOP_eBox4300_60E BSP:

```
; Partial registry listing for COM1
[HKEY_LOCAL_MACHINE\Drivers\BuiltIn\Serial]
 "SysIntr"=dword:14    ; IRQ-4
 "IoBase"=dword:03F8
 "IoLen"=dword:8
 "DeviceArrayIndex"=dword:0
 "Prefix"="COM"
 "IClass"="{CC5195AC-BA49-48a0-BE17-DF6D1B0173DD}"
 "Dll"="Com16550.Dll"
 "Order"=dword:0
 "Flags"=dword:10 ; User MOde: DEVFLAGS_LOAD_AS_USERPROC

; Partial registry listing for COM2
[HKEY_LOCAL_MACHINE\Drivers\BuiltIn\Serial2]
 "SysIntr"=dword:13    ; IRQ-3
 "IoBase"=dword:02F8
 "IoLen"=dword:8
 "DeviceArrayIndex"=dword:1
 "Prefix"="COM"
 "IClass"="{CC5195AC-BA49-48a0-BE17-DF6D1B0173DD}"
 "Dll"="Com16550.Dll"
 "Order"=dword:0
 "Flags"=dword:10 ; User MOde: DEVFLAGS_LOAD_AS_USERPROC
```

The serial port configuration for the eBox-4300-MSJK is different from the default configuration used by CE.

Serial Debugging

By default, even for the release build, Windows Embedded CE captures the first serial port to send out debugging messages and renders the port inaccessible by applications. To fix this problem, we need to disable the serial debugging port by making some changes to the registry.

Following is a listing of the registry entries for the serial debugging port in the platform.reg registry file:

```
; HIVE BOOT SECTION
[HKEY_LOCAL_MACHINE\Drivers\BootArg]
; During load, the system check the SerialDbgX regkey, where X is
; the physical COM port selected for serial debug output.
; Then the system disables the serial driver of the corresponding value
;
  "SerialDbg2"="Drivers\\BuiltIn\\Serial"
IF BSP_SERIAL2
  "SerialDbg1"="Drivers\\BuiltIn\\Serial2"
        ENDIF BSP_SERIAL2

        IF BSP_SERIAL3
                "SerialDbg3"="Drivers\\BuiltIn\\Serial3"
        ENDIF BSP_SERIAL3

; END HIVE BOOT SECTION
```

To disable the serial debugging port, remove the above registry entries. Or, you can wrap the above registry entries with an environment variable, such as BSP_SERIALDEBUG, as follows:

```
IF BSP_SERIALDEBUG
; HIVE BOOT SECTION
[HKEY_LOCAL_MACHINE\Drivers\BootArg]
; During load, the system checks the SerialDbgX regkey, where X is
; the physical COM port selected for serial debug output.
; Then the system disables the serial driver of the corresponding value
;
  "SerialDbg2"="Drivers\\BuiltIn\\Serial"
  IF BSP_SERIAL2
      "SerialDbg1"="Drivers\\BuiltIn\\Serial2"
          ENDIF BSP_SERIAL2

          IF BSP_SERIAL3
                  "SerialDbg3"="Drivers\\BuiltIn\\Serial3"
          ENDIF BSP_SERIAL3

; END HIVE BOOT SECTION
ENDIF BSP_SERIALDEBUG

IF BSP_SERIALDEBUG !
[HKEY_LOCAL_MACHINE\Drivers\BootArg]
    "SerialDbg1"=""
    "SerialDbg2"=""
    "SerialDbg3"=""
ENDIF BSP_SERIALDEBUG
```

With the above change, the serial debugging port is active only when the BSP_SERIALDEBUG environment variable is set.

Useful Registry References

This section includes some useful registry references.

Auto-Flush and Save Registry Settings

Hive-based registry implementation is needed to use the registry in this section.

When the following registry is included in the OS design, changes made to the registry are saved automatically:

```
[HKEY_LOCAL_MACHINE\init\BootVars]
 "RegistryFlags"=dword:1
```

Device Name for USB Removable Storage

To use the registry in this section, the OS design must include support for USB and USB storage class drivers.

The following registry entries enable you to change the device and folder names for removable USB storage:

```
[HKEY_LOCAL_MACHINE\System\StorageManager\Profiles\USBHDProfile]
 "Name"="USB Hard Disk Drive"
 "Folder"="USB Storage"
```

Disable Suspend from the Start Menu

The following registry disables the Suspend option from the Start menu:

```
[HKEY_LOCAL_MACHINE\Explorer]
 "Suspend"=dword:0
```

Internet Explorer Startup Page

The following registry configures the default home page for Internet Explorer:

```
[HKEY_CURRENT_USER\Software\Microsoft\Internet Explorer\Main]
 "Start Page"=http://www.msn.com
```

Static IP Address

The following registry configures the static IP address settings:

```
;  Static IP address settings
[HKEY_LOCAL_MACHINE\Comm\PCI\RTL81391\Parms\TcpIp]
 "EnableDHCP"=dword:0
 "DefaultGateway"=multi_sz:"192.168.2.1"
 "UseZeroBroadcast"=dword:0
 "IpAddress"=multi_sz:"192.168.2.232"
 "Subnetmask"=multi_sz:"255.255.255.0"
```

Windows Embedded CE Device Name

The following registry configures the device name:

```
[HKEY_LOCAL_MACHINE\Ident]
  "Name"="My CE 6.0 Device"
  "Desc"="My CE 6.0 Device built with eBox-4300"
```

Accessing the Registry

To view the target device's registry, we need to use a third-party registry editor, or generate a runtime image with KITL support and use the Remote Registry Editor. The Remote Registry Editor usage is covered in Chapter 6.

There are several third-party registry editors for CE. You can search for them using the Windows CE registry editor keyword.

There is a registry editor for Windows CE available with source code, developed in 2002 by Srinivas Vaithianathan. The code was written using Embedded Visual C++.

For native code developers, using this code as reference, it should be a simple process to migrate the code to support CE 6.0 and compile the code in VS2005. The registry editor for Windows CE is available for download from the following URL: `www.codeproject.com/KB/mobile/redit.aspx`.

Summary

Windows Embedded CE is a flexible OS, allowing you to build customized versions including custom components and selected OS components. When working with a customized OS run time along with custom hardware, problems associated with incorrect hardware configuration and improper software settings are common.

The registry contains much of the configuration and settings data to orchestrate how the OS, application, and hardware work together. Improper registry settings are the source of many of the problems that arise.

When adding device drivers and library components from the CE component catalog to the OS design, the default registry entries may not be configured for the component to load in active mode to perform the expected function. It's good practice to incorporate the review of registry settings as part of the troubleshooting process to resolve problems. Sometimes the OS design does not have a problem at all, but is just missing the necessary registry entries to activate the already included components.

9

Testing with CETK

Ingenious design may yield interesting products. But no matter how ingenious, it's difficult for products to be successful if they can't perform all their intended functions consistently.

Although it's a time- and resource-consuming process, testing to validate the product's ability to perform consistently is vital. It makes good business sense to incorporate testing checkpoints throughout the development process, to validate design features and maintain the quality of the development.

Windows Embedded CE Test Kit

The Windows Embedded CE Test Kit (CETK) provides an easy-to-set-up test environment, with a suite of useful testing tools, provided as part of the Platform Builder installation.

The CETK test kit helps minimize the time and resources needed to perform testing. A developer can set up the CETK test environment quickly without having to dig through piles of documents and spend hours configuring and tweaking the testing environment. The CETK test kit comes in a ready-to-use configuration, with preconfigured tests and common testing parameters.

The CETK's ease of use and setup does not mean that it's a lightweight testing environment. Its tests are thorough and provide credible test data in a standardized report format that can meet rigid testing requirements and provide useful documentation for the project. Microsoft's Windows Embedded product team uses the same CETK tests to perform BSP testing for its BSP certification program. BSPs that have been certified by Microsoft's certification program are listed at the following URL: http://msdn.microsoft.com/en-us/embedded/aa714506.aspx.

This is a good place to find hardware with quality BSPs to support the Windows Embedded CE operating system.

CETK Tests

The CETK is a powerful set of testing tools. It was developed to be easy to use while maintaining a high-quality testing environment and allowing the developer to create customized tests to further enhance the use of the CETK. The test kit can be used to test an individual device driver or the complete hardware platform. Test results and feedback provide useful information that can enhance the reliability of the hardware. The CETK provides a collection of tests for the common peripherals found on most hardware platforms. For each new release of Windows Embedded CE, the CETK introduces new tests to support new technologies and components that were not available in the previous releases.

For the Windows Embedded CE 6.0 R2 release, the CETK test kit provides the following categories of tests:

- Audio
- Bluetooth
- Camera
- Cellular
- Display
- Ethernet
- Filesys
- IR Port
- Keyboard
- Modem
- Mouse
- Multimedia
- NLED
- OAL Cache Tests
- OAL Interrupt Tests
- OAL IOCTL Tests
- OAL KITL Tests
- OAL Timer Tests
- Other Tests
- Parallel Port
- PC Card
- Performance Tests
- Printer
- Serial Port
- Smart Card
- Storage Device
- Touch Panel
- USB Port
- VoIP
- Wi-Fi

Each of the above test categories contains one or more tests, which may or may not be applicable to the target device you are working with.

For example, expanding the Display test node within the CETK program, we can see that there are eight different tests for the Display test category, as follows:

- Direct3D Mobile Driver Comparison
- Direct3D Mobile Driver Verification
- Direct3D Mobile Interface
- Direct3D Mobile Performance
- DirectDraw

❑ DirectDraw Performance

❑ Graphics Device Interface Performance

❑ Graphics Device Interface

The Display test category is not applicable to the headless devices.

Some of the Windows Embedded CE devices built with displays are designed with a display controller that does not support the Direct3D Mobile technology. All the tests involving Direct3D Mobile technology are not applicable to these devices.

Connecting to CETK with KITL and Platform Manager

In this section, we will go over the CETK testing environment using the emulator. Although the emulator is virtual hardware, the steps and processes we work through in this section apply to real-world hardware.

For this exercise, the CETK will connect to the emulator using the Platform Manager with KITL enabled.

Preparing the Test Environment

To work through the CETK exercises, we need to have a target device with the Windows Embedded CE runtime image loaded. We will use the emulator as the target device and the MyOSDesign project from an earlier chapter to generate the runtime image for the emulator.

Open the MyOSDesign project, and perform the following steps:

1. Set the active BSP configuration to MyEmulatorBSP ARMV4I Release. You can set the configuration from the Configuration Manager screen by selecting Build ⇨ Configuration Manager from the VS2005 IDE.

2. Add the Windows Embedded CE Test Kit component from the component library to the OS design, as shown in Figure 9-1.

Figure 9-1

3. From the VS2005 IDE, select Project ⇨ MyOSDesign Properties to bring up the MyOSDesign Property Pages, expand the Configuration Properties node, and navigate to the Build Options screen to select the following options, as shown in Figure 9-2:

❑ Enable eboot space in memory (IMGEBOOT=1).

❑ Enable KITL (no IMGNOKITL=1).

❑ Run-time image can be larger than 32 MB (IMGRAM64=1).

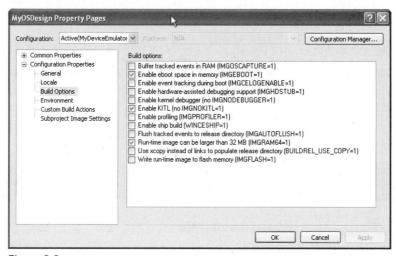

Figure 9-2

4. From the VS2005 IDE, select Build ⇨ Build Solution to generate an OS runtime image for the CETK exercise.

5. After the build process is completed, go through the following steps to download the runtime image to the emulator:

❑ From the VS2005 IDE, select Target ⇨ Connectivity Options to bring up the Target Device Connectivity Options screen.

❑ From the Target Device selection, select the MyEmulator device profile. The MyEmulator device profile was created in Chapter 5, using the Device Emulator (DMA) as the Download and Transport options.

❑ From the VS2005 IDE, select Target ⇨ Attach Device to initiate the download process.

The Emulator window loads as the runtime image is downloading. The Windows Embedded CE 6.0 desktop is shown within the Emulator window after the runtime image is downloaded and launched.

Starting the CETK Host Application

The CETK test environment involves two separate applications. The CETK host application, cetest.exe, is launched from the development workstation. This application controls the tests that run on the target devices and generate test results. The client-side application, clientside.exe, is launched from the target device with parameters to identify and connect to the intended CETK development workstation. Multiple target devices running `clientside.exe` can be connected to the same CETK development workstation.

To launch the CETK host application, `cetest.exe`, select Start ⇨ Windows Embedded CE 6.0 ⇨ Windows Embedded CE 6.0 Test Kit from your development workstation's desktop. The CETK host application will launch, as shown in Figure 9-3.

> When launching the cetest.exe program on a Windows Vista machine, the Program Compatibility Assistant may pop up and display a warning message. This program has known compatibility issues, but click on the Run program button to continue. A warning from the firewall may pop up asking to "Keep Blocking" or "Unblock" the ports necessary to run the application.

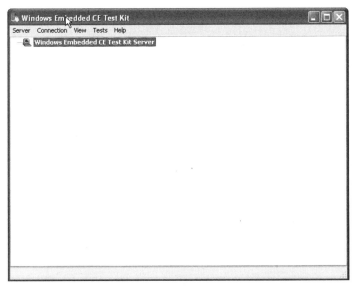

Figure 9-3

The `cetest.exe` application is installed to the following directory on the development workstation:

❑   \PROGRAM FILES\MICROSOFT PLATFORM BUILDER\6.00\CEPB\WCETK.

Connecting CETK to Target Device with Platform Manager

The client-side application, `clientside.exe`, needs to be launched on the target device to establish a connection with the CETK host application.

> The following steps require the Windows Embedded CE 6.0 runtime image, with KITL enabled, to be downloaded to the emulator. The CE 6.0 runtime image is launched on the emulator. Since the emulator runtime image is built with KITL enabled, after the image is downloaded and launched a KITL connection is established between the emulator and the platform builder.

To launch the CETK client-side application on the emulator using the Platform Manager, perform the following steps:

1. From the Windows Embedded CE Test Kit host application screen, select Connection ⇨ Start client to bring up the Device Connection screen, as shown in Figure 9-4.

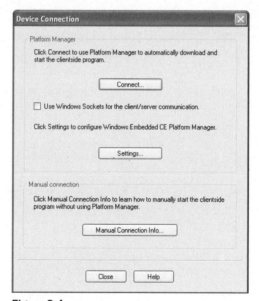

Figure 9-4

2. From the Device Connection screen, click Connect to bring up the "Select a Windows CE Device" screen, as shown in Figure 9-5.

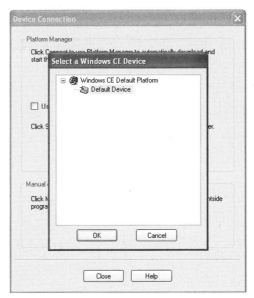

Figure 9-5

3.   From the "Select a Windows CE Device" screen, select Default Device, and click OK to close the screen. The "Connecting to device" screen will show briefly as the Platform Manager is establishing a connection to the emulator, as shown in Figure 9-6. The "Connecting to device" screen will go away after the CETK client-side application, `clientside.exe`, is launched on the emulator.

Figure 9-6

4.   As `clientside.exe` is launched on the emulator and communicates with the CETK host application, the client-side application's communication activities are shown on the Emulator screen, as shown in Figure 9-7.

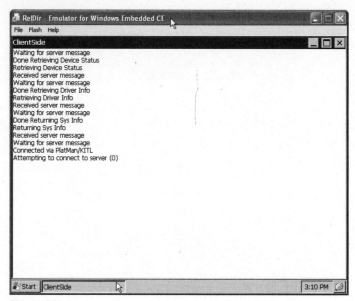

Figure 9-7

5. On the CETK host application screen, the WindowsCE (ARMV4I) node shows up after
   `clientside.exe` is launched on the emulator, indicating that the connection between the CETK
   host application and the CETK client application has been established, as shown in Figure 9-8.
   Expand the WindowsCE (ARMV4I) node to view the available CETK tests.

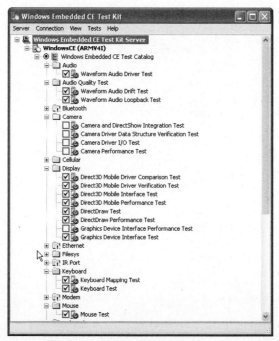

Figure 9-8

By default, the CETK application detects the components available on the connected target device and selects all the tests it determines to be appropriate for the device. The peripheral tests with a checkmark indicate that these tests are detected by the CETK application. The peripheral test with an exclamation point indicates that the device driver for the associated test is not detected.

Running the Tests

The CETK provides a flexible testing environment. We can perform a single test for one of the selected components, or we can perform a suite containing multiple tests for multiple components.

To perform one single test on one of the peripherals, from the Windows Embedded Test Kit screen, right-click the Windows Embedded CE Test Catalog node and select the Deselect All Tests option, as shown in Figure 9-9.

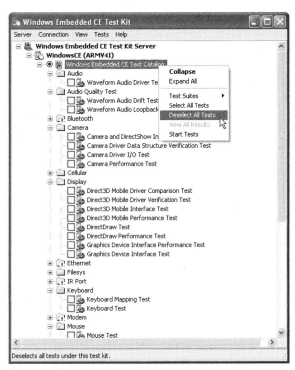

Figure 9-9

Let's select the Mouse Test and work through this single peripheral test. To perform the test, hover the mouse pointer over the Mouse Test node, right-click, and select Quick Start to start the test, as shown in Figure 9-10.

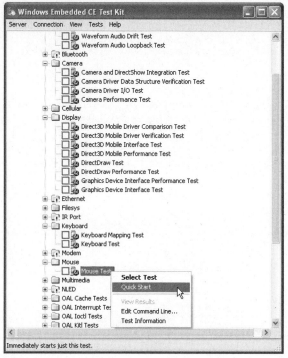

Figure 9-10

As the Mouse Test is launched on the emulator, a series of interactive screens will be launched and will ask the user to interact by using the mouse to work through the Mouse Test. The CETK tests the left, right, and middle buttons and the mouse's scroll wheel. When running the Mouse Test on the emulator, only the left mouse button tests are passed.

CETK Test Results

After the test is completed, right-click on the Mouse Test node and select View Results to bring up the CETKParser showing the test results, as shown in Figure 9-11.

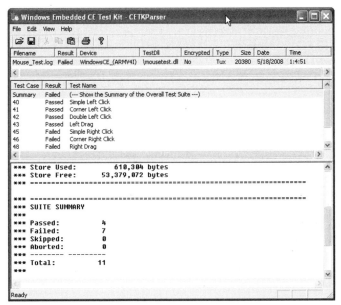

Figure 9-11

The test result in Figure 9-11 shows the summary for the test and lists individual test cases with the results showing the test as passed or failed.

More information is available for the test cases listed on the CETKParser screen. To view additional information for each test case, from the CETKParser screen's top pane, click to highlight the test case you want to see more information on. The additional information will appear in the lower pane of the screen, as shown in Figure 9-12.

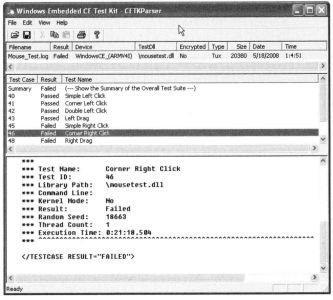

Figure 9-12

Connecting CETK to Target Device Using Sockets

In the previous exercise, the emulator was used to demonstrate the CETK test environment using the Platform Manager and KITL to connect to the target device.

For this exercise, we will use the eBox-4300, physical hardware, as the target device. We'll prepare a runtime image for the eBox-4300, copy the runtime image and `clientside.exe` to its local storage, and launch `clientside.exe` from that local storage.

> You can use other physical hardware with a Windows Embedded CE 6.0 BSP, create an OS design, and generate the appropriate runtime image to work through this CETK exercise.
>
> ❑ SERVERNAME=<Your development workstation name>
>
> ❑ PORTNUMBER=5555
>
> ❑ AUTORUN=0
>
> ❑ DEFAULTSUITE=
>
> When the clientside.exe application is launched on the target device, the eBox-4300, it searches the root of the file system and the \WINDOWS directory for the wcetk.txt file and parses the settings to use as the command-line parameters.

The development workstation and eBox-4300 must be connected to the same network segment using one of the following options:

❑ Both the development workstation and eBox-4300 are connected to the same network segment with a DHCP server to provide IP addresses dynamically.

❑ The development workstation is connected directly to the eBox-4300 using a crossover Ethernet network cable using static IP addresses.

Preparing the Test Environment

Let's go through the following steps to create a runtime image for the eBox-4300, from the MyOSDesign project, and include the `clientside.exe` application with the image:

1. From the VS2005 IDE, open the MyOSDesign project.

2. Set MyeBox-4300BSP x86 Release as the active configuration with the following steps:

    a. From the VS2005 IDE, select Build ⇨ Configuration Manager to bring up the Configuration Manager screen.

    b. From the Configuration Manager screen, select MyeBox-4300BSP X86 Release from the "Active solution configuration," and click Close.

3. From the VS2005 IDE, click the Catalog Items tab to show the component catalog for MyOSDesign, and add the WordPad component to the project, as shown in Figure 9-13. We will

need to use the WordPad program to create the wcetk.txt file for the client-side CETK application, clientside.exe, to run on the eBox-4300.

Figure 9-13

4. The CETK test is intended for testing a target device with a release-mode image. For this exercise, we will launch a release version of the runtime image on the eBox-4300, without the KITL component. Use the following steps to remove the KITL component from the project:

a. From the VS2005 IDE, select Project ⇨ MyOSDesign Properties to bring up the MyOSDesign Property Pages.

b. From the MyOSDesign Property Pages screen, click and expand the Configuration Properties node, and click the Build Options node to bring up the Build Options screen.

c. From the Build Option screen, check the second build option, Enable eboot space in memory (IMGEBOOT=1), and uncheck all the others.

d. From the Build Options screen, click Apply followed by OK to save the change and close the MyOSDesign Property Pages screen.

5. From the VS2005 IDE, select Build ⇨ Build Solution to generate the runtime image.

6. After the runtime image is generated, copy the nk.bin runtime image from the following directory to the eBox-4300's local storage:

_MYOSDESIGN\MYOSDESIGN\RELDIR\MYEBOX4300BSP_X86_RELEASE.

7. Copy the CETK clientside application, clientside.exe, from the following directory on the development workstation to the root directory on eBox-4300's local storage:

_WINCEPROG\CEPB\WCETK\DDTK\X86.

> The clientside.exe application is hardware dependent. Different versions of the application support hardware are built with different CPUs. For example, the application for a hardware platform built with the ARMV4I processor is located in the following directory:
>
> _ WINCEPROG\CEPB\WCETK\DDTK\ARMV4I

Starting the CETK Host Application

If the CETK host application is not already running on the development workstation, select Start ⇨ Windows Embedded CE 6.0 ⇨ Windows Embedded CE 6.0 Test Kit from the workstation's desktop.

Starting the Clientside Application

To launch the `clientside.exe` application on the eBox-4300, go through the following steps:

1. Turn on power to the eBox-4300, and launch the Windows Embedded CE runtime image from the local storage.

   > The nk.bin runtime image and clientside.exe were copied to the eBox-4300's local storage from the previous step.

2. The development workstation's IP address is needed for the next step. From the workstation, open a DOS command window and execute the IPCONFIG command to retrieve the IP address information.

3. From the eBox-4300's Windows desktop, select Start ⇨ Run and enter the following command line, shown in Figure 9-14:

```
\clientside.exe /i=192.168.1.193 /p=5555
```

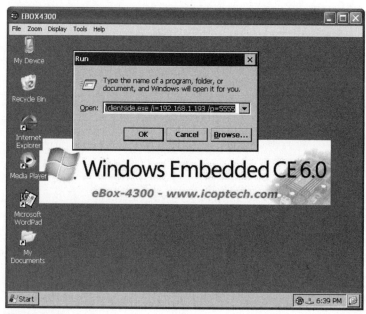

Figure 9-14

The above command can be launched using the computer name, instead of the IP address, as follows:

```
\clientside.exe /n=<Machine Name> /p=5555
```

We can launch `clientside.exe` without command-line parameters by putting a copy of the wcetk.txt file in the target device's root folder or the \WINDOWS folder. The wcetk.txt file contains the following entries:

```
;  Contents for the WCETK.TXT file
SERVERNAME=<Development workstation name>
PORTNUMBER=5555
AUTORUN=0
DEFAULTSUITE=
```

4. After the `clientside.exe` application is launched on the eBox-4300, a connection is established with the CETK host application running on the development workstation. The WindowsCE (x86) node is shown along with the devices on the eBox-4300 detected by the CETK (Figure 9-15).

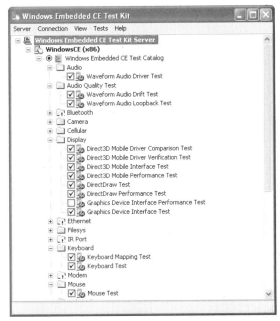

Figure 9-15

Running the Test

On the Windows Embedded CE Test Kit screen, the peripheral tests with a checkmark indicate that the tests are selected by the CETK. By default, the CETK selects the tests it determines are appropriate for the target device.

We are going to work through the Mouse Test exercise. Before starting the test, we need to go through the following steps to deselect all the other selected tests and launch the Mouse Test:

1. Right-click the Windows Embedded CE Test Catalog node, and select Deselect All Tests.

2. Expand the Mouse node, right-click the Mouse Test, and select Quick Start to launch the test.

3. The test requires user interaction and goes through a series of mouse input tests. The screen in Figure 9-16 shows one of the tests.

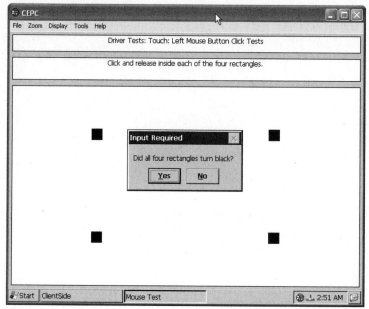

Figure 9-16

CETK Test Results

After the mouse test is completed, right-click the Mouse Test and select View Results to view the test results, as shown in Figure 9-17.

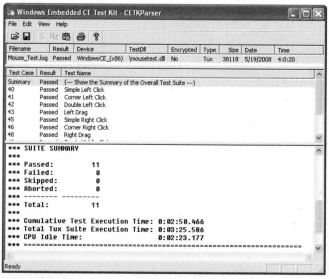

Figure 9-17

The CETK application keeps the test results in the following directory:

\PROGRAM FILES\MICROSOFT PLATFORM Builder\6.0\CEPB\WCETK\RESULTS.

Starting `clientside.exe` with wcetk.txt

In the previous exercise, we started the `clientside.exe` application with command-line parameters as follows:

```
\CLIENTSIDE.EXE /i=192.168.1.193 /p=5555
```

The `/i=192.168.1.193` parameter specifies the IP address for the development workstation. The `/p=5555` parameter specifies that the TCP/IP port number 5555 is used for the communication.

The `clientside.exe` application can be launched without command-line parameters when a wcetk.txt file containing these parameters is present in the target device's root folder or the `\WINDOWS` folder.

For this exercise, let's create a wcetk.txt file in the eBox-4300's root folder using the Wordpad application, include the following entries in the file, and save the file to the root folder.

```
; Development workstation's IP address
SERVERIP=192.168.1.193

; TCP/IP socket
PORTNUMBER=5555

; Automatically start the test when set to 1
AUTORUN=0

; Default test suite
DEFAULTSUITE=
```

Instead of using SERVERIP as in the above code, we can use SERVERNAME, as follows:

```
; Development workstation's name
SERVERNAME=<development workstation name>

; TCP/IP socket
PORTNUMBER=5555

; Automatically start the test when set to 1
AUTORUN=0

; Default test suite
DEFAULTSUITE=
```

With the wcetk.txt file in the root folder, we can launch the `clientside.exe` application without any command-line parameter.

Customizing the Command Line for CETK Test

The Windows Embedded CE Test Kit uses Tux, a test harness that runs the test files. Each of the CETK tests has a Tux command-line entry, containing the parameters for the test.

For example, when testing the Realtek-8139 driver, using the One-Card Network Card Miniport Driver Test with a default command line will yield a failed test result. Let's run the test to view the results. From the Windows Embedded CE Test Kit screen, right-click the One-Card Network Card Miniport Driver and select Quick Start, as shown in Figure 9-18.

Figure 9-18

The driver test, using the default Tux command-line entry, will fail.

To view the test result, right-click the One-Card Network Card Miniport Driver Test and select View Results to bring up the CETKParser screen, as shown in Figure 9-19.

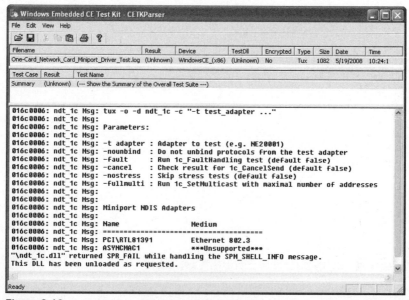

Figure 9-19

The test failed because of improper test parameters. Using the following steps, we can modify the command line for the One-Card Network Card Miniport Driver to reflect the correct test parameter for the Realtek-8139 driver:

1. From the Windows Embedded CE Test Kit screen, right-click the One-Card Network Card Miniport Driver and select Edit Command Line to bring up the Edit Command Line screen.

2. Replace the default command line entry with the following command-line entry, as shown in Figure 9-20, and click OK to complete the change:

```
Tux -o -d ndt_1c -c " -t PCI\RTL81391 -nounbind"
```

Figure 9-20

3. Right-click the One-Card Network Miniport Driver Test and select Quick Start to launch the test again.

4. The One-Card Network Miniport Driver Test for the Realtek-8139 running on eBox-4300 is passed after the Tux command line for the test is changed to the following:

```
Tux -o -d ndt_1c -c " -t PCI\RTL81391 -nounbind"
```

5. To view the test results, right-click the One-Card Network Miniport Driver Test and select View Results to bring up the CETKParser screen, as shown in Figure 9-21.

> **Consult the CETK documentation for more information about the command-line parameters.**

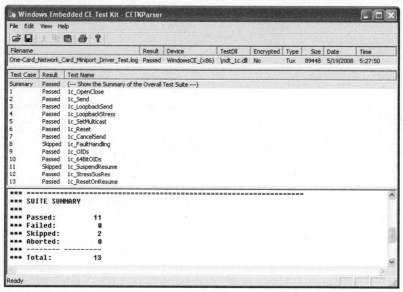

Figure 9-21

Summary

Testing to verify key functions and validate performance consistency is critical to the success of the product. The Windows Embedded CE Test Kit provides the environment to perform the needed testing.

In this chapter, we provided an overview of the Windows Embedded CE Test Kit and worked through the following exercises:

❑ Connecting to the emulator, as the target device, with KITL and Platform Manager

❑ Connecting to the eBox-4300, a physical target device, using Sockets

❑ Customizing the command-line parameters for the CETK test

The Windows Embedded CE Test Kit offers a lot more, and it's well worth the time and effort to explore it further.

More information about the Windows Embedded CE Test Kit is available from the following URL: http://msdn.microsoft.com/en-us/embedded/aa714542.aspx.

10

Application Development

Using the same VS2005 IDE environment to develop managed-code and native-code applications, the application development environment for Windows Embedded CE is quite similar to desktop Windows. Developers with previous experience, who are developing applications for the desktop version of Windows using VS2005, can adapt their knowledge quickly to learning and developing CE applications.

This chapter provides a general overview of the application development environment available in CE.

Although CE is designed from the ground up in a completely different way from desktop Windows, there are a lot of similarities between the two environments. In general, there are two categories of CE applications, native-code and managed-code applications. Just like the desktop version of Windows, a developer can use the VS2005 IDE to develop native-code applications using Visual C++, and managed-code applications using Visual Basic or C#.

Depending on the target device's business scope, required functions, and features, the development process may need to focus on meeting one or more of the following objectives:

- ❑ Real-time
- ❑ Small footprint
- ❑ Existing code base reuse or porting
- ❑ Application binary that can be portable across multiple hardware platforms
- ❑ Application source code that can be portable across multiple hardware platforms

To meet one or more of the above objectives, the application developer may need to develop the solution using managed code, native code, or a combination of both.

> A VS2005 solution may contain multiple projects using different programming languages.

The Development Landscape

When developing an application using C, C++, C#, or Visual Basic, the programming syntax is the same whether it's written for the desktop version of Windows or for CE.

A CE device generally has much less system memory and storage and runs on a slower processor than the desktop computer. When developing applications for a CE device, the developer needs to be conscious of the limited resources and recognize the conveniences available in desktop Windows that are not available in CE.

It's common to see a desktop Windows application with a binary executable file larger than 15 MB. To many desktop application developers, a program using 50 MB, or even 100 MB, of available system memory is not considered to be using a lot. When a Windows desktop computer runs out of system memory during program execution, some of the memory contents can be paged to a swap file on the hard drive to make room for other programs to execute.

In the CE environment, the swap file mechanism is not available. A typical CE runtime image can range from 5 MB to 20 MB. In embedded development, wasting 1 MB of system memory is a lot. Some CE devices are built with 64 MB or less of system memory, with part of that allocated to the filesystem for storage.

When developing applications for CE devices, be conscious of the following:

❑ The target device has limited system memory and limited storage as well as a slow processor.

❑ You should always release resources that are not needed.

❑ The target device may not have display, mouse, or keyboard.

❑ The target device may have a display with very low display resolution.

❑ Instead of keyboard and mouse, the target device may use a button (connect to an I/O line) and touch screen to capture user input.

❑ Power to the device may be turned off unexpectedly.

In addition to the CE device's limited hardware resources, other application development considerations are also different from the desktop Windows environment.

The desktop Windows and CE development environments share the same VS2005 IDE and use the C, C++, C#, and Visual Basic programming languages. Let's take a look at both environments to see the differences.

The Desktop Windows Development Environment

In today's desktop Windows environment, it's safe for the developer to assume that the application will run on a target computer system built with an x86 processor, with the following minimum specifications:

❑ 1 GHz or faster CPU

❑ 512 MB or more system memory (RAM)

❑ Monitor with 1024 × 768 or higher display resolution with 16-bits or better color

❑ Keyboard and mouse for user input

❑ Hard drive with 100 GB or more storage space

In addition to these general assumptions about the computer hardware, the developer can also assume that the user environment has some if not all of the following components:

❑ CD-ROM drive

❑ USB ports

❑ Network interface

❑ Multimedia

❑ Access to the Internet

❑ Browser application such as Internet Explorer

For most desktop application development projects, the development team puts together a minimum hardware requirements list based on the hardware specification generally available at the time. It's the end-user's responsibility to provide computer hardware with adequate processing capability and resources to support the application.

For the desktop computing environment, the application software can be sold separately from the computer hardware. With proper testing and care during the development process, a desktop application can be expected to run flawlessly on most computers with a designated version of Windows installed. For this environment, it's not difficult to develop an application and deploy one set of binaries to support multiple versions of Windows, such as Windows 2000, Windows XP, Windows Server 2003, Windows Server 2008, and Windows Vista.

The CE Development Environment

Other than using the same VS2005 IDE and similar programming languages, the CE development environment is quite different from that of desktop Windows. CE is designed to support hardware built with different processor architecture, including the ARM, MIPS, SH4, and x86 processors. Some CE devices are built without a user interface. Many are built with small display screens and without keyboards, and use a touch-screen interface to capture user input.

A typical CE device is designed to perform a specific set of functions. The device may be a Windows Mobile Smartphone, PocketPC, handheld test instrument, automotive device, cash register, industrial or home automation controller, or set-top box; or have a robotics, medical, or custom function.

Many CE applications are designed to run on one particular family of CE devices, built with a certain user interface, display screen size, and a particular processor. For example, an application written for a Windows Mobile device, built with a 320 × 320 display, with a proprietary alphanumeric keypad but without a touch screen, is meant to run on this family of devices. It will not yield good user experience when running on another Windows Mobile device, built with a 240 × 240 display.

As CE has gained recognition and mindshare among developers, it has been adapted for commercially available products such as the digital camera, PocketPC, Windows Mobile Smartphone, and Windows Network Projector.

During the past few years, the Windows Mobile Smartphone has gained significant market share and established a large base among developers of Windows Mobile applications. Reviews are mixed on Windows Mobile versus CE.

Let's take a look at Windows Mobile and CE in terms of native-code and managed-code application development.

The Windows Mobile OS

The Windows Mobile OS run time is a customized version of CE. Both Windows Mobile 5.0 and Windows Mobile 6.0 are customized versions of the Windows Embedded CE 5.0. In addition to using the components provided by the Platform Builder, additional components and resources are developed specifically for Windows Mobile devices and are not available in general to CE.

To help Smartphone hardware manufacturers minimize time to market, while enabling them to deliver a feature-rich mobile phone, the Windows Mobile team developed a customized version of CE specifically for Windows Mobile devices. In addition to providing the core Windows Mobile run time, the Windows Mobile team also designed the Windows Mobile SDK to support application development for Windows Mobile devices.

To build the Windows Mobile Smartphone, the hardware manufacturer must design the hardware to meet the specifications established by the Windows Mobile team. By having all Windows Mobile Smartphone manufacturers build phones that meet the same specifications, the Windows Mobile team was able to release one set of Windows Mobile SDKs to support devices manufactured by different companies:

❑ **Windows Mobile 6 Standard SDK** — This SDK supports application development for the following Windows Mobile 6 devices, built without touch screen:

    ❑ Windows Mobile 6 standard device with 176 × 220 display resolution

    ❑ Windows Mobile 6 standard device with 240 × 320 display resolution

    ❑ Windows Mobile 6 standard device with 320 × 240 display resolution

❑ **Windows Mobile 6 Professional SDK** — This SDK supports application development for the following Windows Mobile 6 devices, built with touch screen:

    ❑ Windows Mobile 6 Classic with 240 × 320 display resolution

    ❑ Windows Mobile 6 Professional with 240 × 320 display resolution

    ❑ Windows Mobile 6 Professional with 240 × 240 display resolution

    ❏   Windows Mobile 6 Professional with 320 × 320 display resolution

    ❏   Windows Mobile 6 Professional with 480 × 480 display resolution

    ❏   Windows Mobile 6 Professional with 480 × 640 display resolution

❏   **Windows Mobile 5.0 SDK for PocketPC** — Supports application development for the Windows Mobile 5.0-based PocketPC.

❏   **Windows Mobile 5.0 SDK for Smartphone** — Supports application development for the Windows Mobile 5.0-based Smartphone.

❏   **SDK for Windows Mobile 2003-Based PocketPC** — Supports application development for the Pocket PC 2003.

❏   **SDK for Windows Mobile 2003-Based Smartphone** — Supports application development for the Windows Mobile 2003-based Smartphone.

An application written for one particular version of the Windows Mobile device may not be able to run on a different version of the device. Typically, an application targeting multiple Windows Mobile devices needs to deploy with multiple binaries, one for each category of Windows Mobile device.

Windows Embedded CE

In the embedded-device market, each manufacturer generates a customized version of CE and adds additional library components and applications to support the particular device. The manufacturer is responsible for providing the CE SDK needed to support application development for the device and can decide whether or not to allow third-party developers to write programs for it. Not all CE devices are designed with the intention of allowing external application developers to develop programs for the device. Many CE devices are designed as closed systems and do not provide the SDK needed to support application development.

Unlike the desktop computer and Windows Mobile devices, the general CE devices on the market are not built to a common specification. The CE SDK needed to support application development is provided by the company designing the device. Application development for the CE device can be very different from one device to another. A CE application written for one device is not likely to run on a different one. For some CE devices, the company incorporated business secrets into the design, and it is deployed as a closed system that doesn't allow other developers to design for it.

CE Native-Code Applications

A CE native-code application is written in C/C++, targeting a set of software platform APIs specific to the target hardware platform. A native-code application provides the highest performance with the smallest application footprint. The compiled native-application code, the binary executable, can run only on the targeted hardware platform for which the binary is compiled. A native-code application developed for an x86 device will not run on an ARM device.

A CE native-code application can be written using the Win32 API, Microsoft Foundation Classes (MFC), and Active Template Library (ATL).

Using the VS2005 IDE, the new project wizard for native-code smart-device applications provides the following new project templates:

- ❑ ATL smart-device project
- ❑ MFC smart-device ActiveX control
- ❑ MFC smart-device application
- ❑ MFC smart-device DLL
- ❑ Win32 smart-device project

In addition to using the VS2005 IDE to develop native-code applications, the Platform Builder IDE also provides the project wizard to develop Win32 native-code applications.

Managed-Code Applications

Managed-code applications for CE can be written using Visual Basic and C# against the .NET Compact Framework library.

The managed-code application development environment, along with the .NET Compact Framework, hides many of the lower-level complicated APIs from the developer and provides an efficient environment for developing the application. The managed-code environment for CE is quite similar to that of the desktop OS.

Unless the managed-code application uses P-Invoke to access the Win32 API specific to the targeted hardware, a managed-code application written against the standard .NET Compact Framework library is binary-portable across different hardware platforms.

With the .NET Compact Framework and the VS2005 IDE, it's possible to develop Windows form and console applications for CE. The new application project wizard provides the following templates for managed-code applications using C# or Visual Basic:

- ❑ Smart-device Windows form application
- ❑ Smart-device control library
- ❑ Smart-device class library
- ❑ Smart-device console application

The .NET Compact Framework

The .NET Compact Framework is a subset of the desktop version of the .NET Framework, with additional functions designed specifically to support CE devices. For CE 6.0, the .NET Compact Framework version 2.0 is included as one of the available components in the component library. The .NET Compact Framework version 3.5 was released as part of the January 2008 quick-fix engineering (QFE) update for CE 6.0, available for download from the following URL:

```
http://download.microsoft.com
```

❑ Search the above URL for the January 2008 QFE for CE 6.0 using "Windows Embedded CE 6.0 QFE" as the keyword.

A managed-code application is a .NET Compact Framework application and can be developed using Visual Studio 2003, Visual Studio 2005, or Visual Studio 2008, as follows:

❑ The Visual Studio 2003 IDE can develop .NET Compact Framework 1.0 applications.

❑ The Visual Studio 2005 IDE can develop .NET Compact Framework 1.0, 2.0, and 3.5 applications.

❑ The Visual Studio 2008 IDE can develop .NET Compact Framework 2.0 and 3.5 applications.

The .NET Compact Framework components are available in the Platform Builder's component catalog, as shown in Figure 10-1, and can be included in an OS design project and compiled as part of the OS runtime image.

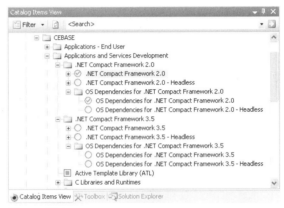

Figure 10-1

For the CE runtime image generated without the .NET Compact Framework library, the library can be installed to the CE runtime image using the software package available for download from the following URLs:

❑ .NET Compact Framework 2.0 Redistributable includes everything needed to run the .NET Compact Framework 1.0 and 2.0 applications:

```
www.microsoft.com/downloads/details.aspx?FamilyID=9655156b-356b-4a2c-
857c-e62f50ae9a55
```

❑ .NET Compact Framework 3.5 Redistributable includes everything needed to run .NET Compact Framework 1.0, 2.0, and 3.5 applications:

```
www.microsoft.com/downloads/details.aspx?familyid=E3821449-3C6B-42F1-
9FD9-0041345B3385
```

Before CE and the .NET Compact Framework, application development for small-footprint, low-cost, and low-power embedded devices was beyond the reach of the managed-code application developer using C# and Visual Basic.

With CE and the .NET Compact Framework, the C# and Visual Basic application developer is able to develop embedded applications targeting the mobile, industrial and home automation, robotics, and a broad range of other embedded devices using small-footprint, low-power, and low-cost embedded hardware.

Other Third-Party Libraries

In addition to the .NET Compact Framework provided by Microsoft, other third-party libraries are available to support managed-code application development for Windows CE:

❑ **OpenNETCF Smart Device Framework** — The OpenNETCF Smart Device Framework community edition (OpenNETCF) is available free for commercial and non-commercial projects. The OpenNETCF contains additional useful functions not provided by the .NET Compact Framework. The OpenNETCF is available for download from the following URL:

```
www.opennetcf.com/Default.aspx?tabid=67
```

❑ **32feet.NET** — The 32feet.NET is a Personal Area Networking library for .Bluetooth, Infrared (IrDA), and more. This 32feet.NET library was developed by Peter Foot as a shared-source project, accessible from the following URL:

```
www.codeplex.com/32feet
```

New Breed of Embedded Devices

CE, VS2005 development tools, the .NET Compact Framework, and a new generation of low-cost, high-performance embedded computing hardware have established a new environment to develop a new breed of intelligent, connected, and low-cost embedded devices.

Consider the following resources and visualize the possibilities provided by the CE and VS2005 development IDE:

❑ The runtime license fee for the CE Core SKU is $3, and the fee for the CE Professional SKU is $16. Visit the following URL for more details:

```
www.microsoft.com/windows/embedded/products/windowsce/default.mspx
```

❑ There is a large pool of hardware devices costing $100 or less.

❑ The eBox-2300SX with its basic configuration costs $90. Different eBox models with different configurations are available from the following URL:

```
http://www.wdlsystems.com/modperl/view_services.cgi?request=ld
.plate&dept_id=24&asibs=no
```

❑ Different models of the Phidgets interface kit with support for CE cost $60 to $100 in Canadian dollars and are available from

```
www.phidgets.com/products.php?category=1
```

❑ The Serializer .NET Robot Controller from Robotics Connection costs about $125 and is available from

```
www.roboticsconnection.com/c-5-robot-controllers.aspx
```

❑ The 300 Mhz Vortex86SX Embedded controller board, built with 128 MB RAM, costs about $100 and is available from

```
www.icoptech.com/products_detail.asp?ProductID=299
```

To find additional resources for CE, visit the Windows Embedded Partner site at

```
www.microsoft.com/windows/embedded/partners/default.mspx
```

Summary

Because of the similarity to the application development environment of desktop Windows, application developers using the VS2005 IDE can develop both native-code and managed-code applications for a broad range of embedded CE devices.

VS2005 developers can leverage their existing programming experience, using the Win32, MFC, ATL, and .NET Framework library from the desktop Windows development environment and adapting their programming skills to develop application for CE.

The new generation of low-cost embedded hardware and the substantially lower cost of licensing for CE have created an ideal environment to develop a new generation of embedded devices, which, in turn, will translate to new opportunities and challenges for the Windows developer community.

11

Visual C# 2005 Applications

Writing C# code for CE devices is quite similar to writing it for XP, Vista, and other versions of Windows. The Visual Studio 2005 IDE provides an efficient and effective environment to develop C# applications for CE devices. Developers with experience writing C# code for the desktop Windows environment can easily adapt their skills to this new task.

When writing code for embedded devices, you need to be conscious of some drawbacks. An embedded device typically has a slower processor with much less system memory and storage compared to the desktop computer. In addition, the embedded device display screen is typically smaller than the desktop computer's and may not have a keyboard or mouse to capture user input. Some embedded devices use the touch screen to capture user input, but some don't have any user interface at all.

In this chapter, you'll go through the steps to develop a C# application for the CE device, using the VS2005 IDE.

Developing C# Applications for CE

To develop a C# application for CE, we need to work with a target device with a CE runtime image, built to support managed-code application development, already launched on the device.

To support the C# application development in this chapter, we will work through the following steps to configure and use the emulator as the target device:

1. Configuring and building a CE OS design for the emulator
2. Adding the necessary component to support C# applications
3. Building and deploying the CE runtime image to the emulator

After the OS design and runtime image are created for the emulator, we will work through the following steps to develop and deploy a simple C# application to the emulator:

1. Create a C# Smart Device application project using the VS2005 IDE.

2. Establish connection to the emulator using CoreCon.

3. Deploy the C# Smart Device application to the emulator.

We will use the emulator as the target device, launching an instance of the VS2005 IDE and using the Platform Builder plug-in within VS2005 to configure a CE design. We'll need to launch a separate instance of the VS2005 IDE to develop the C# application and connect to the target device.

> **Since this exercise involves launching two separate instances of the VS2005 IDE and the emulator, a significant portion of the development workstation's resources will be occupied. It's best to close all other programs while working through the exercise.**

Configuring and Building the Runtime Image

In this section, we will work through the following steps to configure a new OS design and use the emulator as the target device to deploy and execute the C# application:

> **Building a customized runtime image and connecting to the target device were covered in detail in Chapters 4 and 5, and the steps are similar.**

1. Launch a new instance of the VS2005 IDE.

2. From the VS2005 IDE, select File ⇨ New ⇨ Project to create a new project.

3. From the New Project screen, select Platform Builder for CE 6.0 from the Project Type pane on the left, and select OS Design from the Templates pane on the right.

4. Enter **MyOS** as the name for the project, and click OK to bring up the CE 6.0 Design Wizard.

5. From the Design Wizard screen, click Next to bring up the BSP selection screen.

6. Select the Device Emulator: ARM4I, and click Next to bring up the Templates screen.

7. Select the Industrial Device template, and click Next to bring up the Design Template Variants screen.

8. Select the Internet Appliance variant, and click Next to reach the Applications Media screen.

9. Uncheck the Windows Media Audio/MP3 and Windows Media Video/MPEG-4 Video components. Click Next to bring up the Networking Communications screen.

10. Keep the default selection and click Next to bring up the Wizard Complete screen.

11. Click Finish to complete the wizard. At this point, a security warning screen is raised by the NDIS User-mode I/O Protocol Driver, to warn that this component may pose a security risk. Click the Acknowledge button to close the screen.

At this point, the OS Design Project is created. When the VS2005 IDE deploys the application in a CAB file to the target device, the CAB File Installer/Uninstaller component is needed to extract and install the application from the CAB file. Work through the following steps to add this component to the OS design:

1. From the VS2005 IDE, click the Catalog Items View tab to bring up the component catalog.

2. From the Catalog Items View tab, locate and add the CAB File Installer/Uninstaller component to the OS design.

> **The IPCONFIG utility is needed in the process of establishing a connection between the VS2005 development IDE and the target device. This utility is included as part of the Network Utilities component already included in the OS design by the OS Design Wizard.**

To deploy an application from the VS2005 development IDE to the target device running CE, we need to have CoreCon utilities running on the target device, `conmanclient2.exe` and `cmaccept.exe`. These CoreCon utilities and additional required libraries are shipped with VS2005. To run on the target device, the utilities and files need to be copied onto the target device's local storage. These CoreCon component files are installed by the VS2005 installer to the following directory on the development workstation:

_PROGRAMCOMMON)\MICROSOFT SHARED\CORECON\1.0\TARGET\WCE400.

> **_PROGRAMCOMMON = \PROGRAM FILES\COMMON FILES**

There are eight subdirectories under the above directory. Each contains the CoreCon files to support hardware built with different processors. The emulator is based on the ARMV4I processor, and the CoreCon files we need for this exercise are under the \ARMV4I subdirectory.

It's cumbersome and time-consuming to manually copy these files to the CE runtime image running on the target device after each download of the run time. To ease this process, it's best to include these CoreCon files with the OS runtime image.

The VS2005_CoreCon_ARMV4I_WINCE600 component was created to provide an easy path to include the CoreCon files in the OS design. This CoreCon component is available as a self-install file, VS2005_CoreCon_ARMV4I_WINCE600.msi. The file is available for download from the following URL: www.embeddedpc.net/ce6book.

If you have not installed this component, download it from the above URL and install it before continuing.

After the above CoreCon component is installed, take the following step to add this component to the OS design:

❑ From the Catalog Items View window, expand the \Third Party\VS2005 CoreCon\ node and select the VS2005_CoreCon_ARMV4I_WINCE600 component.

Let's review the Build options before compiling the OS design project. Go through the following steps to review the Build options:

1. From the VS2005 IDE, select Build ⇨ Configuration Manager to bring up the Configuration Manager screen.

2. From the Configuration Manager screen, select the Device Emulator ARMV4I Release from the "Active solution configuration" dropdown and click Close.

3. From the VS2005 IDE, select Project ⇨ MyOS Properties to bring up the MyOS Property Pages screen.

4. From the MyOS Property Pages screen's left pane, expand the Configuration Properties node and click the Build Options node to bring up the Build Options screen.

5. Uncheck the Enable kernel debugger (no IMGNOEBUGGER=1) Build option, and select the following three Build options. (Incidentally, *IMGNOEBUGGER* appeared with that spelling on the screen at the time of writing.)

   ❑ Enable eboot space in memory (IMGEBOOT=1)

   ❑ Enable KITL (no IMGNOKITL=1)

   ❑ Enable Runtime image can be larger than 32MB (IMGRAM64=1)

6. From the MyOS Property Pages screen, click Apply followed by OK to save the setting and close the screen.

   Now we are ready to build and generate the OS runtime image for the OS design.

7. From the VS2005 IDE, select Build ⇨ Build Solution to generate the OS design.

> This process may take from 15 to 30 minutes depending on the development workstation's processor speed and performance.

Downloading the Runtime Image to the Emulator

After the Build process is completed, we need to work through the following steps to configure the target device connectivity to download the runtime image to the emulator:

1. From the VS2005 IDE, select Target ⇨ Connectivity Options to bring up the Target Connectivity Options screen.

2. From this screen, select MyEmulator from the Target Device selection. The MyEmulator device profile was created in Chapter 5.

3. From the same screen, select the Device Emulator (DMA) for the Download selection, select the Device Emulator (DMA) for the Transport selection, and select the KdStub for the Debugger selection.

4. Click on the Settings button next to the Download selection to bring up the Emulator Properties screen.

5. From the Emulator Properties screen's General tab, select the "Specify RAM size" checkbox and enter **128** as the RAM size.

6. From the Emulator Properties screen's Display tab, enter **640** for the screen width setting and **480** for the screen height setting.

7. From the Emulator Properties screen's Network tab, select the "Enable NE2000 PCMCIA network adapter and bind to" checkbox, then select the "Connected network card" option, and click OK to close the Emulator Properties screen.

8. The Target Device Connectivity Options screen should look like Figure 11-1. Click on Apply followed by Close to save the changes and close the screen.

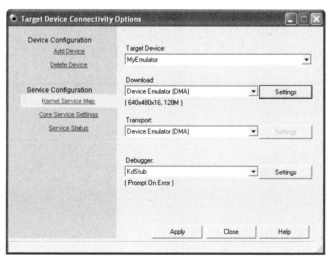

Figure 11-1

9. To download the OS runtime image to the emulator, select Target ⇨ Attach Device from the VS2005 IDE.

After the runtime image is downloaded to the emulator and launched, the CE 6.0 desktop is shown on the Emulator window.

Creating the C# Smart Device Application Project

Let's work through the following steps to create a C# application for the CE device:

1. Launch a new instance of the VS2005.

2. From the VS2005 IDE, select File ⇨ New ⇨ Project to bring up the New Project screen.

3. From the New Project screen's left pane, click and expand the Other Languages node.

4. Click and expand the C# node followed by the Smart Device node, and click on Windows CE 5.0.

> **A Smart Device application generated from the Windows CE 5.0 Smart Device Application template can run on Windows CE 5.0 and CE 6.0.**

5. From the New Project screen's right pane, click on Device Application.

6. Enter **MyCSharpApp** as the application name, as shown in Figure 11-2.

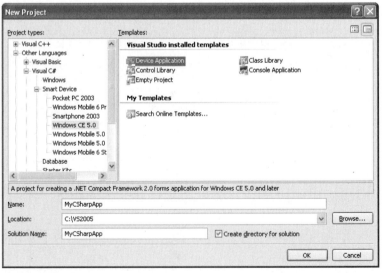

Figure 11-2

7. From the New Project screen, click OK to continue. A blank MyCSharpApp project is created by the VS2005 IDE.

Adding Controls to the Application

After the project is created, an application project with a blank form is created, just like the typical Windows form application. Let's go through the following steps to add some components and code:

1. Right-click Form1 to bring up the Properties tab, and change the Size property from "640, 480" to **320, 240**.

2. From the Form1 properties tab, change the Text property to **My C# Application**.

3. From the VS2005 IDE, select View ⇨ Toolbox to bring up the Toolbox tab.

4. From the Toolbox tab, double-click the TextBox control to add this control to Form1, and move the TextBox1 control on Form1 to the upper middle of the form.

5. From the TextBox1 control's Properties tab, change the Name property to **txtOutput**, clear the Text property, and change the Size property to **200, 23**.

6. From the Toolbox tab, double-click the Button control to add this control to Form1, and position the Button1 control beneath the txtOutput control.

7. From the Button1 control's Properties tab, change the Name property to **btnHelloWorld**, change the Text property to **Hello World**, and change the Size property to **200, 20**.

8. From the Toolbox tab, double-click the Button control to add a second button control to Form1, and position this button control beneath the Hello World button.

9. From the Button1 Properties tab, change the Name property to **btnHelloAgain**, change the Text property to **Hello Again**, and change the Size property to **200, 20**.

10. Position the three controls on Form1 to align in middle of Form1, as shown in Figure 11-3.

Figure 11-3

Adding Codes to the Application

After the TextBox and Button controls are added to the form, we need to work through the following steps to add some code to the application:

1. Double-click the Hello World button to add the following code to the btnHelloWorld button's click event:

```
private void btnHelloWorld_Click(object sender, EventArgs e)
{
    txtOutput.Text = "Hello World!";
}
```

2. Double-click the Hello Again button to add the following codes to the btnHelloAgain button's click event:

```
private void btnHelloAgain_Click(object sender, EventArgs e)
{
    MessageBox.Show ("Hello Again!");
}
```

We created a simple C# application with one textbox and two buttons. When the Hello World button is clicked, the textbox displays the "Hello World!" message. When the Hello Again button is clicked, a message dialog shows and displays the "Hello Again!" message.

We can build and generate the binary executable for this application. From the VS2005 IDE, select Build ⇨ Build Solution to build the application.

Connecting to the Target Device

To work through the exercise in this section, we need to deploy the OS runtime image from the MyOS OS design project to the emulator. We need to have a separate instance of the VS2005 IDE, with the MyCSharpApp application project open, to deploy the MyCSharpApp to the emulator. The emulator should be launched from another instance of VS2005 IDE in the earlier part of this chapter.

We are now working with two separate instances of the VS2005 IDE.

1. The first instance is for the MyOS project, an OS design project. Let's call this instance the *MyOS VS2005 IDE*; it is used to launch the runtime image to the emulator.

2. The second instance is for the MyCSharpApp project, a C# application project. Let's call this instance the *MyCSharpApp VS2005 IDE*. This instance is used to create the C# application.

> To work through this exercise, the development workstation must be connected to a Local Area Network with DHCP service to provide IP addresses dynamically. Both the development workstation and the emulator are dependent on the DHCP service to assign IP addresses.

Now work through the following steps to establish a connection between the MyCSharpApp VS2005 IDE and the emulator:

1. From the MyOS VS2005 IDE, select Target ⇨ Target Control to bring up the Windows CE Command Prompt screen, as shown in Figure 11-4.

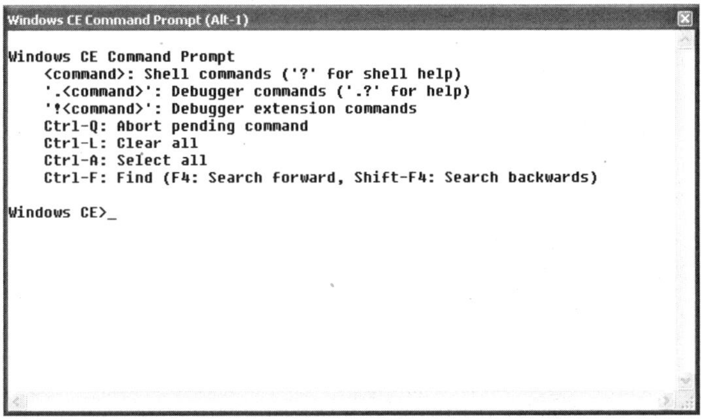

Figure 11-4

2. From the Windows CE Command Prompt screen, enter the following command to retrieve the emulator's IP address:

```
s ipconfig /d
```

> **The above command line is case-sensitive, so use lowercase.**

- ❏ The s in the above command is a Target Control command to start a process. The above command line starts the ipconfig process with the /d switch.

- ❏ The /d switch in the above command redirects the emulator's console output to the MyOS VS2005 IDE's debugging window, as shown in Figure 11-5.

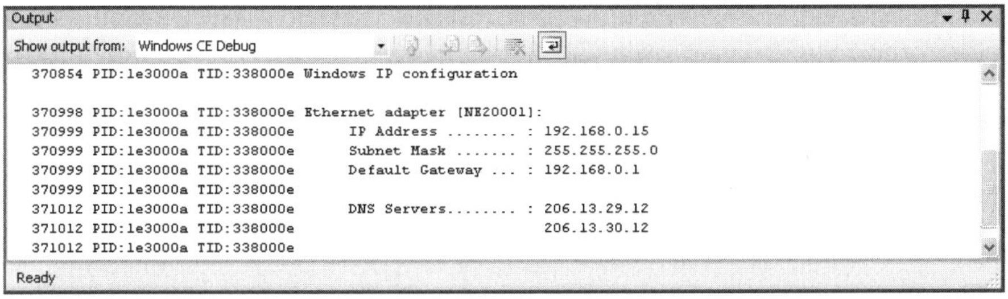

Figure 11-5

3. From the MyOS VS2005 IDE's debugging output window, copy the emulator's IP address to the clipboard.

Switch to the MyCSharpApp VS2005 IDE, and perform the following steps:

1. From the MyCSharpApp VS2005 IDE, select Tools ⇨ Options to bring up the Options screen.

2. From the Options screen's left pane, expand the Device Tools node and click on the Devices node. The Windows CE 5.0 Device should be in the Devices listing, as shown in Figure 11-6.

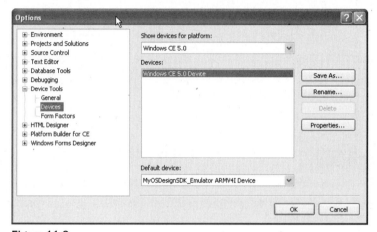

Figure 11-6

3. Click on the Properties button to bring up the Windows CE 5.0 Device Properties screen, with TCP Connect Transport selected for the Transport selection, as shown in Figure 11-7.

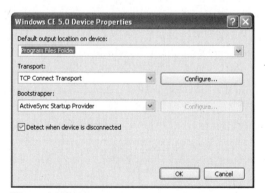

Figure 11-7

4. From the Windows CE 5.0 Device Properties screen, click on Configure to bring up the Configure TCP/IP Transport screen. Then select the "Use specific IP address" option and copy the IP address from the clipboard, as shown in Figure 11-8.

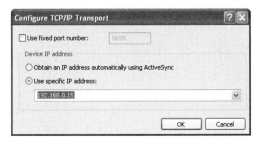

Figure 11-8

5. Click OK to close the Configure TCP/IP Transport screen.

6. Click OK on the Windows CE 5.0 Device Properties screen to close this screen.

7. Click OK on the Options screen to close this screen.

Next, we need to execute the `conmanclient.exe` and `cmaccept.exe` utilities on the emulator to enable the MyCSharpApp VS2005 IDE to connect to the emulator.

Switch to the MyOS VS2005 IDE, and perform the following step:

From the Windows CE Command Prompt screen, enter the following two commands:

```
s conmanclient2
```

```
s cmaccept
```

After the above two commands, it seems like nothing is taking place with the emulator. But something is, and we can run the following command, from the Windows CE Command Prompt screen, to view all the running processes on the emulator, as shown in Figure 11-9:

```
gi proc
```

```
Windows CE Command Prompt (Alt-1)
      Ctrl-A: Select all
      Ctrl-F: Find (F4: Search forward, Shift-F4: Search backwards)

Windows CE>s conmanclient2
Windows CE>s cmaccept
Windows CE>gi proc
PROC: Name            hProcess: CurAKY :dwVMBase:CurZone
  P00: NK.EXE         00400002 00000000 80070000 00000000
  P01: shell.exe      00f80002 00000000 00010000 00000000
  P02: udevice.exe    019e0002 00000000 00010000 00000000
  P03: udevice.exe    01d30002 00000000 00010000 00000000
  P04: udevice.exe    00d20006 00000000 00010000 00000000
  P05: udevice.exe    033f0002 00000000 00010000 00000000
  P06: udevice.exe    03dc0002 00000000 00010000 00000000
  P07: explorer.exe   03e00002 00000000 00010000 00000000
  P08: EmulatorStub.exe 03f20002 00000000 00010000 00000000
  P09: servicesd.exe  03fa0002 00000000 00010000 00000000
  P10: conmanclient2.exe 037f0006 00000000 00010000 00000000
  P11: cmaccept.exe   01e9000a 00000000 00010000 00000000
Windows CE>
```

Figure 11-9

217

> We have 3 minutes after the `cmaccept.exe` utility is executed to establish a connection to the emulator.

Now we need to switch to the MyCSharpApp VS2005 IDE to establish the connection:

1. From the MyCSharpApp VS2005 IDE, select Tools ⇨ Connect to Device to bring up the Connect to Device screen, as shown in Figure 11-10.

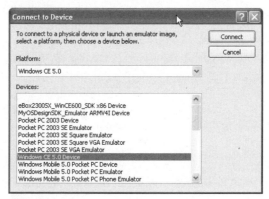

Figure 11-10

2. From the Connect to Device screen, select the Windows CE 5.0 Device from the Devices selection, and click on Connect. The Connecting screen will show, indicating that it is attempting to establish the connection, as shown in Figure 11-11.

Figure 11-11

3. After the connection is established, the "Connection succeeded" message is shown on the Connecting screen, as shown in Figure 11-11. Click Close to close the screen.

> To establish the connection, the `conmanclient.exe` and `cmaccept.exe` utilities need to run on the emulator. The above connection process must happen within 3 minutes after the `cmaccept.exe` utility is executed on the emulator. If the connection fails, you need to restart both instances of the VS2005 IDE and work through the connection process again.

Deploying C# Application to Target Device

With the connection established, we are ready to deploy the application to the emulator. Let's go through the following steps to deploy the MyCSharpApp application to the emulator:

1. From the MyCSharpApp VS2005 IDE, select Debug ⇨ Start Without Debugging to bring up the Deploy MyCSharpApp screen, as shown in Figure 11-12.

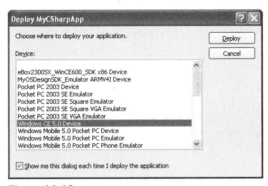

Figure 11-12

2. Select the Windows CE 5.0 Device from the Device selection, and click Deploy.

The MyCSharpApp VS2005 IDE's output window shows the activities while deploying the application's CAB file to the emulator.

After the MyCSharpApp application is deployed and launched on the emulator, the My C# Application screen is shown on the emulator, as shown in Figure 11-13.

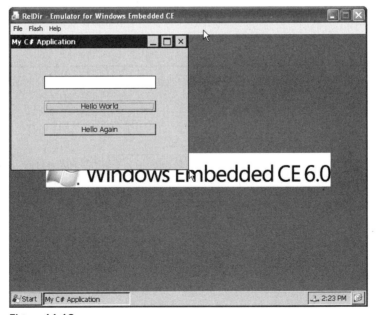

Figure 11-13

3. From the Emulator window, click on the Hello World and Hello Again buttons to verify the application's function.

The MyCSharpApp application is successfully deployed and launched to the emulator.

Debugging the C# Application on Target Device

In the previous steps, we deployed and launched the MyCSharpApp application to the emulator, using the "Start without Debugging" option.

Continuing from the previous session, let's work through the following steps and deploy the MyCSharpApp using the Start Debugging option to set breakpoints in the source code and step through the code as MyCSharpApp is running on the emulator:

1. Close the My C# Application on the emulator.

2. From the MyCSharpApp VS2005 IDE, double-click the Hello Again button to view the code in the btnHelloAgain button's click event.

3. Right-click the following line of code and select Breakpoint ⇨ Insert Breakpoint to set a breakpoint at this line, as shown in Figure 11-14.

```
MessageBox.Show ("Hello Again!");
```

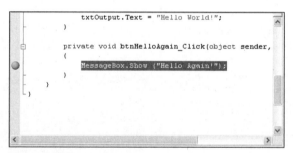

Figure 11-14

4. From the MyCSharpApp VS2005 IDE, select Debug ⇨ Start Debugging to bring up the Deploy MyCSharpApp screen.

5. From the Deploy MyCSharpApp screen, select the Windows CE 5.0 Device from the Device selection, and click Deploy.

Just as in the deployment process we worked through in the previous session, the My C# Application is launched on the emulator.

6. From the My C# Application screen on the emulator, click the Hello World button.

Since we did not set a breakpoint for the btnHelloWorld click event, the code for this click event is processed and displays the "Hello World!" sentence in the textbox.

7. Now, let's click the Hello Again button and see the breakpoint in action.

After clicking on Hello Again, nothing is happening on the My C# Application screen.

On the MyCSharpApp VS2005 IDE, the breakpoint is highlighted in yellow, indicating that the running program is halted by the breakpoint, as shown in Figure 11-15.

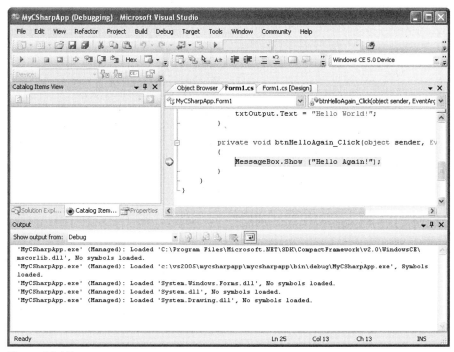

Figure 11-15

8. To resume running the program, from the MyCSharpApp VS2005 IDE, select Debug ⇨ Continue.

On the Emulator window, the My C# Application should resume running and display the Hello Again! message box, as shown in Figure 11-16.

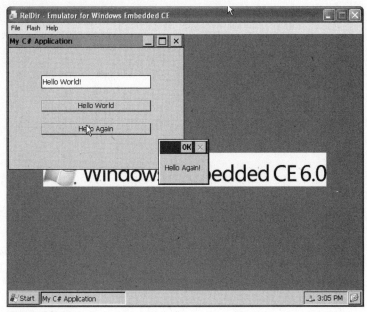

Figure 11-16

Summary

Although the exercise in this chapter deploys the application to the emulator, a virtual target device, the steps and results are the same when working with real-life hardware.

It's a powerful feature to be able to deploy an application in the development mode, to run on the actual target hardware in real time, and be able to set breakpoints to step through the application code one line at a time.

This level of real-time debugging capability helps the developer see how the code behaves when running on the actual target hardware in the development environment. It provides the critical information to help find bugs quickly and design better code.

12

VB 2005 Applications

The Visual Basic programming language has a history going back to the late 1980s. The first version debuted in 1991 and expanded to a huge user base very quickly.

The language has been a popular rapid-application development tool to create user interfaces and database applications. As it evolved over the years, from 16-bit to 32-bit to the current .NET version, a large pool of third-party commercial, shareware, and freeware components has been developed to support the VB community. These third-party components, along with the technologies added for each new version of Visual Basic, help enhance and extend VB's capabilities to create new types of applications.

The Visual Basic migration to support the .NET Framework involved significant changes and improvements and made the new generation of Visual Basic programs more efficient and able to perform tasks that were problematic or impossible in the pre-.NET version.

Visual Basic 2005 (VB 2005) .NET Framework applications execute on top of the same Common Language Runtime (CLR) as Visual C# and Visual C++ .NET Framework applications and have access to the same system resources through the .NET Framework.

With the release of .NET Compact Framework 1.0 in 2002, Visual Basic developers were able to develop applications for CE and Windows Mobile devices. As a subset to the .NET Framework, application development for the .NET Compact Framework was similar to the .NET Framework.

With the 2.0 release able to support headless devices, the .NET Compact Framework enabled Visual Basic developers to write code for a new generation of small-footprint, low-cost embedded devices and to open up a whole new world of opportunities for the Visual Basic developer community.

Visual Basic developers with experience writing code for the desktop version of Windows can easily adapt their skills to write code for the CE environment. Using VB 2005, writing code for the CE is not much different from writing it for Windows, Windows XP, or Windows Vista.

Chapter 11 covered C# application development for CE and used the emulator as the target device.

For this chapter, we will go through a Visual Basic 2005 application exercise using the eBox-4300, a compact computing device.

Developing VB Applications for CE

I'll cover the following subjects to show how to develop Visual Basic 2005 applications for a CE device, using physical hardware as the target device:

❑   Configure and build a CE runtime image for the target device.

❑   Add the necessary components to support managed-code applications such as Visual Basic.

❑   Build and download the CE runtime image to the target device.

❑   Develop a Visual Basic 2005 Smart Device application to access the target device's serial ports.

❑   Establish a connection to download the Visual Basic 2005 Smart Device application to the target device.

❑   Deploy the Visual Basic 2005 Smart Device application to the target device.

We will use the eBox-4300 as the target device. The eBox-4300 is an ultra-compact computing device with all the common peripherals available on a desktop computer. We'll launch the VS2005 IDE and use the Platform Builder plug-in within VS2005 to configure a CE OS design and generate a runtime image to download to the eBox-4300. Since we're working with physical target hardware, we don't need to launch two separate instances of the VS2005 IDE to get things working, as we did in Chapter 11.

The steps to create the OS design project and generate the runtime image are similar to those in Chapter 11 and are necessary to ensure the properly configured runtime image needed to support the exercise in this chapter.

Configuring and Building the Runtime Image

In this section, we will configure a new OS design for the eBox-4300, the target device we use to deploy and execute the Visual Basic 2005 Smart Device application.

To deploy an application from the VS2005 IDE to the target device running CE, we need two software utilities (CoreCon) running on the target device — conmanclient2.exe and cmaccept.exe. Both these utilities and their dependency files, part of the CoreCon component, are shipped with the VS2005. To run on the target device, these two utilities and their dependency files need to be copied onto the target device's local storage. These CoreCon component files are installed by the VS2005 installer to the following directory:

$(_PROGCOMMON) \MICROSOFT SHARED\CORECON\1.0\TARGET\WCE400

_PROGRAMCOMMON = \PROGRAM FILES\COMMON FILES

There are eight subdirectories under the above directory. Each contains the CoreCon files to support hardware built with different processors, corresponding to the directory names.

The eBox-4300 is built with an x86 processor. The CoreCon files we need for this exercise are under the \x86 subdirectory.

It's cumbersome and time-consuming to manually copy these files after each download of the CE runtime image running on the target device. To help ease the development process, it's best to include these CoreCon files with the OS runtime image. The VS2005_CoreCon_x86_WINCE600 component is provided to help make it easy to include the CoreCon files with the OS design. This component is installed by the VS_2005_CoreCon_x86_WINCE600.MSI file.

> **The VS2005_CoreCon_x86_WINCE600 component's installation file, VS2005_CoreCon_x86_WINCE600.msi, is provided as part of the software with this book. This file is available for download from the following URL:** www.embeddedpc.net/ce6book.

Install the VS2005_CoreCon_x86_WINCE600 component before continuing. We will need this component as part of the OS design.

Next, work through the following steps to configure the OS design:

> **Building a customized runtime image and connecting to the target device were covered in Chapters 4 and 5 and can be reviewed there in more detail. The steps below to configure the OS design and build the runtime image have some variations to support the eBox-4300.**

1. Launch a new instance of the VS2005 IDE.

2. From the VS2005 IDE, select File ⇨ New ⇨ Project to create a new OS design project.

3. From the New Project screen, select Platform Builder for CE 6.0 from the Project Type pane on the left, and select OS Design from the Templates pane on the right.

4. Enter **eBox4300** as the Name for the project, and click OK to bring up the CE 6.0 OS Design Wizard.

5. From the Design Wizard screen, click Next to bring up the Board Support Package selection screen.

6. Select the ICOP_eBox4300_60E BSP, and click Next to bring up the Design Templates screen.

7. Select the Industrial Device template, and click Next to bring up the Design Template Variants screen.

8. Select the Internet Appliance variant, and click Next to bring up the Applications Media screen.

9. Keep the default Application Media selections, and click Next to bring up the Networking Communications screen.

10. Keep the default Networking Communications selections, and click Next to bring up the final OS Design Project Wizard screen.

11. Click Finish to complete the Wizard. At this point, a Security Warning screen is raised. The warning is caused by the NDIS User-mode I/O Protocol Driver to warn of potential security problems for this component. Click Acknowledge to close the screen.

At this point, the OS design project is created.

In addition to the components included in the OS design by the Wizard, we need to include the following components in the OS design:

❏ RAM and ROM filesystem

❏ Hive-Based Registry component

Go through the following steps to add the above components to the OS design:

1. From the VS2005 IDE, click the Catalog Items View tab to bring up the component catalog.

2. Add the RAM and ROM File System component from the following folder:

\Core OS\CEBASE\File Systems and Data Store\File System - Internal

3. Add the Hive-Based Registry component from the following folder:

\Core OS\CEBASE\File Systems and Data Store\Registry Storage

4. Add the VIA CN/CX Display Driver component from the following folder:

\Third Party\BSP\ICOP_eBox4300_60E: X86\Device Drivers

When the VS2005 IDE deploys the application in a CAB file to the target device, the CAB File Installer/Uninstaller component is needed to extract and install the application from the CAB file. We need to add this component to the OS design:

❏ From the component catalog, add the CAB File Installer/Uninstaller component from the following folder:

  ❏ \Core OS\CEBASE\Applications - End User

The IPCONFIG utility is needed to query the target device's IP address while establishing a connection between the VS2005 development IDE and the target device. This utility is included as part of the Network Utilities component already included in the OS design by the OS Design Wizard.

The CoreCon component, installed above in this chapter, is needed to establish a connection between the development workstation and eBox-4300, in order to deploy the VB 2005 application. Take the following step to add the CoreCon component to the OS design:

❏ From the Catalog Items View pane, add the VS2005_CoreCon_x86_WINCE600 component from the following folder: \Third Party\VS2005 CoreCon.

Before compiling the OS design project, let's go through the following steps to review the Build options:

1. From the VS2005 IDE, select Project ➪ eBox4300 Properties to bring up the eBox-4300 Property Pages screen.

> **If the Solution tab on the VS2005 IDE is showing, the eBox-4300 Properties option above is not available. Select Project ➪ Properties from the VS2005 IDE to bring up the Property Pages screen.**

2. From the Property Pages screen, click Configuration Properties on the left pane, and then click Configuration Manager on the right to bring up the Configuration Manager screen.

3. From this screen, select the ICOP_eBox4300_60E x86 Release configuration from the "Active solution configuration" selection, and click Close.

4. From the Property Pages screen's left pane, expand the Configuration Properties node, and click on the Build Options node to bring up the Build Options screen.

5. Uncheck all the Build Options.

6. From the Property Pages screen's left pane, click the Environment node to bring up the Environment Variables screen.

7. From this screen, click New to bring up the Environment Variable screen, as shown in Figure 12-1.

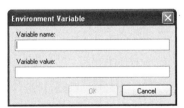

Figure 12-1

8. From the Environment Variable screen, enter **IMGRAM512** as the Variable Name entry and **1** as the Variable Value entry, and then click OK to save and close the screen. The eBox-4300 Property Pages screen should look like Figure 12-2

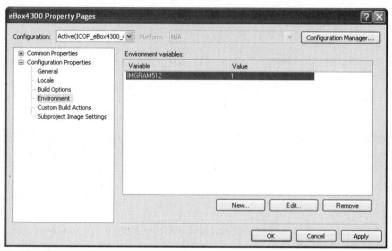

Figure 12-2

> The above environment variable configures the OS design to generate a runtime image to support the eBox-4300 device with 512 MB of system memory.

9. From the eBox-4300 Property Pages screen, click Apply followed by OK to save the settings and close the screen.

Now we are ready to select Build ⇨ Build Solution from the VS2005 IDE to build and generate the runtime image for the OS design.

> This process may take anywhere from 15 to 30 minutes depending on the development workstation's processor speed and performance.

Establishing a Connection to the eBox-4300

After the Build process is completed, we need to establish a connection between the VS2005 development workstation and the eBox-4300 to download the runtime image.

To establish the connection, the VS2005 development workstation and eBox-4300, which are the physical hardware, need to be set up properly. Following are three different variations:

1. The workstation and eBox-4300 are connected to the same Local Area Network (LAN) with DHCP service to assign IP addresses dynamically.

2. The workstation and eBox-4300 are connected to the same network hub, without DHCP service. For this setup, the workstation and eBox-4300 need to use properly configured static IP addresses, as follows:

   a. Configure the workstation's IP address to 192.168.2.100.

   b. Use the provided boot image to boot to a DOS menu, and select Option 3 to launch the boot loader with the preconfigured static IP address 192.168.2.232.

3. The eBox-4300 is connected to the workstation directly using a crossover RJ-45 Ethernet cable. For this setup, the workstation and eBox-4300 need to use properly configured static IP addresses similar to the second option above.

   a. Configure the workstation's IP address to 192.168.2.100.

   b. Using the provided boot image, boot to a DOS menu, and select Option 3 to launch the boot loader with the preconfigured static IP address 192.168.2.232.

> **For this exercise, a computer monitor is connected to the eBox-4300's VGA output, using a standard DB-15 VGA connector. A PS/2 keyboard and mouse are also connected to the eBox-4300 via a PS/2 Y-cable.**

Let's work through the following steps to establish a connection between the VS2005 development workstation and eBox-4300:

1. From the VS2005 IDE, select Target ⇨ Connectivity Options to bring up the Target Connectivity Options screen.

2. From the Target Connectivity Options screen, select the CE Device from the Target Device selection, select Ethernet for the Download option, select Ethernet for the Transport option, and select KdStub for the Debugger option, as shown in Figure 12-3.

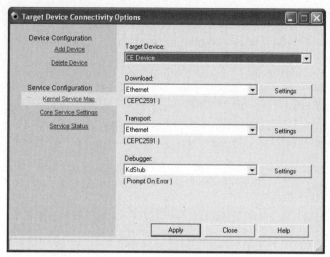

Figure 12-3

3. From the Target Connectivity Options screen, click Settings next to the Download option to bring up the Ethernet Download Settings screen, as shown in Figure 12-4.

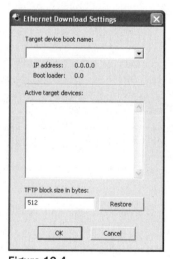

Figure 12-4

4. Power on the eBox-4300.

    The eBox-4300 initially boots to a DOS menu with four options, as shown in Figure 12-5.

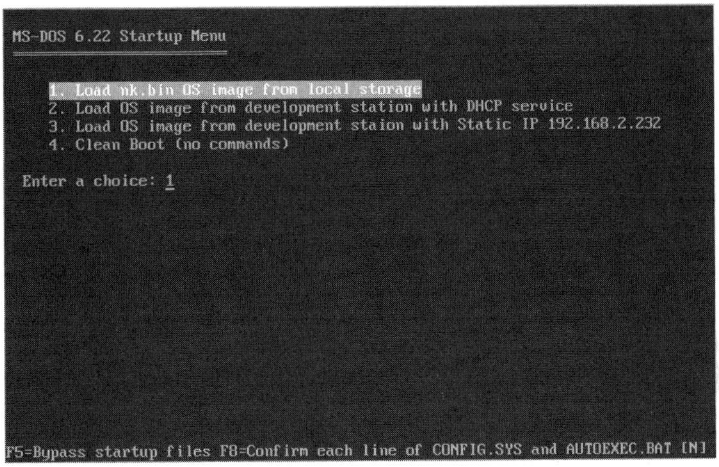

```
MS-DOS 6.22 Startup Menu

1. Load nk.bin OS image from local storage
2. Load OS image from development station with DHCP service
3. Load OS image from development staion with Static IP 192.168.2.232
4. Clean Boot (no commands)

Enter a choice: 1
```

```
F5=Bypass startup files F8=Confirm each line of CONFIG.SYS and AUTOEXEC.BAT [N]
```

Figure 12-5

    a.   The first option, loading the nk.bin OS image from local storage, executes `loadcepc.exe`, a DOS boot loader, to launch the CE runtime image from the local storage, an mk.bin file.

    b.   The second option, loading the OS image from the development station with DHCP service, executes `loadcepc.exe` to launch eboot.bin (Ethernet boot loader) to download a CE runtime image from the VS2005 development workstation. This option requires DHCP service to provide the IP address.

Use the second option when the development workstation and the eBox-4300 are connected to the same local area network with DHCP service to provide IP addresses dynamically.

---

    c.   The third option, loading the OS image from the development station with static IP 192.168.2.232, executes `loadcepc.exe` to launch eboot.bin and download a CE runtime image from the VS2005 development workstation. This option uses a static IP address, preconfigured as 192.168.2.232.

Use the third option when the workstation and the eBox-4300 are connected to a network hub without DHCP service and need to use static IP addresses. Set the IP address to 192.168.2.100 for the VS2005 development workstation.

---

    d.   The fourth option boots the eBox-4300 to a DOS command window.

5. Depending on the network connection between the workstation and the eBox-4300, select Option 2 or 3 to launch the eboot.bin Ethernet boot loader.

6. The eboot.bin Ethernet boot loader broadcasts a bootme message.

7. After detecting the bootme message from the eBox-4300, the Ethernet Download Settings screen shows the detected CEPC#### device on the "Active target devices" list, as shown in Figure 12-6.

Figure 12-6

8. Select the detected CEPC#### device from the "Active target devices" list. The same CEPC#### device is shown as the "Target device boot name" after the device is selected.

> Within the CEPC#### device ID, the "####" is the decimal equivalent for part of the MAC address for the eBox-4300's Network interface.

9. From the Ethernet Download Settings screen, click OK to save the detected device ID settings and close the screen.

10. From the Target Device Connectivity Options screen, click Apply followed by Close to save the settings and close the screen.

Downloading Runtime Image to eBox-4300

The connection between the VS2005 development workstation and eBox-4300 is established. The runtime image generated from the OS design is now ready to download to the eBox-4300 target device.

> The eboot Ethernet boot loader continues to send the bootme messages for about 60 seconds after it launches. After that, the boot loader stops sending, and the eBox-4300 needs to be reset in order to launch the boot loader again.

Let's go through the following steps to download the runtime image to the eBox-4300:

❏ From the VS2005 development workstation, select Target ⇨ Attach Device to bring up the Download Runtime Image to CE Device screen, and start the runtime image download, as shown in Figure 12-7. (The workstation is waiting for a bootme message.)

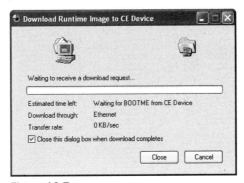

Figure 12-7

If the eBox-4300 is still sending out the bootme message from the previous step, the Download Runtime Image to CE Device will show file download activities shortly. Wait 10 to 20 seconds for the download process to start. If it doesn't start, this means that the eBox-4300 is no longer sending out the bootme message, and you need to go through the following steps to reset the eBox-4300 and launch the appropriate boot option to download the runtime image:

1. Reset the eBox-4300's power to reboot the device.

2. From the eBox-4300's Boot menu, depending on the networking connection between the VS2005 development workstation and the eBox-4300, select Option 2 or 3 to launch the eboot.bin Ethernet boot loader and start sending the bootme message.

3. After detecting the bootme message and establishing the handshake with the connected eBox-4300, the VS2005 development workstation starts to download the runtime image, as shown in Figure 12-8.

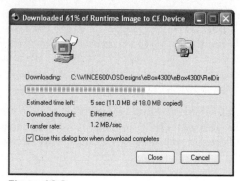

Figure 12-8

After the runtime image is downloaded and launched, the CE desktop is shown on the eBox-4300's display, as shown in Figure 12-9.

Figure 12-9

Creating a VB 2005 Smart Device Application

In this section, we're going to create a Visual Basic 2005 Smart Device application to deploy and execute on the eBox-4300, using the runtime image created in the previous section.

Instead of using the typical Hello World application approach, we're going to develop a simple VB 2005 Smart Device application to access and communicate over the serial port. The serial port is still one of the common interfaces in many of today's industrial automation, home automation, robotics, and other applications.

When serial debugging is enabled, CE captures one of the serial ports to output debugging messages. Improper settings can cause problems for applications trying to access the serial port. When the serial port is captured by CE, that port is not available for applications.

The ICOP_eBox4300_60E BSP used to create the OS design, and which generated the runtime image in the above section, disabled the debugging serial port by default. Within this BSP's platform.reg registry file, the BSP_DEBUGSERIAL environment variable is used to keep the debugging serial port registry from getting into the runtime image.

The following registry entries listings are extracted from the ICOP_eBox4300_60E BSP's platform.reg registry file, located in the following directory:

$(_PLATFORMROOT)\ICOP_EBOX4300_60E\FILES

```
IF BSP_DEBUGSERIAL
    ;
    ; HIVE BOOT SECTION
    [HKEY_LOCAL_MACHINE\Drivers\BootArg]
        ; During load, we check the SerialDbgX regkey, where X is the
        ; physical COM port selected for serial debug output.  Then we
        ; disable the serial driver of the corresponding value.
        ; Be sure that the pointed-to driver is associated with the
        ; same physical COM port (IOBase value).
        ;
        "SerialDbg2"="Drivers\\BuiltIn\\Serial"
        IF BSP_SERIAL2
        "SerialDbg1"="Drivers\\BuiltIn\\Serial2"
        ENDIF BSP_SERIAL2
        ;
        IF BSP_SERIAL3
        "SerialDbg3"="Drivers\\BuiltIn\\Serial3"
        ENDIF BSP_SERIAL3
        ;
    ; END HIVE BOOT SECTION
    ;
ENDIF BSP_DEBUGSERIAL

IF BSP_DEBUGSERIAL !
    ;
    ; HIVE BOOT SECTION
    [HKEY_LOCAL_MACHINE\Drivers\BootArg]
        "SerialDbg1"=""
        "SerialDbg2"=""
        "SerialDbg3"=""
    ; END HIVE BOOT SECTION
    ;
ENDIF BSP_DEBUGSERIAL
```

When using the ICOP_eBox4300_60E BSP to develop an OS design, the BSP_DEBUGSERIAL environment variable must be set in order to enable the serial port for debugging.

Let's work through the following steps to create the VB Smart Device application:

1. Launch the VS2005 IDE.

2. From the VS2005 IDE, select File ⇨ New ⇨ Project to bring up the New Project screen.

3. From the New Project screen's left pane, click on and expand the Other Languages node.

4. Click on and expand the Visual Basic node followed by the Smart Device node, and click Windows CE 5.0.

> **A Smart Device application generated with the Windows CE 5.0 Smart Device application template can run on Windows CE 5.0 and CE 6.0.**

5. From the New Project screen's right pane, click Device Application.

6. Enter **SerialPortApp** as the application name, as shown in Figure 12-10.

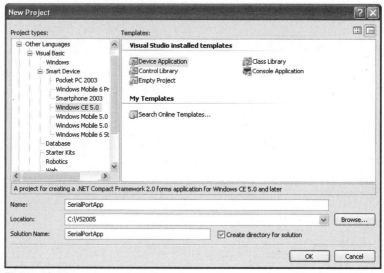

Figure 12-10

7. From the New Project screen, click OK to continue. A blank SerialPortApp project is created by the VS2005 IDE.

Adding Components to the SerialPortApp Application

After the project is created, an application project with a blank form is created, just like the typical Windows Forms application. We need to make some adjustments to the form and add user interface components to it.

By default, the mainMenu control is added to the project. Since we will not need the mainMenu control for this application, right-click on the mainMenu1 control beneath FORM1, and select Delete to remove this control from the application.

We will need to add various components to FORM1, which should look similar to Figure 12-11 after all the components are added. Table 12-1 lists the components added to this form.

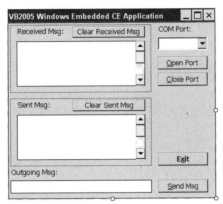

Figure 12-11

Table 12-1: Components Added to the Form

cbSerialPort	Combo box to select the active serial port — COM1, COM2, COM3, or COM4.
btnOpenPort	Opens the selected serial port.
btnClosePort	Closes the active serial port.
btnExit	Terminates the program.
btnSendMsg	Triggers the active serial port to send the message in the txtMsg textbox.
btnClearReceivedMsg	Clears the message listed in the txtReceivedMsg textbox.
btnClearSentMsg	Clears the message listed in the txtSentMsg textbox.
txtReceivedMsg	Textbox to display message received by the active serial port, with multiline enabled.
txtSentMsg	Textbox to display message sent by the active serial port.
txtMsg	Textbox to enter message to be sent out by the active serial port.

Other components, such as the Label and Panel controls, can be used to improve the application's appearance.

Code for the SerialPortApp Application

First, we need to import some references. Add the following import statements to Form1, in the beginning part:

```
Imports System
Imports System.IO.Ports

Public Class Form1
```

Then add the following statement to define the VBSerial object:

```
Public Class Form1
    Dim WithEvents VBSerial As New System.IO.Ports.SerialPort
```

The SerialPortApp is written to perform a few simple tasks, as follows:

❏ When the application launches, the code in the FORM1_Load event performs the following tasks to initialize the user interface:

1. Populates the COM Port selection combo box with detected serial ports.

2. Disables the Close Port button.

3. Disables the Send Msg button.

```
' Here is the source code :om the FORM1_Load event
'
' List all detected serial port to the cbSerialPort combo box
cbSerialPort.DataSource'= SerialPort.GetPortNames
'
' Since the serial port is not active yet
' Disable the btnClosePort and the btnSendMsg button controls
btnClosePort.Enabled = False
btnSendMsg.Enabled = False
```

❏ When the user clicks on Open Port, the code from the btnOpenPort_Click event performs the following tasks:

1. Checks to see if the selected serial port is already opened.

2. If the selected serial port is already opened, it closes the port.

3. Sets the selected serial port's baud rate to 9600.

4. Sets the selected serial port's parity bit to None.

5. Sets the selected serial port's data bit to 8.

6. Sets the selected serial port's stop bit to One.

7. Opens the selected serial port.

8. Displays the selected serial port as the connected port to the labelActivePort label.

9. Enables the Close Port button.

10. Enables the Send Msg button.

11. Disables the Open Port button.

```vb
' Here is the source code from the btnOpenPort_Click event
'
Private Sub btnOpenPort_Click(ByVal sender As System.Object, ByVal e As
    System.EventArgs) Handles btnOpenPort.Click
        '
        ' Check to see if the serial port is already open
        If VBSerial.IsOpen Then
            VBSerial.Close()
        End If
        '
        ' Serial port settings
        With VBSerial
            .PortName = cbSerialPort.Text
            .BaudRate = 9600
            .Parity = Parity.None
            .DataBits = 8
            .StopBits = StopBits.One
        End With
        '
        ' Open the selected serial port
        VBSerial.Open()
        '
        ' Display the active serial port to the labelActivePort label
        labelActivePort.Text = VBSerial.PortName & " Connected."
        '
        btnSendMsg.Enabled = True
        btnClosePort.Enabled = True
        btnOpenPort.Enabled = False
        '
End Sub
```

❑ When the user clicks on Close Port, the code from the btnClosePort_Click event performs the following tasks:

1. Closes the active serial port.

2. Disables the Close Port button.

3. Disables the Send Msg button.

4. Enables the Open Port button.

```vb
' Here are the source codes from the btnClosePort_Click event
'
Private Sub btnClosePort_Click(ByVal sender As System.Object, ByVal e As
    System.EventArgs) Handles btnClosePort.Click
        '
        ' Check to see if the serial port has been closed
```

```
         If VBSerial.IsOpen Then
             ' Serial port is still open
             ' Close the active serial port
             VBSerial.Close()
             '
             btnClosePort.Enabled = False
             btnSendMsg.Enabled = False
             btnOpenPort.Enabled = True
             '
         End If
         '
     End Sub
```

❑   When the user clicks Send Msg, the code from the btnSendMsg_Click event performs the
    following tasks:

    1.   Sends the Outgoing Msg textbox content using the active serial port.

    2.   Clears the Outgoing Msg textbox content.

```
' Here are the source codes from the btnSendMsg_Click event
'
Private Sub btnSendMsg_Click(ByVal sender As System.Object, ByVal e As
   System.EventArgs) Handles btnSendMsg.Click
         '
         Dim strMsg As String
         '
         ' Send the message from txtMsg text box
         strMsg = txtMsg.Text
         VBSerial.Write(strMsg)
         '
         ' Add the sent message to the txtSentMsg text box
         txtSentMsg.Text = txtSentMsg.Text + strMsg
         '
         ' Clear the txtMsg text box content
         txtMsg.Text = ""
         '
     End Sub
```

❑   While the selected serial port is open, when data are received by the serial port, this triggers an
    event. The code in the DataReceived subroutine executes the code and performs the following
    tasks:

    1.   Executes the code in the DataReceived subroutine.

    2.   Calls the UIDelegate to display the received data to the Received Msg textbox.

Add the following DataReceived code to Form1:

```
' Here is the code in the DataReceived subroutine, the Delegate
' declaration and the codes for the processReceivedData subroutine
'
Private Sub DataReceived(ByVal sender As Object,
                         ByVal e As
System.IO.Ports.SerialDataReceivedEventArgs) _
                              Handles VBSerial.DataReceived
        '
        txtReceivedMsg.Invoke(New UIDelegate(AddressOf _
                         processReceivedData), New Object() {})
        '
End Sub

Public Delegate Sub UIDelegate()

Public Sub processReceivedData()
        '
        Dim strMsg As String
        '
        strMsg = VBSerial.ReadExisting
        txtReceivedMsg.Text = txtReceivedMsg.Text & strMsg
        '
End Sub
```

❑ When the user clicks Clear Received Msg, the code in the btnSendMsg_Click event clears the text content for the Received Msg textbox.

```
' Here are the source codes from the btnSendMsg_Click event
'
Private Sub btnClearReceivedMsg_Click(ByVal sender As System.Object, ByVal e
    As System.EventArgs) Handles btnClearReceivedMsg.Click
        '
        txtReceivedMsg.Text = ""
        '
    End Sub
```

❑ When the user clicks Clear Sent Msg, the content in the Sent Msg textbox is cleared.

```
' Here are the source codes from the btnClearSentMsg_Click event
'
Private Sub btnClearSentMsg_Click(ByVal sender As System.Object, ByVal e As
    System.EventArgs) Handles btnClearSentMsg.Click
        '
        txtSentMsg.Text = ""
        '
End Sub
```

❑   When the user clicks Exit, the code in the btnExit_Click event performs the following tasks:

1.   Checks to verify that the selected serial port is open.

2.   If the selected serial port is open, it closes the port and the application.

3.   If the selected serial port is not open, it closes the application.

```
' Here are the source codes from the btnExit_Click event
'
Private Sub btnExit_Click(ByVal sender As System.Object, ByVal e As
   System.EventArgs) Handles btnExit.Click
      '
      If VBSerial.IsOpen Then
         VBSerial.Close()
      End If
      '
      Close()
      '
End Sub
```

The SerialPortApp is created to open one of the available serial ports and provide the user interface to enter text data and send the text data through the active serial port.

When the SerialPortApp is active and connected to one of the available serial ports, the active serial port listens for incoming data, upon which the data-received event displays the data to the textbox on the application screen.

> The complete source code for the VB 2005 SerialPortApp project is provided as part of the software for this book. The C# and C++ versions of this application are available for download from the following URL: www.embeddedpc.net/ce6book.

After all the code for the SerialPortApp is in place, select Build ➪ Build Solution from the VS2005 IDE to build the project.

Establishing a Connection to the eBox-4300

Now let's deploy the SerialPortApp to the eBox-4300 using the CoreCon connection.

To establish a CoreCon connection, the eBox-4300 needs to connect to the VS2005 development workstation, using one of the following options:

❑   Both the eBox-4300 and the workstation are connected to the same local area network with DHCP service to provide IP addresses dynamically.

❑   Both the eBox-4300 and the workstation are connected to the same local area network, or the same network HUB, without DHCP service. In this scenario, the workstation needs to configure with a proper static IP address and subnet, such as 192.168.2.100 with 255.255.255.0 as the subnet mask.

❑ The eBox-4300 is connected to the workstation directly using a crossover RJ-45 Ethernet cable. The VS2005 development workstation needs to configure with a proper static IP address and subnet, such as 192.168.2.100 with 255.255.255.0 as the subnet mask.

Above, a CE runtime image was generated and downloaded to the eBox-4300. We need to perform the following tasks on the eBox-4300 with the CE runtime running:

> **If you don't have the CE runtime (generated above in this chapter) running on the eBox-4300, launch a separate instance of the VS2005 IDE to open the eBox-4300 OS design project and download the runtime image to the eBox-4300. After this has been downloaded and launched, you can close this instance of the VS2005 IDE. A computer monitor, keyboard, and mouse need to be connected to the eBox-4300 to display activities from the eBox-4300 and accept input.**

1. From the keyboard and mouse attached to the eBox-4300, with the CE runtime image running, select Start ⇨ Run, and enter **cmd** in the Run utility screen, as shown in Figure 12-12, to launch the DOS command window.

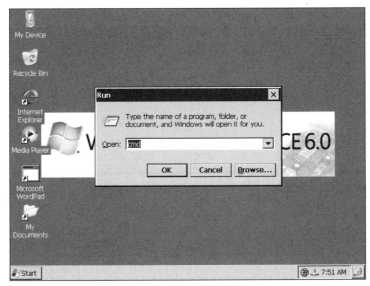

Figure 12-12

2. From the eBox-4300 DOS command window, execute the IPCONFIG utility to display the eBox-4300's IP address, as shown in Figure 12-13. Record the IP address to use in the next step, and keep the DOS command windows open for this later step.

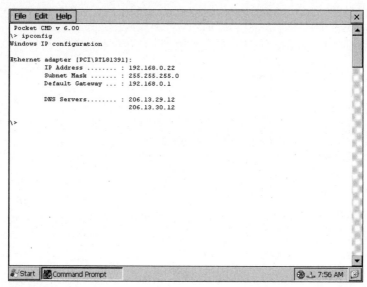

Figure 12-13

3. From the instance of VS2005 with the SerialPortApp open on the development workstation, select Tools ⇨ Options to bring up the Options screen.

4. From the Options screen's left pane, expand the Device Tools node, and click the Devices node to bring up the Devices settings screen.

5. If the Windows CE 5.0 Device is not listed in the Devices list, select the Windows CE 5.0 Device from the "Show devices for platform selection," on the upper right side of the Options screen. Click on

6. Click Properties to bring up the Windows CE 5.0 Device Properties screen.

7. The Transport option should have TCP Connect Transport selected by default on the Windows CE 5.0 Device Properties screen. Click Configure to bring up the Configure TCP/IP Transport screen, as shown in Figure 12-14.

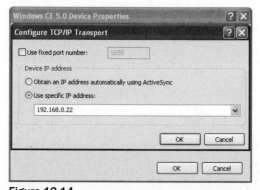

Figure 12-14

8. From the Configure TCP/IP Transport screen, click to select the "Use specific IP address" option, enter the eBox-4300's IP address, and click OK to close the screen.

9. Click OK to close the Window CE 5.0 Device Properties screen.

10. Click OK to close the Options screen.

11. From the eBox-4300's DOS command window, execute the following two commands to run the conmanclient2 utility, followed by the cmaccept utility, as shown in Figure 12-15:

```
\windows\conmanclient2
\windows\cmaccept
```

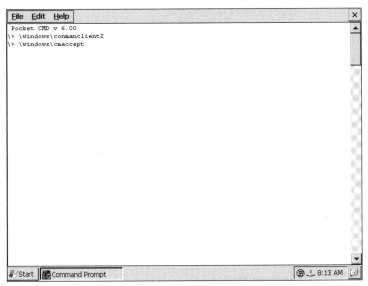

Figure 12-15

After the cmaccept utility is executed, we have 3 minutes to connect to the eBox-4300.

1. From the VS2005 development workstation, select Tools ⇨ Connect to Device to bring up the Connect to Device screen, as shown in Figure 12-16.

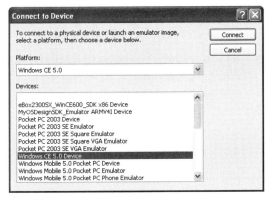

Figure 12-16

2. From the Connect to Device screen, select the Windows CE 5.0 Device, and click Connect to bring up the Connecting screen and display the "Connection succeeded" message, as shown in Figure 12-17. Click Close.

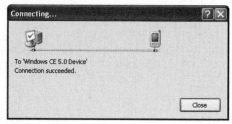

Figure 12-17

Deploying the SerialPortApp to the eBox-4300

With the connection between the VS2005 development workstation and the eBox-4300 in place, let's go through the following steps to deploy the SerialPortApp application to the eBox-4300:

1. From the workstation, select Debug ⇨ Start Without Debugging to bring up the Deploy SerialPortApp screen, as shown in Figure 12-18.

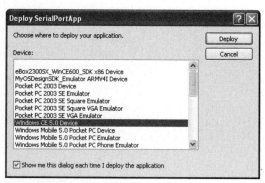

Figure 12-18

2. From the Deploy SerialPortApp screen, select the Windows CE 5.0 Device, and click Deploy to deploy the SerialPortApp to the eBox-4300.

3. After the SerialPortApp is deployed, the application is launched on the eBox-4300 desktop, as shown in Figure 12-19.

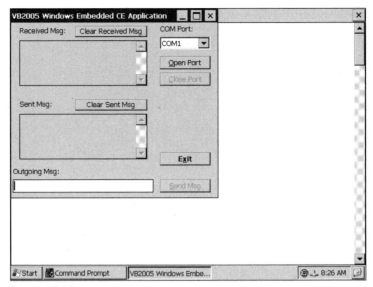

Figure 12-19

With the SerialPortApp running on the eBox-4300, we've concluded the exercise of developing a VB 2005 Smart Device application.

Testing the SerialPortApp on the eBox-4300

Quite a few question are raised in different CE technical forums about accessing the serial port under CE.

Since we have the SerialPortApp deployed to the eBox-4300 with CE 6.0 running, let's take the opportunity to perform a little test to make sure that the SerialPortApp can access both of the serial ports available on the eBox-4300.

When the VS2005 development workstation deployed the SerialPortApp to the eBox-4300, it created the following program folder and copied the `serialportapp.exe` executable to this folder:

\PROGRAM FILES\SERIALPORTAPP

We will work through the following steps to perform the test:

1. Connect a NULL RS-232 serial modem cable between the eBox-4300's COM1 and COM2.

2. From the eBox-4300's desktop, select Start ⇨ Run, and enter the following command to the Run command screen, as shown in Figure 12-20:

```
\Program Files\SerialPortApp\SerialPortApp
```

Figure 12-20

3. After the SerialPortApp is launched on the eBox-4300, select COM1 from the COM Port selection, and click Open Port to open the COM1 serial port.

4. Repeat Step 3 to launch a second instance of the SerialPortApp on the eBox-4300.

5. After the second instance of the SerialPortApp is launched, select COM2 from the COM port selection, and click Open Port to open the COM2 serial port, as shown in Figure 12-21.

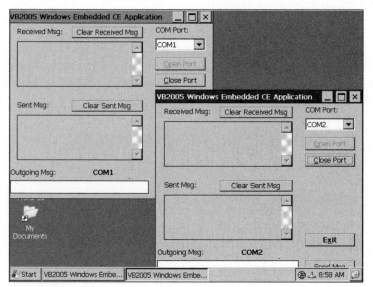

Figure 12-21

At this point, a connection is open between the two serial ports, through the Null serial modem cable. We can enter a message to the Outgoing Msg textbox on one instance and click Send Msg to send the contents to the other SerialPortApp instance's Received Msg textbox, as shown in Figure 12-22.

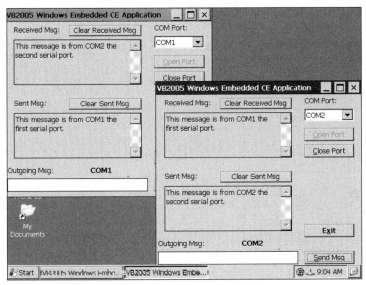

Figure 12-22

Summary

With the CE operating system, the .NET Compact Framework, and VB 2005's ability to support and develop applications with feature-rich graphical user interfaces, as well as console applications for headless devices, VB 2005 becomes an effective and efficient development tool to develop a broad range of embedded applications.

In this chapter, we demonstrated VB 2005's ability to create Smart Device applications rapidly for a CE device. We created an OS design project to generate a runtime image for the eBox-4300, established a connection between the VS2005 development workstation and the eBox-4300 using CoreCon, downloaded the runtime image to the eBox-4300, and deployed the VB 2005 Smart Device application to the eBox-4300.

We worked through the exercise in this chapter using a simple example showing how to access the serial port. Using similar steps from this chapter, and leveraging the CE operating system resources, the .NET Compact Framework, and Visual Basic 2005, we can create feature-rich embedded applications, providing great user experience with the latest in networking, database, multimedia, web services, and security encryption technologies.

13

Native-Code Applications

An application written in *native code* is compiled into a binary executable consisting of CPU instructions *native* to the hardware's processor, and it cannot run on a different type of processor. A native-code application's binary is compiled to run on the ARMV4I processor and cannot run on an x86 platform.

For the general application developer, Visual C++ with the Visual Studio 2005 IDE is the platform of choice when it comes to developing native-code applications for the CE target device.

While the Platform Builder tool itself is a plug-in for the Visual Studio 2005 IDE, the Platform Builder IDE provides its own environment in which to develop native-code applications.

Embedded Visual C++ is another IDE created by Microsoft to develop such native applications for earlier versions of CE. Support for the Embedded Visual C++ is being phased out. If you are new to the CE environment and are planning to develop a new application, the Embedded Visual C++ is not a recommended option and is not covered in this book.

In this chapter, we're going to go over the native-code application development environment and create two native-code applications, a Visual C++ 2005 application and one created with the Platform Builder IDE, to cover the following actions:

❑   Configure an OS design, build the runtime image, and generate an SDK to support native-code applications.

❑   Establish a connection between the target device and the native-code development IDE.

❑   Deploy the native-code application to the target device.

Visual C++ 2005 Native Applications

In this section, we'll create a simple native-code application using Visual C++ 2005.

We'll configure an OS design using the MyEmulatorBSP created in Chapter 3 and use the emulator as the target device.

Although some of the steps are redundant and similar to the OS design in Chapter 11, we'll add the Autolaunch component to the MyEmulatorBSP to enhance the BSP's features. The Autolaunch component can be used to launch one or more applications when CE starts. For the exercise in this section, we'll use the Autolaunch component to launch the CoreCon component when CE starts, and make it easier to establish a connection between the VS2005 development workstation and the target device.

The following tasks are covered in this section:

❑ Add the Autolaunch component to the MyEmulatorBSP.

❑ Configure a CE OS design and generate a runtime image using the emulator as the target device.

❑ Configure and build a Software Development Kit (SDK) from the OS design.

❑ Download the CE runtime image to the target device.

❑ Create a Visual C++ 2005 Win32 Smart Device native-code application.

❑ Establish a connection to the target device using CoreCon.

❑ Deploy the Visual C++ 2005 application to the target device.

The Autolaunch Component

In this section, we will add the `autolaunch.exe` utility to the MyEmulatorBSP and use it to launch the CoreCon component when CE starts. This is a simple process to customize and enhance the BSP's features, using the steps below:

1. Copy the `autolaunch.exe` file to the following directory:

$(_PLATFORMROOT)\MYEMULATORBSP\FILES.

> All of the files placed in the BSP's \files directory will be copied to the OS design's Build release directory during the Build process. The `autolaunch.exe` utility is provided as part of the software for this book, and is available for download from the following URL: www.embeddedpc.net/ce6book.

2. Launch the mydeviceemulatorbsp.pbcxml file using VS2005 from the following directory.

$(_PLATFORMROOT)\MYEMULATORBSP\CATALOG

3. From the VS2005 IDE's Catalog Editor tab, right-click MyEmulatorBSP and select Add Catalog Item, as shown in Figure 13-1, to add a new component to the MyEmulatorBSP.

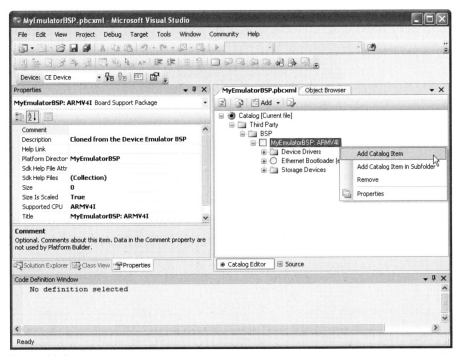

Figure 13-1

4. After the new catalog component is created for the MyEmulatorBSP, the result is shown in Figure 13-2. Depending on the VS 2005 preference settings, your VS2005 IDE may have a different view.

Figure 13-2

5. Right-click on this newly created component, and select Properties to change the component's name and other properties.

6. From the new component's Properties window, change the Title to AutoLaunch Utility, and enter **BSP_Autolaunch** to the Sysgen Variable property, as shown in Figure 13-3.

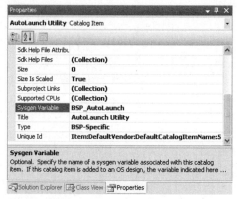

Figure 13-3

7. From the VS2005 IDE, select File ⇨ Save All, and exit this instance of the VS2005.

The Autolaunch utility is now added to the MyEmulatorBSP as a component. When this component is selected in an OS design project, the BSP_Autolaunch environment variable is set for the project and includes the autolaunch binary to the OS design.

Configuring and Building the Runtime Image

Let's work through the following steps to configure the new OS design:

1. Launch a new instance of the VS2005 IDE.

2. From the VS2005 IDE, select File ⇨ New ⇨ Project to create a new project.

3. From the New Project screen, select Platform Builder for CE 6.0 from the Project Type pane on the left, and select OS Design from the Templates pane on the right.

4. Enter **AutoCoreCon** as the name for the project, and click OK to bring up the CE 6.0 OS Design Wizard.

5. From the Design Wizard screen, click Next to bring up the BSP selection screen.

6. Select MyEmulatorBSP, and click Next to bring up the Design Templates screen.

7. Select the Industrial Device template, and click Next to bring up the Design Template Variants screen.

8. Select the Internet Appliance variant, and click Next to bring up the Applications Media screen.

9. Uncheck the Windows Media Audio/MP3 and Windows Media Video/MPEG-4 Video components. Click Next to bring up the Networking Communications screen.

10. Keep the default selection, and click Next to bring up the final OS Design Project Wizard Complete screen.

11. Click Finish to complete the Wizard. A security warning screen is raised. The warning is caused by the NDIS User-mode I/O Protocol Driver, but you should click Acknowledge to close the screen.

At this point, the initial OS design project is created with the components selected during the OS Design Wizard steps. Go through the following steps to add the additional components needed to support the exercise in this chapter (start from the VS2005 IDE by clicking the Catalog Items View tab to bring up the component catalog):

1. Locate and add the CAB File Installer/Uninstaller component to the OS design, from the following folder:

\Core OS\CEBASE\Applications – End User

2. Locate and add the VS2005_CoreCon_ARMV4I_WINCE600 Files Component to the OS design from the following folder:

\Third Party\VS2005 CoreCon

The **VS2005_CoreCon_ARMV4I_WINCE600** component's installation file, **VS2005_CoreCon_ARMV4I_WINCE600.msi**, is provided as part of the software with this book. This file is available for download from the following URL:
www.embeddedpc.net/download

---

3. From the component catalog, locate the MyEmulatorBSP under the Third Party–BSP node, and select the AutoLaunch Utility component, as shown in Figure 13-4.

Figure 13-4

4. Click on the Solution Explorer tab to bring up the Solution Explorer window.

5. From the Solution Explorer window, expand the following folder:

\PARAMETER FILES\MYEMULATORBSP: ARMV4I

6. Double-click on the project.reg file to view and edit the file contents from the VS2005 IDE's center pane.

7. From the VS2005 IDE's center pane, click on the Source icon, next to the RegEdit icon, to view the project.reg file in its source form, as shown in Figure 13-5.

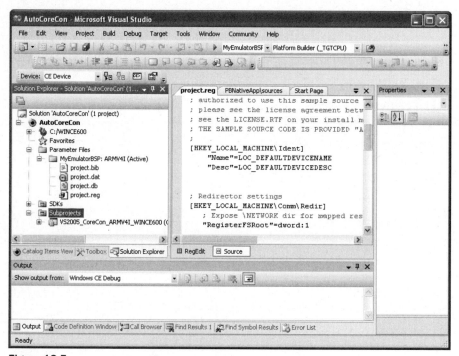

Figure 13-5

8. Scroll to the end of the project.reg file, and add the following entries for the `autolaunch.exe` utility.

```
; Launch by CE during startup
[HKEY_LOCAL_MACHINE\Init]
    "Depend99"=hex:0a,00,14,00,1e,00,32,00
[HKEY_LOCAL_MACHINE\Init]
    "Launch99"="AutoLaunch.exe"

; Launch by AutoLaunch.exe
[HKEY_LOCAL_MACHINE\Startup]
    "Process0"="ConmanClient2.exe"
    "Process0Delay"=dword:00001388        ; delay about 5 seconds

; Without the following registry entry
; CMACCEPT.EXE must be executed for the CoreCon component to function
[HKEY_LOCAL_MACHINE\System]
    "CoreConOverrideSecurity"=dword:1
```

9. From the Solution Explorer window, double-click on the project.bib file to view and edit the file contents from the VS2005 IDE's center pane.

10. Scroll to the end of the project.bib file and add the following entry for the `autolaunch.exe` component:

```
;
FILES
; Name             Path
; ----------------  ------------------------------------------------
AutoLaunch.exe     $(_FLATRELEASEDIR)\AutoLaunch.exe              NK
```

Go through the following steps to review and modify the Build options for the OS design:

1. From the VS2005 IDE, select Project ⇨ AutoCoreCon Properties to bring up the AutoCoreCon Property Pages screen.

2. From the AutoCoreCon Property Pages screen, click on the Configuration Properties node on the left pane, and click on Configuration Manager to bring up the Configuration Manager screen.

3. From the Configuration Manager screen, select the MyEmulatorBSP ARMV4I Release from the "Active solution configuration" selection and click Close.

4. From the AutoCoreCon Property Pages screen's left pane, expand the Configuration Properties node, and click on the Build Options node to bring up the Build Options screen.

5. Uncheck the "Enable kernel debugger (no IMGNOEBUGGER=1)" Build option, and select the following three Build options, as shown in Figure 13-6:

❑ Enable eboot space in memory (IMGEBOOT=1)

❑ Enable KITL (no IMGNOKITL=1)

❑ Enable Runtime image can be larger than 32 MB (IMGRAM64=1)

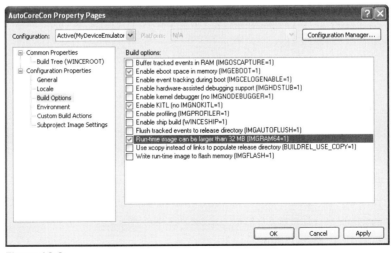

Figure 13-6

257

6. From the AutoCoreCon Property Pages screen, click Apply followed by OK to save the setting and close the screen.

Now, we are ready to build the AutoCoreCon OS design and generate the CE runtime image.

7. From the VS2005 IDE, select Build ⇨ Build Solution to generate the OS design.

> **This process may take anywhere from 15 to 30 minutes depending on the development workstation's processor speed and performance.**

Configuring and Building an SDK

A Software Development Kit (SDK) for the target device is needed to create the Visual C++ 2005 application project. In this section, we will go through the following steps to configure and build an SDK:

1. From the VS2005 IDE, select Project ⇨ Add New SDK to bring up the SDK1 Property Pages, as shown in Figure 13-7.

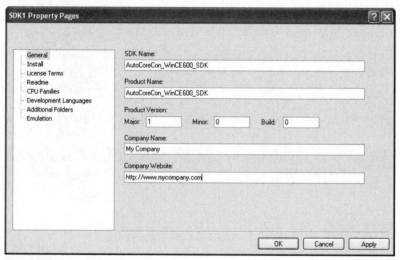

Figure 13-7

2. Enter **AutoCoreCon_WinCE600_SDK** as the SDK Name and Product Name.

3. Enter the Product Version, Company Name, and Company Website.

4. From the SDK1 Property Pages' left pane, click on the Install node, and enter **AutoCoreCon_WinCE600_SDK.msi** as the MSI filename.

5. Click Apply followed by OK to save the changes and close the screen.

6. From the VS2005 IDE, select Build ⇨ Build All SDKs.

After the Build process is completed, the AutoCoreCon_WinCE600_SDK.msi file is generated in the following directory:

$(_MYOSDESIGN)\AUTOCORECON\SDKS\SDK1\MSI

> **_MYOSDESIGN=$(_WINCEROOT)\OSDESIGNS\AUTOCORECON**

7. Close all of the VS2005 IDE instances that are open.

8. From the File Explorer, navigate to the AutoCoreCon_WinCE600_SDK.msi file, and double-click on the file to launch the installation program to install this SDK.

Downloading a Runtime Image to the Emulator

In the previous steps, we configured and built an OS design and the associated SDK. Continuing from the previous steps with the AutoCoreCon OS design project open, let's work through the following steps to configure the target device's connectivity to download the runtime image to the emulator:

1. From the VS2005 IDE, select Target ⇨ Connectivity Options to bring up the Target Connectivity Options screen.

2. From the Target Connectivity Options screen, select DeviceEmulator from the Target Device selection.

3. From the Target Connectivity Options screen, select the Device Emulator (DMA) for the Download selection, select the Device Emulator (DMA) for the Transport selection, and select the KdStub for the Debugger selection.

4. Click on Settings next to the Download selection to bring up the Emulator Properties screen.

5. From the Emulator Properties screen's General tab, select the "Specify RAM size" checkbox, and enter **128** as the RAM size.

6. From the Emulator Properties screen's Display tab, enter **640** for the screen-width setting, and enter **480** for the screen-height setting.

7. From the Emulator Properties screen's Network tab, check the "Enable NE2000 PCMCIA network adapter and bind to" checkbox, and select the "Connected network card" option, as shown in Figure 13-8.

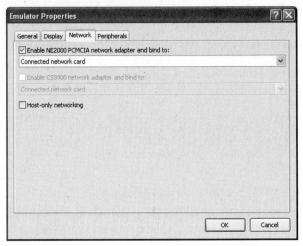

Figure 13-8

8. Click OK to close the Emulator Properties screen.

The Target Device Connectivity Options screen should look like Figure 13-9.

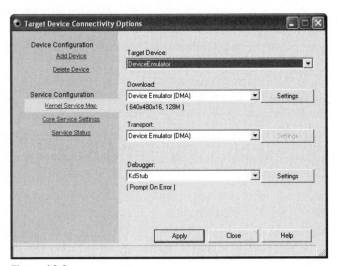

Figure 13-9

9. From the Target Device Connectivity Options screen, click Apply followed by Close to save the changes and close the screen.

Now the runtime image is ready to download to the emulator, as follows:

10. From the VS2005 IDE, select Target ⇨ Attach Device from the VS2005 IDE.

After the runtime image is downloaded to the emulator and launched, the CE 6.0 desktop is shown on the Emulator window.

Creating the Visual C++ 2005 Smart Device Application

In this section, we'll work through the following steps to create a Visual C++ 2005 Smart Device application:

1. Launch a new instance of the VS2005 IDE.

2. From the VS2005 IDE, select File ⇨ New ⇨ Project to bring up the New Project screen.

3. From the New Project screen's left pane, click to expand the Visual C++ node, and click on the Smart Device node to bring up the Smart Device Templates.

4. From the Smart Device Templates on the right pane, select the Win32 Smart Device Project.

5. Enter **MyNativeApp** as the project name, as shown in Figure 13-10.

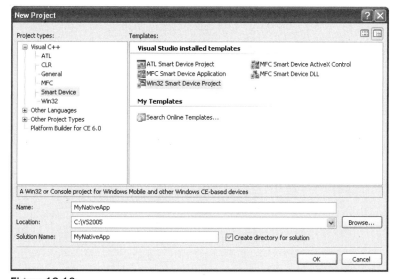

Figure 13-10

> In addition to the Win32 Smart Device application, you can develop MFC Smart Device applications, MFC Smart Device ActiveX controls, and MFC Smart Device DLLs and ATL Smart Device projects using Visual C++ 2005.

6. From the New Project screen, click OK to bring up the Win32 Smart Device Project Wizard.

7. From the Wizard screen, click Next to bring up the Platforms selection screen.

8. From the Selected SDKs pane, click to highlight the Pocket PC 2003 platform, and click on the single left-pointing arrow button to remove the Pocket PC 2003 platform.

9. From the Installed SDKs, click to highlight the AutoCoreCon_WinCE600_SDK, and click on the single right-pointing arrow button to add this SDK as the selected SDK, as shown in Figure 13-11.

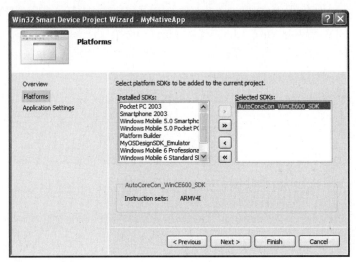

Figure 13-11

10. From the Win32 Smart Device Project Wizard screen, click Next to bring up the Project Settings screen, as shown in Figure 13-12.

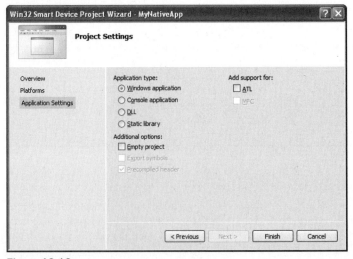

Figure 13-12

11. Keep the default Project Settings selection, and click Finish.

> **The Win32 Smart Device Project Wizard's Project Settings screen provides the option to create different types of applications.**

The Win32 Smart Device Project Wizard created a blank Visual C++ 2005 Smart Device Windows Application project.

The Win32 API within CE is a subset of the Win32 API from the desktop version of Windows. Other than not having all of the Win32 API as the desktop version of Windows does, writing a Win32 program for CE is just the same as writing a Win32 program for Windows XP.

Replace the codes in the case WM_PAINT: statement with the following code:

```
// Codes for the case WM_PAINT:
case WM_PAINT:
    //
    RECT rect;
    GetClientRect (hWnd, &rect);

    hdc = BeginPaint(hWnd, &ps);

    DrawText (hdc, TEXT ("Hello, This is My Native App!"), -1, &rect,
                DT_CENTER | DT_VCENTER | DT_SINGLELINE);

    EndPaint(hWnd, &ps);
```

From the VS2005 IDE, select Build ⇨ Build Solution to build the MyNativeApp application.

Connecting to the Emulator with CoreCon

In the earlier part of this chapter, we configured the AutoCoreCon OS design, generated a runtime image from the OS design, and downloaded the runtime image to the emulator. If you have not downloaded the runtime image to the emulator, launch a new instance of the VS2005 IDE, open the AutoCoreCon OS design, and download the OS.

With the runtime image downloaded, go through the following steps to establish a connection between the MyNativeApp VS2005 IDE and the emulator:

1. From the Emulator window's taskbar, double-click on the networking icon to bring up the network IP settings, as shown in Figure 13-13.

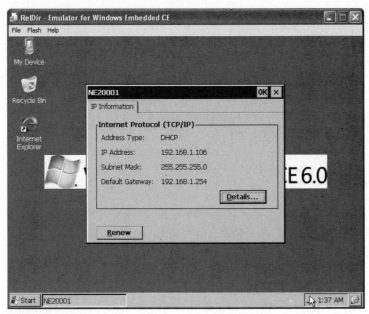

Figure 13-13

2. From the MyNativeApp VS2005 IDE, select Tools ⇨ Options to bring up the project Options screen and expand the Device Tools node on the left pane, as shown in Figure 13-14.

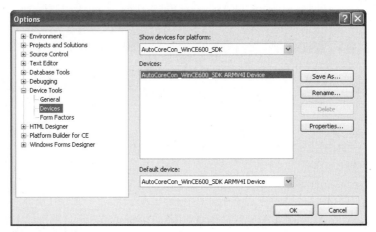

Figure 13-14

3. From the Options screen, select the AutoCoreCon_WinCE600_SDK_ARMV4I device, and click Properties to bring up the AutoCoreCon_WinCE600_SDK_ARMV4I Device Properties.

4. From that Device Properties screen, with the TCP Connect Transport selected as the Transport option, click on Configure to bring up the Configure TCP/IP Transport screen.

5. From the Configure TCP/IP Transport screen, select the "Use specific IP address" option, and enter the emulator's IP address, as shown in Figure 13-15.

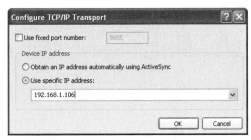

Figure 13-15

6. Click OK to close the Configure TCP/IP Transport screen, click OK to close the AutoCoreCon_ WinCE600_SDK_ARMV4I Device Properties screen, and click OK to close the Options screen.

7. From the MyNativeApp VS2005 IDE, select Tools ⇨ Connect to Device to bring up the Connect to Device screen, as shown in Figure 13-16.

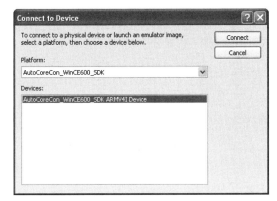

Figure 13-16

8. From the Connect to Device screen, select the AutoCoreCon_WinCE600_SDK device for the Devices selection, and click Connect to connect to the emulator.

9. After successfully connecting to the emulator, the Connecting screen displays the "Connection succeeded" message, as shown in Figure 13-17.

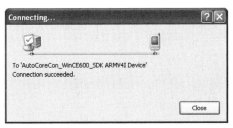

Figure 13-17

Deploying Visual C++ 2005 Application to the Emulator

To deploy the MyNativeApp application to the emulator, select Debug ⇨ Start Without Debugging from the MyNativeApp VS2005 IDE. After the MyNativeApp is deployed to the emulator, the MyNativeApp application screen is shown on the emulator desktop, as in Figure 13-18.

Figure 13-18

Platform Builder Native Application

In this section, we are going to work through the process of creating native-code applications using the Platform Builder IDE. We will use the AutoCoreCon OS design project created earlier in this chapter.

If the emulator is still running, terminate it and select Target ⇨ Detach Device from the AutoCoreCon VS2005 IDE.

For this exercise, we can create the native-code application as part of the AutoCoreCon OS design project.

CE Subproject Wizard

Let's go through the following steps to create a native-code application using the CE Subproject Wizard:

1. From the VS2005 IDE, select Project ⇨ Add New Subproject to bring up the Subproject Wizard screen, as shown in Figure 13-19.

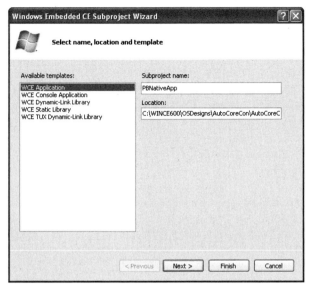

Figure 13-19

2. From the CE Subproject Wizard screen, enter **PBNativeApp** as the Subproject name, and click on Next.

3. From the auto-generated subproject files screen, select a typical "Hello World" application and click Finish, as shown in Figure 13-20.

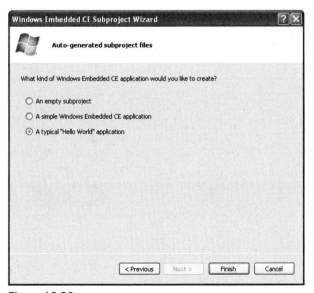

Figure 13-20

The Subproject Wizard created a blank skeleton native-code application subproject in the following directory:

$(_MYOSDESIGN)\AUTOCORECON\PBNATIVEAPP

_MYOSDESIGN = $(_WINCEROOT)\OSDESIGNS\AUTOCORECON

To view and edit the source files for the PBNativeApp native-code application project, go through the following steps:

1. From the VS2005 IDE, click on the Solution Explorer tab.

2. From the Solution Explorer window, expand the Subprojects node and the PBNativeApp node.

3. Expand the Source files node and double-click on the pbnativeapp.cpp file to show the file contents in the VS2005 IDE's Code Editor window, as shown in Figure 13-21.

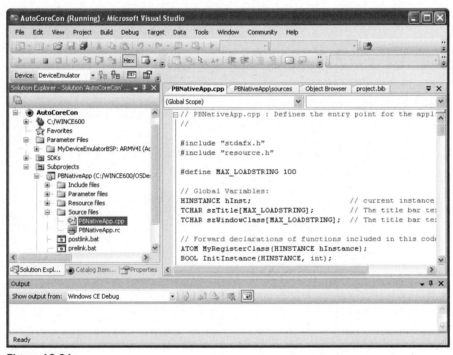

Figure 13-21

4. From the VS2005 IDE's Code Editor window, replace the codes in the case WM_PAINT: statement with the following codes:

```
hdc = BeginPaint(hWnd, &ps);
// TODO: Add any drawing code here...
RECT rt;
GetClientRect(hWnd, &rt);

//DrawText(hdc, szHello, _tcslen(szHello), &rt, DT_CENTER);

DrawText (hdc, TEXT ("Hello, This is PB My Native App!"), -1, &rt,
          DT_CENTER | DT_VCENTER | DT_SINGLELINE);

EndPaint(hWnd, &ps);
break;
```

5. From the Solution Explorer window, right-click on the PBNativeApp, and select Build to build the PBNativeApp subproject, as shown in Figure 13-22.

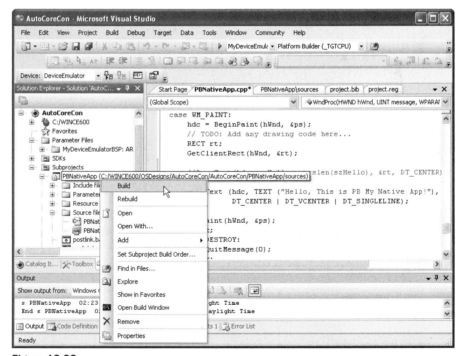

Figure 13-22

Deploying the PBNativeApp Application

We can work with the same instance of the VS2005 IDE to launch the emulator and deploy the application to the emulator.

Go through the following steps to deploy the application:

1. From the VS2005 IDE, select Target ➪ Attach Device to download the CE runtime image to the emulator.

2. After the runtime image is launched to the emulator, select Target ➪ Run Programs from the VS2005 IDE to bring up the Run Program screen, as shown in Figure 13-23.

Figure 13-23

3. From the Run Program screen's available programs, select the pbnativeapp.exe program, and click Run to launch the program.

The pbnativeapp.exe program is launched on the emulator, as shown in Figure 13-24.

Figure 13-24

Summary

In this chapter, we covered Win32 native-code application development for CE, using Visual C++ 2005 and the Platform Builder IDE.

Coding a Win32 application for the CE is very much the same as coding a Win32 application for the desktop version of Windows.

In addition to the Win32 API, CE native-code applications can be developed using MFC and ATL.

14

Autolaunch Applications

A Windows Embedded CE device is generally designed to perform certain designated functions, and it launches one or more applications to perform these functions during start-up.

Different methods are used to automatically launch an application when CE starts. Some applications require certain OS resources to be ready before launching. Some applications need to be launched with command-line parameters. For some CE devices, more than one application needs to be launched in sequence when CE starts.

In this chapter, we'll go through the following methods to autolaunch an application when CE starts:

❑   Configure the registry to automatically launch the application when CE starts.

❑   Autolaunch an application using the Windows\Startup registry.

❑   Develop a utility to launch the application when CE starts.

Autolaunch with the Registry

In this section, we'll work through an exercise to configure the registry to automatically launch an application when CE starts. We'll use the AutoCoreCon OS design project from Chapter 13 for this exercise. If you did not go through the Chapter 13 exercise, you need to work through it now before continuing.

In Chapter 13, we did the following:

❑   Added the `autolaunch.exe` utility to MyEmulatorBSP.

❑   Created the AutoCoreCon OS design project.

❏ Created the PBNativeApp native-code application project to generate the `pbnativeapp.exe` application.

❏ Built the AutoCoreCon OS design project to generate the CE runtime image.

For the exercise in this section, we will exclude the `autolaunch.exe` utility from the OS runtime image and configure the registry to automatically launch the `pbnativeapp.exe` application when CE starts.

Let's go through the following steps to prepare the AutoCoreCon OS design project for the exercise:

1. Launch the VS2005 IDE, and open the AutoCoreCon OS design project.

2. From the Catalog Items View window, expand the Third Party node, expand the BSP node, expand the MyEmulatorBSP node, and unselect the AutoLaunch Utility option, as shown in Figure 14-1.

Figure 14-1

3. From the Solution Explorer window, expand the Parameter Files node, expand the MyEmulatorBSP node, and double-click on the project.reg file to open the file in the center Code Editor window. Click on the Source icon to view the project.reg file contents in source format, and add the following registry entries to the project.reg file:

```
[HKEY_LOCAL_MACHINE\Init]
 ; The Launch99 entry configures the PBNativeApp.exe to launch when
 ; the CE OS starts.
"Launch99"="PBNativeApp.exe"

; The 3C hex value (60 in decimal) in the Depend99
; entry configures the CE OS to wait for application
; launch by the Launch60 process to complete before
; loading the application configured for this process.
"Depend99"=hex:3C,00
```

4. From the VS2005 IDE, select Build ⇨ Advanced Build Commands ⇨ Build Current BSP and Subprojects to generate the CE runtime image.

5. From the VS2005 IDE, select Target ⇨ Connectivity Option to bring up the Target Device Connectivity Options screen. Check to make sure the DeviceEmulator is selected as the target device, with both the Download and Transport options set to Device Emulator (DMA) and the Debugger option set to KdStub.

6. With Device Emulator set as the target device, select Target ⇨ Attach Device from the VS2005 IDE to download the CE runtime image to the emulator.

As the CE runtime image is launched on the emulator, the system scans the HKEY_LOCAL_MACHINE\ Init (HKLM\Init) registry key and launches all the applications configured through the Launchxx entries. As a result, the pbnativeapp.exe application is launched.

In the above steps, we modified the AutoCoreCon OS design to launch the pbnativeapp.exe by configuring the registry.

Let's take a look at the registry entry under the HKLM\Init registry key. As part of the process to compile and generate the CE OS image, all the registry files associated with the BSP, device drivers, and library component selected for the OS design project are combined into the reginit.ini file in the following Build release directory:

$(_MYOSDESIGN)\RELDIR\MYEMULATORBSP_ARMV4I_RELEASE

> **_MyOSDesign = $(_WINCEROOT)\OSDesigns\MyOSDesign\MyOSDesign**

All the registry entries associated with launching applications when CE starts are under the HKLM\Init within the reginit.ini file. Following is the listing of all registry entries under the HKLM\Init key from the AutoCoreCon OS design project:

```
[HKEY_LOCAL_MACHINE\init]
"Launch20"="device.dll"
 "Launch30"="gwes.dll"
 "Depend30"=hex:14,00
 "Launch50"="explorer.exe"
 "Depend50"=hex:14,00,1E,00
 "Launch60"="servicesStart.exe"
 "Depend60"=hex:14,00
 "Launch99"="PBNativeApp.exe"
 "Depend99"=hex:3C,00
```

As the CE kernel initializes, it scans the HKLM\Init registry key looking for Launchxx entries and launches the associated applications in numerical order, going from lower to higher numbers. For our purpose, let's consider each of the Launchxx entries as a process. Each of the Dependxx entries lists the dependencies for the application associated with the corresponding process.

The entries from the above registry would be launched in the following order:

1. `"Launch20"= "device.dll"` — This is the device manager, responsible for loading the audio, battery, keyboard, mouse, NDIS, notification LED, serial, PC Card, USB, and any other drivers that expose the stream interface.

2. `"Launch30"= "gwes.dll"` — The gwes.dll is the graphic windowing and event subsystem, responsible for loading the display, printer, and touch-screen drivers.

> The `"Depend30"=hex:14,00` **entry indicates that gwes.dll is depending on the device.dll from the Launch20 entry. The value 20 in decimal is translated to 14 in hex. The Depend30 entry tells the system to wait until the device.dll launches from the Launch20 process are completed before launching** gwes.dll.type="warning".

3. `"Launch50"= "explorer.exe"` — The `explorer.exe` is the standard desktop shell for CE, similar to the desktop shell for Windows XP and other desktop versions of Windows.

> The `"Depend50"=hex:14,00,1E,00` **entry lists the** `explorer.exe` **dependencies. The hex value 14 is translated to 20 in decimal. The hex value 1E is translated to 30 in decimal. The Depend50 entries tell the system to wait until the device.dll launches from the Launch20 process and gwes.dll launches from the Launch30 process are completed before launching** `explorer.exe.type="warning"`.

4. `"Launch60"="servicesstart.exe"` — The `servicesstart.exe` is associated with the `servicesd.exe`. The `servicesd.exe` is a process that acts as a host to service the DLLs. Applications configured to start early in the boot process that use `servicesd.exe` must be configured to wait for `servicesstart.exe` to be loaded.

5. `"Launch99"= "pbnativeapp.exe"` — The Launch99 process will wait until the dependency application specified in the Depend99 registry entry is launched by CE before launching the `pbnativeapp.exe`. The 3C hex value in the Depend99 entry translates to 60 in decimal. The Launch99 process will wait until the `servicesstart.exe` from the Launch60 process is launched before launching the `pbnativeapp.exe`.

While it's a quick and simple method to configure the registry to launch an application when CE starts, the HKLM\Init registry key cannot be configured to launch applications with command-line parameters.

Autolaunch with Windows\Startup

Another method to autolaunch an application when CE starts is to place a copy of the application executable in the \WINDOWS\STARTUP\ folder. When CE starts, it scans this folder and launches any application found in this folder.

While this is a simple method to implement with an x86 device using the ATAPI block storage device and FAT filesystem, it may not be as straightforward for CE devices built with other processor architecture using different storage devices and filesystems. Some CE devices use battery-backed RAM as the filesystem and aren't able to persist installed programs when the device is powered off.

During the boot process, the boot loader loads the CE OS image, nk.bin, into RAM and launches the OS from RAM. As the CE image boots, it creates the following system folders in RAM. Without implementing a mechanism to persist these folders and their contents during power reset, they all will be lost when the power is off:

- ❏   \APPLICATION DATA
- ❏   \DOCUMENTS AND SETTINGS
- ❏   \MY DOCUMENTS
- ❏   \PROGRAM FILES
- ❏   \TEMP
- ❏   \WINDOWS

For the x86 device, to persist registry settings and installed programs, we need to implement the following components with the OS design to be included in the OS runtime image:

- ❏   **ATAPI Driver** — This is the device driver supporting IDE and SATA storage devices. The IDE flash storage device is built to emulate the IDE hard drive and is supported by the same ATAPI driver.

- ❏   **FAT or exFAT Filesystem** — The FAT and exFAT are filesystem components needed to provide filesystem service for the storage device.

- ❏   **Hive-Based Registry** — The hive-based registry component provides the mechanism to store registry settings in a file, making it possible to save system registry settings when power is off and restore the system settings when CE starts.

- ❏   **Mount the Filesystem as Root** — By mounting the filesystem as the root, \WINDOWS, \PROGRAM FILES, along with the other folders created by CE, are copied to the IDE storage device. When power is off, the IDE storage device preserves these folders and their contents.

Since the emulator does not have a real storage device, we will use the eBox-4300 device and the OS design project created in Chapter 12 to work through the exercises in this section.

In Chapter 12, we worked through the following exercises:

- ❏   Created the eBox4300 OS design project.
- ❏   Created the SerialPortApp managed-code application project to generate the `serialportapp.exe` application.
- ❏   Built the eBox4300 OS design project to generate the CE runtime image.

If you didn't work through the exercises in Chapter 12 to create the eBox4300 OS design project and the SerialPortApp managed-code application project, you need to do so now before continuing.

Using the eBox4300 OS design project and the SerialPortApp managed-code application project, we will work through the following exercises to configure CE to launch the `serialportapp.exe` application from the \WINDOWS\STARTUP folder when it starts:

❑ From the VS2005 IDE, open the eBox4300 OS design project.

❑ Follow the download runtime image to eBox-4300 steps in Chapter 12 to download the CE runtime image to the eBox-4300 device.

In Chapter 12, we generated a debugging version of the `serialportapp.exe` executable. Let's work through the following steps to generate the release version of this executable:

1. Launch a new instance of the VS2005 IDE.

2. From the new instance of VS2005 IDE, open the SerialPortApp project from Chapter 12.

3. From the VS2005 IDE, select Build ⇨ Configuration Manager to bring up the Configuration Manager screen.

4. From the Configuration Manager screen, set the "Active solution configuration" to Release.

5. From the VS2005 IDE, select Build ⇨ Build Solution to generate the release version of the `serialportapp.exe` executable for the project.

6. Follow the Establish Connection to the eBox-4300 steps in Chapter 12 to establish a connection to the eBox-4300 using CoreCon.

7. Follow the Deploy the SerialPortApp to the eBox-4300 steps in Chapter 12 to deploy the `serialportapp.exe` to the eBox-4300 device.

Upon successfully performing the above steps, the eBox-4300 display screen should look similar to Figure 14-2.

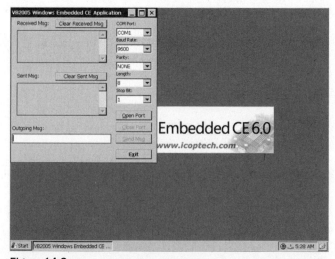

Figure 14-2

When the application is deployed to a CE device from the VS2005 IDE, the application's executable is copied to a folder with the same name as the application's project name in the \PROGRAM FILES directory. For the SerialPortApp project, the `serialportapp.exe` application is copied to the \PROGRAM FILES\SERIALPORTAPP folder.

From the eBox-4300 CE desktop, and with CE downloaded from the eBox4300 project running, double-click on the My Device icon to bring up the file explorer, double-click on the PROGRAM FILES folder, followed by a double click on the SERIALPORTAPP folder, to see that the `serialportapp.exe` executable is copied to the \PROGRAM FILES\SERIALPORTAPP folder as the application is deployed to the eBox-4300 from the VS2005 IDE, as shown in Figure 14-3.

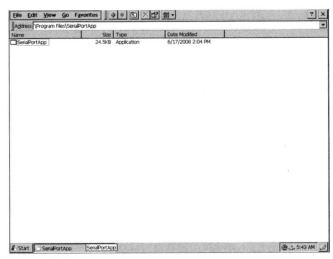

Figure 14-3

The representation for the program files folder on a CE is \PROGRAM FILES. For desktop Windows, the full reference is generally C:\PROGRAM FILES, where "C:" represents the drive letter. The CE filesystem does not use drive letters like the desktop; rather, it refers to the root filesystem with the "\" character.

Copy the `serialportapp.exe` file from the \PROGRAM FILES\SERIALPORTAPP folder to the \WINDOWS\STARTUP folder using the File Explorer.

After the eBox-4300 has finished copying the `serialportapp.exe` to the \WINDOWS\STARTUP folder, reset the eBox-4300, and go through the steps to download the same CE runtime image from the eBox-4300 OS design project to the eBox-4300.

With a copy of the `serialportapp.exe` file in the \WINDOWS\STARTUP file, the CE runtime image as it is loading scans the \WINDOWS\STARTUP folder and launches the `serialportapp.exe` application.

With the filesystem configured to mount as root, when the CE image for the eBox-4300 project is launched for the first time (clean boot), the following folders are created in the eBox-4300's IDE storage:

- ❑ \APPLICATION DATA
- ❑ \DOCUMENTS AND SETTINGS
- ❑ \MY DOCUMENTS
- ❑ \OBJECT STORE
- ❑ \PROGRAM FILES
- ❑ \TEMP
- ❑ \WINDOWS

During the subsequent start-up, the CE image will boot without having to copy the above folder and contents to the IDE storage again. The time required for the system to complete the subsequent boot process is significantly shorter than the initial clean boot.

With the `serialportapp.exe` file copied to the \WINDOWS\STARTUP folder, let's reset the eBox-4300 and download the same eBox-4300 project's CE runtime image from the VS2005 development station.

This time, since the system does not go through a clean boot, the existing file folders and contents will remain intact through the CE image loading process. As the CE runtime is launching, it scans the \WINDOWS\STARTUP folder and automatically launches the `serialportapp.exe` application in the folder.

While this is a quick and easy way to autolaunch an application, it's not a safe method to deploy a commercial CE device. In the event the CE device's registry file becomes corrupted, the system will trigger a clean boot. During the clean boot process, in addition to placing a default registry file in the IDE storage, all the existing system folders created by the previous clean boot will be deleted and copied over by a new set of system folders.

For the hobbyist and academic community, this is an easy and simple method to set up an application to launch when CE starts.

The AutoLaunchApp Utility

The AutoLaunchApp utility can be configured to launch multiple applications and applications with command-line parameters when CE starts. This utility can also be configured to launch the applications with a configurable time delay.

Chapter 14: Autolaunch Applications

> **The AutoLaunch utility is created using Win32 native code and is not part of the Visual Studio 2005 or Windows Embedded CE Platform Builder.**

In this section, we will work through an exercise to add an AutoLaunchApp subproject to the OS design and use it to launch multiple applications with a noticeable time delay between the launching of applications.

For the exercises in this section, we will use the AutoCoreCon OS design project and PBNativeApp application projects created from the exercises in Chapter 13.

Above, in the "Autolaunch with the Registry" section, we also used the AutoCoreCon project to perform the exercise and removed the autolaunch.exe utility from MyEmulatorBSP. For the exercise in this section, the autolaunch.exe utility binary is not needed. Instead, we will create the AutoLaunchApp subproject and add the necessary source code to generate the autolaunchapp.exe utility with similar functionality as the autolaunch.exe utility.

Let's go through the following steps to prepare the AutoCoreCon OS design project, add the AutoLaunchApp subproject, and input the source code for the subproject:

1. Open the AutoCoreCon project using the VS2005 IDE.

2. From the Solution Explorer window, double-click on the project.reg file to open the file in the center Code Editor window, and delete the following registry entries. These entries were added in the earlier section of this chapter for another exercise.

```
[HKEY_LOCAL_MACHINE\Init]
; The Launch99 entry configures the PBNativeApp.exe to launch when
 ; the CE OS starts.
"Launch99"="PBNativeApp.exe"

; The 3C hex value (60 in decimal) in the Depend99
; entry configures the CE OS to wait for application
; launch by the Launch60 process to complete before
; loading the application configured for this process.
 "Depend99"=hex:3C,00
```

Next, we will go through the following steps to add the new AutoLaunchApp subproject:

1. From the VS2005 IDE, select File ⇨ New ⇨ Subproject to bring up the Windows Embedded CE Subproject Wizard screen, as shown in Figure 14-4.

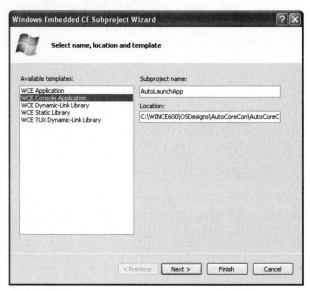

Figure 14-4

2. From the Windows Embedded CE Subproject Wizard screen, select the WCE Console Application from the available templates, enter **AutoLaunchApp** as the Subproject name, use the default location, and click Next to continue.

3. From the autogenerated subproject files screen, select the simple Windows Embedded CE console application option, and click Finish to generate the AutoLaunchApp subproject files.

4. From the Solution Explorer window, double-click on the autolaunchapp.cpp to open the file in the center Code Editor window, delete all the contents, and copy the following code to the autolaunchapp.cpp file:

```
// AutoLaunchApp.cpp :
//

#include "stdafx.h"
#include "winsock2.h"
#include "pkfuncs.h"

#define MAX_APPSTART_KEYNAME 128

void WalkStartupKey();
DWORD WINAPI ProcessThread(LPVOID lpParameter);

typedef struct _ProcessStruct {
    WCHAR szName[MAX_APPSTART_KEYNAME];
    DWORD dwDelay;
} PROCESS_STRUCT, *LPPROCESS_STRUCT;

#define LENGTH_WAIT_FOR_NETWORK_READY 1000 // 1 second
#define MAX_NUM_WAITS_FOR_NETWORK_READY 30 // 30 tries
```

```
#define STR_NAME_OF_CORE_CON_APP TEXT("ConmanClient2.exe")

// Local module functions:
static BOOL IsNetworkReady(void);

int WINAPI WinMain(HINSTANCE hInstance,
                   HINSTANCE hPrevInstance,
                   LPTSTR lpCmdLine,
                   int nCmdShow)
{
    for (int i = 0; i < MAX_NUM_WAITS_FOR_NETWORK_READY; i++)
    {
        if (IsNetworkReady())
        {
                WalkStartupKey();
                break;
        }
        else
        {
            Sleep(LENGTH_WAIT_FOR_NETWORK_READY);
        }
    }

    // RETURN - RETURN: The network was not ready.
    return (-2);
}

BOOL IsNetworkReady()
{
    // Wait up to 2 seconds for the network enumeration API to report
    // ready.
    if (WAIT_OBJECT_0 != WaitForAPIReady(SH_WNET, 2000))
    {
        return (FALSE);
    }

    // Wait up to 2 seconds for the communications API's to report ready.
    if (WAIT_OBJECT_0 != WaitForAPIReady(SH_COMM, 2000))
    {
        return (FALSE);
    }

    // Determine if Winsock is available.
    WSAData wsaData;

    if (WSAStartup(MAKEWORD(1, 1), &wsaData) != 0)
    {
        return (FALSE);
    }

    // Obtain the name of the host we are running on.
    char szHostName[80];

    if (gethostname(szHostName, sizeof(szHostName)) == SOCKET_ERROR)
```

```
        {
            return (FALSE);
        }

        // Obtain the IP addresses of our current host, using
        // the name just retrieved.  There should be at least one
        // IP address if the stack is configured and
        // has received an IP address from the DHCP server.
        struct hostent *pHostEntry = gethostbyname(szHostName);

        if (pHostEntry == NULL || pHostEntry->h_addr_list[0] == NULL)
        {
            return (FALSE);
        }

        WSACleanup();

        // SUCCESS - SUCCESS: The network appears to be functional to return success.
        return (TRUE);
}

void WalkStartupKey()
{
        HKEY    hKey;
        WCHAR   szName[MAX_APPSTART_KEYNAME];
        WCHAR   szVal[MAX_APPSTART_KEYNAME];
        WCHAR   szDelay[MAX_APPSTART_KEYNAME];
        LPWSTR  lpszArg = NULL;
        DWORD   dwTemp, dwType, dwNameSize, dwValSize, i,dwDelay;

        DWORD dwMaxTimeout=0;
        HANDLE hWaitThread=NULL;
        HANDLE ThreadHandles[100];
        int iThreadCount=0;

        if (RegOpenKeyEx(HKEY_LOCAL_MACHINE, TEXT("Startup"), 0, KEY_READ, &hKey) !=
ERROR_SUCCESS) {
                return;
          }

        dwNameSize = MAX_APPSTART_KEYNAME;
        dwValSize = MAX_APPSTART_KEYNAME * sizeof(WCHAR);
        i = 0;
        while (RegEnumValue(hKey, i, szName, &dwNameSize, 0, &dwType,(LPBYTE)szVal,
&dwValSize) == ERROR_SUCCESS) {
                if ((dwType == REG_SZ) && !wcsncmp(szName, TEXT("Process"), 7))
{ // 7 for "Process"
                        // szval
                        wsprintf(szDelay,L"%sDelay",szName);
                        dwValSize=sizeof(dwDelay);
```

```
                        if (ERROR_SUCCESS == RegQueryValueEx(hKey,szDelay,0,&dwType,
        (LPBYTE)&dwDelay,&dwValSize)) {
                                // we now have the process name and the process
        delay - spawn a thread to "Sleep" and then create the process.
                                LPPROCESS_STRUCT ps=new PROCESS_STRUCT;
                                ps->dwDelay=dwDelay;
                                wcscpy(ps->szName,szVal);

                                DWORD dwThreadID;
                                OutputDebugString(L"Creating Thread...\n");

                                HANDLE
        hThread=CreateThread(NULL,0,ProcessThread,(LPVOID)ps,0,&dwThreadID);
                                ThreadHandles[iThreadCount++]=hThread;
                                if (dwDelay > dwMaxTimeout) {
                                        hWaitThread=hThread;
                                        dwMaxTimeout=dwDelay;
                                }
                        }
                }

                dwNameSize = MAX_APPSTART_KEYNAME;
                dwValSize = MAX_APPSTART_KEYNAME * sizeof(WCHAR);
                i++;
        }

        // wait on the thread with the longest delay.
        DWORD dwWait=WaitForSingleObject(hWaitThread,INFINITE);
        if (WAIT_FAILED == dwWait) {
                OutputDebugString(L"Wait Failed!\n");
        }
        for(int x=0;x < iThreadCount;x++) {
                CloseHandle(ThreadHandles[x]);
        }
        RegCloseKey(hKey);
}

DWORD WINAPI ProcessThread(LPVOID lpParameter)
{
        TCHAR tcModuleName[MAX_APPSTART_KEYNAME];
        TCHAR *ptrCmdLine;

        OutputDebugString(L"Thread Created... Sleeping\n");
        LPPROCESS_STRUCT ps=(LPPROCESS_STRUCT)lpParameter;

        Sleep(ps->dwDelay);        // Wait for delay period
        OutputDebugString(L"Done Sleeping...\n");

        PROCESS_INFORMATION pi;
        STARTUPINFO si;
        si.cb=sizeof(si);
```

```
            OutputDebugString(L"Creating Process ");
            OutputDebugString(ps->szName);
            OutputDebugString(L"\n");

            wcscpy(tcModuleName,ps->szName);

            TCHAR *tcPtrSpace=wcsrchr(ps->szName,L' '); // Launch command has a space,
assume command line.
            if (NULL != tcPtrSpace) {
                    tcModuleName[lstrlen(ps->szName)-lstrlen(tcPtrSpace)]=0x00;
// overwrite the space with null, break the app and cmd line.
                    tcPtrSpace++; // move past space character.
            }

            CreateProcess( tcModuleName,  // Module Name
                      tcPtrSpace,     // Command line -- NULL or PTR to command line
                      NULL,           // Process handle not inheritable
                      NULL,           // Thread handle not inheritable
                      FALSE,          // Set handle inheritance to FALSE
                      0,              // No creation flags
                      NULL,           // Use parent's environment block
                      NULL,           // Use parent's starting directory
                      &si,            // Pointer to STARTUPINFO structure
                      &pi );          // Pointer to PROCESS_INFORMATION structure

            OutputDebugString(L"Thread Exiting...\n");

        return 0;
}
```

5. From the Solution Explorer window, double-click on the autolaunchapp.reg registry file to open the file in the center Code Editor window, click on the Source icon to view the file in source format, and enter the following registry entries to the autolaunchapp.reg registry file. CE will launch the `autolaunchapp.exe` application under the HKLM\Init registry key when it starts. In turn, the `autolaunchapp.exe` application will scan the HKLM\Startup registry key and launch all of the programs listed.

```
[HKEY_LOCAL_MACHINE\Init]
 "Depend99"=hex:0a,00,14,00,1e,00,32,00
 "Launch99"="AutoLaunchApp.exe"

[HKEY_LOCAL_MACHINE\Startup]
 "Process1"="cerdisp -c"        ; Remote display application
 "Process1Delay"=dword:00001388
 "Process2"="ConmanClient2.exe" ; CoreCon component
 "Process2Delay"=dword:0
"Process3"="PBNativeApp.exe"
 "Process3Delay"=dword:20       ; Delay 32 seconds
```

6. Open the Sources file in the following directory using a text editor:

_AUTOCORECON\AUTOCORECON\AUTOLAUNCHAPP

_AUTOCORECON = C:\WINCE600\OSDESIGNS\AUTOCORECON
---

7. Delete all of the contents in the Sources file and copy in the following contents:

```
_COMMONPUBROOT=$(_PROJECTROOT)\cesysgen
__PROJROOT=$(_PROJECTROOT)
RELEASETYPE=LOCAL
_ISVINCPATH=$(_WINCEROOT)\public\common\sdk\inc;
_OEMINCPATH=$(_WINCEROOT)\public\common\oak\inc;$(_WINCEROOT)\public\common\
sdk\inc;
TARGETNAME=AutoLaunchApp
FILE_VIEW_ROOT_FOLDER= \
    ReadMe.txt \
    StdAfx.cpp \
    prelink.bat \
    postlink.bat \

FILE_VIEW_RESOURCE_FOLDER= \

FILE_VIEW_INCLUDES_FOLDER= \
    StdAfx.h \

SOURCES= \
    AutoLaunchApp.cpp \

TARGETLIBS= \
    $(_PROJECTROOT)\cesysgen\sdk\lib\$(_CPUINDPATH)\coredll.lib \
    $(_PROJECTROOT)\cesysgen\sdk\lib\$(_CPUINDPATH)\ws2.lib \

PRECOMPILED_PCH=StdAfx.pch
PRECOMPILED_CXX=1
PRECOMPILED_OBJ=StdAfx.obj
PRECOMPILED_INCLUDE=StdAfx.h
TARGETTYPE=PROGRAM
POSTLINK_PASS_CMD=postlink.bat
PRELINK_PASS_CMD=prelink.bat

FILE_VIEW_PARAMETER_FOLDER= \
    AutoLaunchApp.bib \
    AutoLaunchApp.reg \
    AutoLaunchApp.dat \
    AutoLaunchApp.db \
    ProjSysgen.bat \

INCLUDES= \
    $(_WINCEROOT)\public\common\oak\inc \
```

8. We need to add additional applications to the OS design. From the VS2005 IDE's Catalog Items View window, add the following applications from the catalog to the OS design, as shown in Figure 14-5:

❏ Freecell

❏ WordPad

❏ Solitaire

Figure 14-5

9. From the Solution Explorer window, expand the Subprojects node, expand the AutoLaunchApp node, expand the Parameter files node, and double-click on the autolaunchapp.reg file to open the file in the center Code Editor window. Click on the Source icon to view the autolaunchapp .reg file contents in source format, and add the following registry entries to the file:

```
[HKEY_LOCAL_MACHINE\Init]
 ; The Launch90 entry configure the AutoLaunchApp.exe to launch
 ; when the CE OS starts.
"Launch90"="AutoLaunchApp.exe"
```

10. We need to replace the Process1, Process2, and Process3 registry entries as follows to the autolaunchapp.reg file to launch the Freecell, Solitaire, and WordPad applications with the `autolaunchapp.exe` utility:

```
[[HKEY_LOCAL_MACHINE\Startup]
"Process1"="Solitare.exe"          ; Solitare game
"Process1Delay"=dword:00001388     ; 5 seconds delay
"Process2"="Freecell.exe"          ; Freecell game
"Process2Delay"=dword:00003A98     ; 15 seconds delay
"Process3"="PWord.exe"             ; Word Pad
"Process3Delay"=dword:000061A8     ; 25 seconds delay
```

11. From the VS2005 IDE, select Build ⇨ Build Solution to build the OS design and generate the CE OS image for the exercise.

12. After the Build process is completed successfully, select Target ⇨ Connectivity Options to bring up the Target Device Connectivity Options screen. Check to make sure the DeviceEmulator is selected as the target device, with both the Download and Transport options set to Device Emulator (DMA) and the Debugger option set to KdStub.

13. With Device Emulator set as the target device, select Target ⇨ Attach Device from the VS2005 IDE to download the CE runtime image to the emulator.

As the CE runtime image is launched on the emulator, the system scans the HKEY_LOCAL_MACHINE\ Init registry key and launches the autolaunchapp.exe utility.

As this utility is launched, it scans the HKEY_LOCAL_MACHINE\Startup key and launches the solitaire.exe, freecell.exe and pword.exe applications, as shown in Figure 14-6, in the following order:

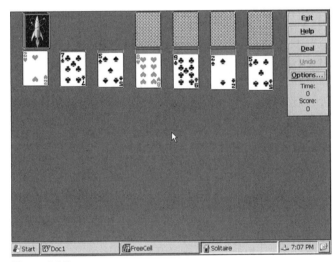

Figure 14-6

1. pword.exe — The 1388 hex value in the Process1Delay registry entry translates to 5000 in decimal, representing 5000 milliseconds, or 5 seconds. The autolaunchapp.exe will delay for 5 seconds after CE is loaded before launching the pword.exe application.

2. freecell.exe — The 3A98 hex value in the Process2Delay registry entry translates to 15000, representing 15,000 milliseconds, or 15 seconds. The freecell.exe application will be launched by the autolaunchapp.exe utility about 10 seconds after the pword.exe application is launched.

3. solitaire.exe — The 61A8 hex value in the Process3Delay registry entry translates to 25000, representing 25,000 milliseconds, or 25 seconds. The solitaire.exe application will be launched by the autolaunchapp.exe utility about 20 seconds after the pword.exe application is launched, or about 10 seconds after the freecell.exe application is launched.

Summary

A CE device is generally designed to perform certain functions and launches the application designed to perform the functions when CE starts. Almost every CE device development project needs to develop one or more applications to launch as CE starts.

We covered launching the application by configuring the HKLM\Init registry key, placing the application in the \WINDOWS\STARTUP folder, and using the AutoLaunch utility.

While it's simple to place a copy of the application executable in the \WINDOWS\STARTUP folder and launch the application when CE starts, this is not a reliable method to deploy on a commercial device.

While we can configure CE to launch the application when CE starts using the HKLM\Init registry key, this is not an option for applications needing command-line parameters.

With just a few lines of code, the AutoLaunch utility is a good way to launch an application when a CE device starts. This utility can be configured to launch multiple applications, in a designated sequence, and to delay the application launching process with a configurable time delay to make certain the applications are launched in the intended order.

15

Customizing the UI

All Windows Embedded CE devices are built with a unique User Interface (UI) designed to capture input and provide output unique to the device's functions and features.

The elements needed for the UI depend on the device's features and function, and can be very different between devices for different application scenarios.

❑ The common input and output interfaces for a CE-based thin-client terminal consist of the following:

 ❑ Standard computer keyboard and mouse

 ❑ Switches to reset the system and turn the system on and off

 ❑ Computer monitor, speaker, and printer port for output

 ❑ Wired and wireless network link for inbound and outbound data

❑ The common input and output interfaces for a CE-based home automation control system include the following:

 ❑ Custom keypad

 ❑ Multiline character display LCD or small graphical display LCD

 ❑ Temperature sensor

 ❑ Humidity sensor

 ❑ Light sensor

❑ In addition to the above input, output, and sensor devices, the home automation control system also uses GPIO (General Purpose Input and Output) to link to LEDs and buttons, and Relay to turn appliances on and off.

In this chapter, I will go over some of the common inputs and outputs you may find on the CE device, and we will work through two exercises to create customized UIs for the device. For the exercises in this chapter, the development workstation is connected to a local area network with a DHCP server to provide IP addresses dynamically.

Input and Output for the CE Device

Applications for the desktop Windows environment are expected to be able to run on different types of computer systems manufactured by different companies, each of which meets certain minimum hardware specifications and has a monitor, keyboard, and mouse. The developer creates applications for the desktop Windows environment based on a generalized set of UIs for all different types of computer systems.

Developing applications for the CE device is different from doing so for the desktop Windows environment. The developer needs to have a good understanding of the specific targeted hardware and the device's intended usage, and create the UI according to these.

The UI for a CE device needs to be designed to work with the inputs and outputs that are specific to the device. Some CE devices may have proprietary inputs and outputs that are protected by patent and may not be available on other devices.

When developing the UI for a CE device, the developer must understand the device's inputs, outputs, intended application, and how the user should use the device to gain the best experience.

The Input

The CE device responds to data received from the input and performs certain tasks based on the received data. The input for the CE device can be one or more of the following, from the user or external peripherals:

❑ **Keyboard** — The keyboard has been a common input interface for the desktop computer and is needed for a CE device with complex input requirements.

❑ **Touch Screen** — While the touch screen is generally designed to capture simple input, it's capable of capturing complex input similar to the keyboard by using the onscreen virtual keyboard.

❑ **Buttons** — Buttons are useful for capturing simple input, such as turning the device on and off, or launching an application.

❑ **Audio Input** — For devices with audio function, the audio input is a source of incoming data and can also be used as a voice command to launch or halt an application.

❑ **Sensor** — Different types of sensors can be common sources of input for a broad range of CE devices. Following is a listing of some common sensors:

  ❑ Temperature, humidity, and light sensors are used as sources of input in the home automation application for controlling the heating, cooling, and lighting systems. These sensors are also used in greenhouse control and other facility control applications.

❏ Different types of gas sensors are used in home automation applications to trigger alerts when unsafe gases are detected. Gas sensors are also used in many industrial automation applications.

❏ Infrared sensors are used commonly in security applications to detect intruders.

❏ **GPIO** — Short for General Purpose Input and Output. When configured as input, the GPIO interface is a common source of input to a CE device to launch an application and to detect an external device's on, off, and operating status.

❏ **Incoming Data** — Incoming data to the CE device can be another kind of input. The incoming data can trigger the application to perform certain tasks according to the contents of that data. Sources of incoming data may include

❏ Local Area Network link

❏ Bluetooth wireless link

❏ IrDA wireless link

❏ WiFi wireless link

❏ GSM/GRPR wireless link

❏ Serial port

❏ USB port

The Output

As the result of carrying out the device's task when it starts or is triggered by inputs, the CE device needs to send certain data to the output. The output for the CE device can be one or more of the following:

❏ **Computer Monitor** — Similar to the desktop Windows environment, the monitor is used to display the CE device's operating status.

❏ **Speaker** — For multimedia devices, the speaker is one of the important outputs providing audio playback function.

❏ **GPIO** — When configured as output, the GPIO can be used to switch an LED on and off to show the device's operating status. The GPIO is also a common output used to control the relay to switch external devices on and off, for home automation, greenhouse control, and industrial automation applications.

❏ **Outbound Data** — Outbound data from the CE device provide another form of output. Upon responding to input and event, the device performs certain tasks and sends the resulting data to the output. The outbound data interface may include one or more of the following data links to the CE device:

❏ Local Area Network link

❏ Bluetooth wireless link

❏ IrDA wireless link

❏ WiFi wireless link

❑   GSM/GRPR wireless link

❑   Serial port

❑   USB port

> In this section, only inputs and outputs from common I/O ports are listed. While certain external peripherals send or receive data to and from the CE device, these peripherals attach to one of the CE device's I/O interfaces. For example, the GPS device is a source of input to the CE device, providing location and time data. An external GPS device is attached to the CE device via the serial or USB port. Even when the GPS device is built in as part of the CE device, it links to the CE device via one of the device's I/O interfaces.

Custom UI for the CE

CE enables the developer to create custom UIs easily. The CE Standard Shell can be replaced by a custom Windows Form application or a browser application. The CE development environment provides useful resources for developing custom UIs, such as providing source code for sample UI projects and for complete application projects that come with customizable UIs. Following is a listing of some of these sample projects:

❑   **IESample** — This is the sample code to a full-feature browser application, in the following directory:

   _WINCEROOT\PUBLIC\IE\OAK\IESAMPLE

❑   **IESimple** — This is the sample code to a full-screen browser without a menu, address bar, or status bar, in the following directory:

   _WINCEROOT\PUBLIC\IE\OAK\IESIMPLE

❑   **Windows Network Projector** — This is the sample code to a fully functional Windows Network Projector application with custom UI, in the following directory:

   _WINCEROOT\PUBLIC\RDP\OAK\PICTOR\PICTORAPP

❑   **Networked Media Device UI** — This is the sample code to the sample UI for a Networked Media Device (NMD). The NMD code provides a good starting point to build a Media Center Extender device to stream audio and video files from the Windows Media Center Server. The code is in the following directory:

   _WINCEROOT\PUBLIC\DIRECTX\OAK\SAMPLES\NMD

In addition to the samples provided, it's possible to develop custom UI applications for a CE device using one of the following programming languages:

❑   Win32 native code

❑   MFC native code

- ❑ C# managed code
- ❑ Visual Basic managed code

Later in this chapter, we will work through an exercise to use Visual Basic to create a custom UI application and deploy the application to the CE target device, using the emulator.

CE with NMD Custom UI

In this section, we will work through an exercise to create an OS design and configure this design with the NMD UI component as the custom UI for CE.

The NMD UI component is written in Win32 native code. The source code for the NMD UI component is provided as part of the Windows Embedded CE Platform Builder installation, in the following directory:

> _WINCEROOT\PUBLIC\DIRECTX\OAK\SAMPLES\NMD

For this exercise, let's work through the following steps to start a clean OS design project, add the needed components, and configure the OS design as needed:

1. Launch the VS2005 IDE, and call this instance the *CustomUI VS2005 IDE.*

2. From the VS2005 IDE, select File ⇨ New ⇨ Project to create a new project.

3. From the New Project screen, select Platform Builder for CE 6.0 from the Project Type pane on the left, and select OS Design from the Templates pane on the right.

4. Enter **CustomUI** as the name for the project, and click OK to bring up the Windows Embedded CE 6.0 OS Design Wizard.

5. From the Design Wizard screen, click Next to bring up the BSP selection screen.

6. Select the MyEmulatorBSP and click Next to bring up the Design Templates screen.

7. Select the Industrial Device template and click Next to bring up the Design Template Variants screen.

8. Select the Internet Appliance variant and click Finish to complete the wizard.

9. A security warning screen will be raised. The security warning is caused by the NDIS User-mode I/O Protocol Driver. Click Acknowledge to close the screen.

The initial OS design project is created by the wizard. For the exercise in this section, we need to add the NMD UI component, which will function as the custom UI for the OS design. Let's go through the following steps to add the NMD UI to the project:

1. From the VS2005 IDE, click on the Catalog Items View tab to bring up the Catalog Items View window.

2. From the Catalog Items View window, add the NMD UI component to the OS design, from the following folder:

   \Core OS\CEBASE\Graphics and Multimedia Technologies\Media

Next, go through the following steps to configure the Build options for the project:

1. From the VS2005 IDE, select ⇨ Configuration Manager to bring up the Configuration Manager screen.

2. From the Configuration Manager screen, select MyEmulatorBSP ARMV4I Release from the "Active solution configuration" selection, and click Close.

3. From the VS2005 IDE, select Project ⇨ CustomUI Properties to bring up the CustomUI Property Pages screen.

4. From the CustomUI Property Pages screen, expand the Configuration Properties node and click on the Build Options node to bring up the Build Options screen.

5. From the Build Options screen, add the following Build option to the project:

   Runtime image can be larger than 32MB (IMGRAM64=1)

6. From the CustomUI Property Pages, click OK to continue.

7. From the VS2005 IDE, select Build ⇨ Build Solution to compile and generate the CE runtime image for the project.

> **It may take 15 to 30 minutes or more to build the OS design project and generate the runtime image.**

After the CE image is generated, go through the following steps to configure the target device connectivity:

1. From the VS2005 IDE, select Target ⇨ Connectivity Options to bring up the Target Device Connectivity Options screen.

2. From the Target Device Connectivity Options screen, select MyEmulator from the Target Device selection.

> **The MyEmulator device profile was created in Chapter 5. The Download and Transport selection are set to Device Emulator (DMA). The Debugger selection is set to KdStub.**

The NMD UI application requires the target device to have 800 × 600 or higher display resolution. To support the NMD UI application, we need to configure the emulator's display resolution to 800 × 600. In addition to the display resolution requirement, the emulator also needs to be configured with a network link for the NMD UI application.

3. To configure the emulator display resolution and network link, go through the following steps:

   a. From the Target Device Connectivity Options screen, with MyEmulator selected as the target device, click the topmost Settings button on the right to bring up the emulator Properties screen.

b. From the Emulator Properties screen, click on the Display tab to bring up the display settings.

c. From the Emulator Properties screen, enter **800** for the screen width and **600** for the screen height settings, as shown in Figure 15-1.

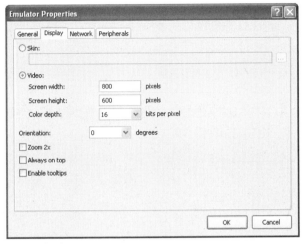

Figure 15-1

4. From the Emulator Properties screen, click Network to bring up the Network settings. Then check the Enable NE2000 PCMCIA network adapter and bind to the Connected network card, as shown in Figure 15-2. Click OK to continue.

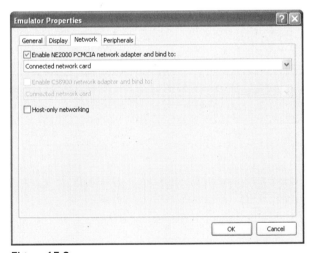

Figure 15-2

5. From the Target Device Connectivity Options screen, click Apply followed by Close to save the settings and continue.

Next, we will download the CE runtime image to the emulator.

6. From the VS2005 IDE, select Target ⇨ Attach Device.

After the image is downloaded to the emulator, we can see that the default CE Explorer shell launches. Shortly after the CE Explorer shell is launched, the NMD UI launches. Since the NMD UI is launched on top of the Explorer shell, the Explorer shell is active, with the default Windows taskbar showing, as in Figure 15-3.

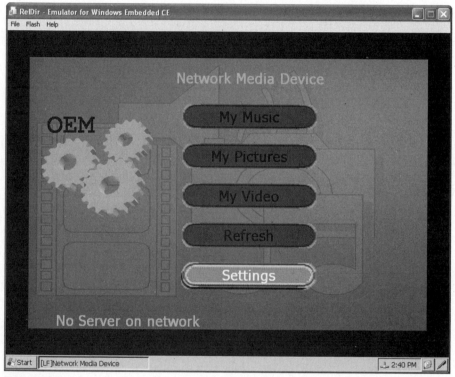

Figure 15-3

When deploying the CE device as an NMD device, the Explorer shell should be disabled from launching. After the device is switched on, only the NMD UI is shown. To accomplish this, go through the following steps to remove the Standard Shell component from the OS design:

1. Close the Emulator screen.

2. From the VS2005 IDE, select Target ⇨ Detach Device to terminate the image downloading process.

3. From the Catalog Items View window, locate the Standard Shell component and remove the OS design from it.

4. From the VS2005 IDE, select Build ⇨ Clean Solution to clear all the libraries generated for the project from the previous Build process.

5. From the VS2005 IDE, select Build ⇨ Build Solution to compile and generate a new OS runtime image.

> **It may take 15 to 30 minutes or more to build the OS design project and generate the runtime image.**

6. After the Build process is completed and the runtime image is generated, select Target ⇨ Attach Device from the VS2005 IDE to download the image to the emulator.

With the Standard Shell component removed, the CE runtime image launches to the NMD UI, as shown in Figure 15-4.

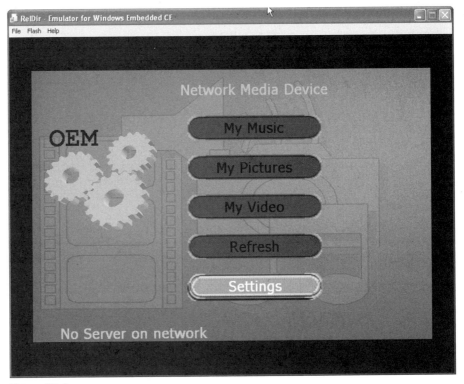

Figure 15-4

Since the Standard Shell component is no longer part of the OS image, the default Windows taskbar no longer appears.

Close the Emulator screen and the VS2005 IDE to continue with the next exercise for this chapter.

VB 2005 Application as the Custom UI

In this section, we will configure the CustomUI OS design to use a VB 2005 managed-code application as the UI and launch a VB 2005 application when the OS starts. We will create a VB 2005 smart device application and configure the CustomUI OS design from the earlier part of this chapter to launch this VB 2005 application.

To accomplish this, we need to configure the CustomUI project by removing the NMD UI component, adding the Standard Shell and VS2005_CorCon_ARMV4I_WINCE600 components to the CustomUI project to generate a runtime image, and use this image to develop and test the VB 2005 application.

After the VB 2005 application is created and tested, we will configure the CustomUI project to include the VB 2005 application that will be launched when the OS starts.

Configure the OS Design for Testing

In this section, we will go through the following steps to configure the CustomUI OS design and use the runtime image from this OS design to develop and test the VB 2005 application in the next section:

1. If it isn't already running, launch the VS2005 IDE and open the CustomUI OS design project created in the earlier part of this chapter, and call this instance the *CustomUI VS2005 IDE*.

2. From the Catalog Items View window, search and remove the NMD UI component from the OS design.

3. From the Catalog Items View window, add the following two components to the OS design:

    ❑   **Standard Shell** — The Standard Shell is needed for application development and testing.

    ❑   **VS2005_CoreCon_ARMV4I_WINCE600** — This CoreCon component is a third-party component, provided as part of this book to perform the book's exercises and needed to establish a connection between the development workstation and target device.

4. From the Solution Explorer window, double-click on project.reg file, to open the file in the center code-editor windows and enter the following registry entries:

```
[HKEY_LOCAL_MACHINE\Init]
    "Depend99"=hex:0a,00,14,00,1e,00,32,00
    "Launch99"="AutoLaunch.exe"

[HKEY_LOCAL_MACHINE\Startup]
    "Process0"="ConmanClient2.exe"
    "Process0Delay"=dword:00001388

[HKEY_LOCAL_MACHINE\System]
"CoreConOverrideSecurity"=dword:1
```

5. From the VS2005 IDE, select Build ⇨ Build Solution to generate a new runtime image.

> **It may take 15 to 30 minutes or more to build the OS design project and generate the runtime image.**

6. After the Build process is completed and the runtime image is generated, select Target ⇨ Attach Device from the VS2005 IDE to download the runtime image to the emulator.

7. After the OS image is downloaded and launched on the emulator, double-click the network icon on the Windows taskbar of the emulator to view the IP address assigned to the emulator, as shown in Figure 15-5, and save this IP address for the exercise in the next section.

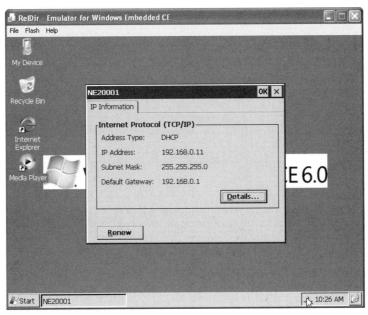

Figure 15-5

Develop the VB 2005 Application

In this section, we will create a simple VB 2005 application using a separate instance of the VS2005 IDE. This application will be used in a later section to demonstrate how a managed-code application can be configured as the custom UI for a CE device.

Let's work through the following steps to create a VB 2005 application:

1. Launch a new instance of the VS2005 IDE, and call this instance the *VBApp VS2005 IDE.*

2. From the VS2005 IDE, select File ⇨ New ⇨ Project to bring up the New Project screen.

3. From this screen, expand the Other Languages node, expand the Visual Basic node, and expand the Smart Device node to select the Windows CE 5.0 project type.

4. From the Templates pane on the right, select the Device Application template.

5. Enter **VBApp** as the name for the project, as shown in Figure 15-6, and click OK to continue.

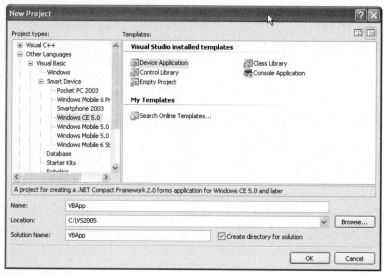

Figure 15-6

The New Project wizard creates the initial VBApp project with a default Windows form, FORM1.VB. Let's go through the following steps to make some changes to FORM1:

1. Remove the mainMenu1 component from FORM1.

2. Add a Label control to FORM1, and place this control in the upper center of the form.

3. Change the Label control's text properties to VB 2005 Custom UI Application for CE.

4. Add a Button control to FORM1, and place this control beneath the Label control.

5. Change the Button control's Text properties to Close.

   At this point, Form1 should look similar to Figure 15-7:

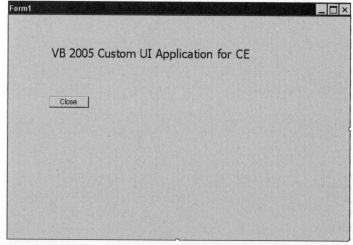

Figure 15-7

6. To launch Form1 in full screen mode, add the following code to the Form1_Load event handler:

```
Private Sub Form1_Load(ByVal sender As System.Object, ByVal e As System.EventArgs)
Handles MyBase.Load

    Me.WindowState = FormWindowState.Maximized
    Me.FormBorderStyle = Windows.Forms.FormBorderStyle.None
    Me.MaximizeBox = False
    Me.MinimizeBox = False
    Me.Text = ""

End Sub
```

7. Add the following code to the Button1_Click event handler:

```
Private Sub Button1_Click(ByVal sender As System.Object, ByVal e As System.EventArgs)
Handles Button1.Click
    Me.Close()
End Sub
```

8. From the VS2005 IDE, select Build ⇨ Configuration Manager to bring up the Configuration Manager screen.

9. From this screen, select Release from the "Active solution configuration" selection, and click Close to continue.

10. From the VS2005 IDE, select Build ⇨ Build Solution to build the application.

Next, work through the following steps to establish a connection to the emulator with the CE runtime image from the CustomUI project running.

From the VBApp VS2005 IDE instance, go through the following steps to establish a connection to the emulator:

1. From the VS2005 IDE, select Tools ⇨ Options to bring up the Options screen.

2. From the Options screen's left pane, expand the Device Tools node and select the Devices option.

3. From the same screen's right pane, select the Windows CE 5.0 Device and click Properties to bring up the Windows CE 5.0 Device Properties screen.

4. From this Properties screen, click Configure to bring up the Configure TCP/IP Transport screen.

5. Enter the IP address from the previous section, configure the OS design for application testing, and click OK to continue.

6. From the VS2005 IDE, select Tools ⇨ Connect to Device to bring up the "Connect to Device" screen.

7. From this screen, select Windows CE 5.0 Device from the Devices list and click Connect.

8. Once the connection is established, the Connecting screen will show the "Connection succeeded" message. Click Close.

With the connection established to the emulator using the CoreCon connection framework, we are ready to deploy the VBApp to run on the emulator:

1. From the VS2005 IDE, select Debug ⇨ Start Without Debugging to bring up the Deploy VBApp screen.

2. From this screen, select the Windows CE 5.0 Device from the Device list, and click Deploy to deploy the application to the emulator, as shown in Figure 15-8.

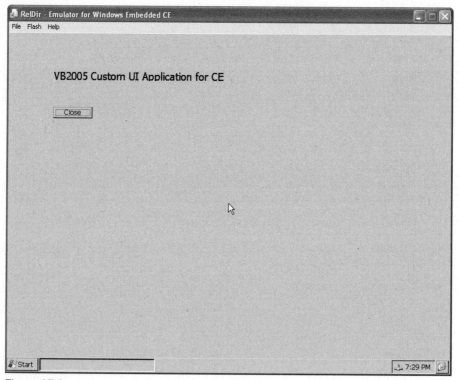

Figure 15-8

Add the VB 2005 Application to the OS Design

With the VBApp application able to deploy and launch on the emulator, we'll work through the exercise in this section to include the VBApp application with the CustomUI OS design project.

The VBApp application binary, vbapp.exe, is compiled into the following directory:

C:\VS2005\VBAPP\VBAPP\BIN\RELEASE

Now we'll work through the following steps to include the vbapp.exe binary in the OS design to be compiled as part of the OS runtime image. To accomplish this, we need to work with the VS2005 IDE instance with the CustomUI OS design project active.

1. If it's still running, terminate the emulator.

2. From the VS2005 IDE, select Target ⇨ Detach Device to release any existing connection.

3. Create the VBAPP folder under the following directory:

   _WINCEROOT\OSDESIGNS\CUSTOMUI\

4. Copy the C:\vs2005\vbapp\vbapp\bin\release\vbapp.exe file to the following directory:

   _WINCEROOT\OSDESIGNS\CUSTOMUI\VBAPP\

5. From the Catalog Items View window, remove the Standard Shell component from the OS design.

6. From the Solution Explorer window, double-click project.bib to open the file in the center Code-Editor window, and enter the following entry under the Files section to include the vbapp.exe application in the OS runtime image:

```
VBApp.exe      $(_WINCEROOT)\OSDesigns\CustomUI\VBApp\VBApp.exe      NK
```

7. From the Solution Explorer window, double-click the project.reg file to open the file in the center Code-Editor window, and delete the following registry entries:

```
[HKEY_LOCAL_MACHINE\Init]
    "Depend99"=hex:0a,00,14,00,1e,00,32,00
    "Launch99"="AutoLaunch.exe"

[HKEY_LOCAL_MACHINE\Startup]
    "Process0"="ConmanClient2.exe"
    "Process0Delay"=dword:00001388

[HKEY_LOCAL_MACHINE\System]
"CoreConOverrideSecurity"=dword:1
```

8. Enter the following registry entries to the project.reg file, needed to launch the vbapp.exe executable when CE starts.

```
[HKEY_LOCAL_MACHINE\init]
    "Launch50"="VBApp.exe"
    "Depend50"=hex:14,00, 1e,00
```

9. From the VS2005 IDE, select Build ⇨ Build Solution to build the OS design and generate a new OS runtime image.

> **It may take 15 to 30 minutes or more to build the OS design project and generate the runtime image.**

After the Build process is completed and the runtime image is generated, select Target ⇨ Attach Device from the VS2005 IDE to download the OS image to the emulator. As the runtime image starts, it launches the vbapp.exe application, as shown in Figure 15-9.

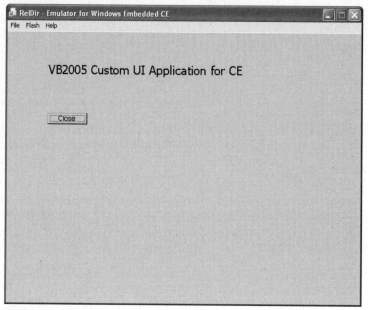

Figure 15-9

Summary

The user interface for a CE device is designed according to the device's hardware and intended application. The CE device's input and output and the device's functions have a strong impact on the device's UI design.

In this chapter, we looked at some of the common inputs and outputs for the CE device and worked through an exercise to create an OS runtime image with custom UI using standard components provided by the Platform Builder. We also created a managed-code VB 2005 application to use as the custom UI for a CE runtime image in another exercise.

The VS2005 IDE and CE development environment provides the resources and makes it easy to create and deploy custom UIs for CE devices.

16

Thin-Client Applications

In all previous chapters, we talked about the CE development environment, worked through exercises to clone BSPs, created OS design projects, generated CE runtime images, and downloaded the images to the target device. Application development and custom user interfaces were also discussed.

So far, I've covered many pieces of CE and the development environment. This and the remaining chapters will discuss application scenarios and cover how we can use CE to build different types of devices. For this chapter, we'll create an OS design using one of the Windows Thin Client OS design templates and configure the OS design as a development platform for different types of information appliance devices, such as information kiosks, self-serve terminals, and digital signage.

The exercises in this chapter can be done using other OS design templates and work just as well. The Windows Thin Client is used for two reasons:

❑ Windows Thin Client is a well-established product. Although it does not have a clearly established specification, Windows Thin Client-capable hardware must be built with the minimum hardware resources to support Windows while having the necessary hardware to support CE.

❑ The thin-client terminal market is one of the key markets for CE. It's an opportunity to introduce the thin-client resources available as part of CE.

The Thin-Client Terminal

With advances in computer hardware technology, server technology, and resources available to support client server computing, demand for the thin-client system has been rising steadily during the past few years.

Similar to the desktop Windows computing system, the Windows Thin Client (WTC) can handle many general computing tasks and can be used with the following types of systems, among others, as a lower-cost alternative to desktop Windows:

❑   Computer workstations for mid-size to large companies, academic institutions, government offices, and many others

❑   Point-of-sale terminals

❑   Information and self-serve kiosks

❑   Digital signage

Although the CE-based WTC does not have all the functions and features of a desktop computer using the full version of Windows XP or Vista, the CE WTC system can perform the common computing tasks required by a typical office.

Most CE-based WTC devices are built using power-efficient components and slower processors and are housed in small enclosures. Many of these WTC devices do not require fans for cooling. The WTC's small size and ability to operate without a fan make these devices attractive options for projects requiring fan-less computer hardware.

The transition from standard desktop computers to thin-client terminals is environmentally friendly. While a common desktop computer requires more than 200 W of power to operate, many thin-client systems require less than 30 W. When deployed in large numbers, these systems can reduce power usage significantly.

Windows Embedded CE is an attractive option for many projects, since it has a lower license fee and an efficient OS kernel able to run on lower-cost computer hardware with fewer resources than Windows XP or Vista.

This chapter covers the following exercises:

❑   Creating an OS design using the Enterprise terminal, a Windows Thin Client design template

❑   Configuring the OS design to generate a runtime image with common thin-client components, showing the similarity between CE and desktop Windows

❑   Configuring the OS design and adding components to generate runtime images suitable for building information appliance devices

The Windows Thin Client OS

In this section, we will create a WTC OS design to generate runtime images with components that perform some general computing tasks similar to those performed in desktop Windows. Using the same WTC OS design, we'll add additional components and configure the OS design to become a browser-based information appliance by launching the web browser and a preconfigured web file when the OS starts.

The Initial WTC OS Design

In this section, we will work through the following steps to create the initial WTC OS design:

1. From the VS2005 IDE, select File ⇨ New ⇨ Project to create a new project.

2. From the New Project screen, select Platform Builder for CE 6.0 from the Project Type pane on the left, and select OS Design from the Templates pane on the right.

3. Enter **WTC** as the name for the project, and click OK to bring up the Windows Embedded CE 6.0 OS Design Wizard.

4. From the Design Wizard screen, click Next to bring up the BSP Selection screen.

5. Select the Device Emulator: ARMV4I BSP, and click Next to bring up the Design Templates screen.

6. Select the Thin Client template, and click Next to bring up the Design Template Variants screen.

7. Select the Enterprise Terminal variant, and click Next to bring up the Applications Media screen.

8. Keep the default selection, and click Next to bring up the Networking Communications screen.

> When the Enterprise Terminal design template is selected in the earlier step, the Remote Desktop Connection components are included to the OS design as dependencies. The Thin Client functions will not work without these components. When creating the OS design for a real device, the Windows Media features are needed to enable the device's multimedia support; the wireless local area network and other networking communication components are needed to support the network interface.

9. From the Networking Communications screen, keep the default selection, and click Next to bring up the final Wizard step.

10. Click Finish to complete the Wizard. A security warning screen will be raised. This warning is caused by the Simple Network Management Protocol (SNMP) and NDIS User-mode I/O Protocol Driver. Click Acknowledge to close the screen.

The initial WTC OS design project is created with the components selected during the OS Design Wizard steps. Go through the following steps to include additional components from the component library in the OS design:

1. From the Catalog Items View window, add the Solitaire components to the OS design from the following folder:

   \Core OS\CEBASE\Applications – End User\Games

The Solitaire card game functions just like the version for desktop Windows.

2. Add the WordPad component, a simple word processor, to the OS design, from the following folder:

   \Core OS\CEBASE\Applications–End User

3. Add the Windows Messenger component, an instant message application similar to the desktop version of Windows Messenger, to the OS design, from the following folder:

   \Core OS\CEBASE\Applications–End User

The above two components are added to the project to show that CE does have general-purpose components similar to those of desktop Windows.

Go through the following steps to configure and further customize the WTC OS design's Build options:

1. From the VS2005 IDE, select Build ⇨ Configuration Manager to bring up the Configuration Manager screen.

2. From this screen, select Device Emulator ARMV4I Release from the "Active solution configuration" selections, and click Close to continue.

3. From the VS2005 IDE, select Project ⇨ WTC Properties to bring up the WTC Property Pages screen. Expand the Configuration Properties node, and select Build Options from the left pane to bring up the Build Options screen.

4. From the Build Options screen, perform the following to edit the Build options, as shown in Figure 16-1:

   a. Unselect the "Enable KITL (no IMGNOKITL=1)" option.

   b. Specify that the "Run-time image can be larger than 32 MB (IMGRAM64=1)."

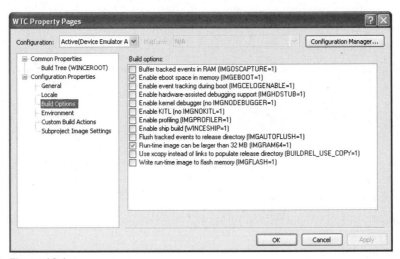

Figure 16-1

> To generate a runtime image that outputs debugging messages, enable the following Build options from the Build Options screen, as seen in Figure 16-1:
>
> 1. Enable kernel debugger (no IMGNODEBUGGER=1).
> 2. Enable KITL (no IMGNOKITL=1).
>
> A runtime image generated in release mode with the above Build options enabled will send debugging information back to the VS2005 IDE through the KITL connection and display the debugging messages in the VS2005's output window.

5. From the WTC Property Pages screen, click Apply followed by OK to close the screen.
6. From the VS2005 IDE, select Build ⇨ Build Solution to generate the OS runtime image.

> It may take 15 to 30 minutes or more to build the OS design project and generate the runtime image.

Configuring a Target Device and Downloading an Image

After the Build process is complete and the runtime image is generated, let's work through the following steps to configure the target device and download the runtime image to the emulator.

1. From the VS2005 IDE, select Target ⇨ Connectivity Options to bring up the Target Device Connectivity Options screen.

2. From the Target Device Connectivity Options screen, select the MyEmulator profile. The MyEmulator profile was created in Chapter 5 with Device Emulator (DMA) selected for the Download and Transport selection and KdStub selected for the Debugger selection. Click Apply followed by Close to save the settings.

3. From the VS2005 IDE, select Target ⇨ Attach Device to download the runtime image to the emulator.

After the runtime image is launched on the emulator, from the CE desktop, select Start ⇨ Programs to view the available applications, as shown in Figure 16-2.

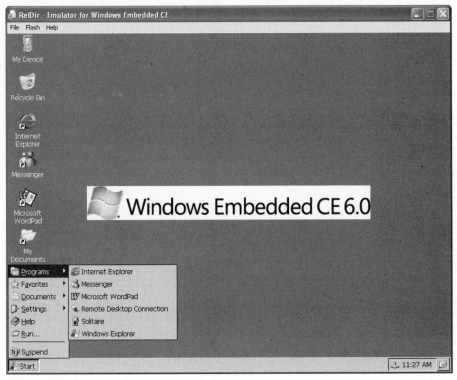

Figure 16-2

The Internet Explorer, Messenger, Microsoft WordPad, Remote Desktop Connection, Solitaire, and Windows Explorer applications provide functions similar to those of their counterparts on desktop Windows.

From the emulator, launch each of the following applications and tinker with the application function to see the similarity to their desktop Windows counterparts:

❑ **Internet Explorer** — This is ported from Internet Explorer 6.0 on desktop Windows.

❑ **Messenger** — The Windows CE Messenger version 5.0 is developed for CE with functions similar to those of Messenger on desktop Windows.

❑ **Microsoft WordPad** — WordPad is a word processor able to support the following types of documents:

  ❑ Plaintext

  ❑ Rich text

  ❑ WordPad

  ❑ WordPad Template

  ❑ Word 97

- ❑ Word 6.0/95

- ❑ Word 97 Template

- ❑ Word 6.0/95 Template

- ❑ Unicode text

❑ **Remote Desktop Connection** — The Remote Desktop Connection application can connect to Windows terminal services and the Windows desktop workstation with Remote Desktop enabled.

❑ **Solitaire** — This is a card game similar to the Solitaire available from desktop Windows.

❑ **Windows Explorer** — Similar to the version running on the desktop Windows, Windows Explorer for CE is used to access the filesystems.

CE is designed from the ground up and is completely different from desktop Windows. In the exercise above, CE feels like a scaled-down version of desktop Windows. This is not surprising and shows that a thin-client terminal built with CE is capable of performing certain Windows PC tasks and can be a cost-efficient alternative to the Windows PC for certain corporate, academic, and government facilities. Often, the thin-client terminal is deployed with an application to perform daily tasks for the office but without allowing the terminal to run other applications. For these scenarios, the thin-client terminal built with CE is a suitable solution.

The similarity to the Windows PC also helps increase acceptance of CE Thin Client as an alternative to Windows PC for certain types of applications.

Customizing the WTC OS Design

Next, we'll work through the following steps to configure the WTC runtime image to launch the Internet Explorer browser and load an HTML file stored locally within the target device. Since the emulator does not have real storage, we will add the files to the OS design and compile into the runtime image.

> This exercise will show how to create a directory and add files to the runtime image.

Follow the steps below to create an HTML file:

1. We need to create a directory to place the HTML file for the exercise. From the development workstation's Windows Explorer, create the \WEBFILE folder in the following directory:

_WINCEROOT\

> When CE 6.0 is installed using the default directory, the _WINCEROOT variable represents C:\WINCE600.

313

2. Using a text editor, create the index.htm file in the _WINCEROOT\WEBFILE directory and add the following contents to the file:

```
<HTML>

<HEAD>
<TITLE>Information Appliance Sample</TITLE>
</HEAD>

<BODY>
<p align="center"> </p>
<p align="center"> </p>
<p align="center"> </p>
<p align="center"><b><font size="6">Hello World</font></b></p>
<p align="center"><font size="6"><b>Information Appliance</b></font></p>
<p align="center"><font size="6"><b>Sample</b></font></p>
</BODY>

</HTML>
```

Follow the steps below to configure the WTC OS design to include the index.htm file in the runtime image:

1. Continuing from the previous exercise, the emulator is still running and connected to the VS2005 IDE. We need to close the emulator and select Target ⇨ Detach Device to terminate the connection before continuing to the next step.

2. From the Solution Explorer window, locate and double-click on the project.bib file under the \Parameter Files\Device Emulator: ARMV4I(Active) node, as shown in Figure 16-3, to open the file for editing in the center Code Editor window.

Figure 16-3

3. From the Code Editor window, add the following entry under the Files section, as shown in Figure 16-4.

```
Index.htm        $(_WINCEROOT)\WEBFILE\Index.htm          NK
```

4. After making changes and additions, select File ⇨ Save All from the VS2005 IDE to save before continuing.

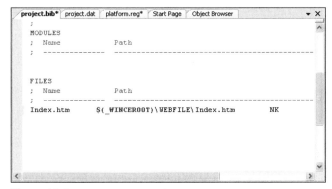

Figure 16-4

5. From the Solution Explorer window, double-click on the project.dat file to open the file for editing in the Editor window.

6. From the Code Editor window, append the following entry to the project.dat file. This entry configures the runtime image to create the \WEBFILE folder in the root of the runtime image.

```
Directory("\"):-Directory("WEBFILE")
```

7. Append the following entry to the project.dat file after the above entry, to copy the index.htm file from the \WINDOWS to the \WEBFILE folder.

```
Directory("\WebFile"):-File("Index.htm", "\Windows\Index.htm")
```

8. From the Solution Explorer window, double-click on the project.reg file to open the file for editing in the Code Editor window. Click on the Source icon on the Code Editor window's lower left to view the file in source-code format, and add the following registry entry to the file:

```
[HKEY_CURRENT_USER\Software\Microsoft\Internet Explorer\Main]
  "Start Page"="\\WEBFILE\\Index.htm"
```

The above registry entry sets the default home page for Internet Explorer.

The Autolaunch Subproject

The following steps will add the Autolaunch subproject to the WTC OS design. This subproject will be used to launch the browser application when CE launches.

1. From the Solution Explorer window, right-click on the Subprojects node and select Add New Subproject to bring up the Windows Embedded CE Subproject Wizard, as shown in Figure 16-5.

Figure 16-5

2. From the CE Subproject Wizard, select WCE Application from the available templates, and enter **Autolaunch** as the subproject name, as shown in Figure 16-6. Click Next to continue.

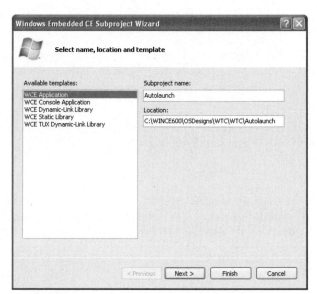

Figure 16-6

3. Select a simple Windows Embedded CE application, and click Finish.

The CE Subproject Wizard created the skeleton code for the Autolaunch subproject. Follow the steps below to add codes to the subproject:

1.   From the Solution Explorer window, expand the Subprojects and Autolaunch nodes to view the files created by the Subproject wizard. Expand the Parameter files folder and double-click on the autolaunch.reg file to open the file for editing in the Editor window.

2.   From the Editor window, click on the Source icon on the lower left to view the contents in source format.

3.   Enter the following registry entries to the autolaunch.reg file:

```
[HKEY_LOCAL_MACHINE\Init]
  "Launch99"="Autolaunch.exe"
  "Depend99"=hex:0a,00,14,00,1e,00

[HKEY_LOCAL_MACHINE\Startup]
  "Process0"="IESample.exe" ; Launch IE browser
  "Process0Delay"=dword:00001388; Delay by 5 seconds
```

The above entries configure CE to launch the `autolaunch.exe` application when it starts. In turn, the `autolaunch.exe` application launches the `iesample.exe`. The Process0Delay entries set the time delay for launching the `iesample.exe` application at about 5 seconds. The "1388" value in hex translates to "5000" in decimal, representing 5,000 milliseconds, or 5 seconds.

4.   From the Solution Explorer window, double-click on the autolaunch.cpp file to open the file in the Code Editor window. This file is located in the following directory:

_WINCEROOT\OSDesigns\WTC\WTC\Autolaunch.

5.   Delete all existing code and enter the following code to the autolaunch.cpp file:

```
// AutoLaunch.cpp : Defines the entry point for the application.
//

#include "stdafx.h"
#include "winsock2.h"
#include "pkfuncs.h"

#define MAX_APPSTART_KEYNAME 128

void WalkStartupKey();
DWORD WINAPI ProcessThread(LPVOID lpParameter);

typedef struct _ProcessStruct {
    WCHAR szName[MAX_APPSTART_KEYNAME];
    DWORD dwDelay;
} PROCESS_STRUCT, *LPPROCESS_STRUCT;

#define LENGTH_WAIT_FOR_NETWORK_READY 1000 // 1 second
#define MAX_NUM_WAITS_FOR_NETWORK_READY 30 // 30 tries
#define STR_NAME_OF_CORE_CON_APP TEXT("ConmanClient2.exe")
```

```c
// Local module functions:
static BOOL IsNetworkReady(void);

int WINAPI WinMain(HINSTANCE hInstance,
                   HINSTANCE hPrevInstance,
                   LPTSTR lpCmdLine,
                   int nCmdShow)
{
    for (int i = 0; i < MAX_NUM_WAITS_FOR_NETWORK_READY; i++)
    {
        if (IsNetworkReady())
        {
                WalkStartupKey();
                break;
        }
        else
        {
            Sleep(LENGTH_WAIT_FOR_NETWORK_READY);
        }
    }

    // RETURN - RETURN: The network was not ready.
    return (-2);
}


BOOL IsNetworkReady()
{
    // Wait up to 2 seconds for the network enumeration API to report
    // ready.
    if (WAIT_OBJECT_0 != WaitForAPIReady(SH_WNET, 2000))
    {
        return (FALSE);
    }

    // Wait up to 2 seconds for the communications API's to report ready.
    if (WAIT_OBJECT_0 != WaitForAPIReady(SH_COMM, 2000))
    {
        return (FALSE);
    }

    // Determine if Winsock is available.
    WSAData wsaData;

    if (WSAStartup(MAKEWORD(1, 1), &wsaData) != 0)
    {
        return (FALSE);
    }

    // Obtain the name of the host we are running on.
    char szHostName[80];

    if (gethostname(szHostName, sizeof(szHostName)) == SOCKET_ERROR)
    {
        return (FALSE);
    }
```

```
            // Obtain the IP addresses of our current host, using
            // the name just retrieved. There should be at least one
            // IP address if the stack is configured and
            // has received an IP address from the DHCP server.
            struct hostent *pHostEntry = gethostbyname(szHostName);

            if (pHostEntry == NULL || pHostEntry->h_addr_list[0] == NULL)
            {
                return (FALSE);
            }

            WSACleanup();

// SUCCESS - SUCCESS: The network appears to be functional to return success.
            return (TRUE);
}

void WalkStartupKey()
{
            HKEY    hKey;
            WCHAR   szName[MAX_APPSTART_KEYNAME];
            WCHAR   szVal[MAX_APPSTART_KEYNAME];
            WCHAR   szDelay[MAX_APPSTART_KEYNAME];
            LPWSTR  lpszArg = NULL;
            DWORD   dwTemp, dwType, dwNameSize, dwValSize, i,dwDelay;

            DWORD dwMaxTimeout=0;
            HANDLE hWaitThread=NULL;
            HANDLE ThreadHandles[100];
            int iThreadCount=0;

if (RegOpenKeyEx(HKEY_LOCAL_MACHINE, TEXT("Startup"), 0, KEY_READ,
  &hKey) != ERROR_SUCCESS) {
                    return;
            }

            dwNameSize = MAX_APPSTART_KEYNAME;
            dwValSize = MAX_APPSTART_KEYNAME * sizeof(WCHAR);
            i = 0;
            while (RegEnumValue(hKey, i, szName, &dwNameSize, 0, &dwType,(LPBYTE)szVal,
&dwValSize) == ERROR_SUCCESS) {
                    if ((dwType == REG_SZ) && !wcsncmp(szName, TEXT("Process"),7))
{ // 7 for "Process"
                            // szval
                            wsprintf(szDelay,L"%sDelay",szName);
                            dwValSize=sizeof(dwDelay);
                            if (ERROR_SUCCESS ==
RegQueryValueEx(hKey,szDelay,0,&dwType,(LPBYTE)&dwDelay,&dwValSize)) {
```

```
                                // we now have the process name and the process
       delay - spawn a thread to "Sleep" and then create the process.
                                LPPROCESS_STRUCT ps=new PROCESS_STRUCT;
                                ps->dwDelay=dwDelay;
                                wcscpy(ps->szName,szVal);

                                DWORD dwThreadID;
                                OutputDebugString(L"Creating Thread...\n");

                                HANDLE
       hThread=CreateThread(NULL,0,ProcessThread,(LPVOID)ps,0,&dwThreadID);
                                ThreadHandles[iThreadCount++]=hThread;
                                if (dwDelay > dwMaxTimeout) {
                                        hWaitThread=hThread;
                                        dwMaxTimeout=dwDelay;
                                }
                        }
                }

                dwNameSize = MAX_APPSTART_KEYNAME;
                dwValSize = MAX_APPSTART_KEYNAME * sizeof(WCHAR);
                i++;
        }

        // wait on the thread with the longest delay.
        DWORD dwWait=WaitForSingleObject(hWaitThread,INFINITE);
        if (WAIT_FAILED == dwWait) {
                OutputDebugString(L"Wait Failed!\n");
        }
        for(int x=0;x < iThreadCount;x++) {
                CloseHandle(ThreadHandles[x]);
        }
        RegCloseKey(hKey);
}

DWORD WINAPI ProcessThread(LPVOID lpParameter)
{
        TCHAR tcModuleName[MAX_APPSTART_KEYNAME];
        TCHAR *ptrCmdLine;

        OutputDebugString(L"Thread Created... Sleeping\n");
        LPPROCESS_STRUCT ps=(LPPROCESS_STRUCT)lpParameter;

        Sleep(ps->dwDelay);        // Wait for delay period
        OutputDebugString(L"Done Sleeping...\n");

        PROCESS_INFORMATION pi;
        STARTUPINFO si;
        si.cb=sizeof(si);
        OutputDebugString(L"Creating Process ");
        OutputDebugString(ps->szName);
```

```
        OutputDebugString(L"\n");

        wcscpy(tcModuleName,ps->szName);

        TCHAR *tcPtrSpace=wcsrchr(ps->szName,L' '); // Launch command has a
    space, assume command line.
        if (NULL != tcPtrSpace) {
                tcModuleName[lstrlen(ps->szName)-lstrlen(tcPtrSpace)
        ]=0x00;// overwrite the space with null, break the app and cmd line.
            tcPtrSpace++; // move past space character.
    }

    CreateProcess( tcModuleName,  // Module Name
                   tcPtrSpace,    // Command line -- NULL or PTR to command line
                   NULL,          // Process handle not inheritable
                   NULL,          // Thread handle not inheritable
                   FALSE,         // Set handle inheritance to FALSE
                   0,             // No creation flags
                   NULL,          // Use parent's environment block
                   NULL,          // Use parent's starting directory
                   &si,           // Pointer to STARTUPINFO structure
                   &pi );         // Pointer to PROCESS_INFORMATION structure

                OutputDebugString(L"Thread Exiting...\n");

    return 0;
    }
```

The above source code compiles into autolaunch.exe. During the WTC OS Design Build process, the autolaunch.exe binary will be compiled into the runtime image. When the runtime image starts, it launches the autolaunch.exe executable. When executed, autolaunch.exe performs the following tasks:

❑   Checks whether the network is ready.

❑   Scans and launches the program under the HKEY_LOCAL_MACHINE\Startup registry key, as follows:

```
[HKEY_LOCAL_MACHINE\Startup]
    "Process0"="program_1.exe"        ; Launch the first program
    "Process0Delay"=dword:00001388    ; Delay by 5 seconds
    "Process1"="program_2.exe"        ; Launch the second program
    "Process1Delay"=dword:00002710    ; Delay by 10 seconds
    "Process2"="program_3.exe"        ; Launch the third program
    "Process2Delay"=dword:00003A98    ; Delay by 15 seconds
```

To compile and build the codes in the autolaunch.cpp file properly, we need to make changes to the source code configuration file. Go through the following steps to change the source code configuration file:

1.   Open the Sources file using a text editor such as notepad.exe from the following directory (the Sources file does not have a file extension):

   _WINCEROOT\OSDESIGNS\WTC\WTC\AUTOLAUNCH

321

2. Delete all of the existing contents in the Sources file, and add the following contents to the file:

```
_COMMONPUBROOT=$(_PROJECTROOT)\cesysgen
__PROJROOT=$(_PROJECTROOT)
RELEASETYPE=LOCAL
_ISVINCPATH=$(_WINCEROOT)\public\common\sdk\inc;
_OEMINCPATH=$(_WINCEROOT)\public\common\oak\inc;$(_WINCEROOT)\public\common\sdk\inc;
TARGETNAME=Autolaunch
FILE_VIEW_ROOT_FOLDER= \
    ReadMe.txt \
    StdAfx.cpp \
    prelink.bat \
    postlink.bat \

FILE_VIEW_RESOURCE_FOLDER= \

FILE_VIEW_INCLUDES_FOLDER= \
    StdAfx.h \

SOURCES= \
    Autolaunch.cpp \

TARGETLIBS= \
    $(_PROJECTROOT)\cesysgen\sdk\lib\$(_CPUINDPATH)\coredll.lib \
    $(_PROJECTROOT)\cesysgen\sdk\lib\$(_CPUINDPATH)\ws2.lib \

PRECOMPILED_PCH=StdAfx.pch
PRECOMPILED_CXX=1
PRECOMPILED_OBJ=StdAfx.obj
PRECOMPILED_INCLUDE=StdAfx.h
TARGETTYPE=PROGRAM
POSTLINK_PASS_CMD=postlink.bat
PRELINK_PASS_CMD=prelink.bat
FILE_VIEW_PARAMETER_FOLDER= \
    Autolaunch.bib \
    Autolaunch.reg \
    Autolaunch.dat \
    Autolaunch.db \
    ProjSysgen.bat \

INCLUDES= \
    $(_WINCEROOT)\public\common\oak\inc \
```

3. From the VS2005 IDE, select Build ➪ Build Solution to build the project and generate the runtime image.

> **It may take 15 to 30 minutes or more to build the OS design project and generate the runtime image.**

After the runtime image is generated, to download the runtime image to the emulator, we need to configure the target device connectivity service. Since the Target Device Connectivity options for image download have been configured above in this chapter, we don't need to configure these again.

4. From the VS2005 IDE, select Target ⇨ Attach Device to download the runtime image to the emulator.

After the OS runtime image is downloaded to the emulator, we can see that the CE desktop launches. Shortly after the CE desktop is launched, Internet Explorer launches with the configured index.htm file, as shown in Figure 16-7.

Figure 16-7

When the OS image in Figure 16-7 is launched, the Explorer shell is launched first. The iesample.exe browser application is launched soon afterward.

Disabling the Explorer Shell

On the CE desktop in Figure 16-7, the Explorer shell taskbar is showing in the lower screen, indicating that explorer.exe, the CE desktop shell, is running.

In this section, go through the following steps to disable the explorer.exe shell:

1. Stop the emulator. From the VS2005 IDE, select Target ⇨ Detach Device to terminate the connection to the emulator, before continuing.

2. From the Solution Explorer window, expand the Subprojects node to view the files created by the Subproject wizard, and double-click on the autolaunch.reg file to open the file for editing in the center Code Editor window.

3. Replace the autolaunch.reg file contents to the following:

```
[HKEY_LOCAL_MACHINE\Init]
    "Launch50"="Autolaunch.exe"
    "Depend50"=hex:0a,00,14,00,1e,00
[HKEY_LOCAL_MACHINE\Startup]
    "Process0"="IESample.exe"          ; Launch IE browser
    "Process0Delay"=dword:00001388     ; Delay by 5 seconds
```

During the Build process, all the registry files, including the shell.reg, for the OS design are merged into the reginit.ini file in the Build release directory. For duplicate registry entries, the entry that appears last in the reginit.ini file is the one that takes effect.

The "Launch50"="explorer.exe" entry, responsible for launching the Explorer shell, is part of the shell.reg file under the HKEY_LOCAL_MACHINE\Init registry key.

The "Launch50"="Autolaunch.exe" entry is part of the autolaunch.reg file under the HKEY_LOCAL_MACHINE\Init registry key.

The contents from shell.reg are merged into the reginit.ini file before the contents from autolaunch.reg are merged. As a result, the "Launch50"="Autolaunch.exe" entry will take effect.

When the OS runtime image starts, it launches the autolaunch.exe executable instead of the Explorer shell.

4. From the VS2005 IDE, select Build ⇨ Advanced Build Commands ⇨ Build Current BSP and Subprojects to generate the runtime image. Since only the registry is changed, it's not necessary to do a full compilation. This advance build command skips part of the Build process and generates the runtime image in a much shorter time.

> It may take 5 to 10 minutes or less to build the OS design project and generate the runtime image.

5. After the Build process is completed, select Target ⇨ Attach Device from the VS2005 IDE to download the runtime image to the emulator.

As CE starts, the Iesample browser launches and loads the index.htm file, as shown in Figure 16-8.

Figure 16-8

Figures 16-7 and 16-8 look similar. For the Emulator screen shown in Figure 16-7, the OS runtime is launched with the Explorer shell, with the Windows taskbar on the bottom of the screen. The OS run time in Figure 16-8 is launched without the Explorer shell. Since the Explorer shell is not active, the taskbar does not appear.

Using the WTC OS design and configuring the browser application to launch in full-screen kiosk mode without the navigation URL, we can build different types of information appliances easily.

In addition to the Iesample browser, the Iesimple browser application is shipped as part of CE with full source code in the following directory:

    _WINCEROOT\PUBLIC\IE\OAK\IESIMPLE

The Iesimple application can be launched as a full-screen browser without menu, address, or status bar. This is an ideal browser application for a kiosk application using the browser as the primary user interface.

The Iesimple browser enables the kiosk to display contents from the Web. By not providing access to the menu, address, and status bar, the application is able to control the contents to be displayed to the kiosk while providing an interactive environment for the user to select the available contents to display.

Summary

In the first portion of this chapter, I provided a brief overview of the thin-client terminal, and we worked through exercises to generate an OS runtime image using one of the WTC OS design templates.

In the later portion, we further configured the OS design to disable the CE Explorer shell and launch the Iesample browser when CE starts.

The exercises in the chapter show that it's a simple and straightforward process to create Information Appliances using CE without having to perform complicated development tasks.

Information Appliances built with CE are able to access web pages locally or over an Internet connection. Information in web-page format is readily available and can be managed with ease.

Using existing resources, a company can deploy CE-based Information Appliances to provide an interactive environment to display web contents based on user input, through a keyboard or touch screen input device, while maintaining control of the contents being displayed.

17

Home Automation Applications

The exercises in previous chapters were done using the emulator. While the emulator is a great tool for general learning, it's a virtual environment and cannot do much beyond simulation.

For this chapter, we will work through various exercises to create simple CE applications that can be used as the starting point for a home automation control application, and work with real hardware.

Since most of us live in an apartment, condominium, or house, the home automation system provides a simple and straightforward application environment we can easily relate to.

Hardware is an integral part of the embedded development environment. Without going through the hands-on process and working with actual hardware, the embedded development learning process is incomplete.

The application developer engaging in embedded development faces many challenges related to hardware. These challenges range from finding hardware with appropriate device drivers to figuring out how to fit all the pieces together, how to interface to the external peripherals, and how to write code to access the hardware.

In this and the subsequent chapters, we will work though CE application development exercises that tinker with hardware.

Home Automation Control

Think of the sprinkler, heating, and air-conditioning systems as simple automation control systems.

Some homes have sprinkler systems to water the lawn. There may be an automatic sprinkler control device to turn the system on and off during certain times each day. Some of these sprinkler controllers use a simple timing device, but others are built with microcontrollers that can be configured to control multiple zones. These sprinklers use a form of automation control system.

The thermostat is one of the must-haves for all dwellings to control heating during the cold winter season and air-conditioning during the hot summer. There are different types of thermostats, ranging from simple units using thermal metallic spring coils with mercury switches to digital thermostats that can set multiple temperatures for different times each day and different days during the week.

Using advanced electronic and computing technologies with networking and wireless capabilities, the modern home automation system is becoming far more advanced. Such a system may contain a central intelligent controller, usually an embedded computing device, interfacing to external peripherals that control home appliances and perform other functions. Using Bluetooth, ZigBee, Z-Wave, and other wireless connectivity technologies to replace cable helps ease the installation process, lowering the overall system cost while enhancing system function and minimizing structural damage caused by wired installations.

Bluetooth, ZigBee, and *Z-Wave* are low-power, short-range wireless technologies being adopted by many companies in the home and building automation field.

The URL to the ZigBee Alliance web site is `www.zigbee.org/en/index.asp`. And following is the URL to the Z-Wave Alliance web site: `www.z-wave.com/modules/Z-Wave-Start`.

To utilize the existing electrical wiring, several powerline network technologies have been developed, targeting the home networking market. There are industry trade groups, such as the Universal Powerline Association (`www.upaplc.org`) and the HomePlug Powerline Alliance (`www.homeplug.org/home`), which work to establish universal standards. Establishing such standards for manufacturers of powerline networking devices enables interoperability between devices and benefits the consumer. Powerline networking is a great resource for home automation projects.

The ability of the system to connect to local area networks and the Internet, using Ethernet or Wi-Fi, enables new features and functions to be developed for home automation.

All these advancements help fuel the home automation system market. As a result, the number of hardware manufacturers developing components for the home automation market is growing, resulting in healthy availability of hardware for such systems.

Since there are broad ranges of hardware, each built differently with different software interfaces, it's necessary to tinker with hardware components when working on home automation projects. Even the software application developer needs access to the hardware to write code that can communicate with and control it.

For application developers who don't want to tinker with low-level layer code to deal with the OS and to access the hardware, CE with the .NET Compact Framework library provides the best development option.

Using a CE-enabled hardware platform, we can minimize the time and frustration of trying to figure out how to get different pieces of hardware to interface with each other and how to write code to access this hardware.

In this chapter, we will use the eBox-4300-MSJK and Phidget devices as the hardware platforms and develop managed-code applications using Visual Basic 2005.

Control Applications

Each generation of modern home automation systems gets more complex with added functionality. Using advanced electronics, the automation control module can pack more control functions in smaller and cheaper packages.

Many features and options are available to build home automation systems. The system may be built with different combinations of the following control systems, with costs ranging from a few hundred dollars to ten of thousands:

❑ **Sprinkler Control System** — Turns the sprinkler valve on and off to water the lawn automatically.

❑ **Lighting Control System** — Turns the lighting system on and off and controls the lighting intensity based on user-configured settings.

❑ **Heating, Ventilation, and Air-Conditioning Control System** — Turns the heating and air-conditioning system on and off based on the temperature setting and time or date.

❑ **Motorized Window Shades and Blinds Control System** — Controls the motor to close or open the shades and blinds.

❑ **Swimming Pool Control System** — Controls the swimming pool circulation, heating, and cleaning to automate the maintenance tasks.

❑ **Control System for the Home Theater** — Controls lighting by automatically turning the lighting and windows shades to a preconfigured state.

❑ **Monitoring System for Hazardous Gases** — While a hazardous-gas sensor device triggers an alarm condition when dangerous levels of a monitored gas are present, it doesn't provide and keep data when hazardous gas doesn't reach the danger level. Gas monitoring systems linked to a smart home automation controller, with the ability to log and analyze the data, provide different levels of *early* warning.

❑ **Water Leak Monitoring System** — Monitors and logs water flow rate during different times of the day to profile water usage. Water flow during an unlikely usage period can provide warning of undetected and invisible water leaks.

Controllers, Relays, Switches, and Sensors

To accomplish the automation control and monitoring tasks for a home automation system, different types of controller, relays, switches, and sensors are needed, such as the following:

❑ **Controller** — This is the brain of the system. In some systems, in addition to the main controller, which is a sophisticated embedded computer, there are other less sophisticated subcontrollers that perform specific tasks and interact with the main controller.

❑ **Relays and Electronic Switches** — Controlled by the controller, relays and electronic switches are used to switch air-conditioning devices, heating devices, lighting, and motors on and off.

❑ **Sensors** — These provide the necessary input to the home automation control system and consist of the following types:

   ❑ On/off sensors used to detect door and window position

   ❑ Temperature sensors used for climate control

   ❑ Humidity sensors used for climate control

   ❑ Light sensors used to control lighting

   ❑ Motion sensors used to detect the presence of people or vehicles

   ❑ Water sensors used to detect water leaks

   ❑ Water flow-rate sensors used to monitor and detect undetected and invisible water leaks

   ❑ Hazardous-gas sensors used to detect dangerous gases

Hardware and Peripherals

Depending on the size of the home and required system functions, the home automation system may be designed with multiple controllers. Typically, most home automation systems have one main controller interfacing to different peripherals.

We will use the following commercially available, low-cost hardware to work through the exercises in this chapter:

❑ eBox-4300-MSJK as the master controller

❑ Phidget devices

The eBox-4300-MSJK

The eBox-4300-MSJK is a 500-MHz compact computing device, with the common features found on a typical computer, as shown in Figure 17-1.

Figure 17-1

The eBox-4300-MSJK configured with CE is used as the master controller for the home automation control system. The three USB interfaces and two serial ports available on an eBox-4300-MSJK interface to input and output devices provide the mechanism to perform automation control functions. The Ethernet network interface, linking to the Local Area Network (LAN) or Internet, provides the connectivity to take advantage of networking and web technologies and enable the system to be controlled and accessed via the network link. The application providing system intelligence runs and resides on the eBox-4300-MSJK.

Below, we will work through the exercises to create an OS design for the eBox-4300-MSJK, including library components to support the Phidget devices, generate an SDK to support VS2005 application development for the system, and create sample applications.

Phidget Devices

Phidget devices are low-cost sensing and control devices, interfacing to the computing hardware through the USB port. These devices are designed with the programmer in mind. The Phidget device driver and software library abstract the hardware layer interface and provide a simple and easy-to-use framework library. The Phidget Framework library is able to support application development using both managed and native code within the VS2005 IDE.

Support libraries for Phidget devices are available for CE and desktop Windows. The latest version of the Phidget Framework requires the .NET Compact Framework 2.0 and later to function.

The Phidget family of I/O devices consists of many interesting and cost-efficient devices. For the exercises in this chapter, we will use the following devices to interface with the eBox-4300-MSJK:

❑ **1203–PhidgetTextLCD** — The PhidgetTextLCD module functions as one of the primary devices interfacing to the eBox-4300-MSJK through the USB port. It has a two-line character LCD screen, eight analog inputs, and eight digital I/Os that can be configured as inputs or outputs. It captures status on the analog and digital I/O and communicates with the host controller through the USB interface. Figure 17-2 shows the front and back view for the PhidgetTextLCD module.

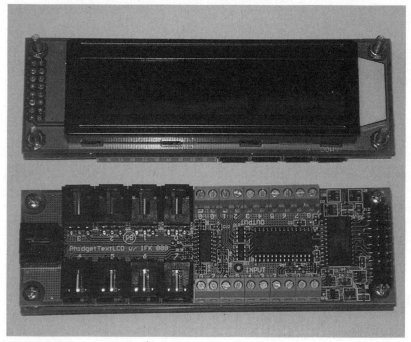

Figure 17-2

❑ **1114–Temperature Sensor** — The temperature sensor, as shown in Figure 17-3, is attached to one of the analog inputs on the PhidgetTextLCD module. Input from the temperature sensor is used to turn the heating and air-conditioning units on or off.

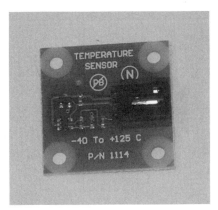

Figure 17-3

❑ **1105–Light Sensor** — The light sensor, as shown in Figure 17-4, is attached to one of the analog inputs on the PhidgetTextLCD module. Input from the light sensor is used to turn the lighting on or off.

Figure 17-4

❑ **1111–Motion Sensor** — The motion sensor, as shown in Figure 17-5, is attached to one of the analog inputs on the PhidgetTextLCD module. Input from the sensor is used to detect when one or more persons are present, and can be used to turn on the light and trigger other controls.

Figure 17-5

❑ **1101–IR Distance Sensor** — The IR distance sensor, as shown in Figure 17-6, is attached to one of the analog inputs on the PhidgetTextLCD module. Input from the distance sensor can be useful in the garage as a parking guidance device for a vehicle. For vehicles entering the garage, the sensor can be set to detect when the vehicle is in the proper position to allow the garage door to close and to trigger an indicator light telling the driver to stop.

Figure 17-6

❑ **1014–PhidgetInterfaceKit 0/0/4** — The PhidgetInterfaceKit 0/0/4, as shown in Figure 17-7, interfaces to the eBox-4300-MSJK's USB port and has four relays on board that can be used to switch appliances, lighting, and other devices on or off.

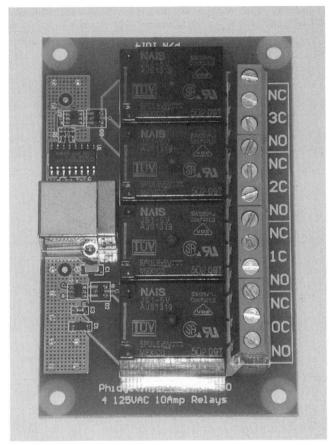

Figure 17-7

To get more information about the above and other Phidget devices, visit this web site:

    www.phidgets.com/

BSP and Software Library

In addition to VS2005 and CE 6.0 R2, the following software libraries need to be installed in the development workstation in order to work through the exercises in this chapter:

- ❏ **ICOP_eBox4300_60E.msi** — This is the CE 6.0 BSP for the eBox-4300-MSJK.

- ❏ **VS2005_CoreCon_x86_WINCE600.msi** — This is the installation file for the CoreCon connection framework. This component is needed to establish a connection between the development workstation and eBox-4300-MSJK for application deployment from the VS2005 IDE.

- ❏ **PhidgetFramework_V214_Library.msi** — This is an installation library to install the Phidget Framework driver for CE 6.0. The Phidget driver for CE is developed as a shared-source project on Codeplex. The source code for the driver is available for download from the following URL:

    www.codeplex.com/PhidgetsWinCEDriver

When developing managed-code smart device applications using the PhidgetFramework library, references are added to this library. For this we need to know the PhidgetFramework installation location. The PhidgetFramework_V214_Library.msi was created for the exercises in this book. The binary files are installed to the following directory:

C:\WINCE600\PUBLIC\PHIDGETFRAMEWORK_V214\PHIDGETBINARIES

> **The CE 6.0 BSP for eBox-4300-MSJK and the CoreCon connection framework component is available for download from** www.embeddedpc.net/ce6book/.

Electronic 101 for Input and Output

There are different types of input and output (I/O) interfaces for an embedded computing system. The wired and wireless network interface is used to send and receive data, the USB interface is used to attach to external storage devices and I/O peripherals, and the VGA interface is used to output video signals to display on the monitor. Keyboard and mouse interfaces are used to capture user input.

For the typical home automation control system, the primary I/Os used to control and capture inputs from home automation-related devices are digital and analog I/Os.

This is a simple 101 introduction to input and output used for automation control. Basically, there are two types of I/O — digital and analog.

Digital Input and Output

A *digital input signal* has two possible states, low and high, and can be used to represent the on and off status for a device. A *digital output signal* has the same two possible states. In electronics terms, these two states translate to 0 V (volts) and 5 V or 0 V and 3.3 V Transistor to Transistor Logic (TTL) level signal for most systems.

> **Most digital and analog I/Os on the embedded computing board are designed using a TTL-level signal interface. This low voltage and low current interface can easily be damaged when not handled correctly. Do not connect devices to I/O interfaces without confirming the signal, voltage, and current compatibilities. Otherwise, it will cause irreversible damage.**

For the home automation system, the digital I/O is typically used as follows:

❑ The digital input is linked to window and door sensors to detect whether each of the windows and doors is open or closed. One digital input interface is needed for each door or window.

❑ Interfacing to a relay, the digital output can control the on and off status of a device, such as the heater, air-conditioning unit, lights, and swimming pool pump.

Analog Input and Output

An analog input has much wider possible value than digital input, depending on the accuracy of the input represented by the number of bits. When used to capture data from the same sensor, an analog input with 10-bit resolution can capture more accurate data than an 8-bit resolution input.

While an analog sensor input with 8-bit resolution can measure the sensor values in 256 different increments, the 10-bit resolution sensor can measure sensor values in 1,024 different increments.

Using an 8-bit analog input to measure a voltage input ranging from 0 V to 120 V, we can measure the input voltage in 256 steps, at 0.46875 of a volt increment for each step.

Using a 10-bit analog input to measure the same voltage input above, we can measure the input voltage in 1,024 steps. At 0.1172 of a volt increment for each step, the 10-bit input is much more accurate than the 8-bit input.

Home automation systems do not require high-precision measurement. An 8-bit analog input is more than sufficient.

For home automation control applications, the analog input is linked to sensors with varying inputs, such as the temperature sensor, humidity sensor, and gas sensor.

The eBoxPhidget OS Design

Before we can develop a CE application, we need to have the CE design and runtime image and generate the SDK to support application development. In this section, we will work through the following steps to create the necessary components to support application development for this chapter:

1. Create an OS design with support for the Phidget devices.
2. Configure and download the runtime image to eBox-4300-MSJK.
3. Generate an SDK from the OS design project to support application development.
4. Create sample VB2005 applications to access different Phidget devices.

Development Environment

For the exercises in this section, the development workstation and eBox-4300-MSJK are connected to the same local area network with DHCP service to assign IP addresses dynamically. The PhidgetTextLCD and PhidgetInterfaceKit 0/0/4 are attached to the eBox-4300-MSJK's USB port. The light, motion, and temperature sensors are attached to the PhidgetTextLCD's analog inputs.

Creating the OS Design

In this section, we will work through the following steps to create an OS design project for the eBox-4300-MSJK, using the ICOP_eBox4300_60E BSP. After the initial project is created, we will configure the project and include additional components to support the Phidget devices and VS2005 application development.

1. From the VS2005 IDE, select File ⇨ New ⇨ Project to bring up the New Project screen.

2. From the Project type selection on the left pane, select the Platform Builder for CE 6.0 option.

3. From the Templates selection on the right pane, select the OS Design option.

4. Enter eBoxPhidget as the project name, and click OK to bring up the OS Design Wizard screen.

5. From the initial wizard screen, click Next to bring up the BSP selection screen.

6. Select ICOP_eBox4300_60E: X86, and click Next to bring up the Design Templates screen.

7. Select Industrial Device, and click Next to bring up the Design Template Variants screen.

8. Select Internet Appliance, and click Next to bring up the Application Media selection screen.

> For the exercises in this chapter, the Internet Browser and multimedia components are not needed and can be removed to build a smaller footprint image. A smaller footprint image helps shorten the boot-up time.

9. Keep the default selection, and click Next to bring up the Networking Communication selection screen.

> In addition to the device driver for the wireless hardware, the Wireless Local Area Network (802.11) component is needed to support the wireless networking features.

10. Keep the default selection, and click Next to bring up the final Wizard screen.

11. From the final OS Design Wizard screen, click Finish.

12. The Security Warning screen is raised to warn that a potential security issue may be caused by the NDIS User-mode I/O Protocol Driver. Click Acknowledge to continue.

At this point, the initial eBoxPhidget OS design project is created.

Additional Needed Components

The OS design needs additional components for the filesystem and application deployment, and to support the Phidget devices. From the Catalog Items View window, locate and add the following components to the project:

- ❑ **VIA CN/CX Display Driver** — Display driver for eBox-4300.

- ❑ **CAB File Installer/Uninstaller** — Provides support to deploy applications from the VS2005 IDE.

- ❑ **RAM and ROM File System** — Provides file storage for the object store in RAM and provides access to ROM.

- ❑ **Hive-Based Registry** — Stores registry data inside files that can be kept on any filesystem and removes the need to perform backup and restore when the device goes through power reset.

- ❑ **PhidgetFrameWork_V214** — Provides device driver support for the Phidget devices.

- ❑ **VS2005_CoreCon_X86_WINCE600** — Provides the CoreCon connection framework needed to establish a connection between the VS2005 development workstation and the eBox-4300-MSJK running CE.

- ❑ **AutoLaunch** — Provides the utility to launch one or more applications when CE starts.

- ❑ **Remote Display Application** — The Remote Display Application is similar to the Remote Desktop for desktop Windows. With this component, we can access the CE's desktop remotely over the Local Area Network.

- ❑ **USB Storage Class Driver** — With this driver loaded, CE is able to read and write to external USB storage devices from different manufacturers. With this feature, we can copy files, using portable USB flash storage, to and from the eBox-4300-MSJK with CE running.

Configuring the Registry

The registry is one of the important system components controlling how the OS launches the components included in the runtime image. We need to configure the Autolaunch registry to launch the CoreCon connection framework needed to support application deployment from the VS2005 IDE.

Go through the following steps to configure the Autolaunch registry:

1. From the VS2005 IDE, click Solution Explorer tab.

2. From the Solution Explorer window, expand the Parameter Files folder.

3. From the Parameter Files folder, expand the ICOP_eBox4300_60E: x86 folder and double-click on the project.reg file to view the file in the Editor window, in the center pane.

4. From the Editor window, click on the Source icon, on the lower left of the Editor window, to view the file in source-code format.

5. Append the following registry entries to the project.reg file:

```
[HKEY_LOCAL_MACHINE\Startup]
    "Process1"="Cerdisp -c"
    "Process2Delay"=dword:00001388
    "Process2"="ConmanClient2.exe"
    "Process2Delay"=dword:0
```

The above registry entries configure the Autolaunch utility to launch the `cerdisp.exe` (Remote Display Application) and `conmanclien2.exe` (CoreCon connection framework) needed to establish a connection between the development workstation and eBox-4300-MSJK for application deployment.

Configuring the Build Option and Build

Before building the project to generate the runtime image, we need to configure the Build options. Go through the following steps to configure these:

1. From the VS2005 IDE, select Build ⇨ Configuration Manager to bring up the Configuration Manager screen.

2. From the Configuration Manager screen, select ICOP_eBox4300_60E x86 Release as the "Active solution configuration," and click Close.

3. From the VS2005 IDE, select Project ⇨ eBoxPhidget Properties to bring up the eBoxPhidget Property Pages.

4. From the eBoxPhidget Property Pages screen, expand the Configuration Properties node and click on the Build Options node to bring up the Build Options page.

5. From the Build Options page, unselect the Enable KITL (no IMGNOKITL=1) option.

6. From the left pane, click on the Environment node to bring up the Environment Variables page.

7. Click New to bring up the new Environment Variable screen, and enter **IMGRAM256** as the variable name and **1** as the variable value, as shown in Figure 17-8.

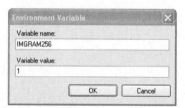

Figure 17-8

8. From the eBoxPhidget Property Pages screen, click Apply followed by OK to save the settings.

9. From the VS2005 IDE, select Build ⇨ Build Solution to build and generate the runtime image.

Target Device Connectivity and Download

After the Build process is completed, go through the following steps to configure the target device connectivity and download the runtime image to the eBox-4300-MSJK target device:

1. From the VS2005 IDE, select Target ➪ Connectivity Options to bring up the Target Device Connectivity Options screen.

2. Select Ethernet for both the Download and Transport selections and KdStub for the Debugger selection, as shown in Figure 17-9.

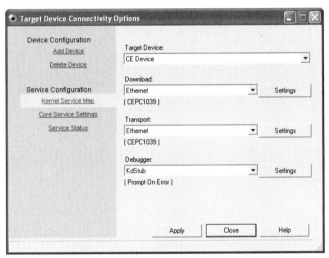

Figure 17-9

3. Click Apply followed by Close.

4. From the VS2005 IDE, select Target ➪ Attach Device to initiate the image download process and bring up the Download Runtime Image to CE Device, as shown in Figure 17-10. Wait for the bootme message from eBox-4300-MSJK.

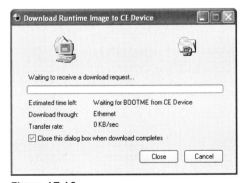

Figure 17-10

341

5. Power up the eBox-4300-MSJK, which boots to DOS and launches a selection menu, as shown in Figure 17-11.

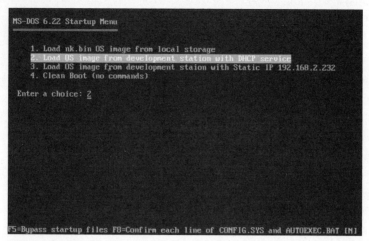

```
MS-DOS 6.22 Startup Menu

   1. Load nk.bin OS image from local storage
   2. Load OS image from development station with DHCP service
   3. Load OS image from development staion with Static IP 192.168.2.232
   4. Clean Boot (no commands)

Enter a choice: 2

F5=Bypass startup files F8=Confirm each line of CONFIG.SYS and AUTOEXEC.BAT [N]
```

Figure 17-11

6. From the eBox-4300-MSJK selection menu, select the second option, loading the OS Image from the development station with DHCP service, to download the runtime image from the development workstation.

After the image is downloaded to eBox-4300-MSJK, CE launches, as shown in Figure 17-12.

Figure 17-12

Configuring and Generating the SDK

In this section, we will configure and generate an SDK for the eBoxPhidget OS design project. Go through the following steps to configure and generate the SDK:

1. From the VS2005 IDE, select Project ⇨ Add New SDK to bring up the SDK Wizard.

2. From the SDK1 Property Pages, enter **eBoxPhidgetSDK** as the SDK name and Product name. Enter **My Company** as the company name and www.mycompany.com as the company web site. Click Apply. The SDK1 Property Pages title changes to "eBoxPhidgetSDK Property Pages."

3. From the left pane, click on the Install node on the right, changing the MSI filename to *eBoxPhidgetSDK.msi*, and click Apply.

4. From the left pane, click on the Development Languages node. On the right, select the checkbox for managed development support, and click Apply followed by OK.

5. From the VS2005 IDE, select Build ⇨ Build All SDKs to build and generate the SDK.

Installing the eBoxPhidgetSDK

After the Build process is completed, the eBoxPhidgetSDK is generated in the following directory:

C:\WINCE600\OSDESIGNS\EBOXPHIDGET\EBOXPHIDGET\SDKS\SDK1\MSI

Close the VS2005 IDE. Navigate to the above directory and double-click on eboxphidgetsdk.msi to install the SDK.

Home Automation Applications

With the runtime image generated from the eBoxPhidget OS design and the eBoxPhidgetSDK generated and installed, we'll move into the next phase to create sample applications for the Phidget devices.

As technologies evolve and new products become available, more technical resources and options are available to develop intelligent home automation applications. For instance, wireless connectivity technologies such as Bluetooth, IrDA, Wi-Fi, ZigBee, and Z-Wave provide cable replacement, remote control, and wireless networking functions that help ease installation challenges and lower overall system costs while enhancing user experience.

In this section, we will work through several short sample applications using different Phidget devices, showing how to write VB2005 code to access the devices and deploy the applications to the eBox-4300-MSJK with the Phidget devices attached for testing.

Temperature Sensor Application

All Phidget sensors are attached to the PhidgetTextLCD module's analog inputs. The application development processes for different Phidget sensors are very similar.

We will develop a VB2005 smart device application to read the temperature sensor value attached to one of the PhidgetTextLCD's analog inputs. The PhidgetTextLCD module is attached to the eBox-4300-MSJK through the USB port. The 1114–Temperature Sensor is attached to port 0 on the PhidgetTextLCD's analog input ports.

Let's go through the following steps in the exercise:

1. Launch a new instance of the VS2005 IDE, and call this instance the *Phidget VS2005 IDE*.

2. From the VS2005 IDE, select File ⇨ New ⇨ Project to bring up the New Project Wizard screen.

3. From the New Project screen's left pane, click and expand the Other Languages node.

4. Click and expand the Visual Basic node followed by the Smart Device node, and click on Windows CE 5.0.

> **A Smart Device application generated with the Windows CE 5.0 Smart Device application template can run on Window CE 5.0 and Windows Embedded CE 6.0.**

5. From the New Project screen's right pane, click Device Application.

6. Enter **VBTempSensor** as the project name, and click OK to continue.

7. The VS2005 New Project Wizard automatically creates the initial project files.

Along with the new project created by the wizard, the form1.vb is created by default with mainMenu1 MainMenu control added. Since the mainMenu1 control is not needed, right-click on the mainMenu1 control and select Delete to remove it.

Go through the following steps to configure the VBTempSensor project and add additional controls to Form1:

1. To use the PhidgetFrameWork library, we need to add references to the library. Select Project ⇨ Add References from the VS2005 IDE to bring up the Add Reference screen.

2. From the Add Reference screen, click on the Browse tab and navigate to the following directory: C:\WINCE600\PUBLIC\PHIDGETFRAMEWORK_V214\PHIDGETBINARIES.

3. Select the Phidget21CE.NET.dll file and click OK to continue.

4. Place a Label control on Form1, and change the Text property to Temperature.

5. Place a second Label control and position the control to the right of the first Label control, and change the control name to *labelTemp*.

6. Place a Button control on Form1. Change the control name to btnRefresh and change the Text property to Refresh.

7. Change the width and height for Form1 to **300** and **200**, respectively.

8. Place a third Label control on Form1. Change both the label's control name and Text property to *labelStatus*. The Text property helps identify the label control's intended function and will be blanked out in the Form1's load event.

9.   Position the third Label control, labelStatus, on the lower edge of Form1. Change the size to fit Form1's entire width and the TextAlign property to TopCenter.

10.   Change the Text property for Form1 to read **Phidget Temperature Sensor**.

After the above steps, the design view for FORM should look like Figure 17-13.

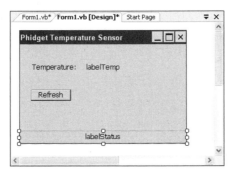

Figure 17-13

Next, go through the following steps to add code:

1.   Right-click on Form1 and select View Code to bring up the Code Editor window.

2.   Enter the following lines of code to define new Phidget InterfaceKit and TextLCD objects. The `bool_PhidgetIOAttached` variable is used to keep track of the `m_PhidgetIO` status, using the Boolean value to show whether the device is attached.

```
Public Class Form1
    Dim WithEvents m_PhidgetIO As Phidgets.InterfaceKit
    Dim WithEvents m_PhidgetLCD As Phidgets.TextLCD
    Dim bool_PhidgetIOAttached As Boolean
    .
    .
    .
```

3.   Add the following code to the Form1's load event to create a new instance of the `m_PhidgetIO` and `m_PhidgetLCD` objects:

```
Private Sub Form1_Load(ByVal sender As System.Object, ByVal e As System.EventArgs)
Handles MyBase.Load
    '
    m_PhidgetIO = New Phidgets.InterfaceKit
    m_PhidgetIO.open()
    '
    m_PhidgetLCD = New Phidgets.TextLCD
    m_PhidgetLCD.open()
    '
    labelTemp.Text = ""
    '
End Sub
```

4. Because of the way the Phidget Framework uses threading and the way the .NET Compact Framework is designed, the following Delegate helper function is needed to display text to the labelStatus label control. Add the following code to Form1:

```
Protected Delegate Sub PrintGUI_delegate(ByVal arg As String)
Private Sub PrintGUI(ByVal arg As String)
        labelStatus.Text = arg
End Sub
```

5. Add the following code for the PhidgetTextLCD's attach event, display the status on Form1's labelStatus label control, and update the LCD on the PhidgetTextLCD module. Add the following code to Form1:

```
Private Sub PhidgetIO_Attach(ByVal sender As Object, ByVal e As
Phidgets.Events.AttachEventArgs) Handles m_PhidgetIO.Attach
        'Initialize relevant properties
        m_PhidgetIO.outputs(0) = False
        m_PhidgetIO.ratiometric = True
        '
        bool_PhidgetIOAttached = True
        '
    End Sub

    Private Sub PhidgetLCD_Attach(ByVal sender As Object, ByVal e As
Phidgets.Events.AttachEventArgs) Handles m_PhidgetLCD.Attach
        '
        m_PhidgetLCD.rows.Item(0).DisplayString = "VB2005 CE 6.0 App"
        m_PhidgetLCD.rows.Item(1).DisplayString = "Temperature Sensor"
        '
        Dim s As String = "Attached: " + e.Device.Name + " " +
e.Device.SerialNumber.ToString()
        Me.Invoke(New PrintGUI_delegate(AddressOf PrintGUI), s)
        '
End Sub
```

Although the PhidgetTextLCD is physically one single module, the Phidget Framework is written as different classes. Each class provides a different set of functions. The PhidgetInterfaceKit and PhidgetTextLCD are two different sets of functions. Both of the above two attached events will take place when the PhidgetTextLCD module is detected.

6. Add the following code for PhidgetTextLCD's detach event, update the labelStatus label control on Form1, and update the value for the bool_PhidgetIOAttached variable.

```
Private Sub PhidgetLCD_Detach(ByVal sender As Object, ByVal e As
Phidgets.Events.DetachEventArgs) Handles m_PhidgetLCD.Detach
        '
        Dim s As String = "Detached: " + e.Device.Name + " " +
e.Device.SerialNumber.ToString()
        Me.Invoke(New PrintGUI_delegate(AddressOf PrintGUI), s)
        '
    End Sub

    Private Sub PhidgetIO_Detach(ByVal sender As Object, ByVal e As
```

```
Phidgets.Events.DetachEventArgs) Handles m_PhidgetIO.Detach
    '
        bool_PhidgetIOAttached = False
    '
End Sub
```

7. Add the following code to the btnRefresh Button control's click event to read the temperature sensor attached to the PhidgetTextLCD.

```
Private Sub btnRefresh_Click(ByVal sender As System.Object, ByVal e As
System.EventArgs) Handles btnRefresh.Click
    '
        Dim temp As Double
    '
        If bool_PhidgetIOAttached Then
            ' Read sensor data from port 0
            temp = m_PhidgetIO.sensors(0).Value
            ' Convert value to temperature and display thru
            ' labelTemp
            temp = (temp / 1000 * 222.22)
            labelTemp.Text = temp.ToString
            '
            m_PhidgetLCD.rows.Item(0).DisplayString = "Current Temperature:"
            m_PhidgetLCD.rows.Item(1).DisplayString = temp.ToString
            '
        Else
            MessageBox.Show("PhidgetInterfaceKit Module is not available.",
"Missing Phidget Device")
        End If
    '
End Sub
```

8. Add the following code to the Form1_Closing event to destroy the event handles and terminate the instances of Phidget objects:

```
Private Sub Form1_Closing(ByVal sender As System.Object, ByVal e As
System.ComponentModel.CancelEventArgs) Handles MyBase.Closing
        RemoveHandler m_PhidgetIO.Attach, AddressOf PhidgetIO_Attach
        RemoveHandler m_PhidgetIO.Detach, AddressOf PhidgetIO_Detach

        RemoveHandler m_PhidgetLCD.Attach, AddressOf PhidgetLCD_Attach
        RemoveHandler m_PhidgetLCD.Detach, AddressOf PhidgetLCD_Detach

        m_PhidgetIO.close()
        m_PhidgetLCD.close()
End Sub
```

9. From the VS2005 IDE, select Build ⇨ Build Solution to build and generate the binary executable.

Preparing eBox-4300-MSJK for Application Deployment

As part of any application development project, we don't expect to get things done right the very first try. The application development process involves trial and error. To put together a more efficient application development environment, let's deploy the OS runtime image created above in this chapter onto the eBox-4300-MSJK. Otherwise, we would have to keep two separate instances of the VS2005 IDE running and would need to download the runtime image from the eBoxPhidget OS design project to eBox-4300-MSJK in order to deploy the VBTempSensor application in this section.

We will use a USB portable flash storage to copy the nk.bin image file from the development workstation to eBox-4300-MSJK. To do this, the eBox-4300-MSJK needs to have one of the CE runtime images built with the USB Storage Class Driver component in order to be able to read from the USB portable flash storage. During the OS design configuration phase, we added the USB Storage Class Driver to the OS design. The resulting runtime image is able to read from the USB storage device.

Go through the following steps to copy the OS runtime image file, nk.bin, to the eBox-4300-MSJK's local storage:

1. If you don't already have the eBoxPhidget OS design project open, launch a new instance of the VS2005 IDE and open this project. Then download the runtime image generated from this project to eBox-4300-MSJK.

2. The runtime image, nk.bin, from the eBoxPhidget OS design is generated in the following directory:

_EBOXPHIDGET\RELDIR\ICOP_EBOX4300_60E_X86_RELEASE

_EBOXPHIDGET=C:\WINCE600\OSDESIGNS\EBOXPHIDGET\EBOXPHIDGET

---

3. Copy the nk.bin file from the above directory to a portable USB flash storage drive. This file is about 18 MB in size.

4. From the eBox-4300-MSJK Windows desktop, with the CE run time from the eBoxPhidget project running, double-click on the MyDevice icon to launch the file explorer and access the root of the filesystem. The default view setting hides the file extension. The NK file is the runtime image file.

5. Insert the USB flash storage device into one of the USB ports on the eBox-4300-MSJK. It takes just a second or two for CE to detect the USB flash storage's presence and display the USB Storage icon, as shown in Figure 17-14.

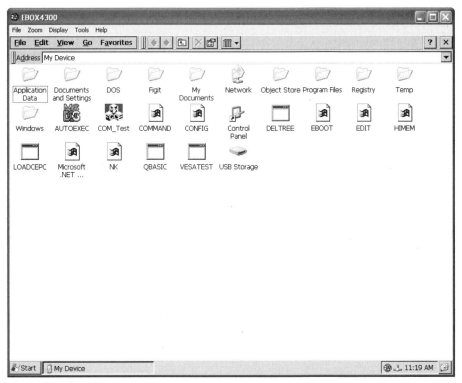

Figure 17-14

6. Use the same routine as you commonly use from desktop Windows to copy a file. Copy the nk.bin file from the USB storage device onto the eBox-4300-MSJK's root filesystem, overwriting the existing nk.bin file.

> The file-copying process may take a few minutes to finish.

7. With the OS runtime image file copied to eBox-4300-MSJK's local storage, we eliminated the need to download the runtime image to eBox-4300-MSJK.

After the nk.bin file is copied to eBox-4300-MSJK's local storage, reset the power. When eBox-4300-MSJK boots up to the DOS selection menu, select the first option to launch the image file from the local storage.

Remote Display Application

During the OS design configuration phase, we added the Remote Display Application (RDA) component to the OS design. The RDA works just like the Remote Desktop available with desktop Windows.

The cerhost.exe application needed to access the RDA is provided as part of the CE installation in the following directory:

C:\WINCE600\PUBLIC\COMMON\OAK\BIN\I386

To access the RDA on eBox-4300-MSJK with CE running, go through the following steps:

1. Locate the cerhost.exe and double-click to launch this application to bring up the Remote Display Control for Windows CE, as shown in Figure 17-15.

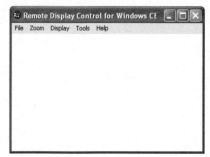

Figure 17-15

2. Select File ⇨ Connect to bring up the Connect screen. When the eBoxPhidget runtime image is launched on eBox-4300-MSJK, the eBox4300 device will show in the "Active target devices," as shown in Figure 17-16.

Figure 17-16

3. From the "Active target devices" window, click to highlight the listed device, and click OK to establish a connection.

After the connection is established, the RDA Application screen pops up, showing the CE desktop from the eBox-4300-MSJK.

Initially, we need to have a display monitor attached to the eBox-4300-MSJK for the development environment to develop the OS runtime image.

After a stable runtime image is created, we can add the Remote Display Application component to the runtime image and the Autolaunch utility to launch the Remote Display Application when the runtime image starts, thus eliminating the need to use a monitor for the eBox-4300-MSJK. Using the Remote Display Application, we can redirect eBox-4300-MSJK's display to the development workstation's display and help save precious desktop or workbench space.

Deploying Applications to eBox-4300-MSJK

We will use the CoreCon connection framework to deploy applications from the VS2005 IDE to the eBox-4300-MSJK. To accomplish this, we need to identify the eBox-4300-MSJK's IP address, with CE running, and set this IP address as the target device's IP address from the VS2005 IDE.

Go through the following steps to establish a connection between the VS2005 IDE and eBox-4300-MSJK using the CoreCon connection framework:

1. From the CE desktop running on eBox-4300-MSJK, double-click on the network icon on the CE desktop's taskbar to bring up the PCI\RTL81391 IP Information screen, as shown in Figure 17-17.

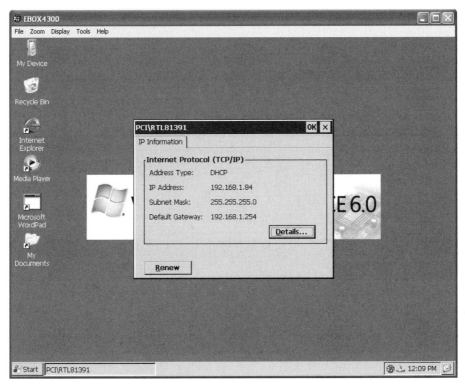

Figure 17-17

2. Record the IP address settings for the eBox-4300-MSJK.

Next, we need to configure the CoreCon connection framework for the Phidget VS2005 IDE to connect to the eBox-4300-MSJK.

1. From the Phidget VS2005 IDE, select Tools ➪ Options to bring up the Options screen.

2. From the Options screen's left pane, expand the Device Tools node and click on the Devices node.

3. From the "Show devices for platform" selection, select eBoxPhidgetSDK, as shown in Figure 17-18.

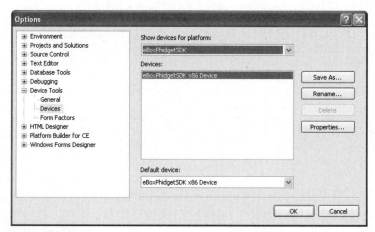

Figure 17-18

4. From the Options screen, click Properties to bring up the eBoxPhidgetSDK x86 Device Properties screen, as shown in Figure 17-19.

Figure 17-19

5. From the eBoxPhidgetSDK x86 Device Properties screen, click Configure to bring up the Configure TCP/IP Transport screen, and enter the IP address for eBox-4300-MSJK, as shown in Figure 17-20.

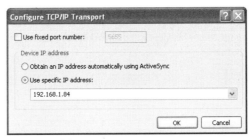

Figure 17-20

6. After the IP address for eBox-4300-MSJK is entered, click OK to close the Configure TCP/IP Transport screen.

7. Click OK to close the eBoxPhidgetSDK x86 Device Properties screen.

8. Click OK to close the Options screen.

9. From the VS2005 IDE, select Project ⇨ Change Target Platform to bring up the Change Target Platform screen.

10. From the Change Target Platform screen, select eBoxPhidgetSDK from the "Change to" selection, as shown in Figure 17-21.

Figure 17-21

11. From the Change Target Platform screen, click OK to accept the change. A Microsoft Visual Studio message box will show; click Yes to accept. The project will close and reopen with the new settings.

12. From the VS2005 IDE, select Tools ⇨ Connect to Device to bring up the Connect to Device screen, as shown in Figure 17-22.

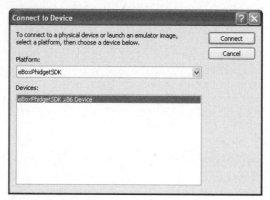

Figure 17-22

13. From the Connect to Device screen, click Connect. Upon successful connection, the Connecting screen shows the "Connection succeeded" message, as shown in Figure 17-23.

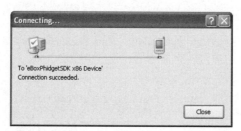

Figure 17-23

14. Click Close to close the Connecting screen.

With the CoreCon connection framework connected, we can deploy the VBTempSensor application to the eBox-4300-MSJK. In the event the connection is lost, select Tools ⇨ Connect to Device from the VS2005 IDE to reconnect.

Go through the following steps to deploy the VBTempSensor application to eBox-4300-MSJK:

1. From the VS2005 IDE, select Debug ⇨ Start Without Debugging to bring up the Deploy VBTempSensor screen, as shown in Figure 17-24.

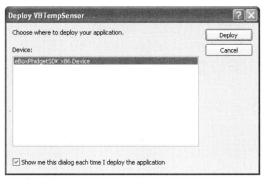

Figure 17-24

2. From the Deploy VBTempSensor screen, click Deploy to deploy the application to eBox-4300-MSJK. The application will launch on the CE desktop on eBox-4300-MSJK, as shown in Figure 17-25.

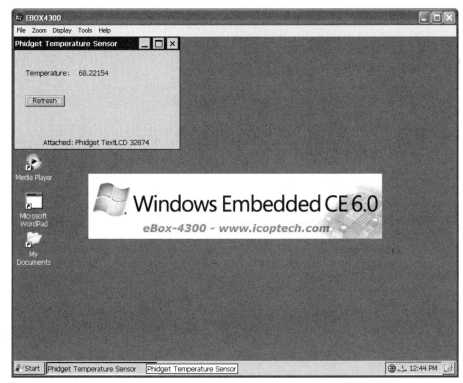

Figure 17-25

To deploy the application, and be able to step through the code when a pre-set breakpoint is reached, use the Start Debugging option instead of the Start Without Debugging option.

Phidget Relay Switching Application

Continuing from the previous section and using the same VBTempSensor application, we will add code to control a relay to the project.

Go through the following steps to add the code:

1. Place a CheckBox control on Form1. Change the Text property to "Relay control," and change the Name property to chkboxRelay, as shown in Figure 17-26.

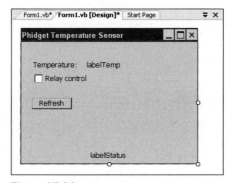

Figure 17-26

2. Double-click on the chkboxRelay checkbox control to bring up the Code Editor window and view the code in the chkboxRelay_CheckStateChanged event, and add the following code:

```
Private Sub chkboxRelay_CheckStateChanged(ByVal sender As System.Object, ByVal e As
System.EventArgs) Handles chkboxRelay.CheckStateChanged
        '
        If chkboxRelay.Checked Then
            '
            m_PhidgetIO.outputs(2) = True
            '
        Else
            '
            m_PhidgetIO.outputs(2) = False
            '
        End If
        '
End Sub
```

With the application running, when clicking on the chkbox_Relay control, the above code will execute and switch the associated digital output signal high or low, to engage or disengage the relay.

Compile the code to generate an updated application executable to deploy and test the function.

Other Phidget Sensors

As we pointed out above in the "Temperature Sensor Application" section, all Phidget sensors are attached to the PhidgetTextLCD module's analog inputs. The application development processes for different Phidget sensors are very similar.

In this section, we will continue to use the existing VBTempSensor application and add additional code to capture input from the light and motion sensors.

Go through the following steps to add the code to the project:

1. Place a Label control on Form1, and change the Text property to Light Sensor.

2. Place another Label control on Form1. Position this label control horizontally next to the Light Sensor label above, and change the Name property to labelLight.

3. Place another Label control on Form1, and change the Text property to Motion Sensor.

4. Place another Label control on Form1. Position this label control horizontally next to the Motion Sensor label above, and change the Name property to labelMotion.

5. Place another Label control on Form1. Position this label on the topmost part of Form1, and change the Name property to labelTime.

6. Place a Checkbox control on Form1. Position this control horizontally next to the Refresh button. Change the Name property to chkboxAuto.

7. Add a Timer control to the project.

After the above steps, organize the control on Form1 similar to Figure 17-27.

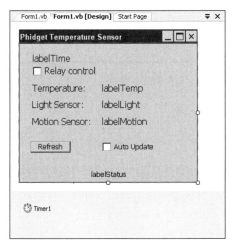

Figure 17-27

Go through the following steps to add code to the project:

1. Add the following code to the Form1_Load event to initial display for the label controls and the Timer1:

```
        labelTime.Text = ""
        labelLight.Text = ""
        labelMotion.Text = ""
        '
  Timer1.interval=1000
        Timer1.Enabled = True
```

2. Add the following Delegate helper function to display captured sensor data to the label control:

```
Protected Delegate Sub PrintGUI_Temp_delegate(ByVal arg As String)
Private Sub PrintGUI_Temp(ByVal arg As String)
        labelTemp.Text = arg
End Sub

Protected Delegate Sub PrintGUI_Light_delegate(ByVal arg As String)
Private Sub PrintGUI_Light(ByVal arg As String)
        labelLight.Text = arg
End Sub

Protected Delegate Sub PrintGUI_Motion_delegate(ByVal arg As String)
Private Sub PrintGUI_Motion(ByVal arg As String)
        labelMotion.Text = arg
End Sub
```

3. Add the following code to the btnRefresh Button control's click event, btnRefresh_Click:

```
' Read sensor data from port 1 - Light sensor
temp = m_PhidgetIO.sensors(1).Value
  labelLight.Text = temp.ToString
'
' Read sensor data from port 1 - Motion sensor
temp = m_PhidgetIO.sensors(2).Value
labelMotion.Text = temp.ToString
```

4. Add the following code to the Timer1_Tick event:

```
Private Sub Timer1_Tick(ByVal sender As System.Object, ByVal e As System.EventArgs)
Handles Timer1.Tick
        '
        Dim dt As Date = DateTime.Now
        Dim s As String
        Dim temp As Double
        '
        s = dt.ToString("G")
        Me.Invoke(New PrintGUI_Time_delegate(AddressOf PrintGUI_Time), s)
        '
```

```
        If bool_PhidgetIOAttached Then
            If chkboxAuto.Checked Then
                temp = m_PhidgetIO.sensors(0).Value
                ' Convert value to temperature and display thru
                ' labelTemp
                temp = (temp / 1000 * 222.22)
                s = temp.ToString
                Me.Invoke(New PrintGUI_Temp_delegate(AddressOf PrintGUI_Temp), s)
                '
                ' Read sensor data from port 1 - Light sensor
                temp = m_PhidgetIO.sensors(1).Value
                If temp < 180 Then
                    chkboxRelay.Checked = True
                Else
                    chkboxRelay.Checked = False
                End If
                s = temp.ToString
                Me.Invoke(New PrintGUI_Light_delegate(AddressOf PrintGUI_Light), s)
                '
                ' Read sensor data from port 1 - Motion sensor
                temp = m_PhidgetIO.sensors(2).Value
                s = temp.ToString
                Me.Invoke(New PrintGUI_Motion_delegate(AddressOf PrintGUI_Motion), s)
                '
                'chkboxRelay


                '
            End If
        End If
        '
End Sub
```

The code in the Timer1_Click event will execute once every second. When the Auto Update checkbox is checked, the code in the Timer1_Click event will capture the temperature, light, and motion sensors data and update the display.

With the Auto Update checkbox checked, and when the light sensor data dips below 180, the following code in the Timer1_Click event will set the chkboxRelay's Checked property to True, which, in turn, will trigger the code in the chkboxRelay_CheckStateChanged event to execute and control the relay by setting the PhidgetTextLCD's digital output connected to the relay.

❑   Code in the Timer1_Click event being executed when the light sensor data dips below 180:

```
        If temp < 180 Then
            chkboxRelay.Checked = True
        Else
            chkboxRelay.Checked = False
        End If
```

❑   Code from the chkboxRelay_CheckStateChanged event:

```
Private Sub chkboxRelay_CheckStateChanged(ByVal sender As System.Object, ByVal e As
System.EventArgs) Handles chkboxRelay.CheckStateChanged

    If chkboxRelay.Checked Then

        m_PhidgetIO.outputs(2) = True

    Else

        m_PhidgetIO.outputs(2) = False

    End If

End Sub
```

5.   Compile the code to generate an updated application executable to deploy and test the added code, to capture additional sensor data, and to check the auto update function.

Summary

In this chapter, using the home automation system as a learning tool, we worked though a series of exercises and created the following:

❑   The eBoxPhidget OS design configured to support I/O peripherals, the Phidget devices, needed for the home automation application exercise.

❑   The VBTempSensor application, using VB2005. We started with a simple project to read the temperature sensor data, and code to control the relay and to automatically read additional sensor data was added.

In addition, we also learned how to use the Remote Display Application and worked through the exercise showing how to place the CE runtime image file into the eBox-4300-MSJK's local storage to help ease the application development process.

Complicated sample applications are difficult to explain and create confusion, defeating the teaching purpose. We worked through the exercises using simple, easy-to-follow examples. Although the sample application is simple, there is more complicated code running as part of CE, the .NET Compact Framework, and Phidget Framework, isolating much of the complexity from the managed-code development environment.

RFID Security Access Control Applications

Working to resolve modern security concerns, the security industry has evolved rapidly to develop more effective and cost-efficient solutions, creating new technologies and improved products and services. Radio Frequency Identification (RFID) is one of these technologies that has gone through tremendous growth and gained widespread global adoption in different segments of industry, government, and academia.

Following the home automation sample applications in the previous chapter, we'll now work through the exercises in this chapter to add RFID applications to the project. The sample application for the exercise in this chapter shows how to interact with the RFID reader using the PhidgetFramework library and can be used as the building block or starting point for a security access control application.

Radio Frequency Identification — RFID

The application potential for RFID technology is huge. We can find RFID tags in the everyday products we purchase, embedded in credit cards, and tracking inventory in warehouses. RFID is part of the employee card for security access control, of contactless payment for mass transit, and of government and academic identification cards. It's even embedded in casino chips. This book is not about RFID and does not go into technical detail about RFID technology. But it will tell you enough for a general idea of the subject.

The RFID tag is like a transponder, responding to the RFID reader's radio frequency and "magically" sending the RFID data to the reader. There are different types of RFID tags working on different frequencies.

The PhidgetRFID Reader

We will use the PhidgetRFID reader for the exercise in this chapter. This is a low-cost reader, working with an RFID tag that uses the EM4102 protocol and can read tags within about 3 inches of its antenna.

The PhidgetRFID reader is 3.25 inches by 2.75 inches in size, as shown in Figure 18-1.

Figure 18-1

The PhidgetRFID reader comes with a USB interface and is powered by the USB port, which we will use to interface with one of the USB ports on the eBox-4300.

RFID Reader Applications

In this section, we will work through an exercise to develop a simple RFID reader application to work with the PhidgetRFID device. We will use the same runtime image generated from the eBoxPhidget OS design in Chapter 17.

Hardware Component for the Application

We will use the following Phidget devices to work through the exercise:

❏   **PhidgetTextLCD** — Provides LCD display to simulate the real environment, where there will not be a computer monitor at each RFID reader.

❏   **Relay Module** — Connects to one of the PhidgetTextLCD module's digital output ports to simulate door lock and unlock functions.

❏   **PhidgetRFID** — Captures data from RFID tag.

❏   **eBox-4300** — Runs CE and functions as the primary controller for the system.

Software Component for the Application

We will create a managed-code application using VB2005. In Chapter 17, the eBoxPhidget OS design was created with the .NET Compact Framework component. In addition, the Phidget Framework was added to support the Phidget devices. Using the same eBoxPhidget OS design, we can start writing the code without having to make any change to the OS design or runtime image.

In Chapter 17, we worked through the process to copy the runtime image from the eBoxPhidget OS design project onto eBox-4300. For this chapter, we just need to power up the eBox-4300 and start writing the program.

Creating the RFIDApp

We will create a new VS2005 application project and name this project *RFIDApp*. After the PhidgetRFID reader has captured the RFID data, this application will compare the data against a list of RFID data stored on the system and display the result.

Let's go through the following steps to create the application:

1. Launch a new instance of the VS2005 IDE, and call this instance *RFID VS2005 IDE*.
2. From the VS2005 IDE, select File ⇨ New ⇨ Project to bring up the New Project Wizard screen.
3. From the New Project screen's left pane, click on and expand the Other Languages node.
4. Click on and expand the Visual Basic node followed by the Smart Device node, and click Windows CE 5.0.
5. From the New Project screen's right pane, click Device Application.
6. Enter **RFIDApp** as the project name, and click OK to continue.
7. The VS2005 New Project Wizard automatically creates the initial project files with the default Form1.

To access the PhidgetRFID reader function, we need to add a reference to the PhidgetFrameWork library. Go through the following steps to add the reference:

1. From the RFID VS2005 IDE, select Project ⇨ Add References to bring up the Add Reference screen.
2. From the Add Reference screen, click on the Browse tab and navigate to the following directory: C:\WINCE600\PUBLIC\PhidgetFrameWork_V214\PhidgetBinaries.
3. Select the Phidget21CE.NET.dll file, and click OK to continue.

Next, go through the following steps to configure and add additional components to the application:

1. Since we don't need the mainMenu1 control, right-click on the mainMenu1 control and select Delete.
2. Change Form1's width and height properties to **390** and **340**, respectively.

3. Add a textbox control to Form1, and use the default control name, *TextBox1*; keep the default Text property, TextBox1. Change the ReadOnly and MultiLine properties to True. Change the ScrollBars property to Vertical. Change the width and height properties to **325** and **215**, respectively. Position the TextBox1 control at about the center on Form1.

4. Add a label control to Form1. Change both the control Name and Text property to *labelTime*, and position this control just above the TextBox1 control, on the left side.

5. Add a label control to Form1. Change both the control Name and Text property to *labelRelay*, and position this control just above the TextBox1 control, on the right side.

6. Add a Button control to Form1. Keep the default control name, *Button1*. Change the button Text property to read **Turn On RFID**. Change the width and height properties to **110** and **20**, respectively. Position this control below the TextBox1 control, on the right side.

7. Add a radio Button control to Form1. Change the control Name to *rbtnNormal*, and change the Text property to Normal mode. Position this control under the TextBox1 control, on the left side.

8. Add a second radio Button control to Form1. Change the control name to *rbtnAdmin*, and change the Text property to Admin mode. Position this control under the other radio Button control, rbtnNorml.

9. Add the Timer control to Form1, and use the default control Name, *Timer1*.

10. Change the Form1's Text property to PhidgetRFID Reader Application, as shown in Figure 18-2.

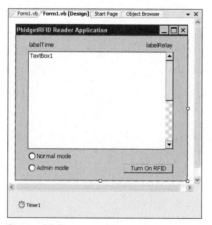

Figure 18-2

Next, go through the following steps to add code to the project:

1. Right-click on Form1 and select View Code to bring up the Code Editor window.

2. Enter the following code to define the Phidget InterfaceKit, TextLCD and RFID objects, and a `bool_Admin` variable for keeping tracking of whether the application is running in Administrative mode.

```
Public Class Form1
    Dim WithEvents m_PhidgetIO As Phidgets.InterfaceKit
    Dim WithEvents m_PhidgetLCD As Phidgets.TextLCD
    Dim WithEvents m_PhidgetRFID As Phidgets.RFID
    Dim bool_Admin As Boolean
    Dim bool_PhidgetIOAttached As Boolean
    Dim bool_PhidgetRFIDAttached As Boolean
    Dim bool_PhidgetRFIDAtennaOn As Boolean
```

3. Add the following code to the Form1's load event to create a new instance of the `m_PhidgetIO`, `m_PhidgetLCD`, and `m_PhidgetRFID` objects, and initialize the controls on the form.

```
Private Sub Form1_Load(ByVal sender As System.Object, ByVal e As System.EventArgs)
Handles MyBase.Load
    '
        bool_Admin = False
        bool_PhidgetIOAttached = False
        bool_PhidgetRFIDAttached = False

        m_PhidgetIO = New Phidgets.InterfaceKit
        m_PhidgetIO.open()
        '
        m_PhidgetLCD = New Phidgets.TextLCD
        m_PhidgetLCD.open()
        '
        m_PhidgetRFID = New Phidgets.RFID
        m_PhidgetRFID.open()
        '
        Dim dt As Date = DateTime.Now
        labelTime.Text = dt.ToString("G")
        '
        labelRelay.Text = "OFF"
        rbtnNormal.Checked = True
        rbtnAdmin.Checked = False
        TextBox1.Text = ""
        '
        Button1.Text = "Turn On RFID"
        '
        Timer1.Interval = 5000
        Timer1.Enabled = True
        '
    End Sub
```

4. Add the following Delegate helper function, needed to update GUI display components:

```
Protected Delegate Sub PrintGUI_delegate(ByVal arg As String)

Private Sub PrintGUI_labelTime(ByVal arg As String)
        labelTime.Text = arg
End Sub

Private Sub PrintGUI_labelRelay(ByVal arg As String)
        labelRelay.Text = arg
End Sub

Private Sub PrintGUI_TextBox1(ByVal arg As String)
        TextBox1.Text = arg + vbNewLine + TextBox1.Text
End Sub
```

5. Add the following code to the Phidget device's attach and detach events to update TextBox1, showing when a device is attached or detached.

```
Private Sub PhidgetRFID_Attach(ByVal sender As Object, ByVal e As
Phidgets.Events.AttachEventArgs) Handles m_PhidgetRFID.Attach
        '
        bool_PhidgetRFIDAttached = True

        Dim s As String = "Attached: " + e.Device.Name + " " +
e.Device.SerialNumber.ToString()
        Me.Invoke(New PrintGUI_delegate(AddressOf PrintGUI_TextBox1), s)
End Sub

Private Sub PhidgetLCD_Attach(ByVal sender As Object, ByVal e As
Phidgets.Events.AttachEventArgs) Handles m_PhidgetLCD.Attach
        '
        m_PhidgetLCD.rows.Item(0).DisplayString = "Windows CE 6.0"
        m_PhidgetLCD.rows.Item(1).DisplayString = "RFID Application"
        '
        Dim s As String = "Attached: " + e.Device.Name + " " +
e.Device.SerialNumber.ToString()
        Me.Invoke(New PrintGUI_delegate(AddressOf PrintGUI_TextBox1), s)
        '
End Sub

Private Sub PhidgetIO_Attach(ByVal sender As Object, ByVal e As
Phidgets.Events.AttachEventArgs) Handles m_PhidgetIO.Attach
        '
        bool_PhidgetIOAttached = True
        m_PhidgetIO.outputs(0) = False
        m_PhidgetIO.ratiometric = True
        '
        bool_PhidgetIOAttached = True
        Dim s As String = "Attached: " + e.Device.Name + " " +
e.Device.SerialNumber.ToString()
        Me.Invoke(New PrintGUI_delegate(AddressOf PrintGUI_TextBox1), s)
```

```
End Sub

Private Sub PhidgetRFID_Detach(ByVal sender As Object, ByVal e As
Phidgets.Events.DetachEventArgs) Handles m_PhidgetRFID.Detach
        '
        bool_PhidgetRFIDAttached = False
        Dim s As String = "Detached: " + e.Device.Name + " " +
e.Device.SerialNumber.ToString()
        Me.Invoke(New PrintGUI_delegate(AddressOf PrintGUI_TextBox1), s)
End Sub

Private Sub PhidgetLCD_Detach(ByVal sender As Object, ByVal e As
Phidgets.Events.DetachEventArgs) Handles m_PhidgetLCD.Detach
        '
        Dim s As String = "Detached: " + e.Device.Name + " " +
e.Device.SerialNumber.ToString()
        Me.Invoke(New PrintGUI_delegate(AddressOf PrintGUI_TextBox1), s)
        '
End Sub

Private Sub PhidgetIO_Detach(ByVal sender As Object, ByVal e As
Phidgets.Events.DetachEventArgs) Handles m_PhidgetIO.Detach
        '
        bool_PhidgetIOAttached = False
        Dim s As String = "Detached: " + e.Device.Name + " " +
e.Device.SerialNumber.ToString()
        Me.Invoke(New PrintGUI_delegate(AddressOf PrintGUI_TextBox1), s)
        '
End Sub
```

6. Add the following code to the Button1_Click event to turn the RFID antenna on and off:

```
Private Sub Button1_Click(ByVal sender As System.Object, ByVal e As
System.EventArgs) Handles Button1.Click
        '
        If Button1.Text = "Turn On RFID" Then
            If bool_PhidgetRFIDAttached Then
                m_PhidgetRFID.Antenna = True
                Button1.Text = "Turn Off RFID"
            End If
        Else
            If bool_PhidgetRFIDAttached Then
                m_PhidgetRFID.Antenna = False
                Button1.Text = "Turn On RFID"
            End If
        End If
        '
End Sub
```

7. Add the following code to the Form1_Closing event to destroy the event handles and terminate active instances of Phidget objects:

```
Private Sub Form1_Closing(ByVal sender As System.Object, ByVal e As
System.ComponentModel.CancelEventArgs) Handles MyBase.Closing
        RemoveHandler m_PhidgetIO.Attach, AddressOf PhidgetIO_Attach
        RemoveHandler m_PhidgetIO.Detach, AddressOf PhidgetIO_Detach

        RemoveHandler m_PhidgetLCD.Attach, AddressOf PhidgetLCD_Attach
        RemoveHandler m_PhidgetLCD.Detach, AddressOf PhidgetLCD_Detach

        RemoveHandler m_PhidgetRFID.Attach, AddressOf PhidgetRFID_Attach
        RemoveHandler m_PhidgetRFID.Detach, AddressOf PhidgetRFID_Detach

        m_PhidgetIO.close()
        m_PhidgetLCD.close()
        m_PhidgetRFID.close()
End Sub
```

8. Add the following code to read the RFID tag from the PhidgetRFID_Tag event. This is the event where the RFID tag's data are captured:

```
Private Sub PhidgetRFID_Tag(ByVal sender As Object, ByVal e As
Phidgets.Events.TagEventArgs) Handles m_PhidgetRFID.Tag
        '
        Dim s As String = "RFID Read: [" + e.Tag + "]"
        Me.Invoke(New PrintGUI_delegate(AddressOf PrintGUI_TextBox1), s)
        '
        Dim s_TagID As String = " + e.Tag + "
        '
        ' s_TagID is the RFID data captured from the PhidgetRFID reader
        '
        If bool_Admin Then
            ' Add code to handle the RFID data in Administrative mode.
            ' Such as, add the RFID data to the user database to grant access
            '
        Else
            ' Add code to handle the RFID data in normal mode.
            ' Such as, search and compare this captured RFID Data
            ' With the user database.
            '
        End If
        '
End Sub
```

9.   Add the following code to the Timer1_Tick event. The Timer1_Tick event is triggered every 5 seconds to update the date and time information on the application screen.

```
Private Sub Timer1_Tick(ByVal sender As System.Object, ByVal e As System.EventArgs)
Handles Timer1.Tick
    '
    Dim dt As Date = DateTime.Now
    Dim s As String
    '
    s = dt.ToString("G")
    Me.Invoke(New PrintGUI_delegate(AddressOf PrintGUI_labelTime), s)
    '
End Sub
```

10.   From the VS2005 IDE, select Build ⇨ Build Solution to build and generate the binary executable for the application.

In Chapter 17, the CE runtime image from the eBoxPhidget OS design was copied onto the eBox-4300 target device. Follow the steps from Chapter 17 to deploy the RFIDApp application to the eBox-4300.

With the application deployed to the eBox-4300, as the Phidget modules are being attached or detached from the eBox-4300, the attached and detached events are logged to the TextBox on the PhidgetRFID Reader Application screen. With the Phidget RFID module attached, as the module detects and reads the RFID tag, the captured RFID information is also logged to the TextBox, as shown in Figure 18-3.

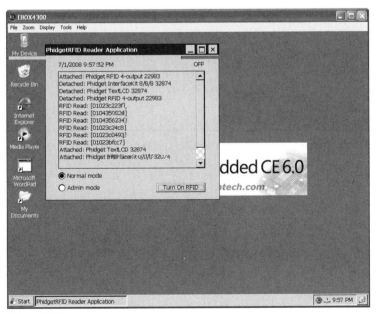

Figure 18-3

On the PhidgetRFID Reader Application screen, the button on the lower right is showing "Turn On RFID," indicating that the Phidget RFID reader's antenna is not enabled. When you click the "Turn On RFID" button, the application enables the Phidget RFID reader's antenna and changes the text caption on the button to "Turn Off RFID." When you click on the button again, the application disables the Phidget RFID reader's antenna and changes the text caption back to "Turn On RFID."

Summary

Continuing from Chapter 17, a simple managed-code application is created in this chapter to read an RFID tag's data using the PhidgetRFID module.

The combination of Windows Embedded CE, the .NET Compact Framework, the Phidget Framework, and the VS2005 IDE provides an efficient application development platform and enables the developer to create complex applications with ease.

In any security access control system, one of the key components for the system is the module that captures the users' security access credentials. These credentials can come in different formats, such as an identification card with a magnetic strip, an identification card with RFID, or an access code.

In this chapter, we created a simple RFID reader application, which can be used as the starting point or one of the building blocks to create a more complex security access control application using RFID as the security access credential.

Robotic Applications

Robotic applications provide an interactive and interesting way to learn and engage in the embedded development environment. The robotic applications can be complex, involving different type of sensors, responding to the sensors' data, and using complicated algorithms to maneuver the robots. At the same time, robotic applications can be simple, controlling a simple robot's movements. For academic institutions, robotics has been a learning resource for engineering students around the world.

For the hobbyist community, there is a huge audience who like to tinker with robotic hardware and develop applications for different types of robotic devices.

For the academic, hobbyist, and commercial developer community, Windows Embedded CE's real-time capability, wireless networking resources, multimedia resources, small footprint, and quick start-up time, along with the efficient Visual Studio IDE, provide the best development environment for a broad range of robotic applications.

In this chapter, we will cover simple robotic applications for CE, using C#, to help all levels of robotic enthusiasts engage in and develop CE robotic applications.

We will use a Stinger robot built with a CE-enabled robotic controller, the Serializer WL robot controller board, and the eBox-4300 running CE 6.0 to work through the exercises in this chapter. Even without the Stinger CE Robot, it's worthwhile to go through this chapter thoroughly to get an idea of how a CE-enabled robotic controller works.

The Stinger CE Robot

The Stinger CE Robot uses the eBox-4300 running CE as the host controller and the Serializer WL Board to interface with motors and sensors. The Stinger Robot is a simple, low-cost robot platform designed with two DC gear head motors and line sensors with expansion options to add additional sensors and other peripherals.

The eBox-4300 is mounted on the Stinger Robot's top deck, as shown in Figure 19-1.

Figure 19-1

As shown in Figure 19-2, the Serializer Robot Controller board is mounted in the same compartment where the two DC motors and the DC-to-DC voltage regulator are mounted. The DC-to-DC voltage regulator is needed to convert the battery power, at 9.6 V, to 5 V DC to power the eBox-4300. The electronic circuit board with five sensors, mounted between the two front wheels, is the line sensor module.

Figure 19-2

The Serializer WL Robot Controller

Before getting into the exercise, it's helpful to know about the robotic hardware.

The Serializer Robot Controller has an onboard microcontroller designed with the necessary electronic components to interface with various sensors and motors for robotic applications. The Serializer has built-in General Purpose Input and Output (GPIO), an analog-to-digital converter (A2D), I2C bus, and pulse width modulation (PWM) for motor control. In addition, the Serializer is available with Serial, USB, and Bluetooth interfaces. The Serializer firmware implements a serial interface protocol that allows an external controller to communicate with and control the board's function.

A general-purpose embedded computing device like the eBox-4300 does not have the proper I/O needed to interface with the large selection of robotic sensors on the market. The Serializer serves as the intermediate hardware bridging the gap between the general-purpose computing device and the robotic sensors and motors.

The Serializer is connected to the eBox-4300 through a serial port connection. The eBox-4300 sends commands to the Serializer and receives sensor data through the same serial port connection.

It's possible to control the Serializer function and receive sensor data by sending formatted command strings to the serial port and parsing the received data from the serial port to read the sensor data. The Serializer Robot Controller provides an easy-to-use .NET library to control low-level robotic hardware. We will work through an exercise to control the Serializer using standard serial port communication. Then we'll work through another exercise to perform the same function using the Serializer .NET library to show how much easier it is to use the .NET library.

There are different variations of the Serializer, as shown in Figure 19-3, with an RS-232 interface, and Figure 19-4, with a USB interface.

Figure 19-3

Figure 19-4

Following is a listing of the I/O provided by the Serializer:

❑   One TTL serial I/O port

❑   Two encoder ports

❑   Two DC motor controls

❑   One I2C port

❑   One analog port with six analog inputs

❑   One general-purpose I/O port with 10 I/O lines

❑   LEDs to indicate operating status

How Does the Serializer Work?

Before getting into writing code to control the Serializer, let's briefly go over the Serializer board's function and how it works.

When power is applied to the Serializer, the firmware boots up and waits for commands from the serial port. Once a command is received over the serial port from the host controller, the command is parsed, validated, and executed. After the command is received and executed, the Serializer board sends a response back to the host controller.

There are three possible scenarios for the Serializer board's response to the host controller:

1.   After receiving an invalid command from the host controller, the Serializer board responds to the host control with the NACK message.

2.   After receiving a valid command from the host controller requesting sensor data, the Serializer board responds to the host controller by sending back the requested sensor data.

3.   After receiving a valid command from the host controller to control the servo or DC motor or set the status of the GPIO pins, without having to send back data, the Serializer board responds to the host controller by sending the ACK message to indicate that the command has been executed.

The Serializer board is connected to the eBox-4300 through a serial port with the following settings:

19200 baud, 8 data bits, no parity, and 1 stop bit

To provide a consistent method of communicating with the host controller, the firmware for the Serializer incorporates a set of serial communication protocols with commands to control motor velocity and direction of movement, and to request sensor data for the sensor attached to the Serializer.

Since it's not within the scope of this chapter to talk about this serial communication protocol, it will not be covered. The *Serializer WL User Guide* provides detailed information about the serial communication protocol. The guide is available for download from the following URL:

www.roboticsconnection.com/p-16-serializer-net-robot-controller.aspx

Below in this chapter, we will use some of the serial communication protocol to work through the exercises.

Simple Robotic Control Applications

In this section, we will work through the exercises to create two C# applications. One of the exercises uses the serial port class within the .NET Compact Framework 2.0 to send commands to the robot. The other uses the Serializer .NET library to control the robot. Both applications will perform the same tasks, as follows:

- ❑ After initialization, the robot will travel a short distance in a straight line and perform a 180-degree U-turn after the designated travel distance is reached.

- ❑ After the U-turn, the robot will continue traveling in a straight line.

- ❑ After the designated distance is reached, the robot will make another U-turn and repeat the process.

Before getting into developing the applications, we must install the Serializer .NET library, which is needed for one of the exercises. The Serializer .NET library installer is available for download from the following URL:

    www.embeddedpc.net/ce6book/

Download and install the Serializer .NET library before continuing.

Windows Embedded CE Design

In addition to the Serializer .NET library, we need to work with an OS design to generate a runtime image for the eBox-4300 target device, with the necessary components included to support the managed-code applications created from the exercises in this chapter.

We can create a new OS design or use the one created in Chapter 12. In either case, we need to work with an OS design.

In Chapter 12, we created the eBox-4300 OS design with all the necessary components needed to support VS2005 managed-code applications running on the eBox-4300 target device. Let's use this OS design for the exercises in this chapter. If you did not work through the exercise and create the OS design, follow the steps in Chapter 12 to create the OS design before continuing.

Robotic Application Using the Serial Port Class

In this section, we will create a VS2005 managed-code smart device application using C#. This application uses a serial port class to communicate with the Serializer board and send commands to the Serializer board to perform the following tasks:

- ❑ Drive straight forward a specified distance.
- ❑ Rotate 180 degrees.
- ❑ Drive straight forward a specified distance.
- ❑ Rotate 180 degrees.
- ❑ Repeat the above processes.

Launch a new instance of the VS2005 IDE and work through the following steps to create a smart device application:

1. From the VS2005 IDE, select File ⇨ New ⇨ Project to bring up the New Project screen.

2. From the Project Types window on the left pane, expand the Other Languages.

3. Click on and expand the Visual C# node followed by the Smart Device node, and select Windows CE 5.0.

4. From the New Project screen's Template selection windows on the right pane, select Console Application.

5. Enter **SerialPortClass** as the name for the project, as shown in Figure 19-5, and click OK to continue.

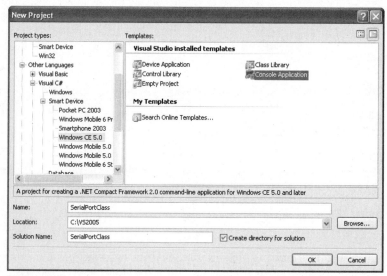

Figure 19-5

At this point, a blank console application project is created. The program.cs source code file should be opened in the VS2005 IDE's Code Editor window in the center.

By default, the following namespaces are generated for the new project:

```
using System;
using System.Collections.Generic;
using System.Text;
```

Let's work through the following steps to add codes to the SerialPortClass project:

1. Add the following three namespaces to program.cs, just after the above three using statements:

```
using System.IO.Ports;
using System.Threading;
using System.Diagnostics;
```

2. Add the following codes to define an instance of the SerialPort class, sp, and two other variables, portName and baudRate, as shown below. Since we plan to connect the Serializer board to the eBox-4300's COM2 at 19200 baud, the portName variable is assigned a string value, COM2. The baudRate variable is assigned an integer value, 19,200.

```
private enum RotateDirection
{
    Left,
    Right
}
private static SerialPort sp;
private const string portName = "COM2";
private const int baudRate = 19200;
```

3. In the Main() routine, we need to create an instance of the SerialPort class and provide the parameters to the constructor to configure the port properly. The Serializer board communicates by default at 19200 baud (defined above), using 8 data bits, 1 stop bit, and no parity. We also set the ReadTimeOut property to 300 milliseconds. To handle errors and unexpected events, the try-finally block of code is added to handle errors gracefully, as shown below:

```
static void Main(string[] args)
{
    // Instantiate a serial port
    sp = new SerialPort(portName, baudRate, Parity.None, 8, StopBits.One);
    sp.ReadTimeout = 300;

    try
    {
        sp.Open();

    }
    // The try-finally block handle all exception.
    // Insuring the SerialPort will get cleaned up properly.
    finally
    {
        sp.Close();
    }
}
```

4. Next, add a function to send data to the Serializer and receive data from the Serializer board. We will create a method called SendReceive(). This method will send a command to the Serializer board and receive a response from the board. This method sends commands using ASCII text format and receives responses in the same format.

There are two local variables within this method, attemptCounter and resp. The attemptCounter variable is used to keep track of the number of attempts to send the command. The resp variable is used to hold the response from the Serializer.

A try-catch block is implemented to help handle unexpected errors gracefully and log the number of failed attempts. Once a valid response is received, or after three failed attempts, the program execution breaks out of the loop. If a valid response was not received, a debug statement is printed to the output window, and an empty response is returned. Otherwise, the SendReceive() method sends back the requested data or the ACK message to indicate that the command was executed successfully, as shown in the following block of code:

```
// Handles Serial Communications Protocol with Serializer
// (Read more about the Serializer Protocol in Serializer User's Guide)
static string SendReceive(string cmd)
{
    uint attemptCounter;
    string resp = "";

    // Attempt to send the command 3 times...
    for (attemptCounter = 0; attemptCounter < 3; attemptCounter++)
    {
        try
        {
            // Send the command:
            SerialPortWriteLine(cmd);

            // Process the response:
            resp = SerialPortReadLine();

            // Did the Serializer ACK, or NACK on the command?
            if (resp != "NACK")
            {
                // Yes, we're done!
                break;
            }
        }
        catch (TimeoutException e)
        {
            Debug.WriteLine(String.Format("{0}: {1} -> {2}", attemptCounter,
                cmd, e.Message));
        }
    }

    // Serializer Didn't respond:
    if (attemptCounter > 3)
    {
        Debug.WriteLine(String.Format("#: aborting {0} after {1} tries",
            cmd, attemptCounter));
    }

    return resp;
}
```

5. Next, add the `SerialPortReadLine()` method, a helper function to read the response from the Serializer and parse the message. The Serializer sends all responses back with the \r\n> character sequence appended to the end of the message. This is done to support terminal applications such as Hyperterminal.

We can configure the `SerialPort` object to look for this character sequence by setting the NewLine property equal to \r\n> and treating it as an end-of-message marker. Doing this will enable the program to process one response at a time. Since the new line character sequence does not have any useful purpose, the response message is parsed to discard the \r\n> character by adding the `Substring(3)` function before sending the response back for further processing:

```
// Reads a response from the Serializer over the serial port:
static string SerialPortReadLine()
{
    // Every command returned from the Serializer has
    // a "\r\n>" appended to it.
    sp.NewLine = "\r\n>";

    // Remove "\r\n>":
    return sp.ReadLine().Substring(3);
}
```

6. Now add the `SerialPortWriteLine()` method, a helper function, to add the \r character to the command before sending it to the Serializer. The Serializer requires that the command sent to it end with the \r character, the carriage return character.

```
// Sends a command to the Serializer over the serial port:
static void SerialPortWriteLine(string s)
{
    // The Serializer expects every command to end in a '\r' character
    sp.NewLine = "\r";
    sp.WriteLine(s);
}
```

We have written the methods needed to handle the transmission of commands to the Serializer and reception of responses from the Serializer. In the subsequent steps, we will add code that sends commands to the Serializer board.

1. Let's start by adding the `ResetSerializer()` method. This method will send the `reset` command string telling the Serializer to reset itself. This is useful to bring the Serializer to a known state before sending commands to perform critical actions. If the Serializer is operating in an abnormal state, sending the `reset` command initially will cause the Serializer to send back a NACK message. After the `reset` command is repeated, the command should be interpreted as a valid command.

```
// Sends a command to reset the Serializer
static string ResetSerializer()
{
    Return SendReceive("reset");
}
```

2. In this step, add the `QueryFirmwareVersion()` method. This method sends an `fw` command string to the Serializer, requesting the firmware version number. This is a useful function to check whether the Serializer is equipped with the correct version of firmware.

```
// Send a command to query the Serializer's firmware
static string QueryFirmwareVersion()
{
    Return SendReceive("fw");
}
```

3. Next add the `DriveDistance()` method, sending a command to the Stinger Robot to drive forward a specified distance, using the `digo` (distance go) command.

The `digo` command leverages the Serializer's internal PID (proportional–integral–derivative) algorithm built into the firmware, along with the wheel encoder information, to command the robot to drive an exact distance. The PID algorithm also monitors motor velocity. This is useful when the robot starts to slow down while traveling up a hill or over an obstacle or speeds up when traveling downhill.

The parameters for the `DriveDistance()` method are distance and velocity. We will use the `String.Format()` function to build the command string and send it to the Serializer. The `digo` command requires the command to be in the following format:

```
digo 1:<distance1>:<velocity1>2:<distance2>:velocity2>
```

Since we want the robot to drive a straight line, both `distance1` and `distance2` must be identical, and `velocity1` and `velocity2` must be identical. Otherwise, the robot will travel in an arc.

> The Stinger Robot has two DC motors attached to two wheels to propel the robot. In the `digo` command, the `distance1` and `velocity1` variables control the number of rotations and rotation velocity for the left wheel. The `distance2` and `velocity2` variables control the number of rotations and rotation velocity for the right wheel.

```
// Sends a command to the Serializer
// to drive both motors forward a specified distance and velocity
// using the digo PID motor control command
static void DriveDistance(int distance, int vel)
{
    // Calculate the number of ticks required to travel the specified distance,
    // since the digo PID command wants the distance in encoder ticks.
    // Stinger Wheel Diameter: 2.25"->Wheel Circumference: 8.75"
    // Motor encoder resolution: 624 ticks/rev
    // ticks = (distance * ( 1 rev/8.75") * 624 ticks/rev)
    int distanceTicks = (int)(distance * ((1 / 8.75) * 624));
    string DriveCmd = String.Format("digo 1:{0}:{1} 2:{2}:{3}", distanceTicks, vel,
distanceTicks, vel);
}
```

4. Next, add the code for the `Rotate180()` method to command the robot to rotate 180 degrees. We will leverage the RotateDirection enumeration defined in Step 2 to determine the robot's rotating direction, left or right. This method is similar to the `DriveDistance()` method using the `digo` command. We assigned a negative value for the distance to one of the motors to cause the motor on one side to rotate in the opposite direction and make the robot spin around. We need to calculate the number of ticks required to rotate the robot exactly 180 degrees, using physical robot parameters such as wheel circumference, wheel track, and encoder resolution:

```
// Sends a command to the Serializer to command it
// to drive both motors in opposite directions,
// for a specified angle and velocity using the
// 'digo' PID motor control command.
static void Rotate180(RotateDirection dir, int vel)
{
    string driveCmd;

    // Calculate the distance required to rotate 180 degrees.
    // Stinger Track: 8.75" (Distance between centerline of wheels)
    // Stinger Track Circumference: 27.48
    // Since we're rotating 180 degrees, we can take half of
    // the entire rotational distance.
    double rotationalDistance = (27.48 / 2);

    // Determine how many wheel revolutions it'll take to travel this distance:
    double wheelRevs = rotationalDistance / 8.75;

    // Determine how many ticks it'll take to go the specified distance,
    // since the digo PID command wants the distance in encoder ticks.
    int distanceTicks = (int)(wheelRevs * 624);

    // Determine which motor needs reversing to rotate
    // NOTE: To reverse the direction of a motor using the digo command,
    // you must set a negative distance, not a negative velocity!
    if (dir == RotateDirection.Right)
    {
        driveCmd = String.Format("digo 1:{0}:{1} 2:-{2}:{3}",
                            distanceTicks, vel, distanceTicks, vel);
    }
    else
    {
        driveCmd = String.Format("digo 1:-{0}:{1} 2:{2}:{3}",
                            distanceTicks, vel, distanceTicks, vel);
    }

    SendReceive(driveCmd);
}
```

Chapter 19: Robotic Applications

5. Next, add the code for the `Stop()` method, to stop the motors. This method simply sends the `stop` command string to the Serializer.

```
// Sends a command to stop the Serializer's motors
static void Stop()
{
    SendReceive("stop");
}
```

Let's go back to the `Main()` function and add code to command the robot to drive a short distance, rotate 180 degrees, and then drive back, over and over.

1. After the call to `sp.Open()` to initialize the serial port, call the `ResetSerializer()` function to set the Serializer to a known state, followed by a call to `QueryFirmwareVersion()`, and print the Serializer version using `Debug.WriteLine()`.

2. Add a `while (true)` loop, and add calls to `DriveDistance()` and `Rotate180()` within the `while` loop to make the robot behave as described above. Since it takes time for the robot to travel the commanded distance, a call to `Thread.Sleep()` is added after the `DriveDistance()` and `Rotate180()` function calls to create time for these two functions to be completed.

```
static void Main(string[] args)
{
    // Instantiate a serial port
    sp = new SerialPort(portName, baudRate, Parity.None, 8, StopBits.One);
    sp.ReadTimeout = 300;

    try
    {
        sp.Open();

        // Send command to reset the Serializer
        ResetSerializer();

        // Query Serializer firmware version
        Debug.WriteLine("Serializer Firmware: " + QueryFirmwareVersion());

        // The following command within the while loop will keep on repeating
        //    send command to the Serializer to drive the robot forward 15 inches
        //    wait for the robot to complete traveling 15 inches
        //    send command to the Serializer to rotate the robot by 180 degrees
        //    wait for the robot to complete the rotation
        //
        while (true)
        {
            // drive forward 20 inches
            Debug.WriteLine("Driving Forward");
            DriveDistance(20, 24);

            // Sleep and wait 8 seconds for the DriveDistance() function to finish
            Thread.Sleep(8000);

            // Rotate 180 degrees
```

```
                    Debug.WriteLine("Rotate 180 degrees");
                    Rotate180(RotateDirection.Right, 20);

                    // Sleep and wait for the Rotate180() function to finish
                    Thread.Sleep(5000);

                }
            }
            // This ensures that not matter what exception gets thrown
            // the SerialPort will get cleaned up properly.
            finally
            {
                sp.Close();
            }
        }
```

3. Build the SerialPortClass project and generate the `serialportclass.exe` executable.

This concludes the SerialPortClass application, using the `SerialPort` object to communicate with the Serializer. You can build the SerialPortClass application and launch the application to run on the Stinger Robot with eBox-4300 running CE as the controller. We will work through the steps to launch the application on the Stinger Robot toward the end of this chapter.

Source Code Listing for SerialPortClass Project

Below is the complete source code for the SerialPortClass application:

```
// SerialPortClass project listing
using System;
using System.Collections.Generic;
using System.Text;
using System.IO.Ports;
using System.Threading;
using System.Diagnostics;

namespace SerialPortClass
{
    class Program
    {
        #region PRIVATES
        private enum RotateDirection
        {
            Left,
            Right
        }
        private static SerialPort sp;
        private const string portName = "COM2";
        private const int baudRate = 19200;
        #endregion

        #region MAIN
        static void Main(string[] args)
```

```
        {
            // Instantiate a serial port
            sp = new SerialPort(portName, baudRate, Parity.None, 8, StopBits.One);
            sp.ReadTimeout = 300;

            try
            {
                sp.Open();

                // Send command to reset the Serializer
                ResetSerializer();

                // Query Serializer Firmware Version
                Debug.WriteLine("Serializer Firmware: " + QueryFirmwareVersion());

                // The commands within the while loop will keep on repeating
                //    command to the Serializer to drive the robot forward 15 inches
                //    wait for the robot to complete traveling 15 inches
                //    command to the Serializer to rotate the robot by 180 degrees
                //    wait for the robot to complete the rotation
                //
                while (true)
                {
                    // drive forward 20 inches
                    Debug.WriteLine("Driving Forward");
                    DriveDistance(20, 24);

                    // Sleep and wait 8 seconds for the DriveDistance()
                    // function to finish
                    Thread.Sleep(8000);

                    // Rotate 180 degrees
                    Debug.WriteLine("Rotate 180 degrees");
                    Rotate180(RotateDirection.Right, 20);

                    // Sleep and wait 8 seconds for the Rotate180()
                    // function to finish
                    Thread.Sleep(5000);
                }
            }
            // This ensures that no matter what exception gets thrown
            // the SerialPort will get cleaned up properly.
            finally
            {
                sp.Close();
            }
        }
        #endregion

        #region HELPER FUNCTIONS

        // Handles Serial Communications Protocol with Serializer
```

```
// (Read more about the Serializer Protocol in Serializer User's Guide)
static string SendReceive(string cmd)
{
    uint attemptCounter;
    string resp = "";

    // Attempt to send the command 3 times...
    for (attemptCounter = 0; attemptCounter < 3; attemptCounter++)
    {
        try
        {
            // Send the command
            SerialPortWriteLine(cmd);

            // Process the response:
            resp = SerialPortReadLine();

            // Did the Serializer ACK, or NACK on the command?
            if (resp != "NACK")
            {
                // Yes, we're done!
                break;
            }
        }
        catch (TimeoutException e)
        {
            Debug.WriteLine(String.Format("{0}: {1} -> {2}",
attemptCounter, cmd, e.Message));
        }
    }

    // Serializer Didn't respond:
    if (attemptCounter > 3)
    {
        Debug.WriteLine(String.Format("#: aborting {0} after
{1} tries", cmd, attemptCounter));
    }

    return resp;
}

// Reads a response from the Serializer over the serial port:
static string SerialPortReadLine()
{
    // Every command returned from the Serializer has
    // a "\r\n>" appended to it.
    sp.NewLine = "\r\n>";

    // Remove "\r\n>":
    return sp.ReadLine().Substring(3);
}

// Sends a command to the Serializer over the serial port:
static void SerialPortWriteLine(string s)
```

```
    {
        // The Serializer expects every command to end in a '\r' character
        sp.NewLine = "\r";
        sp.WriteLine(s);
    }

#endregion

#region SERIALIZER METHODS
// Sends a command to the Serializer to command it
// to drive both motors forward a specified
// distance and velocity using the
// 'digo' PID motor control command.
static void DriveDistance(int distance, int vel)
{
    // Calculate the number of ticks required to travel the specified
    // distance, since the digo PID command wants the distance in encoder
    // ticks.
    // Stinger Wheel Diameter: 2.25"->Wheel Circumference: 8.75"
    // Motor encoder resolution: 624 ticks/rev
    // ticks = (distance * ( 1 rev/8.75") * 624 ticks/rev)
    //
    int distanceTicks = (int)(distance * ((1 / 8.75) * 624));

    string DriveCmd = String.Format("digo 1:{0}:{1} 2:{2}:{3}",
distanceTicks, vel, distanceTicks, vel);

    SendReceive(DriveCmd);
}

// Sends a command to the Serializer to command it
// to drive both motors in opposite directions,
// for a specified angle and velocity using the
// 'digo' PID motor control command.
static void Rotate180(RotateDirection dir, int vel)
{
    string driveCmd;

    // Calculate the distance required to rotate 180 degrees.
    // Stinger Track: 8.75" (Distance between centerline of wheels)
    // Stinger Track Circumference: 27.48
    // Since we're rotating 180 degrees, we can take half of
    // the entire rotational distance.
    double rotationalDistance = (27.48 / 2);

    // Determine how many wheel revolutions it'll take to travel
    // this distance:
    double wheelRevs = rotationalDistance / 8.75;

    // Determine how many ticks it'll take to go the specified distance,
    // since the digo PID command wants the distance in encoder ticks.
```

```
            int distanceTicks = (int)(wheelRevs * 624);

            // Determine which motor needs reversing to rotate
            // NOTE: To reverse the direction of a motor using the digo command,
            // you must set a negative distance, not a negative velocity!

            if (dir == RotateDirection.Right)
            {
                driveCmd = String.Format("digo 1:{0}:{1} 2:-{2}:{3}",
        distanceTicks, vel, distanceTicks, vel);
            }
            else
            {
                driveCmd = String.Format("digo 1:-{0}:{1} 2:{2}:{3}",
        distanceTicks, vel, distanceTicks, vel);
            }

            SendReceive(driveCmd);
        }

        // Sends a command to the Serializer to command it to stop both motors:
        static void Stop()
        {
            SendReceive("stop");
        }

        // Sends a command to the Serializer to query the firmware version:
        static string QueryFirmwareVersion()
        {
            return SendReceive("fw");
        }

        // Sends a command to the Serializer to reset it:
        static string ResetSerializer()
        {
            return SendReceive("reset");
        }
        #endregion
    }
}
```

In the next section, we will create another C# application, using the Serializer .NET library performing the identical tasks to show how much simpler it is to develop a managed-code smart-device CE application with a good set of .NET libraries.

Robotic Application Using the Serializer .NET Library

In this section, we will create a C# managed-code application to perform the identical task as the SerialPortClass application in the previous section, using the Serializer .NET library instead of the `SerialPort` object.

To work through the exercise in this section, the Serializer .NET library is needed. If you have not installed the Serializer .NET library, install it now before continuing.

Work through the following steps to create a new C# smart device application:

1. From the VS2005 IDE, select File ⇨ New ⇨ Project to bring up the New Project screen.

2. From the Project Types window on the left pane, expand the Other Languages.

3. Click and expand the Visual C# node follow by the Smart Device node, and select Windows CE 5.0.

4. From the New Project screen's Template selection windows on the right pane, select Console Application.

5. Enter **SerializerNET** as the name for the project, and click OK to continue.

Add Reference to the Serializer .NET Library

At this point, a blank console application project is created. To use the Serializer .NET library, we need to add a reference to the library. Work through the following steps to add a reference to the Serializer .NET library:

1. From the Solution Explorer window, right-click on the References node and select Add Reference, as shown in Figure 19-6, to bring up the Add Reference screen.

Figure 19-6

2. From the Add Reference screen, select Serializer.CompactFramework, and click OK to continue, as shown in Figure 19-7.

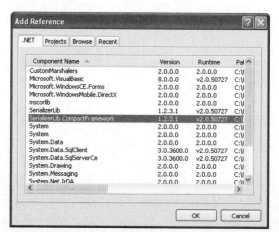

Figure 19-7

Adding Code to the Project

In this section, we will add code to the SerializerNET application to perform the same tasks as the SerialPortClass application, using the `SerialPort` object.

1. From the Solution Explorer window, double-click on and open the program.cs file for editing inthe center Code Editor window, and work through the following steps to add codes to program.cs.

By default, the following namespaces are generated for the new project:

```
using System;
using System.Collections.Generic;
using System.Text;
```

2. Add the following namespaces to program.cs:

```
using RoboticsConnection.Serializer;
using RoboticsConnection.Serializer.Components;
using RoboticsConnection.Serializer.Controllers;
using RoboticsConnection.Serializer.Ids;
using RoboticsConnection.Serializer.Sensors;
using System.Diagnostics;
using System.Threading;
```

3. Next, define the private static variable `mySerializer`, as an instance of the Serializer. Define another private static variable, `pid`, as an instance of the PIDMotorController:

```
private static Serializer mySerializer
private static PIDMotorController pid;
```

4. In the `Main()` routine, we need to create an instance for each of the two variables above, and set the PortName and BaudRate properties for the Serializer object. We then instantiate the `PIDMotorController` class, passing in mySerializer, one of the Serializer instances.

Next, we need to sign up for the CommunicationStarted event, which is signaled once the Serializer library has established communication with the Serializer robot controller board. This is needed to establish communication between the Serializer .NET library and the Serializer controller board. After we have signed up for the CommunicationStarted event, we can invoke `StartCommunication()` on mySerializer, one of the Serializer instances.

```
static void Main(string[] args)
{
    mySerializer = new Serializer();
    mySerializer.PortName = "COM2";
    mySerializer.BaudRate = 19200;

    // Create a new PIDMotorController object
    // to control the motors.
    pid = new PIDMotorController(mySerializer);

    // Sign up to receive a notification once the Serializer Library
    // has established communication with the Serializer.
    mySerializer.CommunicationStarted += new
                    SerializerEventHandler(mySerializer_CommunicationStarted);
    mySerializer.StartCommunication();

}
```

5. Next, we need to add an infinite `while` loop to the `Main()` routine, where we will add code to perform the same tasks as the SerialPortClass application in the earlier section.

The following code in the `while` loop will drive the robot 24 inches forward by setting the pid.Distance property and calling the `pid.TravelDistance()` function. Then the `pid.QueryStatus()` function is called within a `while` loop to wait for the `pid` algorithm to finish. The next portion of the code drives the robot to rotate 180 degrees by setting the pid.RotationAngle and calling the `pid.Rotate()` function. After the `pid.QueryStatus()` function is called within a `while` loop to wait for the `pid` algorithm to finish, the whole process will repeat, over and over again.

```
While (true)
{
    // The mySerializer.PumpEvents() function call let the Serializer object send
    // out events associated with sensors and function call, such as
    // DistanceChanged event.
    mySerializer.PumpEvents();

    // Set the exact distance to travel
    // Command the robot to travel the specified distance
    pid.Distance = 24;     // 24 inches
    pid.TravelDistance();

    // Wait until the pid algorithm has finished
    While (pid.QueryStatus()) {}

    // Set the angle to rotate
    // Command the robot to rotate the specified angle
    Pid.RotationAngle = 180;
    Pid.Rotate();

    // Wait until the pid algorithm has finished
    While (pid.QueryStatus()) {}

}
```

Since we signed up for the Serializer CommunicationStarted event, we need to add a handler for it. We can add the handler below, `mySerializer_CommunicationStarted()`. The static handler takes a single Serializer object as a parameter. All we are doing here is writing a few debugging statements. The `mySerializer.GetFirmwareVersion()` function call performs the same job as the `QueryFirmwareVersion()` function in the SerialPortClass project:

```
// CommunicationStarted Event Handler
static void mySerializer_CommunicationStarted(Serializer sender)
{
    Debug.WriteLine("CommunicationStarted");
    Debug.WriteLine("Serializer Firmware version: {0}",
                                    mySerializer.GetFirmwareVersion());
}
```

6. Build the SerializerNET project and generate the `serializernet.exe` executable.

This concludes the SerializerNET application, using the Serializer .NET library to communicate with the Serializer Robot Controller board. You can build the SerializerNET application and launch the application to run on the Stinger Robot with eBox-4300 running CE as the controller. We will work through the steps to launch the application on the Stinger Robot in the next section.

Complete Source Code Listing for SerializerNET Project

Below is the complete source code for the SerializerNET application. Compared to the code for the SerialPortClass application, performing the identical tasks, this application is much simpler and shorter.

```
// SerializerNET project listing
using System;
using System.Collections.Generic;
using System.Text;
using RoboticsConnection.Serializer;
using RoboticsConnection.Serializer.Components;
using RoboticsConnection.Serializer.Controllers;
using RoboticsConnection.Serializer.Ids;
using RoboticsConnection.Serializer.Sensors;
using System.Diagnostics;
using System.Threading;

namespace SerializerNET
{
    class Program
    {
        private static Serializer mySerializer;
        private static PIDMotorController pid;

        static void Main(string[] args)
        {
            mySerializer = new Serializer();
            mySerializer.PortName = "COM2";
            mySerializer.BaudRate = 19200;

            // Create a new PIDMotorController object
```

```
        // to control the motors
        .pid = new PIDMotorController(mySerializer);

        // Sign up to receive a notification once the Serializer Library
        // has established communication with the Serializer
        .mySerializer.CommunicationStarted += new
                    SerializerEventHandler(mySerializer_CommunicationStarted);
        mySerializer.StartCommunication();

        while (true)
        {
            // The mySerializer.PumpEvents() function call let the Serializer
            // object send out events associated with a sensor
            // (e.g. DistanceChanged event)
            mySerializer.PumpEvents();

            // Set the exact distance to travel
            // Command the robot to travel the specified distance
            pid.Distance = 24;    // 24 inches
            pid.TravelDistance();

            // Wait until pid algorithm has finished
            while (pid.QueryStatus()) { }

            // Set the angle to rotate
            // Command the robot to rotate the specified angle
            pid.RotationAngle = 180;
            pid.Rotate();

            // Wait until pid algorithm has finished
            while (pid.QueryStatus()) { }
        }
    }

    //
    static void mySerializer_CommunicationStarted(Serializer sender)
    {
        Debug.WriteLine("CommunicationStarted");
        Debug.WriteLine("Serializer Firmware version: {0}",
                    mySerializer.GetFirmwareVersion());
    }
    }
}
```

Launching the Robotic Application

In this section, we will configure the eBox-4300 OS design to generate a runtime image to launch and test the SerialPortClass and SerializerNET applications.

Since both the SerialPortClass and SerializerNET applications are console, headless applications, they do not have user interfaces to show the function performed.

We need to configure the OS design, generate the runtime image for each application, and deploy the runtime image and application to the Stinger CE Robot to test and see how each program performs.

Configuring the OS Design for SerialPortClass Application

We need to configure the eBox-4300 OS design and generate a runtime image to launch the SerialPortClass application when CE starts.

Work through the following steps to configure the OS design:

1. Launch the VS2005 IDE, and open the eBox-4300 OS design project.

2. From the Solution Explorer window, expand the Parameter Files folder, and then expand the ICOP_eBox4300_60E: x86 folder.

3. Double-click on project.reg to open the file for editing in the center Code Editor window.

4. Click on the Source icon to view the content in source form.

5. Add the following registry entries to the end of the project.reg file:

```
[HKEY_LOCAL_MACHINE\Init]
    "Depend99"=hex:0a,00,14,00,1e,00
    "Launch99"=\\App\\SerialPortApp.exe
```

The above registry entries configure the runtime image to launch the `serialportclass.exe` application from the \APP\ folder.

Since we've already built the eBox-4300 OS design project and generated a runtime image for this project in Chapter 12, we can use the advance Build option to save time.

1. From the VS2005 IDE, select Build ⇨ Advanced Build Commands ⇨ Build Current BSP and Subprojects to build the project and generate the runtime image.

2. If you did not work through the exercise and build a runtime image for the eBox-4300 project, select Build ⇨ Build Solution to generate one now.

Next, we need to copy the runtime image and the `serialportclass.exe` executable to the eBox-4300. In the above steps, the registry is configured to launch the `serialportclass.exe` executable from the \APP directory under the root of the filesystem. We need to create the APP directory at the root of the eBox-4300's storage and copy the `serialportclass.exe` to the \APP directory.

Launching `serialportclass.exe` on the Stinger CE Robot

With the runtime image from the previous section copied to the eBox-4300 on the Stinger Robot and the `serialportclass.exe` executable copied to the \APP directory at the root of eBox-4300's storage, the Stinger CE Robot is ready to run the test.

After the power is on, as CE starts it launches the `serialportclass.exe` application. Once this application is launched, the Stinger CE Robot will drive itself forward, make a 180-degree U-turn, drive forward, make another U-turn, and keep repeating the process.

Configuring the OS Design for SerializerNET Application

We need to configure the eBox-4300 OS design and generate a new runtime image to launch the SerializerNET application when CE starts.

In this section, we'll work through the same steps to configure the OS design as we did for the SerialPortClass application:

1. Launch the VS2005 IDE, and open the eBox-4300 OS design project.

2. From the Solution Explorer window, expand the Parameter Files folder, and then expand the ICOP_eBox4300_60E: x86 folder.

3. Double-click on project.reg to open the file for editing in the center Code Editor window.

4. Click on the Source icon to view the content in source form.

5. Add the following registry entries to the end of the project.reg file:

```
[HKEY_LOCAL_MACHINE\Init]
    "Depend99"=hex:0a,00,14,00,1e,00
    "Launch99"=\\App\\SerializerNET.exe
```

The above registry entries configure the runtime image to launch the `serializernet.exe` application from the \APP\ folder.

Since we've already built the eBox-4300 OS design project and generated a runtime image for this project in Chapter 12, we can use the advanced Build option to save time.

1. From the VS2005 IDE, select Build ➪ Advanced Build Commands ➪ Build Current BSP and Subprojects to build the project and generate the runtime image.

2. Next, copy the runtime image to eBox-4300's storage, and copy the `serializernet.exe` executable to the \APP folder in the root of the eBox-4300's filesystem.

Launching `serializernet.exe` *on the Stinger CE Robot*

With the new runtime image copied to the eBox-4300 on the Stinger Robot and the `serializernet.exe` executable copied to the \APP directory at the root of eBox-4300's storage, the Stinger CE Robot is ready to run the test.

After the power is on, as CE starts it launches the `serializernet.exe` application and performs the same tasks as the `serialportclass.exe`.

Summary

In this chapter, using the robotic application's interactive environment, we created two applications to perform the same tasks. One uses the `SerialPort` object and one uses the Serializer .NET library, to show the efficiency and simplicity provided by the Serializer .NET library.

As part of the exercise, a simple formula is used to calculate distance traveled versus the wheel diameter. Another simple formula is used to calculate the travel distance for each wheel to rotate the robot by 180 degrees.

20

Deploying a CE 6.0 Device

In the preceding chapters, we covered the CE development environment, tools, how to develop applications using the VS2005 IDE, and sample applications. For most of these chapters, we used the emulator to work through the exercises. In some of the chapters, we worked through the exercises with the eBox-4300 target device, using a DOS-based boot loader.

While the DOS-based boot loader is a great tool for the development process, DOS is a commercial product and requires a separate license to be distributed as part of another commercial product. In this chapter, we will show how to deploy a CE 6.0 device using the BIOS Loader to eliminate the need for booting to DOS and using the DOS-based boot loader to launch the CE runtime image.

We will work through an exercise to build and deploy a CE 6.0 device, using the eBox-4300 as the target device with the BIOS Loader to eliminate the need to use DOS. In addition, we will work through an exercise showing how to clone the sample code under the _WINCE600\PUBLIC directory to the OS design for customization.

We will use the Windows Network Projector (WNP) OS design template to build a Windows Network Projector CE 6.0 device and use the BIOS Loader as the boot loader to launch the CE runtime image when the device power is on. We will also work through an exercise to clone the WNP sample application to the OS design in order to customize the WNP application.

The CE device created through the exercises in this chapter can be used to upgrade an existing computer video projector with the same functions and features available from the new generation of Windows Network Projectors.

To work through the exercises in this chapter, the development workstation and the eBox-4300 device are connected to a Local Area Network (LAN) with DHCP service to assign IP addresses dynamically. We will work through the following exercises in this chapter:

❑   Create an OS design with the Windows Network Projector template.

❑   Clone the Windows Network Projector user interface application for customization.

- ❑ Configure and build the OS design.

- ❑ Configure the eBox-4300 to boot using the BIOS Loader, to eliminate the need for DOS, and configure the BIOS Loader to launch CE.

Windows Network Projector

As a useful tool to project information from the computer to a large display screen, enabling large numbers of people to view and share the information, the computer video projector has become an essential component for the conference room, lecture hall, and training facility.

To project video through the video projector, in addition to having an available VGA output interface to connect to the video projector, the computer system must adjust the display resolution and refresh rate to match the video projector. Older computer video projectors have the following disadvantages:

- ❑ Attaching the computer's video output to the projector is a cumbersome process. Plugging and unplugging the cable to the fragile portable computer VGA output interface can be problematic and can potentially damage the computer.

- ❑ Some of the compact notebook computers are built without the VGA video output interface and are unable to connect to older projectors.

- ❑ The computer's display resolution must be adjusted manually during each use.

The Windows Network Projector represents a new generation of video projectors. In addition to connecting the VGA video interface for direct connection between the computer system and the projector, a Vista computer can connect to the WNP projector through a wired or wireless LAN. When connected, the computer system will prompt the user to accept the automatically adjusted display resolution to match the video projector's resolution.

Although the exercises in this chapter are simple, using the Pictor application that comes as part of the WNP OS design template, the code from the template is fully functional without requiring any modification. The devices built from the exercises, using the eBox-4300, are not far from being production-quality devices.

The WNP project is a wired or wireless network-enabled computer video projector. Using remote desktop technology, the WNP can enable a computer with Windows Vista Home Premium, Business, Enterprise, or Ultimate OS to use the Connect to Network Projector feature, provided as part of Vista. With this it can connect to a WNP through a wired or wireless LAN without the need to attach cumbersome cables. When connected, the computer's display resolution is also adjusted automatically.

For more information about the Windows Vista Connect to Network Projector feature and the Windows Network Projector, search the `http://msdn.microsoft.com` web site using the following key words:

- ❑ Windows Network Projector Overview
- ❑ Connecting to a Windows Network Projector

Windows Network Projector OS Design

In this section, we will create an OS design using the ICOP_eBox4300_60E BSP and the WNP OS design template to generate a runtime image.

The WNP OS design template includes the Pictor sample application with the runtime image. The Pictor sample application source code is installed as part of the CE Platform Builder installation to the following directory:

> _WINCEROOT\PUBLIC\RDP\OAK\PICTOR

In addition to the WNP OS design, we will work through the process of cloning part of the Pictor application source code from the Public directory to the WNP OS design project directory for customization.

Creating the Initial OS Design

Let's work through the following steps to create the OS design:

1. From the VS2005 IDE, select File ⇨ New ⇨ Project to bring up the New Project screen.

2. From the New Project screen's Project Types pane on the left, select the Platform Builder for CE 6.0 project type.

3. From the New Project screen's Templates pane on the right, select OS Design and enter **WNPOSDesign** as the project name, and click OK to bring up the OS Design Wizard.

4. Click Next on the first OS Design Wizard screen to bring up the BSP selection screen.

5. From this BSP screen, select the ICOP_eBox4300_60E BSP, and click Next to bring up the Design Templates selection screen.

6. From this screen, select the Thin Client template, and click Next to bring up the Design Template Variants selection screen.

7. From the Variants selection screen, select the Windows Network Projector variant, and click Finish.

8. When clicking Finish from the previous step, the Catalog Item Notification screen shows up with a security warning. This warns that the web server, included in the OS design, can be a potential source of security breaches for the device. Click Acknowledge to close the Security Warning screen and continue.

At this point, the initial OS design project for the WNPOSDesign project is created.

Configuring, Customizing, and Building the OS Design

Next, we'll go through the following steps to further configure the OS design to generate the runtime image for the eBox-4300 target device:

1. From the Catalog Items View window, include the VGA Linear (Flat) Framebuffer component to the OS design from the following folder: \Device Drivers\Display.

> The Pictor application requires 800 × 600 and higher display resolution to function. Although the Via video driver provided as part of the ICOP_eBox4300_60E can support display resolutions well beyond 800 × 600 resolution, the Pictor application is not able to detect the Via display driver's resolution. To avoid having to make complicated code changes and keep the exercise simple, we will use the VGA Linear (Flat) Framebuffer display driver instead.

2. From the Catalog Items View windows, check to confirm that the VIA CN/CX Display Driver is not selected, as shown in Figure 20-1.

Figure 20-1

For this exercise we are creating an OS design to generate a retail release-mode runtime image to deploy to the eBox-4300. Go through the following steps to further configure the OS design:

1. From the VS2005 IDE, select Build ⇨ Configuration Manager to bring up the Configuration Manager screen.

2. From the Configuration Manager screen, select the ICOP_eBox4300_60E x86 Release option from the "Active solution configuration" selection, and click Close to continue.

3. From the VS2005 IDE, select Project ⇨ WNPOSDesign Properties to bring up the WNPOSDesign Property Pages screen.

4. From the Property Pages screen, expand the Configuration Properties node, and click on the Build Options node to bring up the Build Options selection screen.

5. From this selection screen, change the following Build options for the resulting Build options, as shown in Figure 20-2:

❑ Unselect the "Enable KITL (no IMGNOKITL=1)" option.

❑ Select the "Enable ship build (WINCESHIP=1)" option.

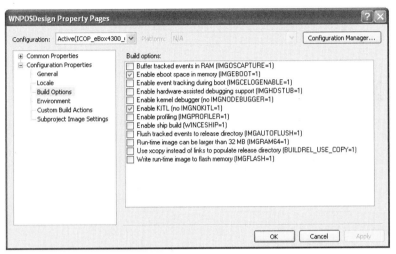

Figure 20-2

6. From the WNPOSDesign Property Pages screen, click Apply followed by OK to save the changes and close the WNPOSDesign Property Pages screen.

7. From the VS2005 IDE, select Build ⇨ Build Solution to build the project and generate an OS runtime image for the emulator.

> **It may take 15 to 30 minutes or more to build the OS design project and generate the runtime image.**

Target Connectivity and OS Image Download

After the CE image is generated, work through the following steps to configure the Target Connectivity needed to establish a connection to download the runtime image:

1. From the VS2005 IDE, select Target ⇨ Connectivity Options to bring up the Target Device Connectivity Options screen.

2. From this options screen, select Ethernet for the Download and Transport selection. Select KdStub for the Debugger selection, and click Apply.

3. Click on the topmost Settings button to bring up the Ethernet Download Settings screen.

4. With both the eBox-4300 and development workstation connected to the same LAN with DHCP service, power on the eBox-4300.

5. After the eBox-4300 boots to a DOS selection menu, select the second option from the available options, and load the OS image from the development workstation with DHCP service.

6. After detecting the bootme packet from the eBox-4300, a device ID is shown in the "Active target devices" window. Click to highlight the device in the "Active target devices" window, and click OK to continue.

7. From the Target Device Connectivity Options screen, click Apply followed by Close to continue.

8. From the VS2005 IDE, select Target ⇨ Attach Device to start the download process.

9. If the download runtime image to the CE device does not start, it means that the eBox-4300 is timed out. Do not cancel or close the image download process.

10. Reset the eBox-4300's power for it to boot to the DOS selection menu again, and select the second option that will send the bootme packet to download the image.

11. After the image is downloaded and launched on the eBox-4300, the display from eBox-4300 should look like Figure 20-3.

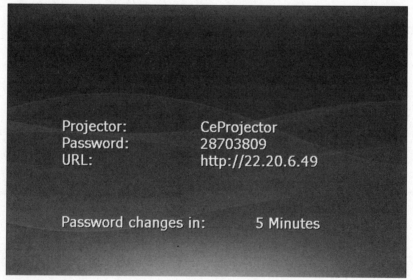

Figure 20-3

Cloning the Pictor Application

In the previous section, the runtime image from the WNPOSDesign is downloaded to the target device and able to launch successfully. Next, we need to clone a portion of the Pictor application source code to the OS design for customization.

When selecting the Windows Network Project OS design template during the OS Design Wizard steps to create the OS design, the Pictor application is included as the start-up application with the OS design. The source code for the Pictor application is in the following directory:

WINCEROOT\PUBLIC\RDP\OAK\PICTOR

It's not recommended to make changes to source code under the _WINCEROOT\PUBLIC directory. Routine QFE updates from Microsoft may contain new code for the source code in the Public directory. To modify and customize the source code for the Pictor application, you should clone the source code as a subproject to the OS design and modify the cloned source code.

Since the WNPOSDesign uses the Pictor application under the _WINCEROOT\PUBLIC directory, let's take the opportunity to work through the process and show how to clone part of the Pictor application's source code for customization from the following directory:

WINCEROOT\PUBLIC\RDP\OAK\PICTOR\PICTORAPP\MAIN

Creating a Blank Subproject

To clone the Pictor application source code, we need to create an empty subproject and copy the Pictor application code to this subproject.

Let's work through the following steps to create the WNPMain subproject:

1. From the VS2005 IDE, select Project ⇨ Add New Subproject to bring up the Windows Embedded CE Subproject Wizard screen, as shown in Figure 20-4.

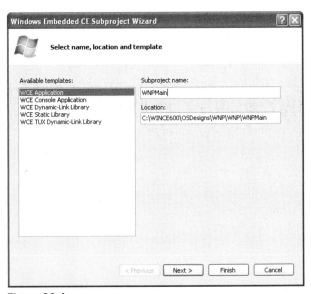

Figure 20-4

2. From the Windows Embedded CE Subproject Wizard screen, enter **WNPMain** as the name for the subproject, and click Next to continue.

3. Select an empty subproject, and click Finish to create the empty subproject.

As part of the subproject creation, a Sources file is also created in the subproject directory. This file contains the information about the WNPMain subproject needed to build and generate the binary executable file. When we copy the source code from the Pictor application in the later steps, the Sources file from the Pictor application will also be copied and overwrite the current Sources file.

Some of the entries from the current Sources file are needed to build the subproject, so navigate to the current Sources file and rename it *sources.bak* in the following directory:

_WINCEROOT\OSDESIGNS\WNP\WNP\WNPMAIN

Copying the Pictor Application Source Code

Copy all the files from the _WINCEROOT\PUBLIC\RDP\OAK\PICTOR\PICTORAPP\MAIN directory to the _WINCEROOT\OSDESIGNS\WNP\WNP\WNPMAIN folder. This portion of the code compiles into `pictorapp.exe`, which is configured to launch when CE starts.

To keep the exercise simple, we'll clone only this part of the Pictor application code.

Modifying the Sources File

After copying the Pictor application source code to the WNPMain subproject directory, we need to edit the Sources file and configure the project to generate the `wnpmain.exe` binary executable to the WNP OS design's build release directory.

Open the _WINCE600\OSDESIGNS\WNP\WNP\WNPMAIN\SOURCES file using a text editor such as `notepad.exe`, and perform the following:

1. Copy the contents from sources.bak to the beginning part of the Sources file.

2. Delete the following entries from the file:

- ❑ TARGETNAME=PictorApp
- ❑ TARGETTYPE=LIBRARY
- ❑ RELEASETYPE=OAK

3. When the WNPMain subproject was created in the earlier step, the Project Wizard created the Sources file and included the above three entries as follows:

- ❑ TARGETNAME=WNPMain
- ❑ TARGETTYPE=PROGRAM
- ❑ RELEASETYPE=LOCAL

4. The above three entries configure the build system to generate the wnpmain.exe executable in the OS design's release directory.

In the Includes section of the Sources file, change the following:

1. Add the following entry:

$(_WINCEROOT)\PUBLIC\RDP\OAK\INC; \

2. Change the "..\INC;" entry, relative path, to

$(_WINCEROOT)\PUBLIC\RDP\OAK\PICTOR\PICTORAPP\INC;, absolute path

3. Change "$(_COMMONPUBROOT)\OAL\WTL\INCLUDE;" to

_WINCEROOT\PUBLIC\COMMON\OAK\WTL\INCLUDE;

4. In the Targetlibs section of the Sources file, add the following entries:

- ❑ $(_PROJECTROOT)\CESYSGEN\SDK\LIB\$(_CPUINDPATH)\URLMON.LIB \
- ❑ $(_PROJECTROOT)\CESYSGEN\SDK\LIB\$(_CPUINDPATH)\COMMCTRL.LIB \
- ❑ $(_WINCEROOT)\PUBLIC\RDP\OAK\LIB\$(_CPUINDPATH)\ PASSWORDMANAGER.LIB \
- ❑ $(_PROJECTROOT)\CESYSGEN\OAK\LIB\$(_CPUINDPATH)\ATLS.LIB \
- ❑ $(_PROJECTROOT)\CESYSGEN\OAK\LIB\$(_CPUINDPATH)\ATLOSAPIS.LIB \

5. Add the following line to the Sources file, just before the WINCETARGETFILES line:

RESFILE=PictorApp.res

The following is a listing of the Sources file after the modifications:

```
!if 0
Copyright (c) Microsoft Corporation.  All rights reserved.
!endif
!if 0
Use of this sample source code is subject to the terms of the Microsoft
license agreement under which you licensed this sample source code. If
you did not accept the terms of the license agreement, you are not
authorized to use this sample source code. For the terms of the license,
please see the license agreement between you and Microsoft or, if
 applicable,
see the LICENSE.RTF on your install media or the root of your tools
 installation.
THE SAMPLE SOURCE CODE IS PROVIDED "AS IS", WITH NO WARRANTIES.
!endif

_COMMONPUBROOT=$(_PROJECTROOT)\cesysgen
__PROJROOT=$(_PROJECTROOT)
RELEASETYPE=LOCAL
_ISVINCPATH=$(_WINCEROOT)\public\common\sdk\inc;
```

```
_OEMINCPATH=$(_WINCEROOT)\public\common\oak\inc;$(_WINCEROOT)\public\common\
   sdk\inc;
TARGETNAME=WNPMain
FILE_VIEW_ROOT_FOLDER= \
    ReadMe.txt \
    prelink.bat \
    postlink.bat \

FILE_VIEW_RESOURCE_FOLDER= \

FILE_VIEW_INCLUDES_FOLDER= \

SOURCES= \

TARGETLIBS= \
    $(_PROJECTROOT)\cesysgen\sdk\lib\$(_CPUINDPATH)\coredll.lib \

TARGETTYPE=PROGRAM
POSTLINK_PASS_CMD=postlink.bat
PRELINK_PASS_CMD=prelink.bat
FILE_VIEW_PARAMETER_FOLDER= \
    WNPMain.bib \
    WNPMain.reg \
    WNPMain.dat \
    WNPMain.db \
    ProjSysgen.bat \

WINCEOEM=1
COPYRES=1
RCADDNULL=1
WINCEATL80=1

RESFILE=PictorApp.res
WINCETARGETFILES= $(_RELEASELIBDIR)\$(TARGETNAME).res \

INCLUDES= \
  $(INCLUDES) \
 $(_WINCEROOT)\public\rdp\oak\pictor\pictorapp\inc; \
 $(_WINCEROOT)\public\servers\oak\inc; \
 $(_WINCEROOT)\public\servers\sdk\inc; \
 $(_WINCEROOT)\public\common\ddk\inc; \
 $(_WINCEROOT)\public\rdp\oak\inc; \
    $(_WINCEROOT)\public\common\oak\wtl\include; \
    $(_WINCEROOT)\public\shell\oak\OwnerDrawLib; \


SOURCES= \
  PictorApp.cpp \
  EditPage.cpp \
  SplashScreen.cpp \
  PictorApp.rc \
 debugSettings.c \
```

```
ProjectorInfo.cpp

TARGETLIBS=$(_PROJECTROOT)\cesysgen\sdk\lib\$(_CPUINDPATH)\coredll.lib \
  $(_PROJECTROOT)\cesysgen\sdk\lib\$(_CPUINDPATH)\ole32.lib \
  $(_PROJECTROOT)\cesysgen\sdk\lib\$(_CPUINDPATH)\uuid.lib \
  $(_PROJECTROOT)\cesysgen\sdk\lib\$(_CPUINDPATH)\mmtimer.lib \
  $(_PROJECTROOT)\cesysgen\sdk\lib\$(_CPUINDPATH)\Oleaut32.lib \
  $(_PROJECTROOT)\cesysgen\sdk\lib\$(_CPUINDPATH)\Iphlpapi.lib \
  $(_PROJECTROOT)\cesysgen\sdk\lib\$(_CPUINDPATH)\Ws2.lib \
  $(_PROJECTROOT)\cesysgen\sdk\lib\$(_CPUINDPATH)\wininet.lib \
  $(_PROJECTROOT)\cesysgen\sdk\lib\$(_CPUINDPATH)\urlmon.lib \
  $(_PROJECTROOT)\cesysgen\sdk\lib\$(_CPUINDPATH)\commctrl.lib \
  $(_PROJECTROOT)\cesysgen\oak\lib\$(_CPUINDPATH)\atls.lib \
  $(_PROJECTROOT)\cesysgen\oak\lib\$(_CPUINDPATH)\atlosapis.lib \
  $(_WINCEROOT)\public\rdp\oak\lib\$(_CPUINDPATH)\PasswordManager.lib \
  $(_WINCEROOT)\public\rdp\oak\lib\$(_CPUINDPATH)\PictorUI_Core.lib \
  $(_WINCEROOT)\public\rdp\oak\lib\$(_CPUINDPATH)\PictorUI_UI.lib \
  $(_WINCEROOT)\public\shell\oak\lib\$(_CPUINDPATH)\ODLib.lib \
  $(_WINCEROOT)\public\rdp\oak\lib\$(_CPUINDPATH)\PictorCore.lib \
```

Modifying the Registry File

Next, go through the following steps to modify the WNPMain subproject's registry and assign a default projector name for the project:

1. From the Solution Explorer window, expand the WNPMain node and then the Parameter Files node, double-click on wnpmain.reg, and open this file in the center Code Editor window.

2. Enter the following entries to the wnpmain.reg file:

```
[HKEY_LOCAL_MACHINE\Ident]
"Name"="Windows Network Projector"

[HKEY_LOCAL_MACHINE\Software\Microsoft\PictorService]
"ProjectorName"="Windows Network Projector"
"AdhocSSID"="WNP-1000"
```

Customizing the WNPMain Program

To show that the WNPMain program is actually compiled from the code in the WNP OS design directory, we will go through the process and modify the display graphic for the WNPMain program in the following directory:

    _WINCE600\OSDESIGNS\WNP\WNP\WNPMAIN

The screen_start.png, a blue-shaded graphic, is provided in the above directory as the default backdrop for the WNPMain program. Use a graphic editor to add some wording to the screen_start.png graphic file, as shown in Figure 20-5, to help visually identify that the WNPMain program is compiled from the code in the above directory.

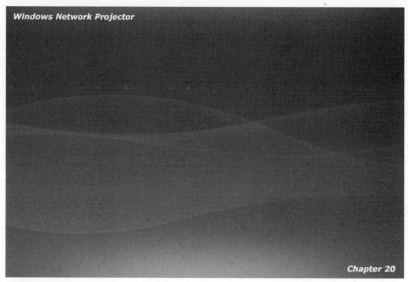

Figure 20-5

Building the Project

Now, we are ready to build the OS design to generate an updated runtime image with the binary executable compiled from the WNP OS design project.

From the VS2005 IDE, select Build ⇨ Build Solution to build the project.

After the build process is completed, download the updated runtime image to test on the eBox-4300 target device. The runtime image should launch with the updated WNPMain executable, as shown in Figure 20-6.

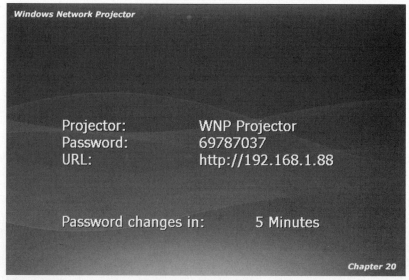

Figure 20-6

Configuring to Boot from BIOS Loader

As we can see from Figure 20-6, the runtime image functions as expected. Next, we need to configure the eBox-4300 to launch CE without having to boot to DOS.

To accomplish this, we will use the BIOS Loader, provided as part of the CEPC BSP by Microsoft. The compiled binary as well as the source code for the BIOS Loader is provided as part of the Platform Builder installation.

The BIOS Loader is provided as part of the CEPC BSP in the following directory:

_WINCEROOT\PLATFORM\CEPC\SRC\BOOTLOADER\BIOSLOADER

The files we will use for the exercise in this chapter are located in the \DISKIMAGES\SETUPDISK folder under the above directory. Following is a list of the files:

❑ **ATTRIB.EXE** — DOS utility to set file attributes

❑ **AUTOEXEC.BAT** — DOS batch file that executes during boot up

❑ **BLDR** — BIOS Loader binary, does not have any file extension.

❑ **BOOT.INI** — Boot parameter file contains system settings such as which image file to boot from, display resolution, and debugging serial port settings

❑ **BSECT.IMG** — Boot sector image file

❑ **CESYS.EXE** — DOS utility used to copy the bsect.img file to the boot partition

❑ **EBOOT.BIX** — Ethernet boot loader

❑ **FDISK.EXE** — DOS utility used to prepare the partition on the storage device

❑ **FORMAT.COM** — DOS utility used to format the storage partition using FAT filesystem format

❑ **MKDISK.BAT** — DOS batch file containing command sequence to prepare storage device and copy the necessary BIOS Loader files to the storage device and enable the device to boot from the BIOS Loader

❑ **SPLASH.BMX** — Graphic file for the splash screen display when the BIOS Loader launches

In addition to the above files, a bootable floppy image file, setupdisk.144, is also provided. This floppy image contains all of the above files and can be found in the following directory:

_WINCEROOT\PLATFORM\CEPC\SRC\BOOTLOADER\BIOSLOADER\DISKIMAGES

There is a `makeimagedisk.exe` utility provided as part of the CE installation to extract the setupdisk.144 image file onto a floppy disk, in the following directory:

\PROGRM FILES\MICROSOFT PLATFORM BUILDER\6.00\CEPB\UTILITIES

Typically, an embedded device does not have a floppy drive or CD-ROM to boot from. Without the proper tools and knowledge, it's a challenging task to prepare the eBox-4300's internal flash storage to boot to the BIOS Loader, which, in turn, loads CE.

The eBox-4300's BIOS can be configured to boot from a USB floppy drive, USB CD-ROM drive, or USB flash storage.

We will work through two exercises to install the BIOS Loader to the eBox-4300's IDE flash storage. The first exercise uses a USB floppy drive; the second uses a USB flash storage. To work through these two exercises, we need to have a monitor and keyboard connected to the eBox-4300.

Installing BIOS Loader Using USB Floppy Drive

To install the BIOS Loader to the eBox-4300's IDE flash storage using a USB floppy drive, we need to go through the following steps to create a bootable floppy disk from the setupdisk.144 image file:

1. Double-click on the `makeimagedisk.exe` utility to install the utility to the system. The system does not appear to do anything when you double-click on this utility.

2. Insert a blank floppy disk into the development workstation's floppy drive.

3. Double-click on the setupdisk.144 image file to bring up the Web Image NT screen, as shown in Figure 20-7.

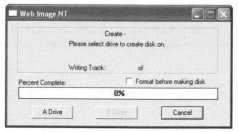

Figure 20-7

4. Click on "A Drive" to start extracting the image file onto the floppy disk. This floppy disk is bootable to DOS version 6.22.

After the bootable floppy set-up disk is created, we need to configure the eBox-4300 system BIOS to boot from the USB floppy drive.

Go through the following steps to enter the BIOS Settings menu and configure the settings:

1. Before applying power to the eBox-4300, attach the USB floppy drive to one of the USB ports on the eBox-4300.

2. Within 5 to 10 seconds after power is applied to the eBox-4300, press the Del key on the keyboard multiple times to enter the BIOS Settings menu.

3. From the main menu, use the arrow left or right key to navigate to the Boot menu.

4. From the Boot menu, use the arrow up or down key to navigate to the Boot Device Priority settings, and press Enter to bring up the Boot Device Priority menu.

5. From the Boot Device Priority menu, use the arrow up or down key to navigate to the 1st Boot Device, and press Enter to bring up the Options screen.

6. From the Options screen, use the arrow up or down key to select the USB: <Floppy drive model> option, and press Enter.

7. Press F10, and select OK to save the change and exit the BIOS Settings mode.

Now the eBox-4300 is configured to boot from the USB floppy drive. Go through the following steps to install the BIOS Loader onto the eBox-4300:

1. Power on the eBox-4300, and let it boot from the floppy drive.

2. After the boot process is done, copy the existing eboot.bin file on the eBox-4300's internal flash storage to the floppy, since we will need this in later steps.

3. From the DOS command, format the flash storage using the following command:

```
FORMAT C:
```

4. If the storage device does not have a drive partition yet, use the `fdisk.exe` utility to create a bootable partition before formatting.

5. After the formatting is done, enter the following command to copy the boot sector and the BIOS Loader files:

```
MKDISK C:
```

The above steps will have configured the eBox-4300's internal flash to boot using the BIOS Loader. However, we still need to copy the CE runtime file onto the eBox-4300's internal flash.

A typical CE runtime file ranges from 10 MB to 20 MB, too large to copy using the floppy disk. We need to copy the CE runtime image to the eBox-4300.

1. During the BIOS Loader installation process, we kept a copy of the eboot.bin file from the eBox-4300 on the BIOS Loader set-up floppy.

2. Copy the eboot.bin file back to the eBox-4300's flash storage, and rename the file *nk.bin*.

3. Because the eboot.bin file's name is changed to *nk.bin*, the BIOS Loader will launch this file when it starts.

Since the floppy disk's capacity is too small for copying the CE runtime image file, nk.bin, we will copy this file through the LAN. To do this, we need to launch VS2005 IDE and open one of the eBoxPhidget OS design projects. Download the runtime image to the eBox-4300. With CE running, we can access the LAN to copy the CE runtime image file to the eBox-4300's local storage.

The CE runtime image generated from the WNP OS design in this chapter does not have the needed utility to copy files from shared folders over a network connection.

The runtime image for the eBoxPhidget OS design has already been generated. Go through the following steps to download the image to the eBox-4300. For this to work, both the VS2005 development workstation and the eBox-4300 must be attached to the same LAN with DHCP service to assign the IP address dynamically.

1. From the VS2005 IDE, select Target ➪ Connectivity Options to bring up the Target Connectivity Options screen.

2. From this options screen, click on the topmost Settings button to bring up the Ethernet Download Settings screen.

3. Power on the eBox-4300. After the BIOS Loader starts, it launches the eboot.bin file, renamed *nk.bin*, and broadcasts a series of bootme packets.

4. As the development workstation receives the bootme packets with the Ethernet Download Settings screen active, the device identification for the eBox-4300 is shown on the "Active target devices" window. Click to highlight the device listed in the "Active target devices" window, and then click OK to continue.

5. From the VS2005 IDE, select Target ➪ Attach Device to start the download process.

6. The download process should begin shortly. If not, the bootme process is timed out. Reset the eBox-4300's power to download the image.

With the eBox-4300 running CE, go through the following steps to copy the WNP runtime image:

1. From the VS2005 development workstation, copy the nk.bin image file from the WNP project to a folder with network share enabled.

2. From the eBox-4300's CE desktop, double-click on the My Device icon to view the root of the filesystem using File Explorer.

   From the File Explorer screen, we can see the NK file icon without file extension. We need to copy the nk.bin image file from the WNP OS design project, through the network-shared folder, and overwrite the nk.bin file currently in the eBox-4300's root folder. The syntax for accessing network-shared folders for CE is similar to that for desktop Windows, as shown in Figure 20-8:

   \\<computer name>\<folder name>\

Figure 20-8

Preparing to Boot to BIOS Loader Using USB Flash Storage

To install the BIOS Loader to the eBox-4300's internal IDE flash using USB flash storage, we need to go through the following steps to prepare the USB flash storage and configure the flash to become bootable:

1. Follow the manufacturer's instructions to configure the USB flash storage to become bootable to DOS. Usually, the USB flash is configurable to boot to Windows 98 or Windows Millennium DOS.

2. After the USB flash storage is configured to be bootable, copy all the following files from the _CEPC\ SRC\BOOTLOADER\BIOSLOADER\DISKIMAGES\SETUPDISK folder to the USB flash storage.

_CEPC = _WINCEROOT\PLATFORM\CEPC

❑ `attrib.exe` — The `attrib.exe` file provided is from DOS version 6.22. We need to replace it with the equivalent `attrib.exe` file compatible with the version of DOS configured for the USB flash storage.

❑ **autoexec.bat** — This is a DOS batch file that executes during boot up.

❑ **BLDR** — BIOS Loader binary, does not have any file extension

❑ **boot.ini** — Boot parameter file, contains system settings such as which image file to boot from, display resolution, and debugging serial port settings

❑ **bsect.img** — Boot sector image file

❑ `cesys.exe` — DOS utility used to copy the bsect.img file to the boot partition

❑ **eboot.bix** — Ethernet boot loader

❑ `fdisk.exe` — The `fdisk.exe` provided is from DOS version 6.22. We need to replace this with the equivalent `fdisk.exe` file compatible with the version of DOS configured for the USB flash storage.

❑ **format.com** — The format.com file provided is from DOS version 6.22. We need to replace this with the equivalent format.com file compatible with the version of DOS configured for the USB flash storage.

❑ **mkdisk.bat** — DOS batch file containing the command sequence to prepare storage device and copy the necessary BIOS Loader files to the storage device and enable the device to boot from the BIOS Loader

❑ **splash.bmx** — Graphic file for the splash screen display when the BIOS Loader launches

The CE runtime image ranges from about 10 MB to 20 MB, rarely larger than 30 MB. The USB flash storage has sufficient storage space to hold a copy of the CE runtime image.

3. Using the USB flash storage already made bootable from the previous step, copy the nk.bin runtime image file from the WNPOSDesign project onto the USB storage.

Next, we need to configure the eBox-4300 to boot from the USB flash storage. Go through the following steps to enter the BIOS settings menu and configure the settings:

1. Before applying power to the eBox-4300, attach the USB flash storage to one of the USB ports.

2. Within 5 to 10 seconds after power is applied to the eBox-4300, press the Del key on the keyboard multiple times to enter the BIOS settings menu.

3. From the main menu, use the arrow left or right key to navigate to the Boot menu.

4. From the Boot menu, use the arrow up or down key to navigate to the Hard Disk Drives settings, and press Enter to bring up the Hard Disk Drives setting menu.

5. Use the arrow up or down key to navigate to the first drive, and press Enter.

6. Use the arrow up or down key to select the USB: <device manufacturer name>, and press Enter.

7. Press F10 and OK to save the change and exit the BIOS settings mode.

Now the eBox-4300 is configured to boot from the USB flash storage. Go through the following steps to configure the BIOS Loader onto the eBox-4300 using the USB flash storage:

1. Before applying power to the eBox-4300, attach the USB flash storage to one of the USB ports on the eBox-4300.

2. Power on the eBox-4300, and let it boot from the USB flash storage.

3. After the boot process is done, enter the following command to format the flash storage:

```
FORMAT C:
```

   If the storage device does not have a drive partition yet, use the `fdisk.exe` utility to create the primary partition, make the partition bootable, and execute the Format command above.

4. After the formatting is done, enter the following command to copy the boot sector and the BIOS Loader files to the internal flash storage:

```
MKDISK C:
```

5. After the Mkdisk command is done, from the USB flash storage, enter the following command to copy the CE runtime image file to the eBox-4300's internal flash storage. There are two different command lines, depending on how the USB flash storage is configured.

   Some USB flash storage emulates the floppy drive and boots as Drive A. For this type of USB flash, use the following command to copy the nk.bin file to the eBox-4300's internal IDE flash storage:

```
Copy A:\NK.BIN C:\
```

   Some USB flash storage emulates the hard drive and boots as Drive C. For this type of USB flash, use the following command to copy the nk.bin file to the eBox-4300's internal IDE flash storage:

```
Copy C:\NK.BIN D:\
```

Launching nk.bin with BIOS Loader

From the previous step, the eBox-4300's internal IDE flash storage is configured to boot to the BIOS Loader, which, in turn, will launch the CE runtime image, nk.bin.

We need to configure the BIOS Loader to launch CE with 1,024 × 768 display resolution. To accomplish this, we need to edit the boot.ini file. This file is installed in the IDE flash storage's root directory.

We can use a text editor to edit the boot.ini file. To do this, we need to copy the boot.ini file from the eBox-4300's IDE flash storage to the portable USB flash storage and edit the file from the development workstation.

Let's work through the following steps to edit the boot.ini file:

1. Open the boot.ini file using a text editor.

2. Locate and change the DisplayWidth, DisplayHeight, DisplayDepth, PhysicalWidth, and PhysicalHeight entries as follows:

```
DisplayWidth = 1024
DisplayHeight = 768
PhysicalWidth = 1024
PhysicalHeight = 768
```

3. Save and close the boot.ini file. If the boot.ini file was copied onto the USB flash storage and uses the development workstation to edit the file, we need to copy this updated boot.ini file back to the eBox-4300's internal flash storage.

4. After this is done, overwriting the existing boot.ini file, reset the eBox-4300's power.

After power reset, the eBox-4300 boots to the BIOS Loader. During the boot process, a Windows Embedded CE 6.0 splash screen is shown while loading the OS image into RAM. As CE starts, it launches the wnpmain.exe application, as shown in Figure 20-6.

Windows Network Projector Usage

In order for the Windows Network Projector attached to a LAN with DHCP service to provide IP addresses dynamically, configuration is not needed.

Press the F3 key to enter the network settings menu. Use the Escape key to exit the current setting screen and go back to the previous screen. Press Home to go back to the Windows Network Projector's main menu.

Summary

In this chapter, we worked through a few exercises, using the Windows Network Projector template to create an OS design, cloning the Pictor application source code to the WNPOSDesign project folder, and generating the runtime image for the eBox-4300 target device.

With the WNPOSDesign run time, the eBox-4300 becomes a fully functional, production-quality CE device capable of upgrading existing computer projectors and enabling projectors with the Windows Network Projector feature.

Using the Connect to Network Projector feature provided as part of the Windows Vista Home Premium or higher version, the computer is able to connect to a Windows Network Projector through a LAN using a wired or wireless connection.

Using the BIOS Loader, the eBox-4300 is able to boot and launches the CE image without DOS.

Windows Embedded CE References

A large pool of information resources is available for Windows Embedded CE. By searching the Internet with the correct keywords, you can find the helpful information and avoid what's unnecessary. The challenge in locating information on the Internet is providing the correct keywords to the search engine.

This appendix provides a list containing Windows Embedded CE resources with brief descriptions.

Online Resources from Microsoft

Windows Embedded Home Page

Following is the URL to the Windows Embedded home page, for all Windows Embedded products. From here, you can navigate and find different Windows Embedded product information:

```
www.microsoft.com/Windows/embedded/default.mspx
```

Windows Embedded CE 6.0 Online Documentation

Following is the URL to Windows Embedded CE 6.0 online documentation:

```
http://msdn.microsoft.com/en-us/library/aa924073.aspx
```

Windows Embedded eHow-Tos and Tutorials

In the following URL, you can find links to video and webcast sessions covering different Windows Embedded technical subjects:

```
http://msdn2.microsoft.com/en-us/embedded/aa731296.aspx
```

Windows Embedded Virtual Labs

The following URL provides links to Windows Embedded CE virtual lab exercises covering different subjects:

```
http://msdn2.microsoft.com/en-us/virtuallabs/aa740455.aspx
```

Mike Hall's Blog

If there is something happening with Windows Embedded technologies, Mike Hall knows about it. On his blog, you can find tons of Windows Embedded technical information and resources:

```
http://blogs.msdn.com/mikehall/
```

Windows Embedded CE Base Team Blog

The Windows Embedded CE development team blogs about different subjects related to CE. On this blog, you can find a lot of useful technical information coming directly from the development team:

```
http://blogs.msdn.com/ce_base/
```

Windows Embedded News Groups

Windows Embedded news groups are monitored by the Microsoft development team and expert MVPs working in the Windows Embedded field. These news groups are active:

```
http://msdn2.microsoft.com/en-us/embedded/aa731160.aspx
```

To find support information related to OS design development using the Platform Builder tool, check out the following news group:

```
www.microsoft.com/communities/newsgroups/en-us/
default.aspx?dg=microsoft.public.windowsce.platbuilder
```

To find support information related to application development for Windows Embedded CE, check out the following news group:

```
www.microsoft.com/communities/newsgroups/en-us/
default.aspx?dg=microsoft.public.windowsce.app.development
```

Windows Embedded Technical Chat

The Windows Embedded CE product team holds routine technical chat online, providing the opportunity for you to ask questions and get help with technical issues:

```
www.microsoft.com/communities/chats/default.mspx
```

Other Learning Resources

Introduction to Embedded System Using Windows Embedded CE

This Embedded System curriculum was developed by James Hamblen at Georgia Institute of Technology. It provides materials and labs for an introductory embedded systems class, using Windows Embedded CE as a tool for teaching students about embedded systems development.

```
www.academicresourcecenter.net/curriculum/pfv.aspx?ID=6676
```

Drivers and Shared-Source Projects

This section provides references to online information resources related to CE device driver and shared-source projects.

USB Webcam Driver for Windows Embedded CE

This is a CE 60 USB webcam driver from Microsoft:

```
http://www.microsoft.com/downloads/
details.aspx?FamilyID=2ef087c0-a4ae-42cc-abd0-c466787c11f2&DisplayLang=en
```

Windows CE Webcam Project

This shared-source project provides a Windows CE USB video webcam driver that supports Windows CE 4.2, 5.0, and 6.0:

```
www.codeplex.com/cewebcam
```

Phidgets Driver for Windows Embedded CE

This is a shared-source Windows Embedded CE device driver to support the Phidgets devices:

```
www.codeplex.com/PhidgetsWinCEDriver
```

Open SSH for Windows CE

This is a shared-source project for a Secure Shell (SSH) network protocol to support Windows Embedded CE:

```
www.codeplex.com/CESSH
```

32feet.NET — Personal Area Networking for .NET

This is a personal area network for .NET shared-source projects with programming libraries to support Bluetooth, IrDA, and Object Exchange:

```
www.codeplex.com/wiki/view.aspx?projectname=32feet
```

LSP Samples for Windows CE

This shared-source project provides the code necessary to create a Layered Service Provider (LSP) on Windows Embedded CE and Windows Mobile devices.

```
http://www.codeplex.com/wiki/view.aspx?projectname
=LSPSamplesWindowsCE
```

Windows CE WLAN Driver for Atheros AR-60001

This is a shared-source project providing a Windows Embedded CE device driver for the AR6001 wireless LAN network card:

```
http://www.codeplex.com/wiki/view.aspx?projectname
=CEWifiDriverAR6000
```

Other Online Resources

Smart Device Framework

The Smart Device Framework is a useful programming library, filling many of the gaps not supported by the .NET Compact Framework. This framework was developed by the OpenNETCF team, consisting of veteran Windows Embedded developers.

The OpenNETCF team releases a community version of the Smart Device Framework free of charge to any developer wanting to take advantage of this library:

```
www.opennetcf.com
```

EmbeddedPC.NET

This site provides information resources useful to developers new to Windows Embedded CE:

```
www.embeddedpc.net
```

LearningCE.COM

This site is hosted by James Y. Wilson, a Windows Embedded MVP. James wrote a Windows Embedded CE book for version 3.0. He routinely posts useful technical information on his site:

```
www.learningce.com
```

Hardware Vendors

This section lists some of the hardware available with support for Windows Embedded CE.

Supported Board Support Packages

One of the good places to find hardware that supports Windows Embedded CE is the Supported Board Support Packages URL on MSDN. This site provides a long list of hardware from different manufacturers with board support packages to support Windows Embedded CE:

    http://msdn.microsoft.com/en-us/library/aa913454.aspx

CompactPC

The eBox-4300 used for exercises in some of the chapters is available from CompactPC. In addition to the eBox-4300, CompactPC has a full line of small-footprint computing devices with support for Windows Embedded CE:

    www.compactpc.com.tw

ICOP Technology

ICOP Technology designs and manufactures embedded x86 processor boards. It focuses on providing PC/104 small-footprint, low-power, and low-cost embedded processor boards:

    www.icoptech.com

Through Microsoft's SPARK program, ICOP is making available two low-cost Windows Embedded CE 6.0 R2 jump-start kits, which include the full version of Windows Embedded CE 6.0 and Visual Studio 2005 Professional. Here is the URL to Microsoft's SPARK program:

    www.microsoft.com/windows/embedded/products/spark/
    default.mspx

Here is the URL to ICOP's SPARK jump-start kits:

    www.icoptech.com/spark/

Phidgets

The Phidgets Company provides a family of small devices consisting of different type sensors, servo and relay controllers, and the PhidgetFramework library to support CE applications:

    www.phidgets.com

Robotics Connection

The Stinger CE Robot in Chapter 19 is from Robotics Connection. Robotics Connection designed and built the Serializer Board, a robot controller, and developed the Serializer .NET library to support application development for desktop Windows and CE:

    www.roboticsconnection.com

B

Installation and Software

The Windows Embedded CE 6.0 R2 development environment requires multiple pieces of software and updates for the software. Improper installation and missing software are the two major causes for many of the problems encountered by developers new to the Windows Embedded CE environment. This appendix provides information regarding installation and the software needed to work through the exercises in the book.

Windows Embedded CE 6.0 R2

The exercises in this book are written for CE 6.0 R2. The initial CE 6.0 was released in 2006. During November 2007, CE 6.0 R2 was released.

The CE 6.0 development tool, Platform Builder, is a plug-in for the Visual Studio 2005 IDE and does not function in the Visual Studio 2008 IDE.

Whether you purchased the full version of Windows Embedded CE 6.0 R2 or received the evaluation version, Visual Studio 2005 Professional is provided as part of the CE 6.0 R2 software kit. For the evaluation version of the CE 6.0, an evaluation version of the Visual Studio 2005 Professional software kit is included.

On April 15, 2008, Microsoft introduced the SPARK program. Through hardware vendors participating in this program, you can purchase a low-cost Windows Embedded CE 6.0 R2 hardware kit, with the full version of Windows Embedded CE 6.0 R2 and Visual Studio 2005 software kit included.

Here is the URL to the SPARK program home page:

```
www.microsoft.com/windows/embedded/products/spark/default.mspx
```

Here is the URL to download the evaluation version of Windows Embedded CE 6.0 R2:

```
www.microsoft.com/windows/embedded/products/windowsce/
getting-started.mspx
```

CE 6.0 R2 Installation

The CE 6.0 R2 installation involves installing multiple pieces of software.

Visual Studio 2005

CE 6.0 is a plug-in for VS2005. VS2005 must be the first thing installed. If you've already installed and use VS2005 for other development tasks, you can use the existing VS2005 IDE.

If your development workstation does not have VS2005 installed, go through the following steps to install VS2005:

1. Install Visual Studio 2005.

2. Install the Visual Studio 2005 Service Pack 1.

    Although you can install and use CE 6.0 without the VS2005 Service Pack installed, some of the CE 6.0 functions will not work. You can install the VS2005 Service Pack 1 before or after the CE 6.0 installation. Here is the URL to download the VS2005 Service Pack 1:

    ```
    www.microsoft.com/downloads/details.aspx?FamilyID=bb4a75ab-e2d4-4c96-
    b39d-37baf6b5b1dc&
    ```

3. Install Visual Studio 2005 SP1 Update for Vista.

    This update only applies to the Windows Vista workstation and should be installed after the VS2005 Service Pack 1 above. Here is the URL to download the VS2005 SP1 Update for Vista:

    ```
    www.microsoft.com/downloads/details.aspx?FamilyID=90e2942d-3ad1-4873-
    a2ee-4acc0aace5b6&
    ```

Windows Embedded CE 6.0 R2

Before you can install CE 6.0 R2, you need to go through the following steps to install CE 6.0 and Service Pack 1:

1. Install Windows Embedded CE 6.0.

2. Install Windows Embedded CE 6.0 Service Pack 1.

    CE 6.0 Service Pack 1 needs to be installed before installing CE 6.0 R2. If you purchased the full version of the software kit, Service Pack 1 is provided on one of the CDs. Otherwise, download Service Pack 1 from the following URL:

    ```
    www.microsoft.com/downloads/details.aspx?FamilyID=bf0dc0e3-8575-4860-
    a8e3-290adf242678&
    ```

3. Install Windows Embedded CE 6.0 R2.

   CE 6.0 R2 is an update that installs on top of an existing CE 6.0 installation. CE 6.0 Service Pack 1 must be installed before installing CE 6.0 R2. If you purchased the full version of CE 6.0 R2, a separate CD containing CE 6.0 R2 is provided. Otherwise, download CE 6.0 R2 from the following URL:

   ```
   www.microsoft.com/downloads/details.aspx?FamilyID=f41fc7c1-f0f4-4fd6-
   9366-b61e0ab59565&
   ```

Installing Other Software

In this section, we will go over the board support package and other software library items needed for the exercise.

ICOP_eBox4300_60E BSP

This BSP is needed for developing the OS design to generate a runtime image for the eBox-4300. There are different versions of BSPs available for the eBox-4300. The ICOP_eBox4300_60E BSP used in the book is configured differently from the other versions.

The ICOP_eBox4300_60E BSP is available for download from the following URL:

```
www.embeddedpc.net/ce6book/
```

CoreCon Connection Framework

The CoreCon connection framework is needed to establish a connection between the development workstation and the target device.

The CoreCon component files are installed as part of the VS2005 installation. There are different CoreCon files for each of the supported processors. These files are located in the following directory: \Program Files\Common Files\Microsoft Shared\CoreCon\1.0\Target\wce400\.

There are eight folders under the above directory. Each folder contains the CoreCon files to support the processor corresponding to the folder name. CoreCon files to support the x86 processor are under the \x86 folder. CoreCon files to support the ARMV4I processor are under the \ARMV4I folder.

To use the CoreCon connection framework, the CoreCon files must be copied to the target device with the runtime image already launched. To help ease the process, the VS2005_CoreCon_x86_WINCE600 and VS2005_CoreCon_ARMV4I_WINCE600 CoreCon components for CE 6.0 were created to make it easy to include the CoreCon files into the OS design and compile them into the runtime image.

The following two CoreCon components are used in this book:

❑ VS2005_CoreCon_X86_WINCE600 (to support the x86 processor)

❑ VS2005_CoreCon_ARMV4I_WINCE600 (to support the ARMV4I processor and the emulator)

Both of the above two components are available for download from the following URL:

```
www.embeddedpc.net/ce6book/
```

Autolaunch Utility

The Autolaunch utility is used to launch one or more applications when the CE runtime starts. By including this utility with the runtime image, you can configure the Autolaunch utility to launch one or more applications through the following registry configuration:

```
[HKEY_LOCAL_MACHINE\Startup]
    "Process0"="app1.exe"              ; first app
    "Process0Delay"=dword:00001388     ; delay 5 seconds
    "Process1"="app2.exe"              ; second app
    "Process1Delay"=dword:2710         ; delay 10 seconds
    "Process2"="app3.exe"              ; third app
    "Process2Delay"=dword:3A98         ; delay 15 seconds
```

The AutoLaunch_x86 component is available for download from the following URL:

```
www.embeddedpc.net/ce6book/
```

PhidgetFramework Library

The PhidgetFramework Library provides VS2005 application development support for all Phidget devices. The PhidgetFramework Library source code is available through the shared-source project hosted on Codeplex, in the following URL:

```
www.codeplex.com/PhidgetsWinCEDriver
```

The Phidget shared-source project does not provide instructions showing how to include the PhidgetFramework Library in the runtime image. A self-install PhidgetFramework library is created to make it easier to include this library with the runtime image.

The PhidgetFramework_V214_Library component used in Chapters 17 and 18 is available for download from the following URL:

```
www.embeddedpc.net/ce6book/
```

Sample Applications and OS Design Projects

A series of OS Design and application development exercises is provided throughout the chapters in this book. Some of these projects require certain versions of the programming library and board support package to function. When attempting to compile and build the sample project files provided as part of the software for this book, using mismatched versions of libraries and BSPs will generate errors. This appendix provides more detailed information about the sample projects and shows how to modify the projects to support different versions of the libraries or BSPs, when possible. This appendix also provides information about additional sample projects.

In addition to the code used for the exercises in this book, other code is available for download from

    www.embeddedpc.net/ce6book/

Robotic Remote Control Application

This application uses the TCP/IP network to send commands and retrieve robot sensors' data. There are two parts to the application — the server running on the CE robot and a client application with user interface that runs on a desktop PC or PocketPC equipped with the Wi-Fi wireless network. The robot is equipped with the 802.11 b/g Wi-Fi wireless network.

The client application sends commands and retrieves sensor data from the robot using the wireless network connection.

The full source code for the applications will be posted on the following URL:

    www.embeddedpc.net/ce6book/

Serial Port Communication Application

In Chapter 12, a serial port communication application was created using VB 2005.

There are two other versions, using C# and Visual C++, that provide the same function. Both these applications are available for download with full source from the following URL:

    www.embeddedpc.net/ce6book/

Source Code for the Exercises

This section lists all the source codes for the exercises provided as part of software for this book.

Chapter 1: Windows Embedded CE

Chapter 1 does not have any code.

Chapter 2: Development Environment and Tools

Chapter 2 does not have any code.

Chapter 3: Board Support Package

This chapter works through three exercises and clones the following three BSPs:

- ❑ MyCEPCBSP is cloned from the CEPC.
- ❑ MyEmulatorBSP is cloned from the Device Emulator.
- ❑ MyeBox4300BSP is cloned from the ICOP_eBox4300_60E.

The codes for the three cloned BSPs are created in the following three directories:

- ❑ C:\WINCE600\Platform\MyCEPCBSP
- ❑ C:\WINCE600\Platform\MyEmulatorBSP
- ❑ C:\WINCE600\Platform\MyeBox4300BSP

Codes for the three cloned BSPs in this chapter are provided in three separate folders:

- ❑ \MyCEPCBSP
- ❑ \MyEmulatorBSP
- ❑ \MyeBox4300BSP

To use the above code, simply copy the complete BSP folder to the C:\WINCE600\PLATFORM directory. If you worked through the exercises in Chapter 3 and created the folders with the same names, you need to remove or rename these folders before copying the provided codes.

Chapter 4: Building a Customized CE 6.0 Runtime Image

The code for the MyOSDesign, created with support for the three BSPs cloned in Chapter 3, is provided as part of the software for this chapter in the following folder:

\MyOSDesign

To use the code from this chapter, simply copy the \MyOSDesign folder along with all the files and subfolders to the C:\WINCE600\OSDesigns directory, and use VS2005 to launch the MyOSDesign.sln project file, from the C:\WINCE600\OSDesigns\MyOSDesign directory. If you worked through the exercises in this chapter and created the C:\WINCE600\OSDesigns\MyOSDesign, you need to rename or remove this folder before copying the provided code.

Chapter 5: Connecting to Target Device

The exercises in this chapter did not involve writing code. The DOS files from the CEPC and eBox-4300 BSP are provided for you to use as references.

The code is provided in the following folders:

❑ \CEPC_Floppy

❑ \eBox4300_DOS_Files

Chapter 6: Debugging and Debugging Tools

Chapter 6 does not have any code.

Chapter 7: Boot Loader Overview

The exercises in this chapter made changes to the MyCEPCBSP's BIOS Loader code. The MyCEPCBSP folder with the modified code is provided for this chapter.

The exercises in this chapter modify the MyCEPCBSP BSP created in Chapter 3 and maintain the same BSP name. The modified code is provided in the following folder:

\MyCEPCBSP

If you want to use the MyCEPCBSP code from this chapter, you need to remove or rename the existing \MyCEPCBSP. Then copy the \MyCEPCBSP to the C:\WINCE600\Platform directory.

Chapter 8: The Registry

Chapter 8 does not have any code.

Chapter 9: Testing with CETK

Chapter 9 does not have any code.

Chapter 10: Application Development

Chapter 10 does not have any code.

Chapter 11: Visual C# 2005 Applications

An OS design and a C# application project were created in this chapter. The code is provided in the following two folders:

- ❏ \MyOS
- ❏ \MyCSharpApp

The code in the \MyOS folder is the OS design. To use this code, copy the complete folder to C:\WINCE600\OS Designs. If you worked through the exercises in this chapter and created the MyOS OS design, you need to remove or rename the project before copying the provided code.

The code in the \MyCSharpApp is a C# application. To use this code, you can copy this folder to a temp folder and open the MyCSharpApp.sln project file, under the \MyCSharpApp folder, using VS2005.

Chapter 12: VB 2005 Applications

In this chapter, an OS design project with support for the eBox-4300 target device was created along with a VB 2005 serial port application, SerialPortApp.

Code for the OS design and VB 2005 application projects is provided in the following two folders:

- ❏ \eBox4300
- ❏ \SerialPortApp

The code in the \eBox4300 folder is the OS design. To use this code, copy the complete folder to C:\WINCE600\OSDesigns. If you worked through the exercises in this chapter and created the eBox4300 OS design, you need to remove or rename the project before copying the provided code.

The code in the \SerialPortApp folder is a VB 2005 serial port communication application.

> **The C# and Visual C++ versions of the serial port communication application are available for download from** www.embeddedpc.net/ce6book/.

Chapter 13: Native-Code Applications

In this chapter, the MyCEPCBSP was edited to add the autolaunch.exe component. An OS design was created, along with the SDK, to support the native-code exercises. In addition, this chapter steps through two exercises to develop MFC and Win32 native-code applications.

The modified BSP codes, utility, and sample application for this chapter are provided in the following folders:

- ❏ \MyCEPCBSP
- ❏ \AutoCoreCon
- ❏ \AutoLaunch

- ❑ \SDK
- ❑ \MyNativeApp
- ❑ \PBNativeApp

The \MyCEPCBSP folder contains the complete BSP code with modifications added from this chapter. To use this code, copy the complete folder to C:\WINCE600\Platform. Before copying, you need to remove or rename the existing MyCEPCBSP folder, created from the previous exercises.

The \AutoCoreCon folder contains the OS design. To use this code, copy the complete folder to C:\WINCE600\OSDesigns. If you worked through the exercises in this chapter and created the AutoCoreCon OS design, you need to remove or rename the AutoCoreCon folder before copying the provided code.

The \AutoLaunch folder contains the autolaunch.exe utility to support the x86 processor.

The \SDK folder contains the SDK generated from the AutoCoreCon OS design.

The \MyNativeApp folder contains the Visual C++ MFC native-code application.

The \PBNativeApp folder contains the Win32 native-code application.

Chapter 14: Autolaunch Applications

In this chapter, the MyEmulatorBSP was edited to add the autolaunch.exe component, and you worked through additional exercises using the MyOSDesign.

The modified OS design and BSP code along with the utility for this chapter are provided in the following folders:

- ❑ \AutoLaunch
- ❑ \AutoLaunchApp
- ❑ \MyEmulatorBSP
- ❑ \MyOSDesign

The \AutoLaunch folder contains the autolaunch.exe utility to support the ARMV4I processor.

The \AutoLaunchApp folder contains the OS design subproject source code. To use this code with the MyOSDesign, copy the complete \AutoLaunchApp folder to the MyOSDesign's folder, C:\WINCE600\OSDesigns\MyOSDesign\MyOSDesign. If you worked through the exercises and created the \AutoLaunchApp, remove or rename the existing folder before copying the provided code.

The \MyEmulatorBSP folder contains the modified code for the BSP.

The \MyOSDesign folder contains the code for the OS design project from the exercises in this chapter.

Chapter 15: Customizing the UI

A new OS design is created in this chapter to work through the custom user interface exercises. The same OS design is configured with different settings to support the chapter's two exercises.

The codes are provided in the following folders:

- ❏ \CustomUI_NMD
- ❏ \CustomUI_VB
- ❏ \VBApp

The CustomUI_NMD folder contains the OS design used for the first exercise, using the NMD custom user interface. To use this code, copy the complete \CustomUI_NMD folder to C:\WINCE600\ OSDesigns, and rename the folder \CustomUI.

The \CustomUI_VB folder contains the OS design used for the second exercise, using a managed-code application as the custom user interface. To use this code, copy the complete \CustomeUI_VB to C:\WINCE600\OSDesigns, and rename the folder \CustomUI.

The \VBApp folder contains the managed-code application used as the custom user interface for the second exercise. The code in this folder is provided as reference and is already included in the \CustomUI_VB folder.

Chapter 16: Thin-Client Applications

A new OS design and a simple HTML file are created to work through the thin-client exercise.

The codes are provided in the following folders:

- ❏ \WTC
- ❏ \WebFile

The \WTC folder contains the thin-client OS design. To use this code, copy the complete folder to C:\WINCE600\OSDesigns.

The \WebFile folder contains the HTML file used in the thin-client exercise. To use this code, copy the complete folder to C:\WINCE600.

Chapter 17: Home Automation Applications

A new OS design and a managed-code application are created to work through the exercise in this chapter.

The codes are provided in the following folders:

- ❏ \eBoxPhidget
- ❏ \VBTempSensor

The \eBoxPhidget folder contains the OS design with the PhidgetFramework included. To use this code, copy the complete \eBoxPhidget folder to C:\WINCE600\OSDesigns. In addition, the PhigetFramework_V214 library and ICOP_eBox4300_60E BSP are needed for this OS design.

The \VBTempSensor folder contains the VB 2005 managed-code application created from the exercise in this chapter.

Chapter 18: RFID Security Access Control Applications

This chapter uses the same eBoxPhidget OS design from Chapter 17 and a managed-code application to work through the exercise in this chapter.

The code is provided in the following folder:

    \RFIDApp

The \RFIDApp folder contains the VB 2005 managed-code application created from the exercise in this chapter.

Chapter 19: Robotic Applications

This chapter uses the eBox-4300 OS design created in Chapter 12, which created two managed-code applications for the exercises.

The codes are provided in the following folders:

❑   \SerialPortClass
❑   \SerializerNET

The \SerialPortClass folder contains a simple robotic application code, using the serial port object to send commands to the robot with the serial port.

The \SerializerNET folder contains a simple robot application code, performing the same tasks as the SerialportClass application above, using the Serializer.NET library.

Chapter 20: Deploying a CE 6.0 Device

A new OS design is created to support the eBox-4300 target device to work through the exercises in this chapter.

The codes are provided in the following folder:

    \WNPOSDesign

The \WNPOSDesign folder contains the code for an OS design.

Index

C

R

customized, 61–83, 429
development, 42
eBox-4300, 228–242
eBox-4300-MSJK, downloading, 98–99, 104–105
emulator, 211–212, 259–261
Ethernet, 79
flash memory, 76
generating, 76–78
HKEY_LOCAL_MACHINE\Init, 289
MyCEPCBSP, 78–80
MyeBox4300BSP, 80–83, 94
MyEmulator, 90–91
native-code applications, 254–258
Platform Builder, 76–78
release-mode, 114–115
WNP OS design, 411–412
WTC, 311
Run-time image can be larger than 32 MB, 75

S

s, 143
s ipconfig /d, 214
SAPI. *See* **Speech Application Programming Interface**
save, registry, 175
Sboot loader, 152
Sboot.bin, 106
SDK. *See* **Software Development Kit**
_SDKROOT, 32
SDP. *See* **Session Description Protocol**
Secure Digital controller drivers, 7
Secure Shell (SSH), 419
Secure Socket Layer (SSL), 7
Security, 68, 164
security, 14
security warning screen, 69
SendReceive(), 377
sensors, 292–293, 330
Phidgets, 357–360
serial ports, 54
applications, communication, 428
boot loader, 152
CEPC, 110–112, 172
debugging, 144–146, 173–174, 235
eBox-4300, 81
eBox-4300-MSJK, 173
home automation system controller, 234
incoming data, 293
industrial automation controller, 234
outbound data, 294
registry, 171–173
robotic controller, 234
robotics applications, 375–383
SerialPortApp, 242
target device, 85
x86, 173
Serializer .NET library, 373
robotics applications, 387–392
Serializer Robot Controller, 205, 372–374
eBox-4300, 373

GPIO, 373
I/O, 374
.NET library, 373
SerializerNET
code, 391–392
OS design, 394
serializernet.exe
code, 391–392
registry, 394
Stinger CE Robot, 395
SerialPort, 379
SerialPortApp, 236–237, 277–278
code, 238–242
CoreCon, 242–246
eBox-4300, 242–249
deploying, 246–247
testing, 247–249
serial ports, 242
TCP/IP, 244–245
serialportapp.exe, 277–278
\WINDOWS\STARTUP, 280
serialportclass.exe
code, 383–387
eBox-4300, 393
Stinger CE Robot, 394
SerialPortReadLine(), 379
SerialPortWriteLine(), 379
Server Authentication, 7
Server Message Block (SMB), 29
servicesd.exe, 276
servicestart.exe, 276
Session Description Protocol (SDP), 10
Session Initiation Protocol (SIP), 10
VoIP, 35
Settings Application, 11
Set-Top Box, 11
SETUPDISK.144, 161
SH-4, 5, 6
ship build, 75
Short Message Service (SMS), 8
SIM. *See* **Subscriber Identity Module**
SIP. *See* **Session Initiation Protocol**
Small Footprint, 5, 11, 65, 371
Smart Device
applications
C#, 212
Visual C++, 261–263
ATL, 261
MFC, 261
VB 2005 applications, 234–242
Visual C++, 252
Smart Device Framework, 419
Smart Drive applications, Win32, 261, 263
Smart-device class library, 202
Smart-device console applications, 202
Smart-device control library, 202
Smart-device Windows form applications, 202
SMB. *See* **Server Message Block**
SMS. *See* **Short Message Service**
sockets, CETK, target devices, 196

445